高 橋 和 希

IN THE BEGINNING, I HAD A FEW IDEAS FOR A COMIC. SINCE
IT WAS A SHONEN MANGA, I DECIDED TO USE "BATTLE" AS
A THEME. BUT FIGHTING MANGA HAD BEEN DONE TO DEATH
AND I COULDN'T COME UP WITH A NEW IDEA...THAT'S WHEN
I DECIDED TO CREATE A FIGHTING MANGA WHERE THE MAIN
CHARACTER NEVER HITS ANYBODY. THIS LIMITATION GAVE
ME A HARD TIME, BUT WHEN I SUDDENLY THOUGHT OF
"GAME" AS THE KEYWORD, A PATH OPENED UP IN FRONT OF
MY EYES. THAT'S HOW I CAME UP WITH YU-GI-OH!.
    —KAZUKI TAKAHASHI, 1999

Artist/author Kazuki Takahashi first tried to break into
the manga business in 1982, but success eluded him
until Yu-Gi-Oh! debuted in the Japanese **Weekly
Shonen Jump** magazine in 1996. **Yu-Gi-Oh!**'s themes
of friendship and fighting, together with Takahashi's
weird and wonderful art, soon became enormously
successful, spawning a real-world card game, video
games, and two anime series. A lifelong gamer,
Takahashi enjoys Shogi (Japanese chess), Mahjong,
and tabletop RPGs, among other games.

D1260440

YU-GI-OH!: DUELIST VOL. 9
The SHONEN JUMP Graphic Novel Edition

STORY AND ART BY
KAZUKI TAKAHASHI

Translation & English Adaptation/Joe Yamazaki
Touch-up Art & Lettering/Eric Erbes
Design/Andrea Rice
Editor/Jason Thompson

Managing Editor/Elizabeth Kawasaki
Director of Production/Noboru Watanabe
Vice President of Publishing/Alvin Lu
Vice President & Editor in Chief/Yumi Hoashi
Sr. Director of Acquisitions/Rika Inouye
Vice President of Sales & Marketing/Liza Coppola
Publisher/ Hyoe Narita

YU-GI-OH! © 1996 by Kazuki Takahashi. All rights reserved. First published in Japan in 1996 by SHUEISHA Inc., Tokyo. English translation rights in the United States of America and Canada arranged by SHUEISHA Inc. The stories, characters and incidents mentioned in this publication are entirely fictional.

In the original Japanese edition, YU-GI-OH! and YU-GI-OH!: DUELIST are known collectively as YU-GI-OH!. The English YU-GI-OH!: DUELIST was originally volumes 8-31 of the Japanese YU-GI-OH!.

Printed in the U.S.A.

Published by VIZ Media, LLC
P.O. Box 77010
San Francisco, CA 94107

SHONEN JUMP Graphic Novel Edition
10 9 8 7 6 5 4 3 2 1
First printing, September 2005

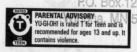

THE WORLD'S MOST POPULAR MANGA

www.viz.com

www.shonenjump.com

SHONEN JUMP GRAPHIC NOVEL EDITION

YU-GI-OH!™ DUELIST

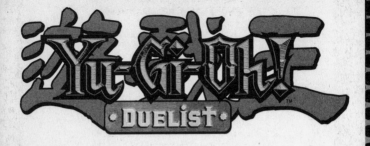

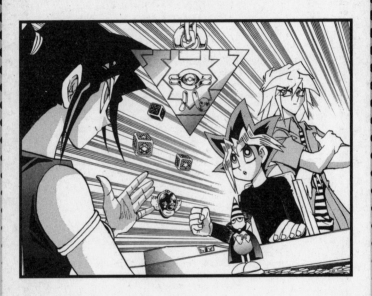

Vol. 9

DUNGEON DICE MONSTERS

STORY AND ART BY

KAZUKI TAKAHASHI

YUGI MUTOU/ YU-GI-OH

When 10th grader Yugi solved the Millennium Puzzle, another spirit took up residence in his body…Yu-Gi-Oh, the King of Games, a dark avenger who challenges evildoers to "Shadow Games" of life and death!

YUGI FACES DEADLY ENEMIES!

Using his gaming skills, Yugi fights ruthless adversaries like Seto Kaiba, obsessive gamer and teenage corporate president, and Ryo Bakura, whose friendly personality turns evil when he is possessed by the spirit of the Millennium Ring. When he defeats Kaiba at the collectible card game "Duel Monsters," Yugi attracts the attention of Maximillion Pegasus, the game's creator…and bearer of the soul-stealing Millennium Eye. By kidnapping Yugi's grandpa and Kaiba's brother, Pegasus forces Kaiba and Yugi to fight each other in a "Duel Monsters" tournament on his private island, Duelist Kingdom. Faced with a common enemy, Yugi and Kaiba come to respect each other as rivals. Pegasus defeats Kaiba, but Yugi avenges him, defeating Pegasus and rescuing Kaiba's soul.

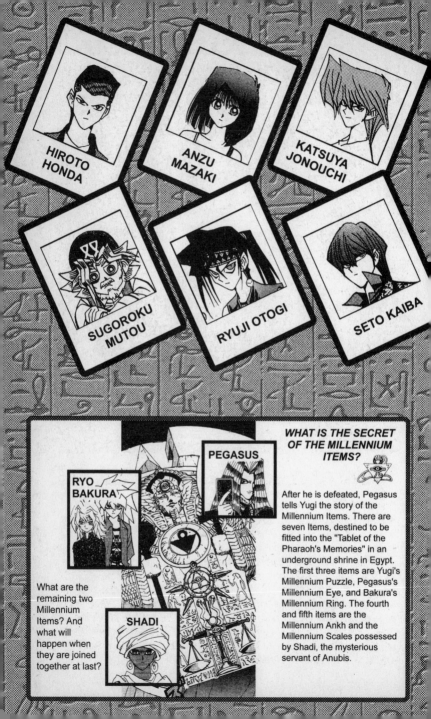

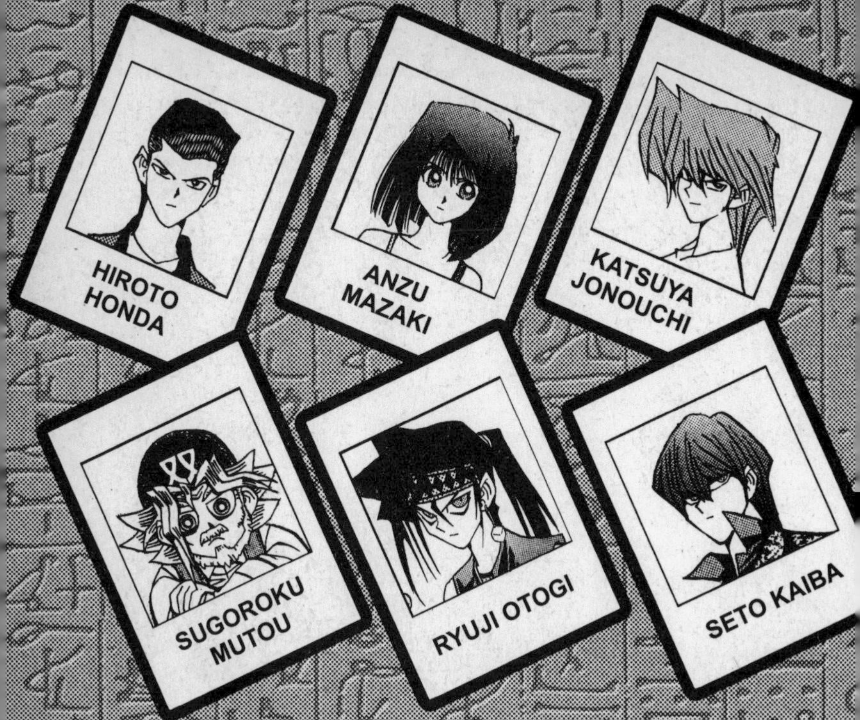
HIROTO HONDA
ANZU MAZAKI
KATSUYA JONOUCHI
SUGOROKU MUTOU
RYUJI OTOGI
SETO KAIBA

WHAT IS THE SECRET OF THE MILLENNIUM ITEMS?

After he is defeated, Pegasus tells Yugi the story of the Millennium Items. There are seven Items, destined to be fitted into the "Tablet of the Pharaoh's Memories" in an underground shrine in Egypt. The first three items are Yugi's Millennium Puzzle, Pegasus's Millennium Eye, and Bakura's Millennium Ring. The fourth and fifth items are the Millennium Ankh and the Millennium Scales possessed by Shadi, the mysterious servant of Anubis.

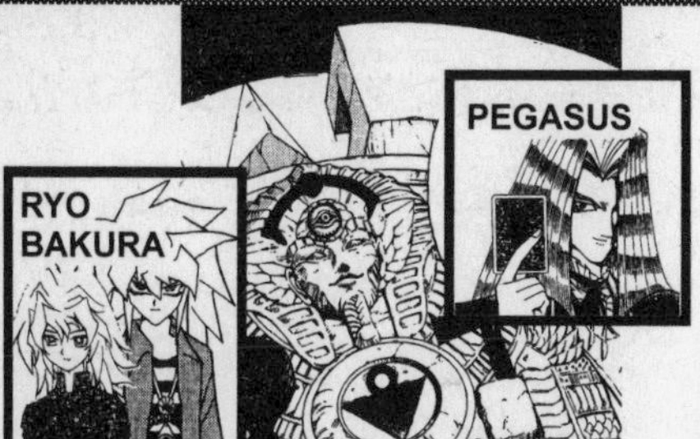
PEGASUS
RYO BAKURA

What are the remaining two Millennium Items? And what will happen when they are joined together at last?

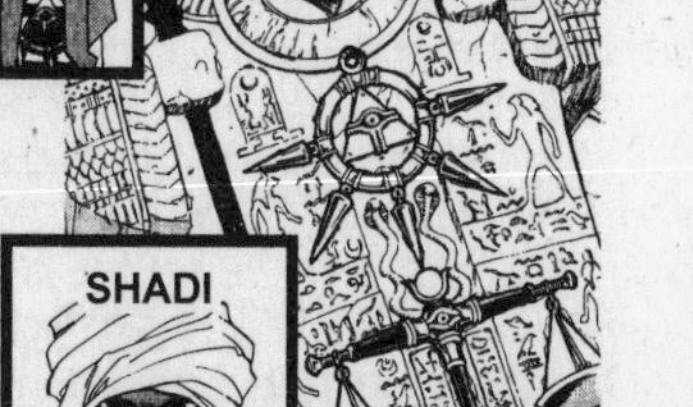
SHADI

YU-GI-OH! DUELIST

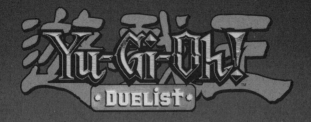

Vol. 9

CONTENTS

Duel 75: The New Game

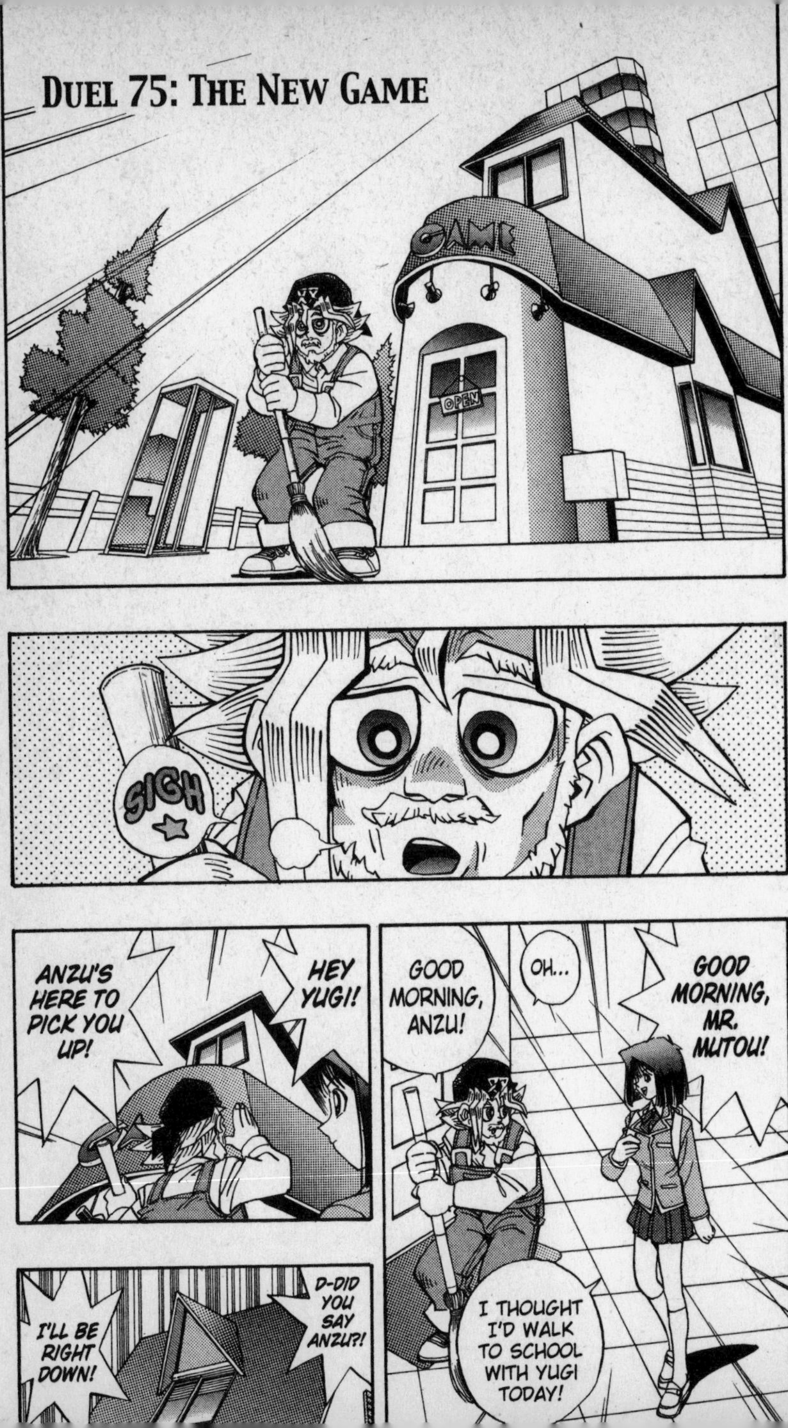
SIGH
GOOD MORNING, MR. MUTOU!
OH...
GOOD MORNING, ANZU!
I THOUGHT I'D WALK TO SCHOOL WITH YUGI TODAY!
HEY YUGI!
ANZU'S HERE TO PICK YOU UP!
D-DID YOU SAY ANZU?!
I'LL BE RIGHT DOWN!

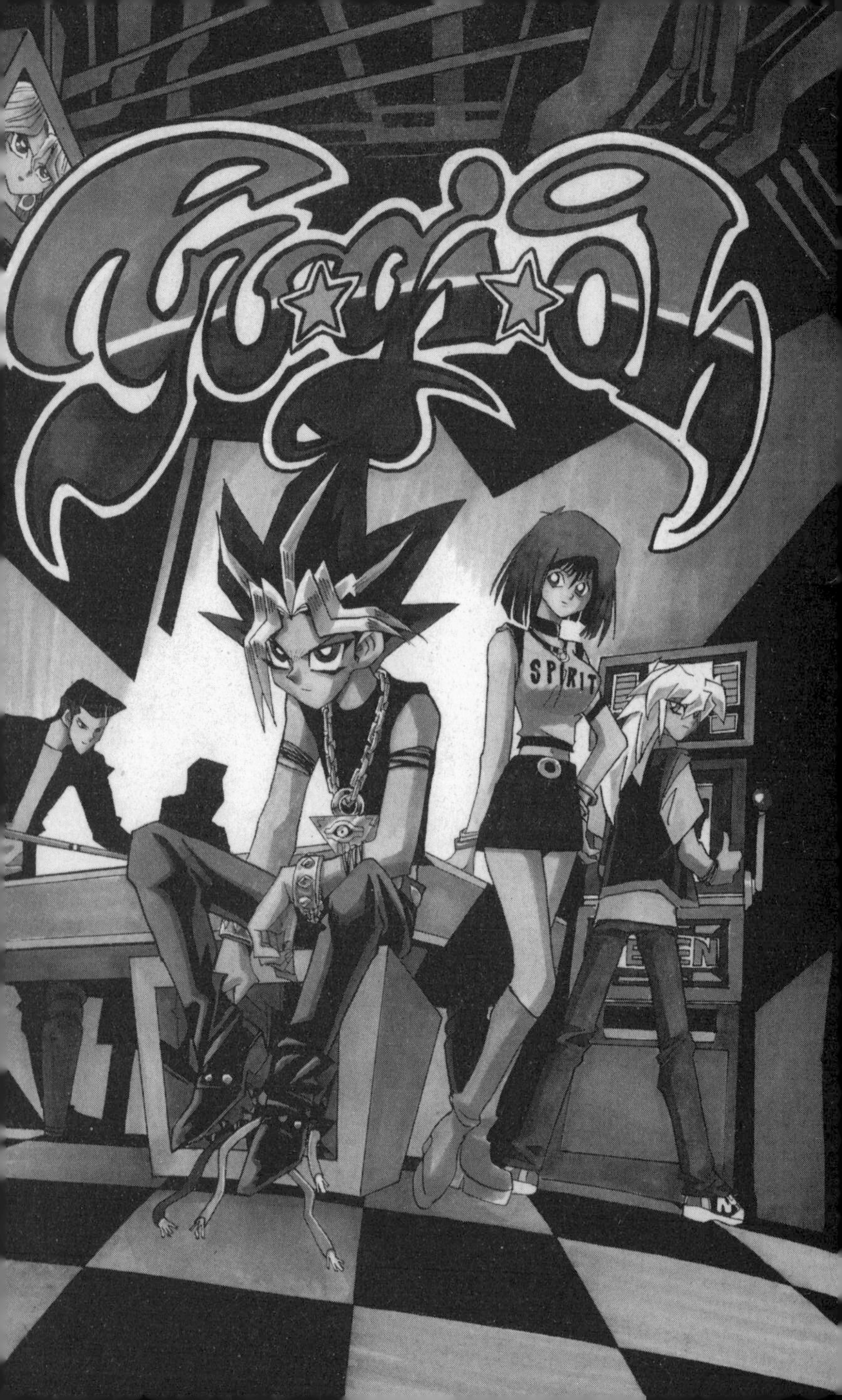
SPIRIT

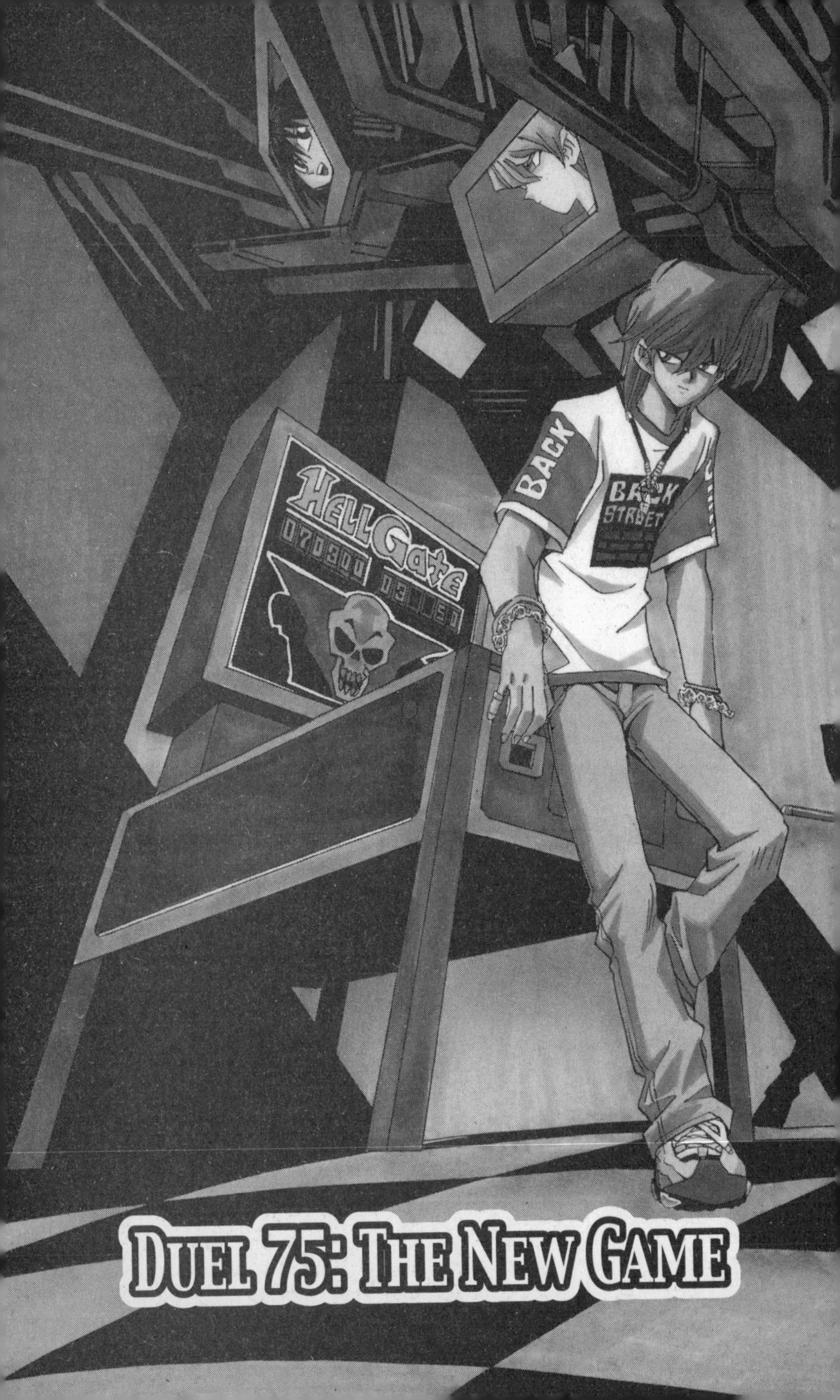
HELL Gate
BACK
BACK STREET

DUEL 75: THE NEW GAME

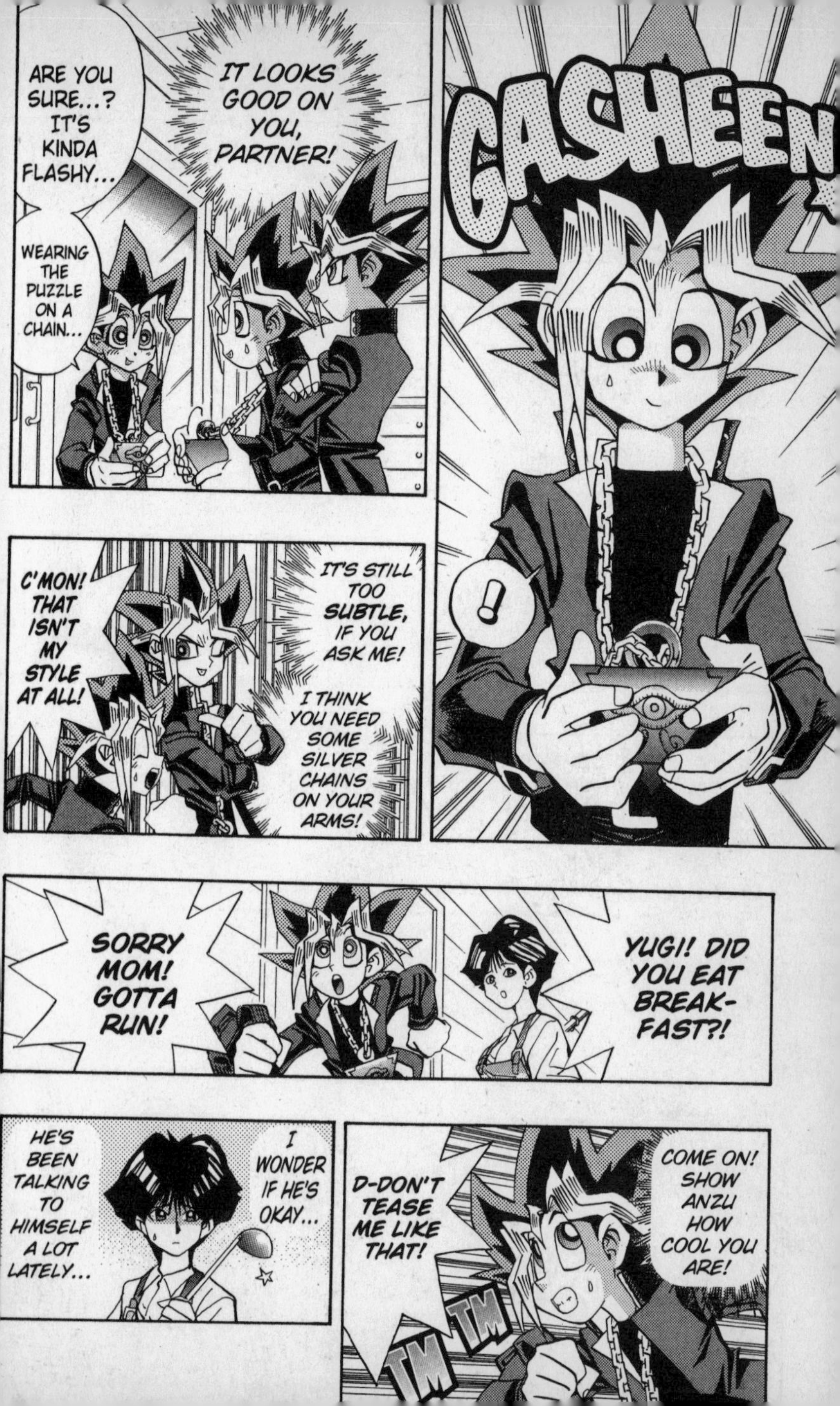
GASHEEN
!
IT LOOKS GOOD ON YOU, PARTNER!
ARE YOU SURE...? IT'S KINDA FLASHY...
WEARING THE PUZZLE ON A CHAIN...
IT'S STILL TOO SUBTLE, IF YOU ASK ME!
I THINK YOU NEED SOME SILVER CHAINS ON YOUR ARMS!
C'MON! THAT ISN'T MY STYLE AT ALL!
YUGI! DID YOU EAT BREAK-FAST?!
SORRY MOM! GOTTA RUN!
COME ON! SHOW ANZU HOW COOL YOU ARE!
D-DON'T TEASE ME LIKE THAT!
TM TM
I WONDER IF HE'S OKAY...
HE'S BEEN TALKING TO HIMSELF A LOT LATELY...

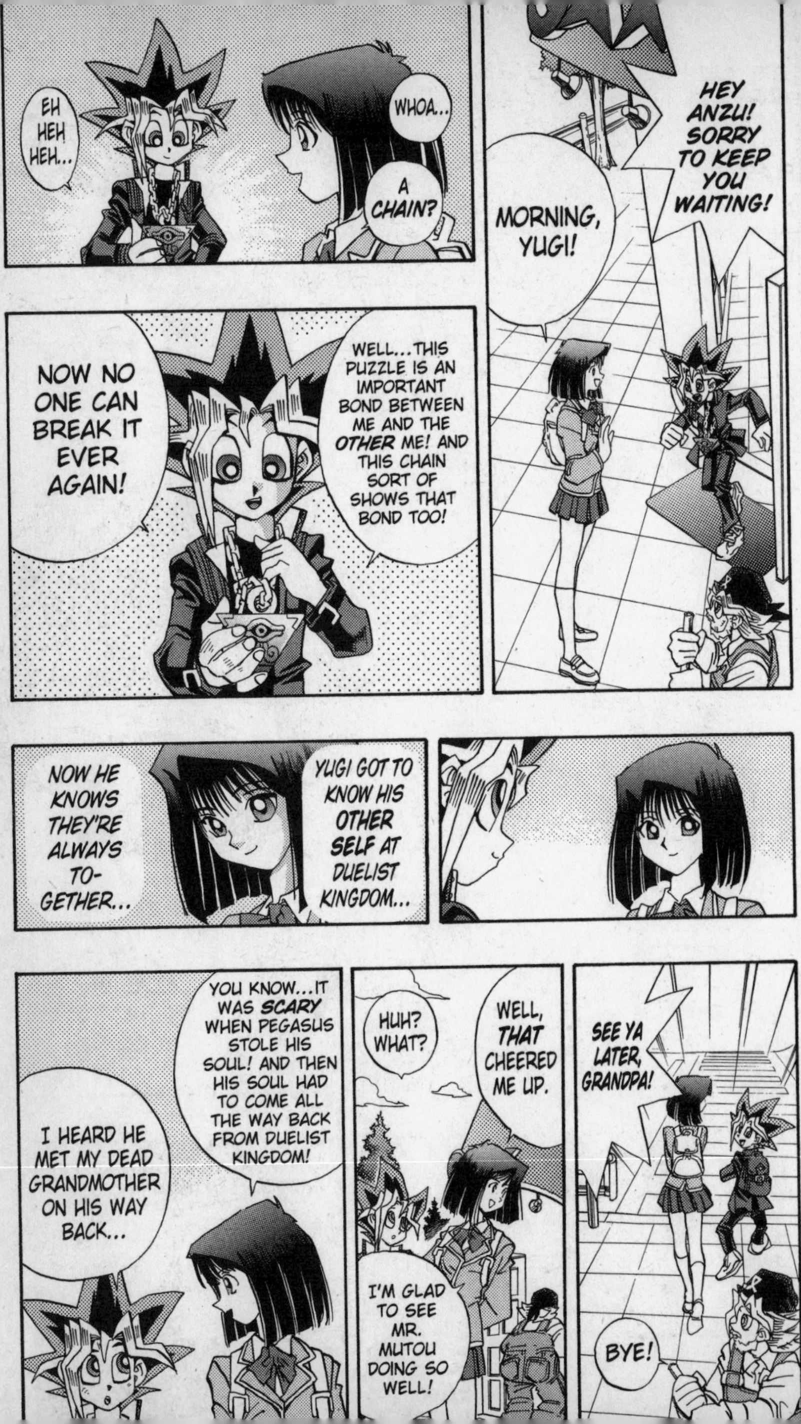
HEY ANZU! SORRY TO KEEP YOU WAITING!
MORNING, YUGI!
WHOA...
A CHAIN?
EH HEH HEH...
WELL...THIS PUZZLE IS AN IMPORTANT BOND BETWEEN ME AND THE OTHER ME! AND THIS CHAIN SORT OF SHOWS THAT BOND TOO!
NOW NO ONE CAN BREAK IT EVER AGAIN!
YUGI GOT TO KNOW HIS OTHER SELF AT DUELIST KINGDOM...
NOW HE KNOWS THEY'RE ALWAYS TO-GETHER...
SEE YA LATER, GRANDPA!
BYE!
WELL, THAT CHEERED ME UP.
HUH? WHAT?
I'M GLAD TO SEE MR. MUTOU DOING SO WELL!
YOU KNOW...IT WAS SCARY WHEN PEGASUS STOLE HIS SOUL! AND THEN HIS SOUL HAD TO COME ALL THE WAY BACK FROM DUELIST KINGDOM!
I HEARD HE MET MY DEAD GRANDMOTHER ON HIS WAY BACK...

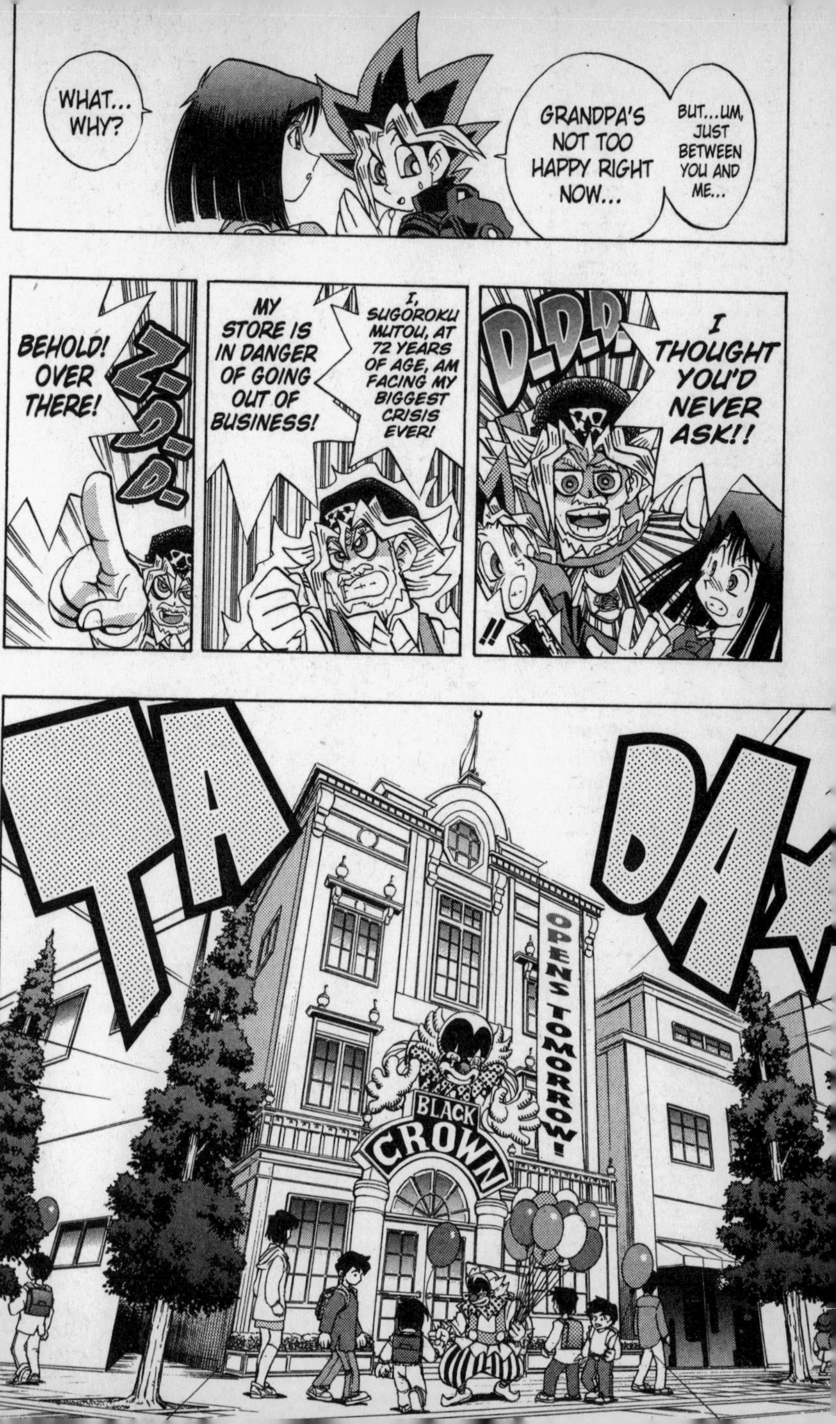
BUT...UM, JUST BETWEEN YOU AND ME...
GRANDPA'S NOT TOO HAPPY RIGHT NOW...
WHAT... WHY?
D.D.D.
I THOUGHT YOU'D NEVER ASK!!
!!
I, SUGOROKU MUTOU, AT 72 YEARS OF AGE, AM FACING MY BIGGEST CRISIS EVER!
MY STORE IS IN DANGER OF GOING OUT OF BUSINESS!
BEHOLD! OVER THERE!
TA
DA
OPENS TOMORROW!
BLACK CROWN

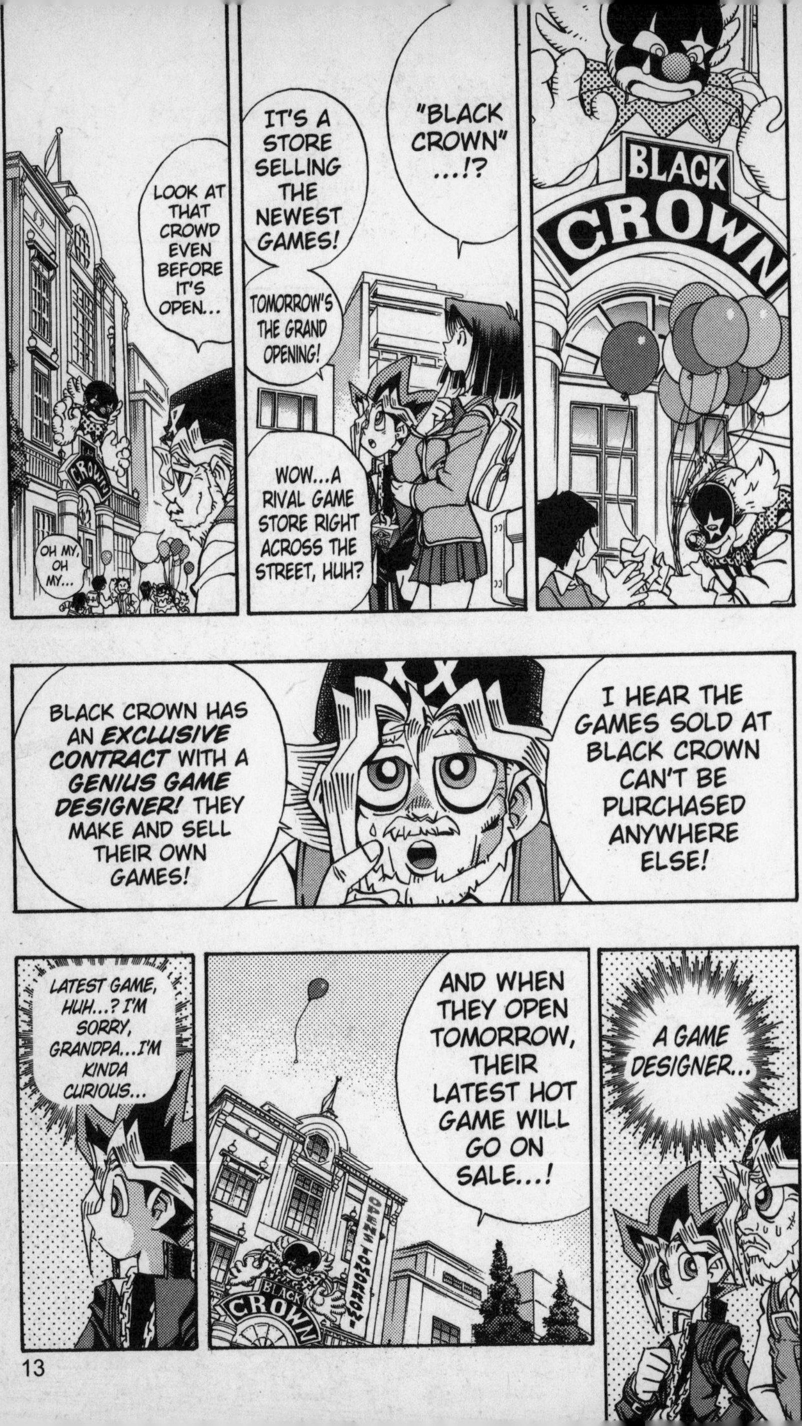
BLACK CROWN
"BLACK CROWN"...!?
IT'S A STORE SELLING THE NEWEST GAMES!
TOMORROW'S THE GRAND OPENING!
WOW...A RIVAL GAME STORE RIGHT ACROSS THE STREET, HUH?
LOOK AT THAT CROWD EVEN BEFORE IT'S OPEN...
CROWN
OH MY, OH MY...
I HEAR THE GAMES SOLD AT BLACK CROWN CAN'T BE PURCHASED ANYWHERE ELSE!
BLACK CROWN HAS AN ***EXCLUSIVE CONTRACT*** WITH A ***GENIUS GAME DESIGNER!*** THEY MAKE AND SELL THEIR OWN GAMES!
A GAME DESIGNER...
AND WHEN THEY OPEN TOMORROW, THEIR LATEST HOT GAME WILL GO ON SALE...!
OPENS TOMORROW!
BLACK CROWN
LATEST GAME, HUH...? I'M SORRY, GRANDPA...I'M KINDA CURIOUS...

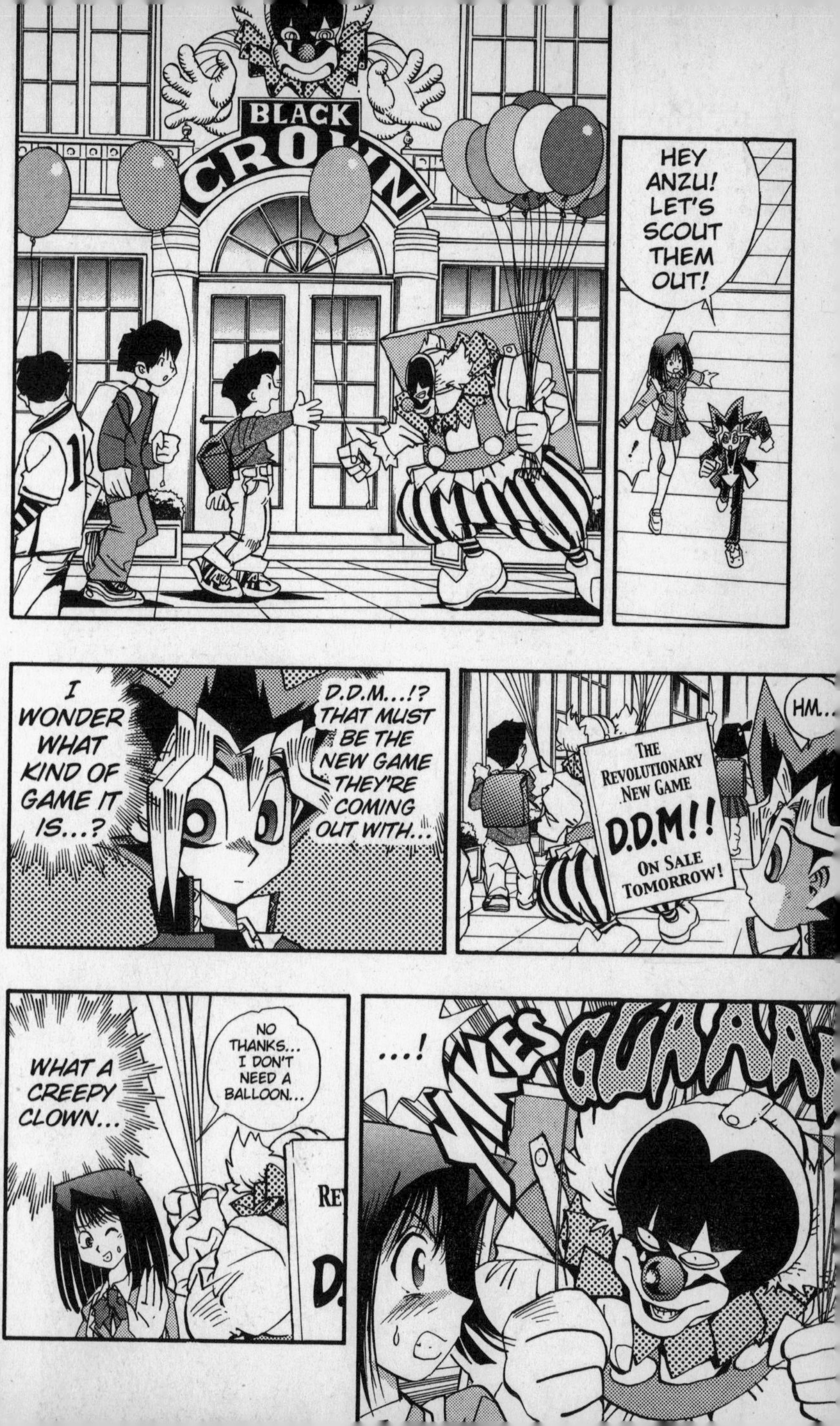
BLACK CROWN
HEY ANZU! LET'S SCOUT THEM OUT!
HM...
THE REVOLUTIONARY NEW GAME D.D.M!! ON SALE TOMORROW!
D.D.M...!? THAT MUST BE THE NEW GAME THEY'RE COMING OUT WITH...
I WONDER WHAT KIND OF GAME IT IS...?
...!
YIKES
GUAAA
NO THANKS... I DON'T NEED A BALLOON...
WHAT A CREEPY CLOWN...

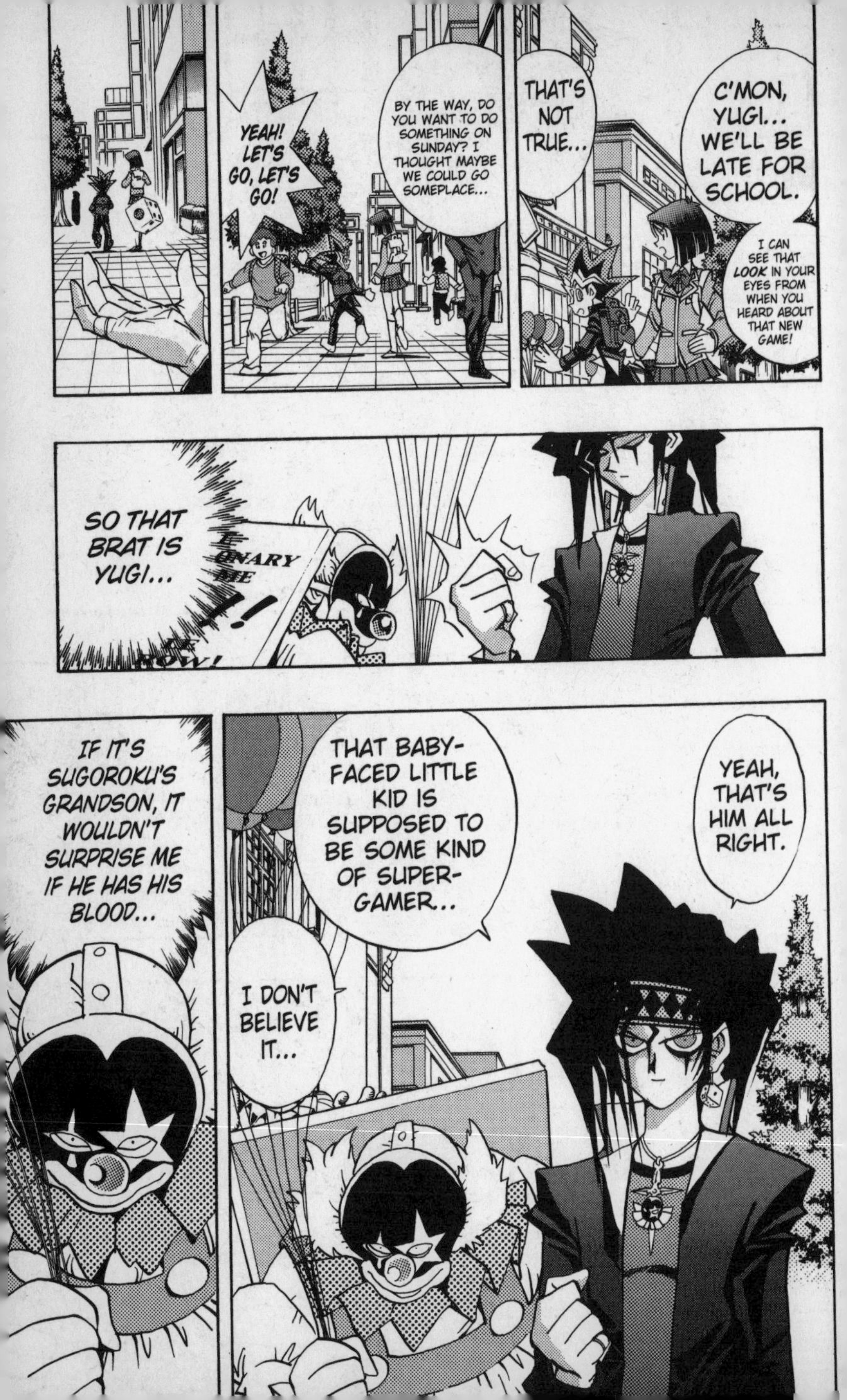
C'MON, YUGI... WE'LL BE LATE FOR SCHOOL.
I CAN SEE THAT LOOK IN YOUR EYES FROM WHEN YOU HEARD ABOUT THAT NEW GAME!
THAT'S NOT TRUE...
BY THE WAY, DO YOU WANT TO DO SOMETHING ON SUNDAY? I THOUGHT MAYBE WE COULD GO SOMEPLACE...
YEAH! LET'S GO, LET'S GO!
SO THAT BRAT IS YUGI...
YEAH, THAT'S HIM ALL RIGHT.
THAT BABY-FACED LITTLE KID IS SUPPOSED TO BE SOME KIND OF SUPER-GAMER...
I DON'T BELIEVE IT...
IF IT'S SUGOROKU'S GRANDSON, IT WOULDN'T SURPRISE ME IF HE HAS HIS BLOOD...

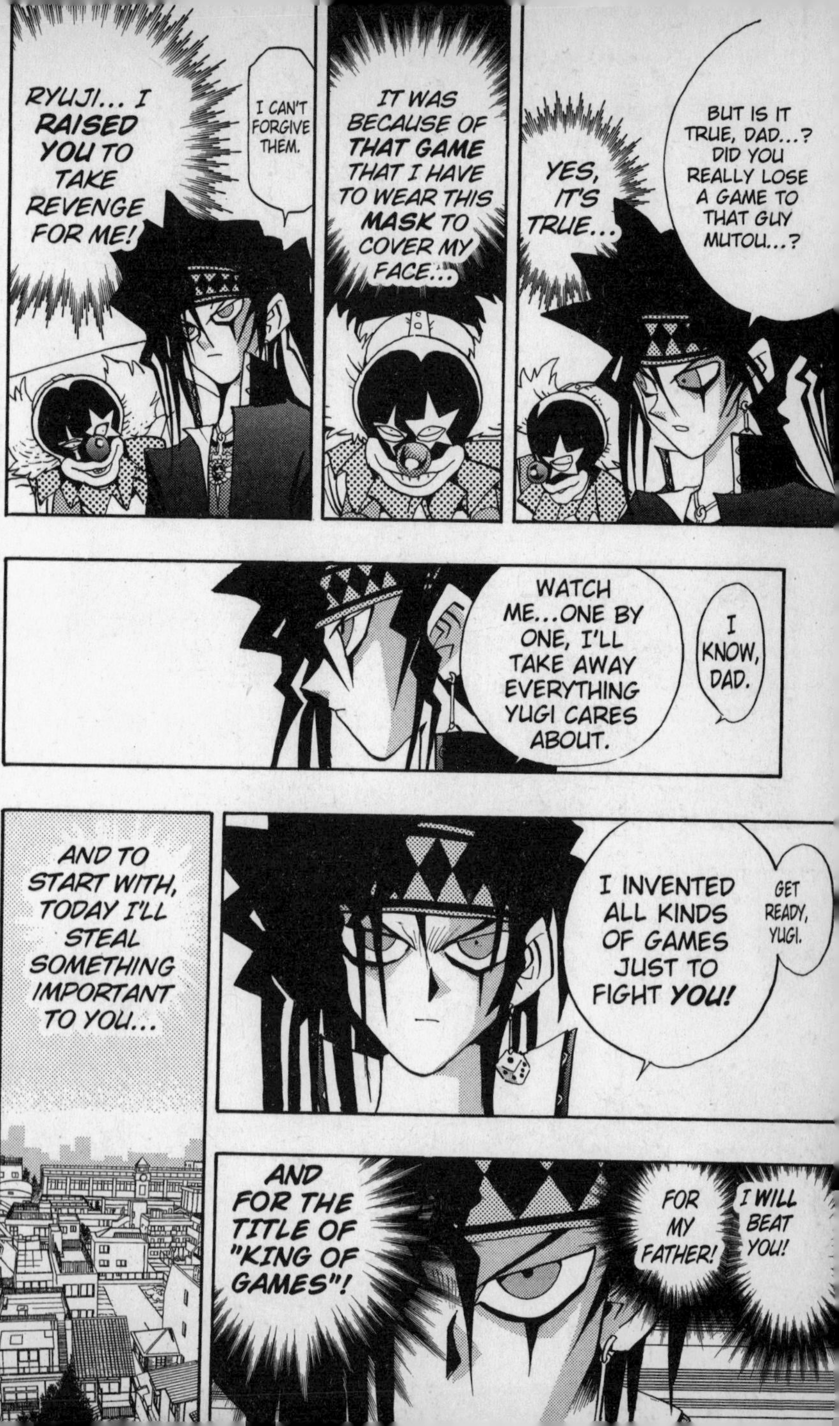
BUT IS IT TRUE, DAD...? DID YOU REALLY LOSE A GAME TO THAT GUY MUTOU...?
YES, IT'S TRUE...
IT WAS BECAUSE OF THAT GAME THAT I HAVE TO WEAR THIS MASK TO COVER MY FACE...
I CAN'T FORGIVE THEM.
RYUJI... I RAISED YOU TO TAKE REVENGE FOR ME!
I KNOW, DAD.
WATCH ME...ONE BY ONE, I'LL TAKE AWAY EVERYTHING YUGI CARES ABOUT.
GET READY, YUGI.
I INVENTED ALL KINDS OF GAMES JUST TO FIGHT YOU!
I WILL BEAT YOU!
FOR MY FATHER!
AND FOR THE TITLE OF "KING OF GAMES"!
AND TO START WITH, TODAY I'LL STEAL SOMETHING IMPORTANT TO YOU...

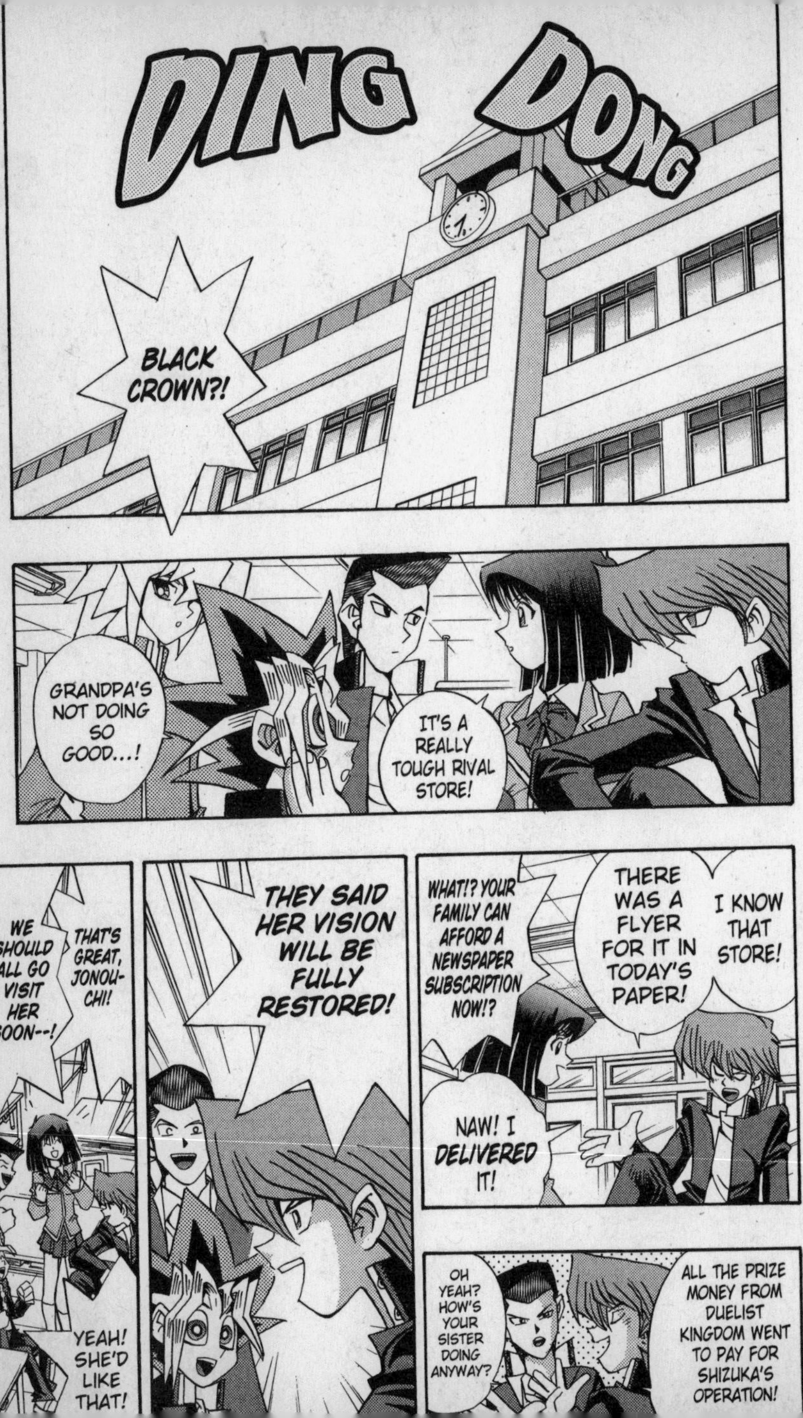
DING DONG
BLACK CROWN?!
GRANDPA'S NOT DOING SO GOOD...!
IT'S A REALLY TOUGH RIVAL STORE!
I KNOW THAT STORE!
THERE WAS A FLYER FOR IT IN TODAY'S PAPER!
WHAT!? YOUR FAMILY CAN AFFORD A NEWSPAPER SUBSCRIPTION NOW!?
NAW! I DELIVERED IT!
OH YEAH? HOW'S YOUR SISTER DOING ANYWAY?
ALL THE PRIZE MONEY FROM DUELIST KINGDOM WENT TO PAY FOR SHIZUKA'S OPERATION!
THEY SAID HER VISION WILL BE FULLY RESTORED!
THAT'S GREAT, JONOU-CHI!
WE SHOULD ALL GO VISIT HER SOON--!
YEAH! SHE'D LIKE THAT!

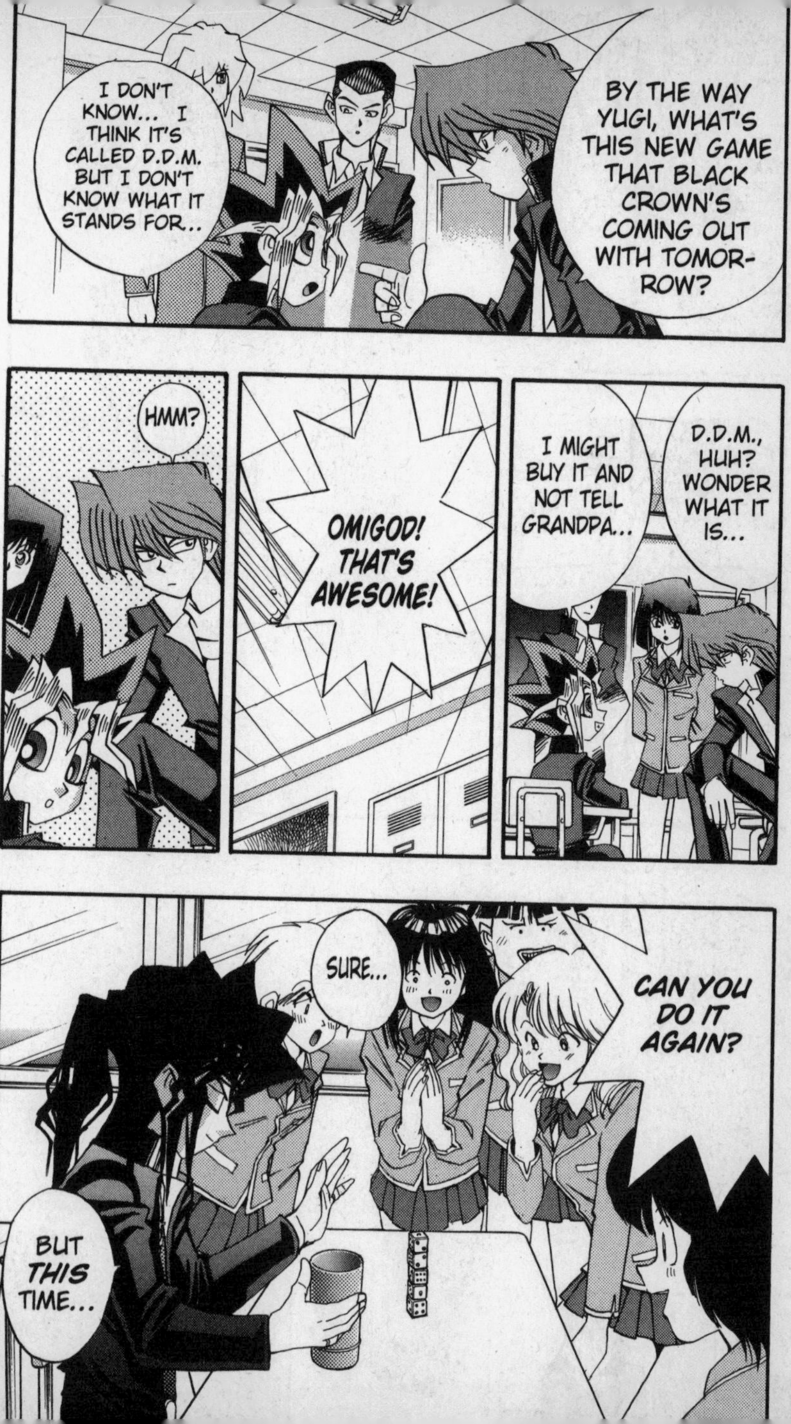
BY THE WAY YUGI, WHAT'S THIS NEW GAME THAT BLACK CROWN'S COMING OUT WITH TOMORROW?
I DON'T KNOW... I THINK IT'S CALLED D.D.M. BUT I DON'T KNOW WHAT IT STANDS FOR...
D.D.M., HUH? WONDER WHAT IT IS...
I MIGHT BUY IT AND NOT TELL GRANDPA...
OMIGOD! THAT'S AWESOME!
HMM?
CAN YOU DO IT AGAIN?
SURE...
BUT THIS TIME...

I'LL DO IT WITH *SIX* DICE!

THIS TIME...

LET'S *BET* SOMETHING!

YOU'LL BUY ME LUNCH!

LET'S SAY...

IF THIS WORKS...

NOW WATCH...

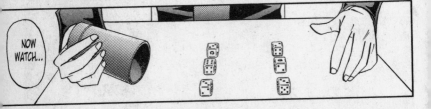

BAM

SHAKA☆

SHAKA☆

FWP

SHAKA☆

...

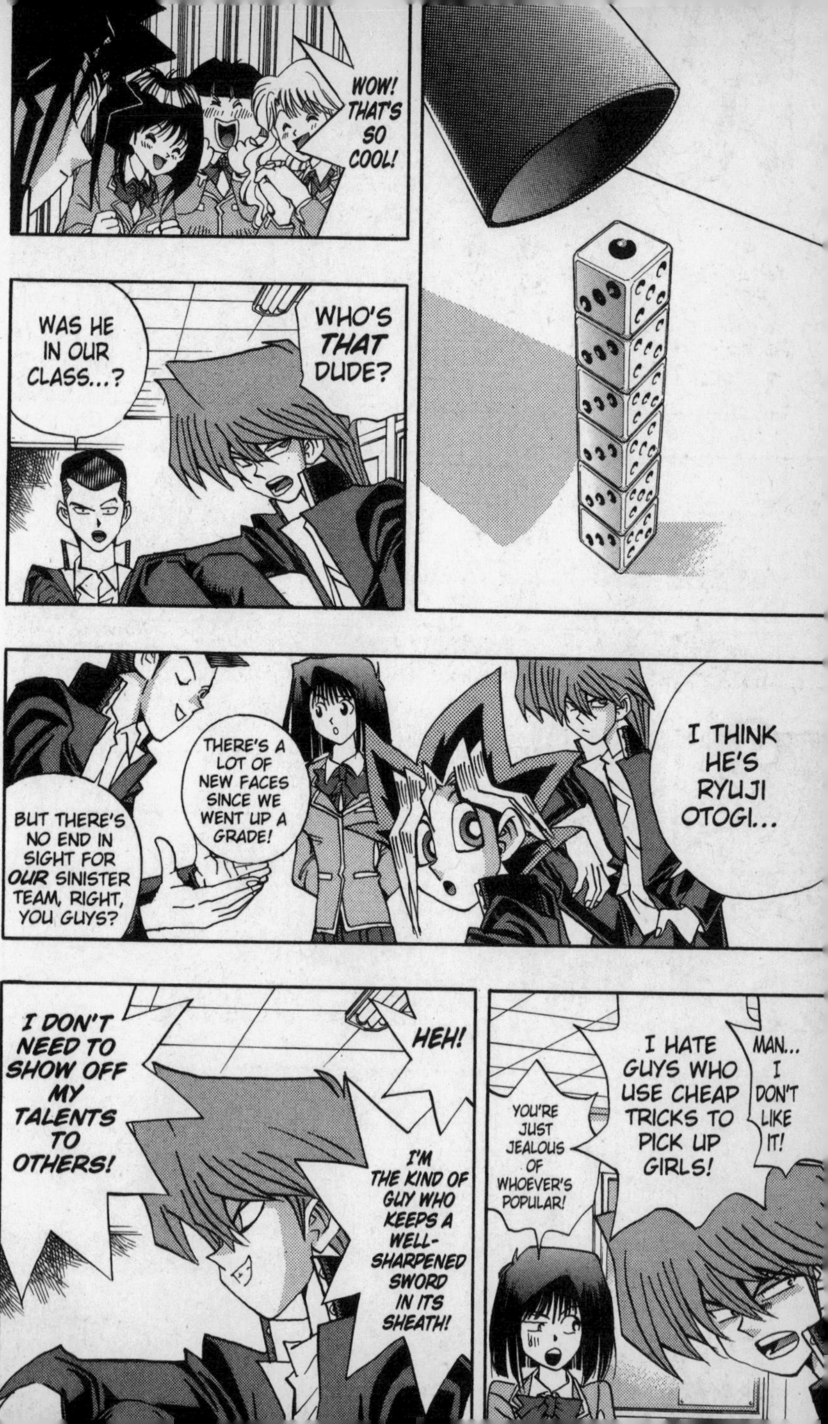
WOW! THAT'S SO COOL!
WHO'S THAT DUDE?
WAS HE IN OUR CLASS...?
I THINK HE'S RYUJI OTOGI...
THERE'S A LOT OF NEW FACES SINCE WE WENT UP A GRADE!
BUT THERE'S NO END IN SIGHT FOR OUR SINISTER TEAM, RIGHT, YOU GUYS?
MAN... I DON'T LIKE IT!
I HATE GUYS WHO USE CHEAP TRICKS TO PICK UP GIRLS!
YOU'RE JUST JEALOUS OF WHOEVER'S POPULAR!
HEH!
I DON'T NEED TO SHOW OFF MY TALENTS TO OTHERS!
I'M THE KIND OF GUY WHO KEEPS A WELL-SHARPENED SWORD IN ITS SHEATH!

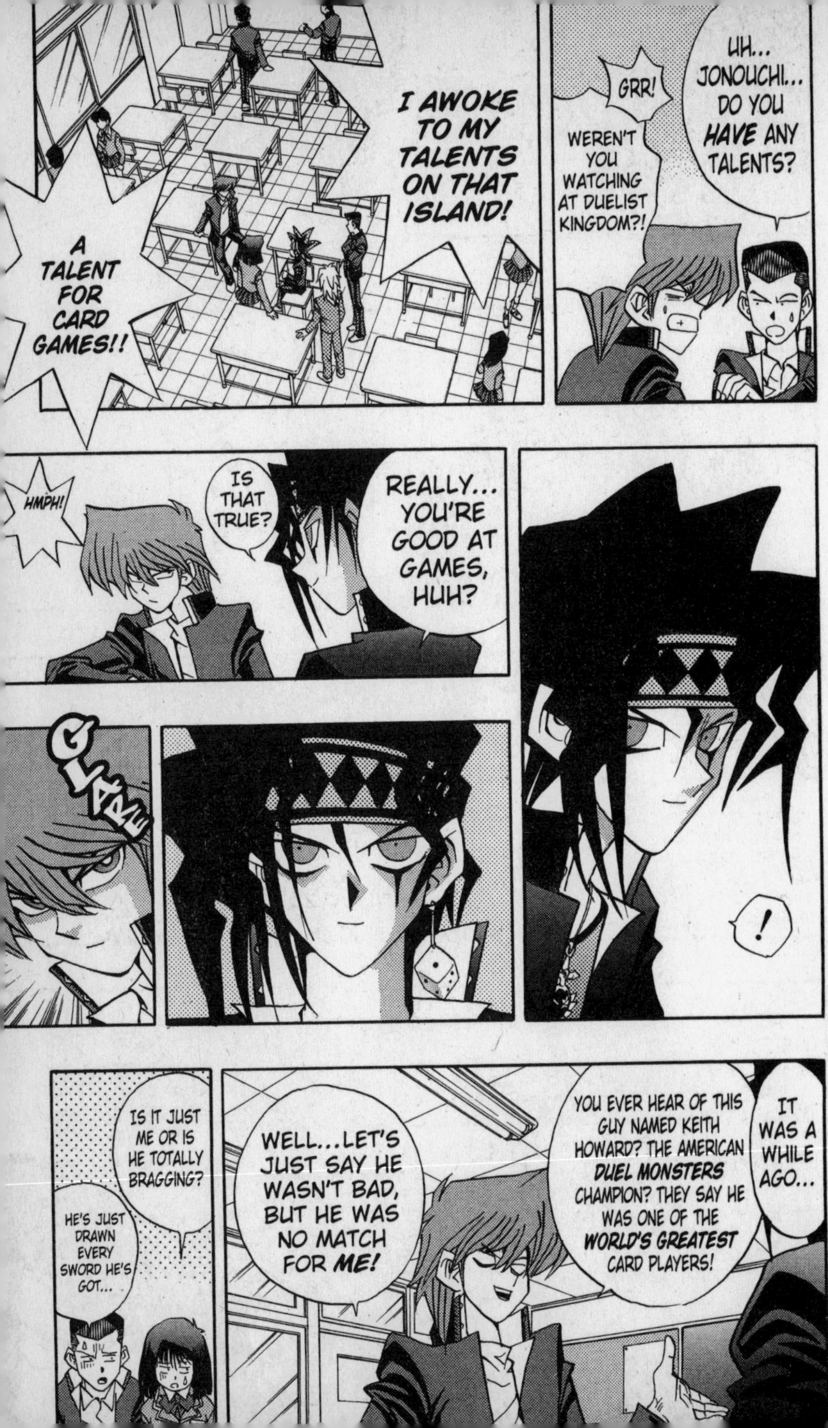
UH... JONOUCHI... DO YOU HAVE ANY TALENTS?
GRR!
WEREN'T YOU WATCHING AT DUELIST KINGDOM?!
I AWOKE TO MY TALENTS ON THAT ISLAND!
A TALENT FOR CARD GAMES!!
!
REALLY... YOU'RE GOOD AT GAMES, HUH?
IS THAT TRUE?
HMPH!
GLARE
IT WAS A WHILE AGO...
YOU EVER HEAR OF THIS GUY NAMED KEITH HOWARD? THE AMERICAN DUEL MONSTERS CHAMPION? THEY SAY HE WAS ONE OF THE WORLD'S GREATEST CARD PLAYERS!
WELL...LET'S JUST SAY HE WASN'T BAD, BUT HE WAS NO MATCH FOR ME!
IS IT JUST ME OR IS HE TOTALLY BRAGGING?
HE'S JUST DRAWN EVERY SWORD HE'S GOT...

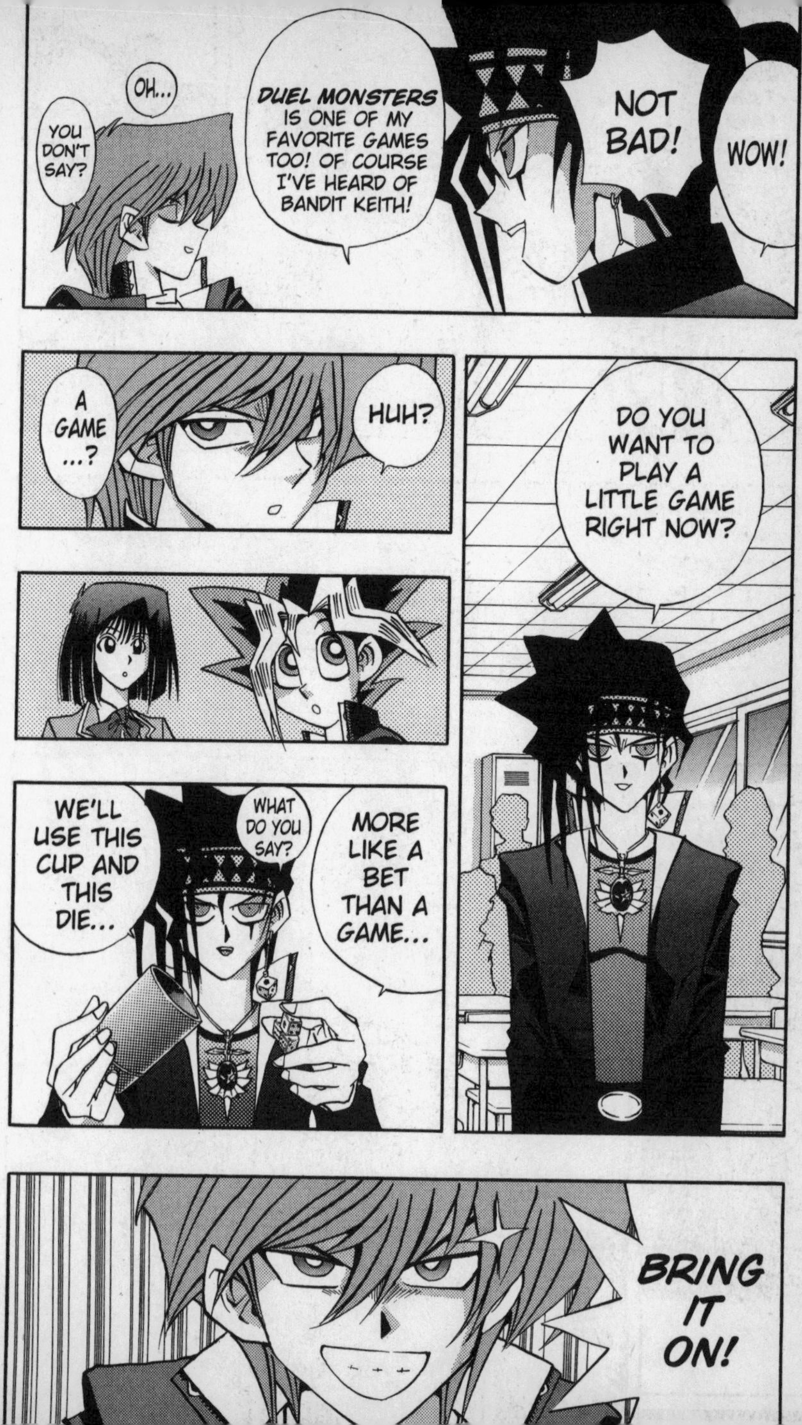
WOW!
NOT BAD!
DUEL MONSTERS IS ONE OF MY FAVORITE GAMES TOO! OF COURSE I'VE HEARD OF BANDIT KEITH!
OH...
YOU DON'T SAY?
DO YOU WANT TO PLAY A LITTLE GAME RIGHT NOW?
HUH?
A GAME ...?
MORE LIKE A BET THAN A GAME...
WHAT DO YOU SAY?
WE'LL USE THIS CUP AND THIS DIE...
BRING IT ON!

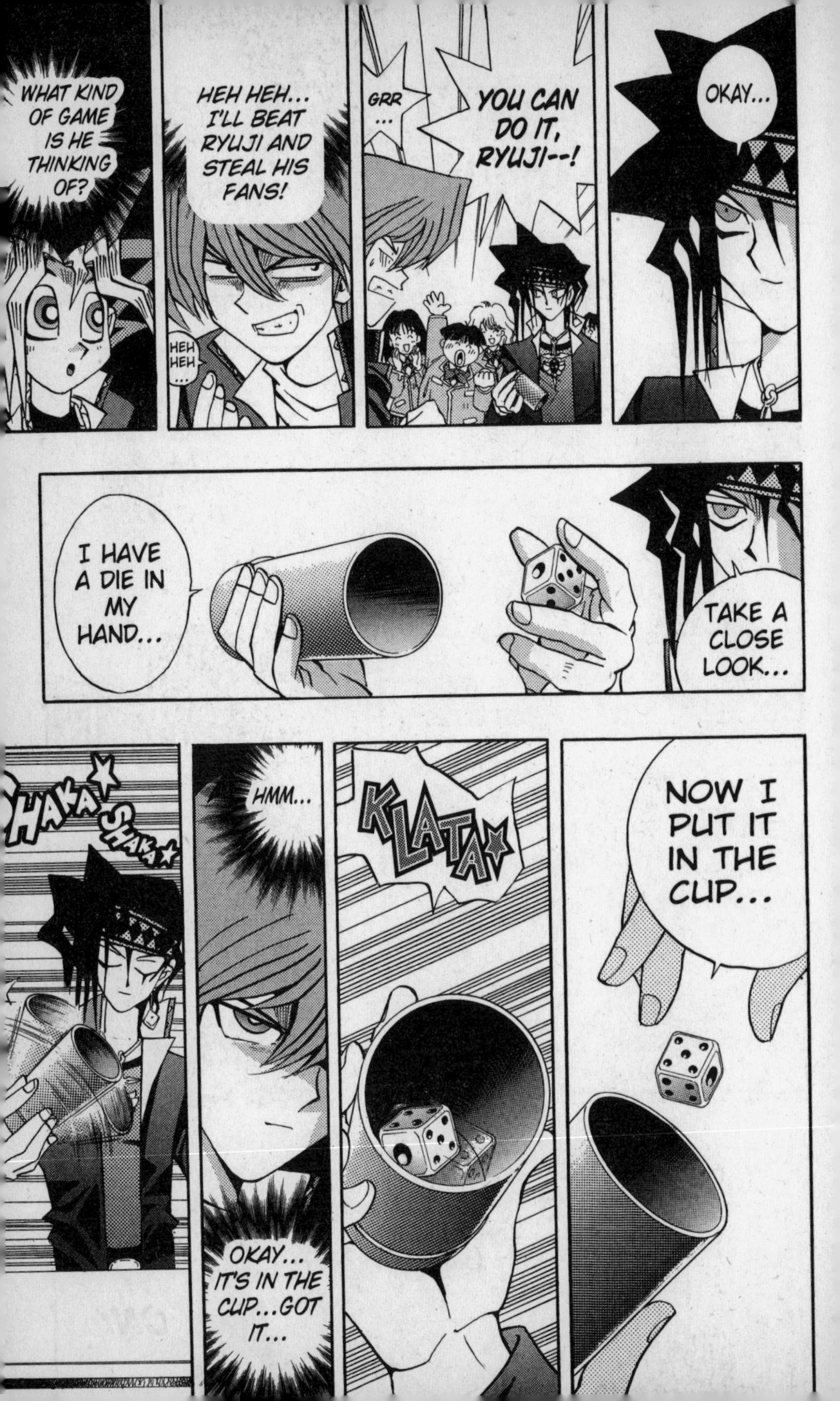
OKAY...
YOU CAN DO IT, RYUJI--!
GRR ...
HEH HEH... I'LL BEAT RYUJI AND STEAL HIS FANS!
HEH HEH ...
WHAT KIND OF GAME IS HE THINKING OF?
I HAVE A DIE IN MY HAND...
TAKE A CLOSE LOOK...
NOW I PUT IT IN THE CUP...
KLATA
HMM...
OKAY... IT'S IN THE CUP...GOT IT...
SHAKA SHAKA

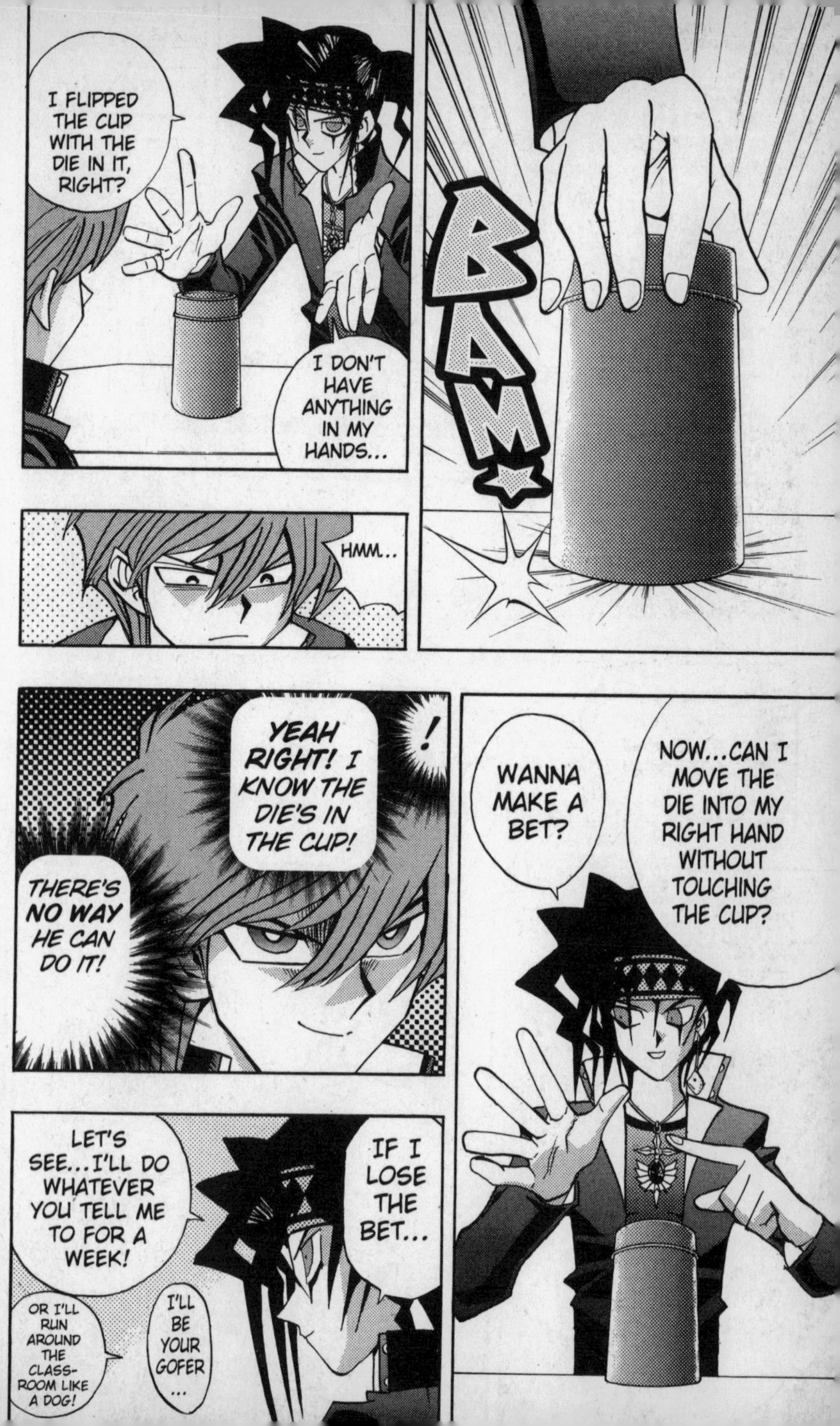
BAM
I FLIPPED THE CUP WITH THE DIE IN IT, RIGHT?
I DON'T HAVE ANYTHING IN MY HANDS...
HMM..
NOW...CAN I MOVE THE DIE INTO MY RIGHT HAND WITHOUT TOUCHING THE CUP?
WANNA MAKE A BET?
!
YEAH RIGHT! I KNOW THE DIE'S IN THE CUP!
THERE'S NO WAY HE CAN DO IT!
IF I LOSE THE BET...
LET'S SEE...I'LL DO WHATEVER YOU TELL ME TO FOR A WEEK!
I'LL BE YOUR GOFER...
OR I'LL RUN AROUND THE CLASS-ROOM LIKE A DOG!

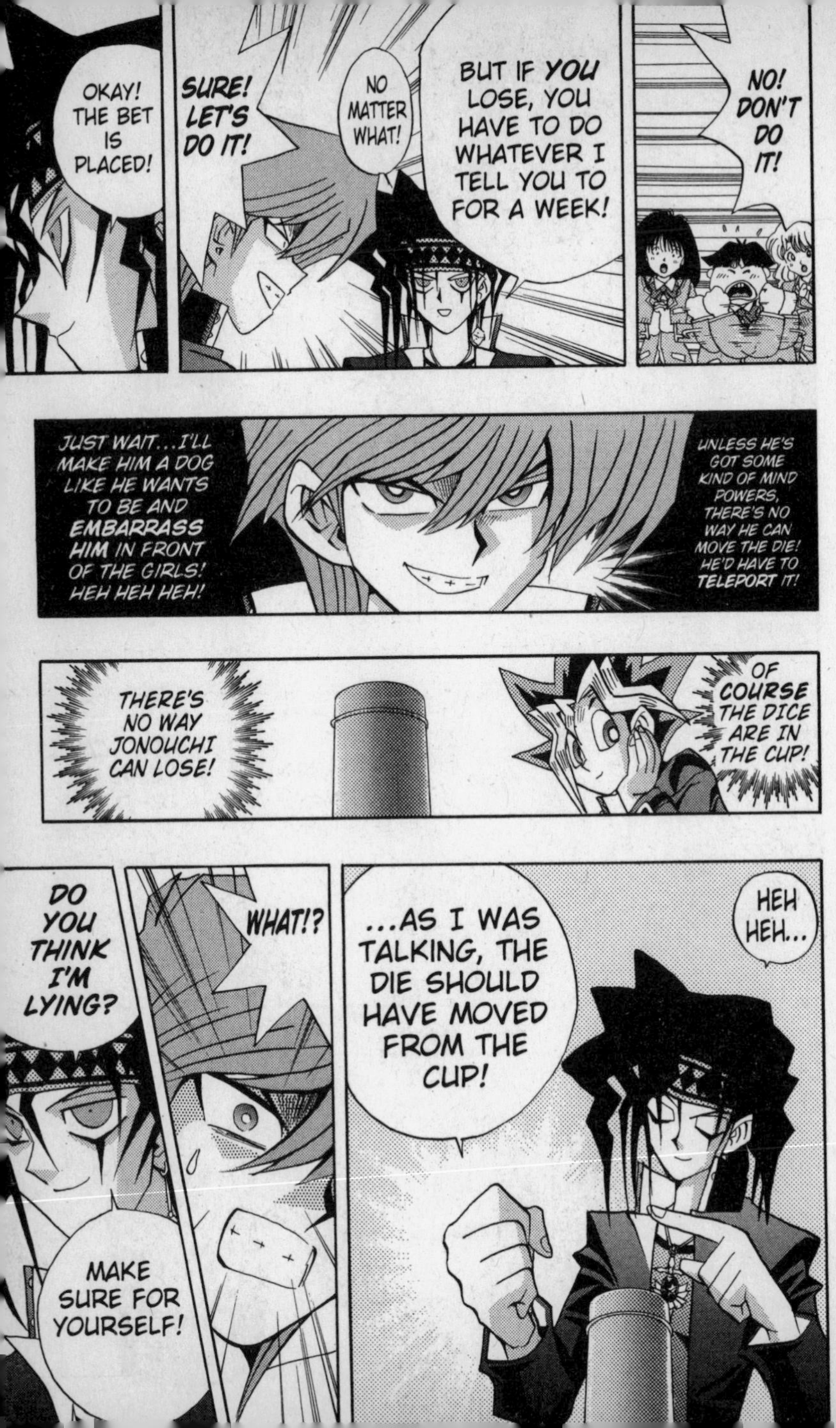
NO! DON'T DO IT!
BUT IF YOU LOSE, YOU HAVE TO DO WHATEVER I TELL YOU TO FOR A WEEK!
NO MATTER WHAT!
SURE! LET'S DO IT!
OKAY! THE BET IS PLACED!
UNLESS HE'S GOT SOME KIND OF MIND POWERS, THERE'S NO WAY HE CAN MOVE THE DIE! HE'D HAVE TO TELEPORT IT!
JUST WAIT...I'LL MAKE HIM A DOG LIKE HE WANTS TO BE AND EMBARRASS HIM IN FRONT OF THE GIRLS! HEH HEH HEH!
OF COURSE THE DICE ARE IN THE CUP!
THERE'S NO WAY JONOUCHI CAN LOSE!
HEH HEH...
...AS I WAS TALKING, THE DIE SHOULD HAVE MOVED FROM THE CUP!
WHAT!?
DO YOU THINK I'M LYING?
MAKE SURE FOR YOURSELF!

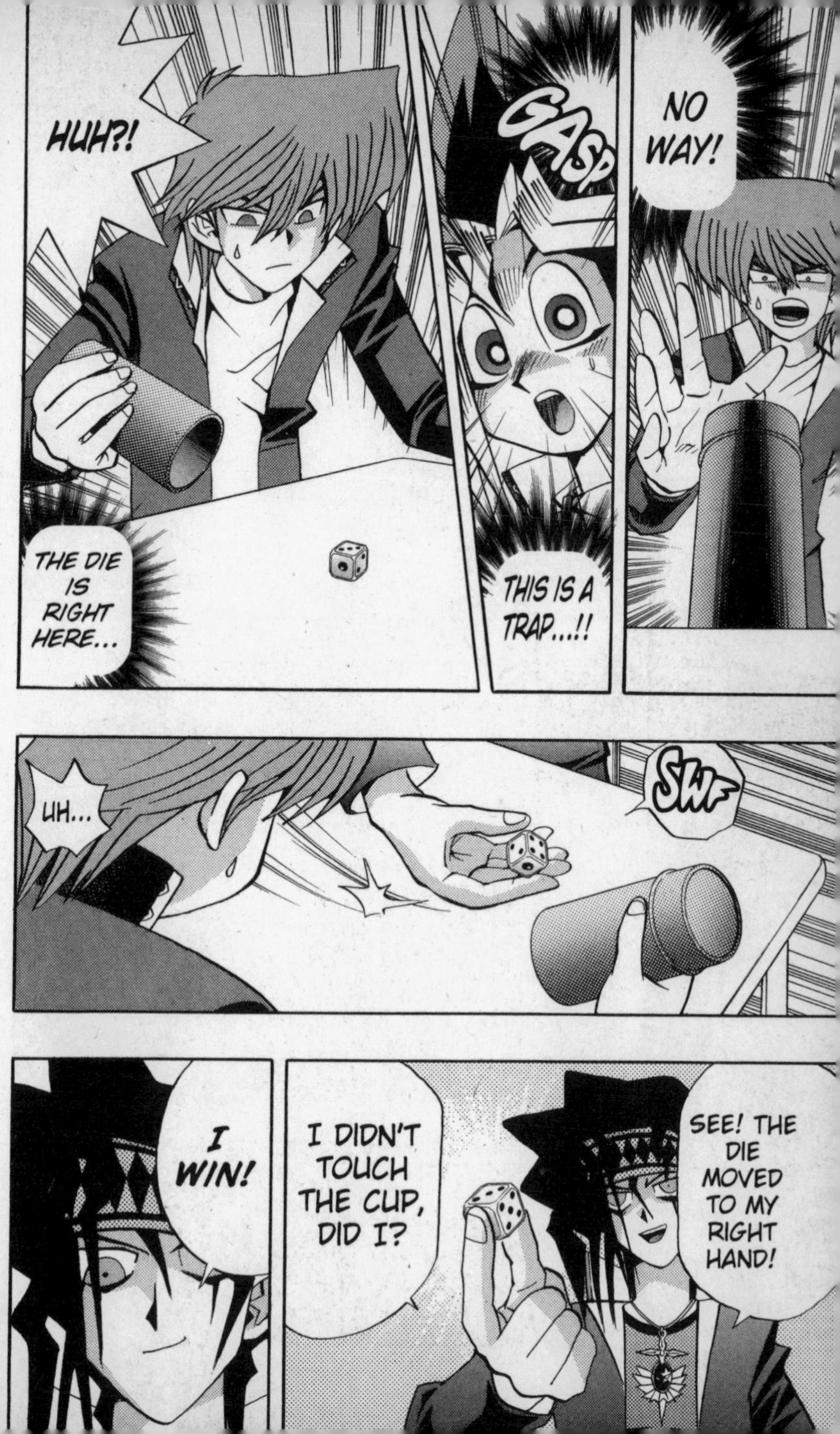
NO WAY!
GASP
THIS IS A TRAP...!!
HUH?!
THE DIE IS RIGHT HERE...
SWF
UH...
SEE! THE DIE MOVED TO MY RIGHT HAND!
I DIDN'T TOUCH THE CUP, DID I?
I WIN!

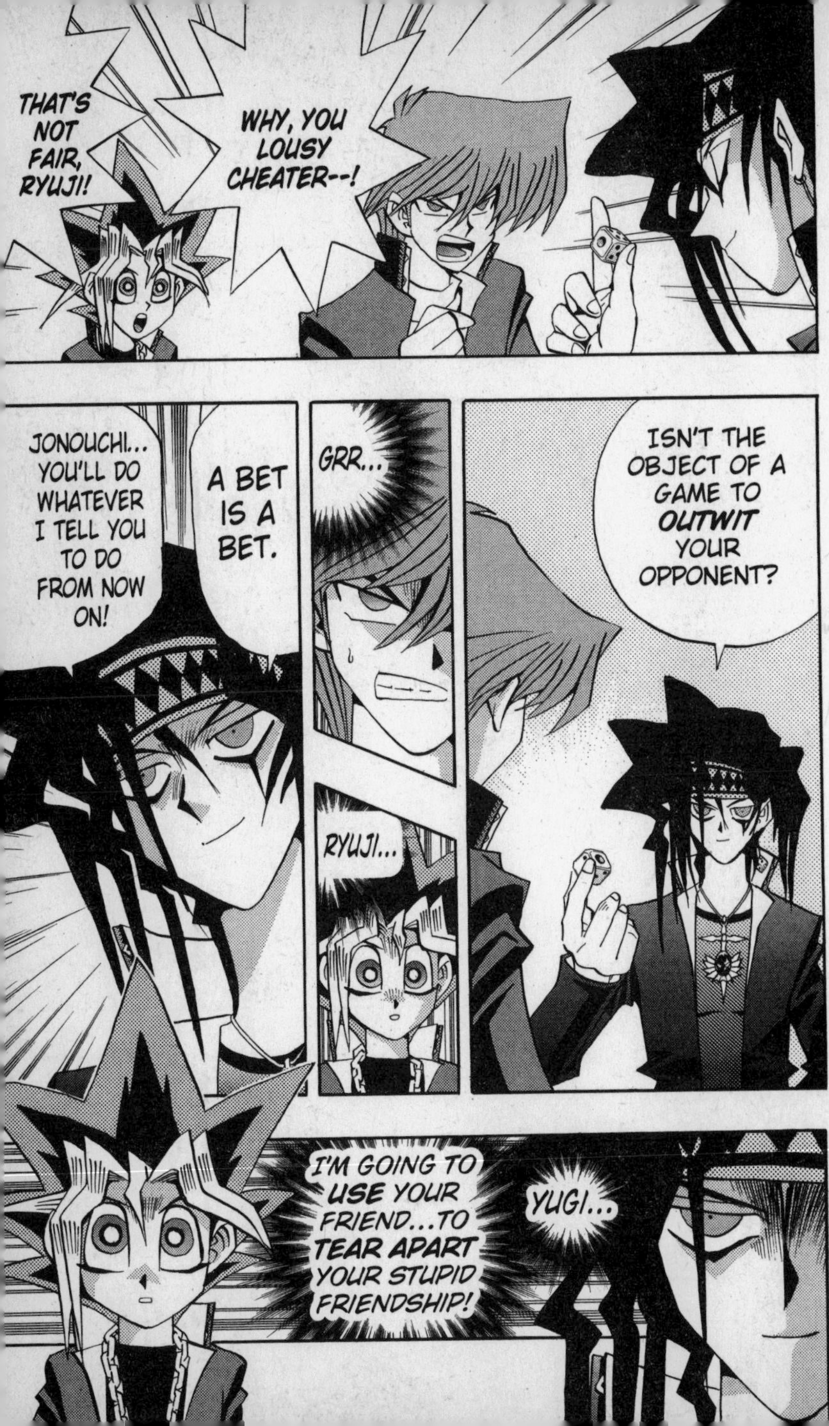
WHY, YOU LOUSY CHEATER--!
THAT'S NOT FAIR, RYUJI!
ISN'T THE OBJECT OF A GAME TO OUTWIT YOUR OPPONENT?
GRR...
RYUJI...
A BET IS A BET.
JONOUCHI... YOU'LL DO WHATEVER I TELL YOU TO DO FROM NOW ON!
YUGI...
I'M GOING TO USE YOUR FRIEND...TO TEAR APART YOUR STUPID FRIENDSHIP!

Duel 76: Rigged!

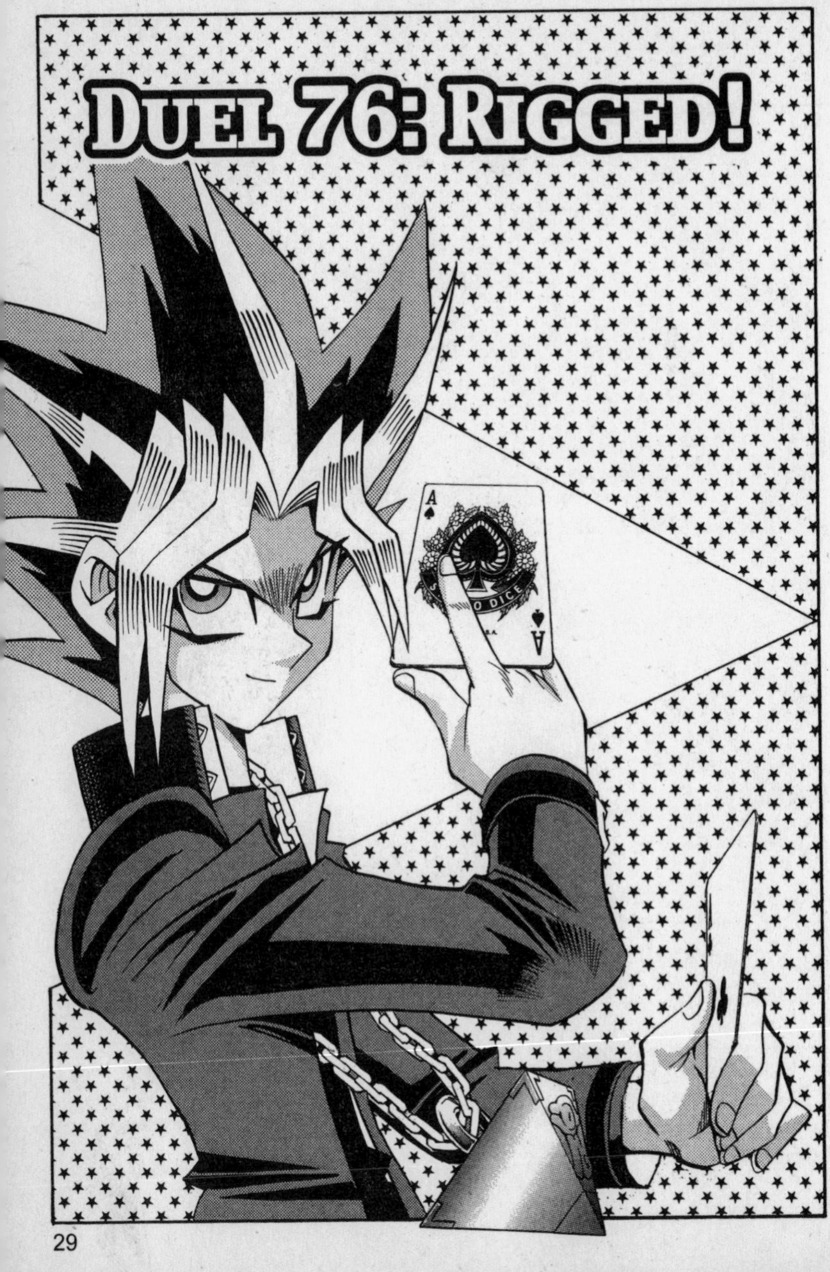

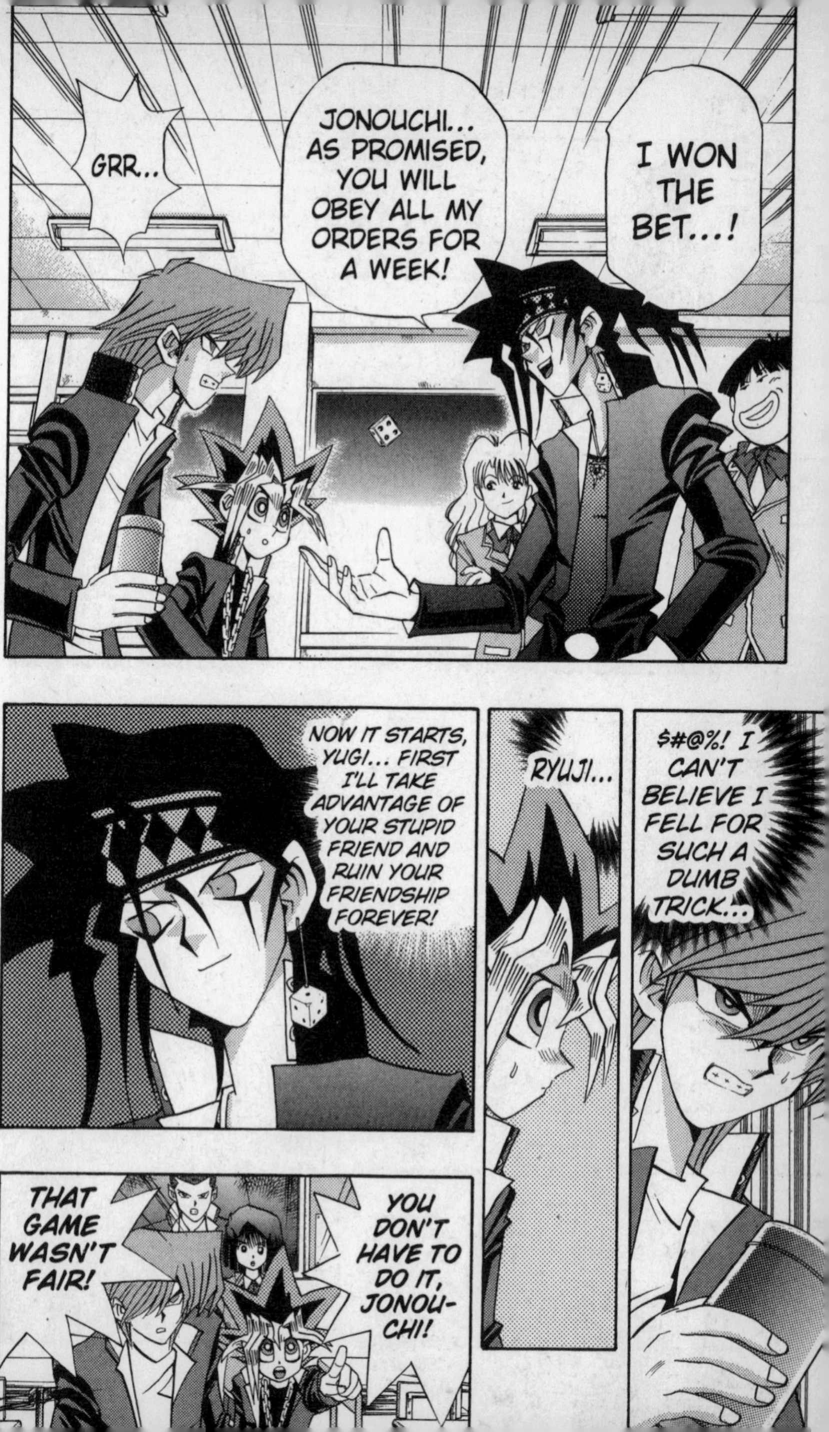
I WON THE BET...!
JONOUCHI... AS PROMISED, YOU WILL OBEY ALL MY ORDERS FOR A WEEK!
GRR...
$#@%! I CAN'T BELIEVE I FELL FOR SUCH A DUMB TRICK...
RYUJI...
NOW IT STARTS, YUGI... FIRST I'LL TAKE ADVANTAGE OF YOUR STUPID FRIEND AND RUIN YOUR FRIENDSHIP FOREVER!
YOU DON'T HAVE TO DO IT, JONOU-CHI!
THAT GAME WASN'T FAIR!

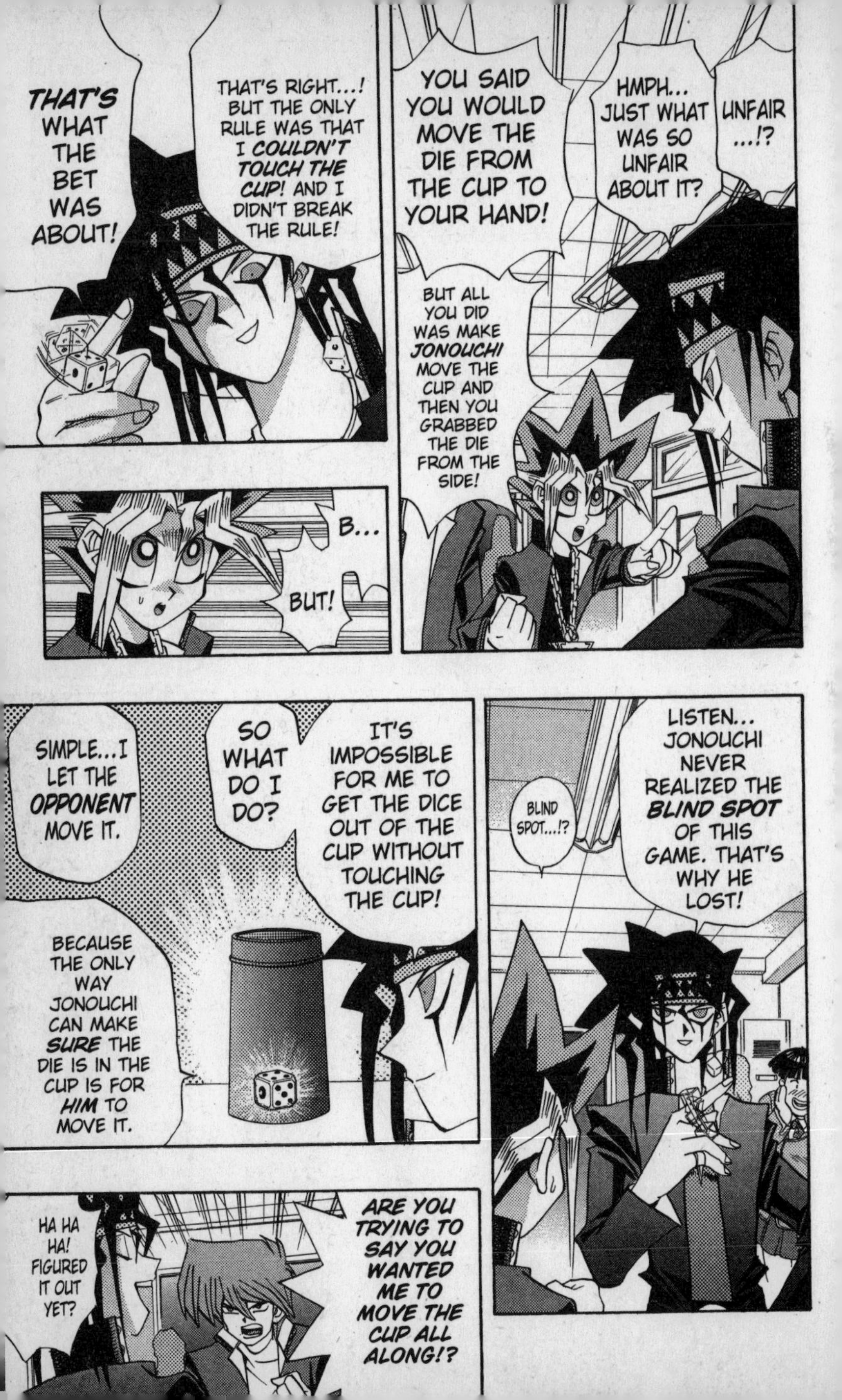
UNFAIR ...!?
HMPH... JUST WHAT WAS SO UNFAIR ABOUT IT?
YOU SAID YOU WOULD MOVE THE DIE FROM THE CUP TO YOUR HAND!
BUT ALL YOU DID WAS MAKE JONOUCHI MOVE THE CUP AND THEN YOU GRABBED THE DIE FROM THE SIDE!
THAT'S RIGHT...! BUT THE ONLY RULE WAS THAT I COULDN'T TOUCH THE CUP! AND I DIDN'T BREAK THE RULE!
THAT'S WHAT THE BET WAS ABOUT!
B... BUT!
LISTEN... JONOUCHI NEVER REALIZED THE BLIND SPOT OF THIS GAME. THAT'S WHY HE LOST!
BLIND SPOT...!?
IT'S IMPOSSIBLE FOR ME TO GET THE DICE OUT OF THE CUP WITHOUT TOUCHING THE CUP!
SO WHAT DO I DO?
SIMPLE...I LET THE OPPONENT MOVE IT.
BECAUSE THE ONLY WAY JONOUCHI CAN MAKE SURE THE DIE IS IN THE CUP IS FOR HIM TO MOVE IT.
ARE YOU TRYING TO SAY YOU WANTED ME TO MOVE THE CUP ALL ALONG!?
HA HA HA! FIGURED IT OUT YET?

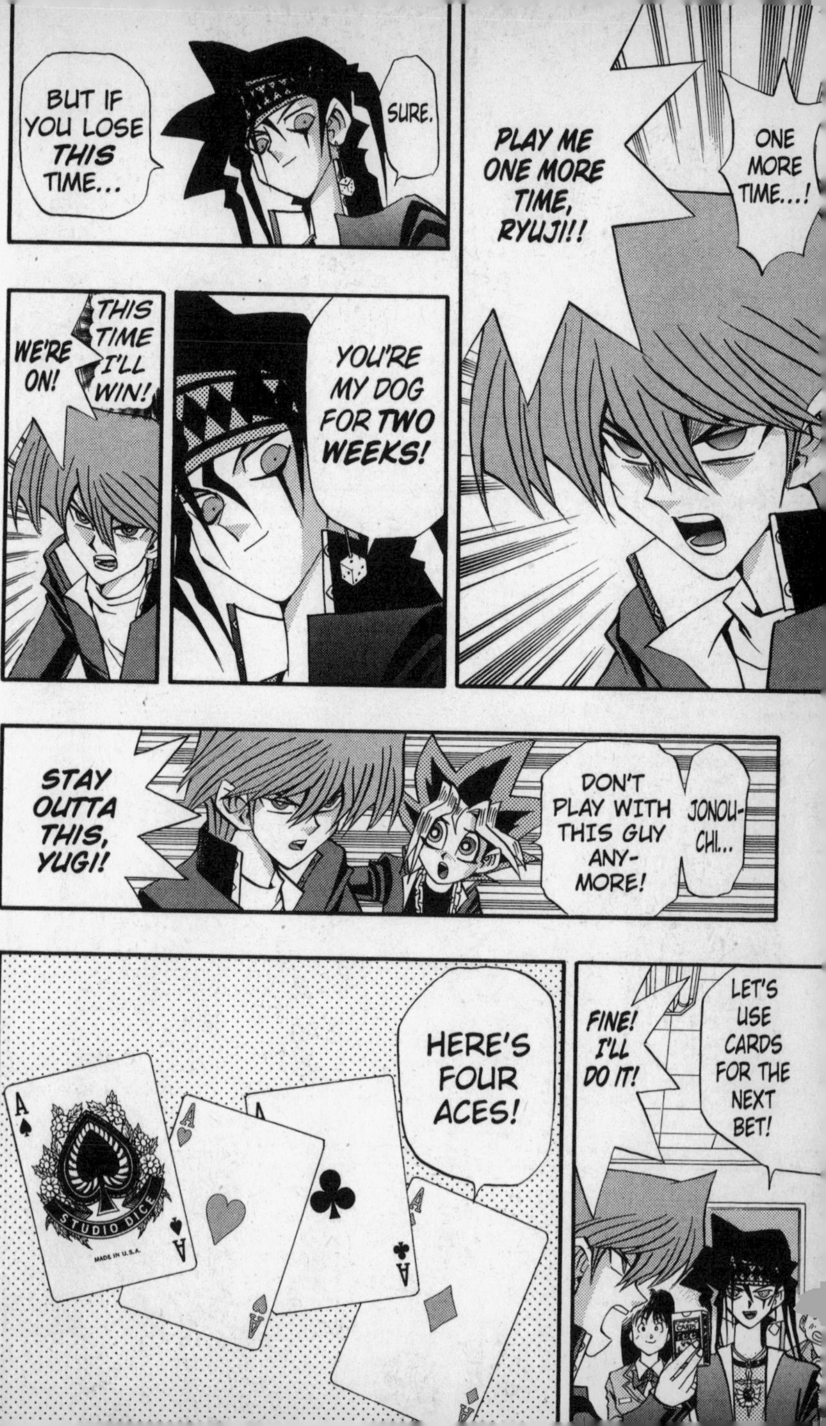
ONE MORE TIME...!
PLAY ME ONE MORE TIME, RYUJI!!
SURE.
BUT IF YOU LOSE THIS TIME...
YOU'RE MY DOG FOR TWO WEEKS!
THIS TIME I'LL WIN!
WE'RE ON!
JONOU-CHI...
DON'T PLAY WITH THIS GUY ANY-MORE!
STAY OUTTA THIS, YUGI!
LET'S USE CARDS FOR THE NEXT BET!
FINE! I'LL DO IT!
HERE'S FOUR ACES!
STUDIO DICE
MADE IN U.S.A.

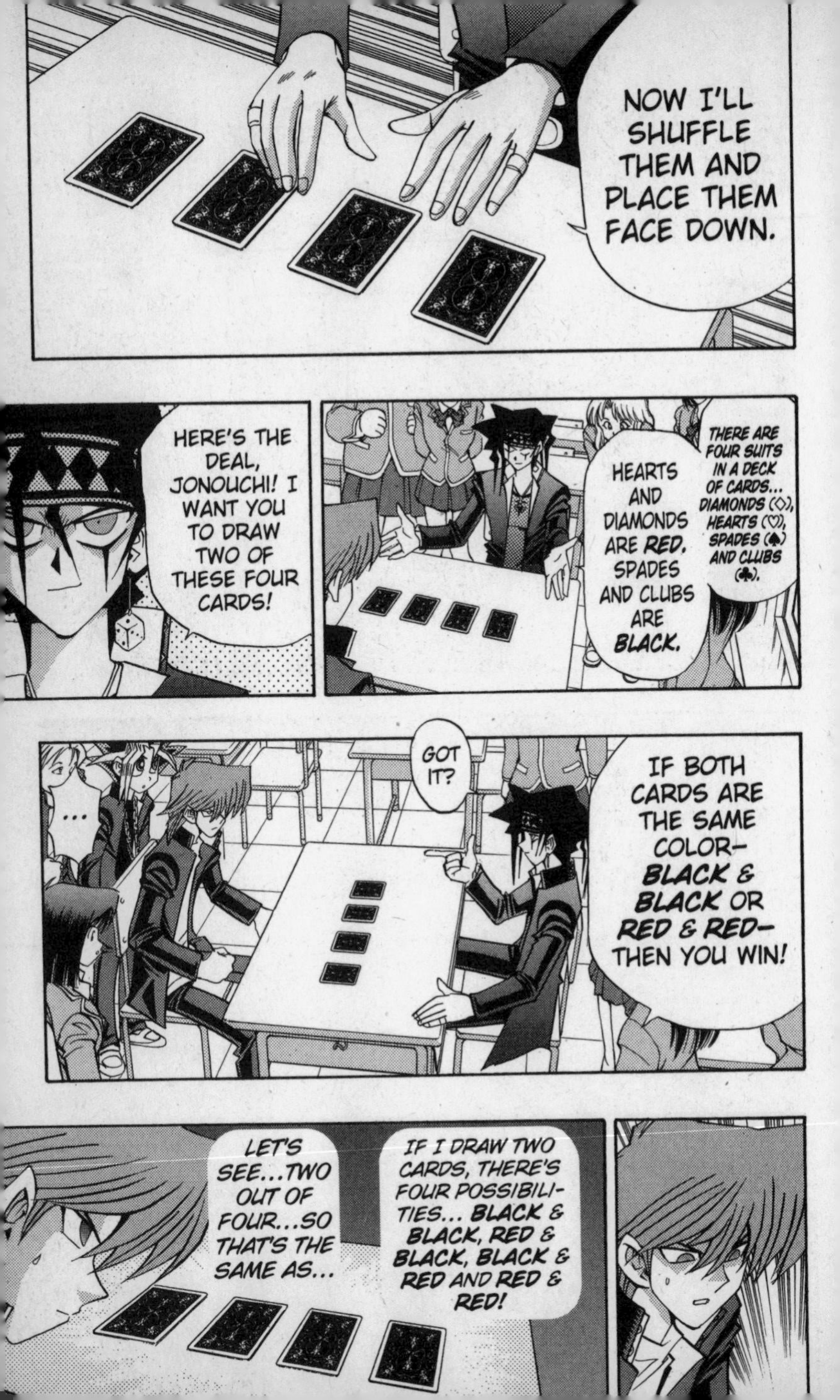
NOW I'LL SHUFFLE THEM AND PLACE THEM FACE DOWN.
THERE ARE FOUR SUITS IN A DECK OF CARDS... DIAMONDS (◇), HEARTS (♡), SPADES (♠) AND CLUBS (♣).
HEARTS AND DIAMONDS ARE RED, SPADES AND CLUBS ARE BLACK.
HERE'S THE DEAL, JONOUCHI! I WANT YOU TO DRAW TWO OF THESE FOUR CARDS!
IF BOTH CARDS ARE THE SAME COLOR– BLACK & BLACK OR RED & RED– THEN YOU WIN!
GOT IT?
...
IF I DRAW TWO CARDS, THERE'S FOUR POSSIBILI- TIES... BLACK & BLACK, RED & BLACK, BLACK & RED AND RED & RED!
LET'S SEE...TWO OUT OF FOUR...SO THAT'S THE SAME AS...

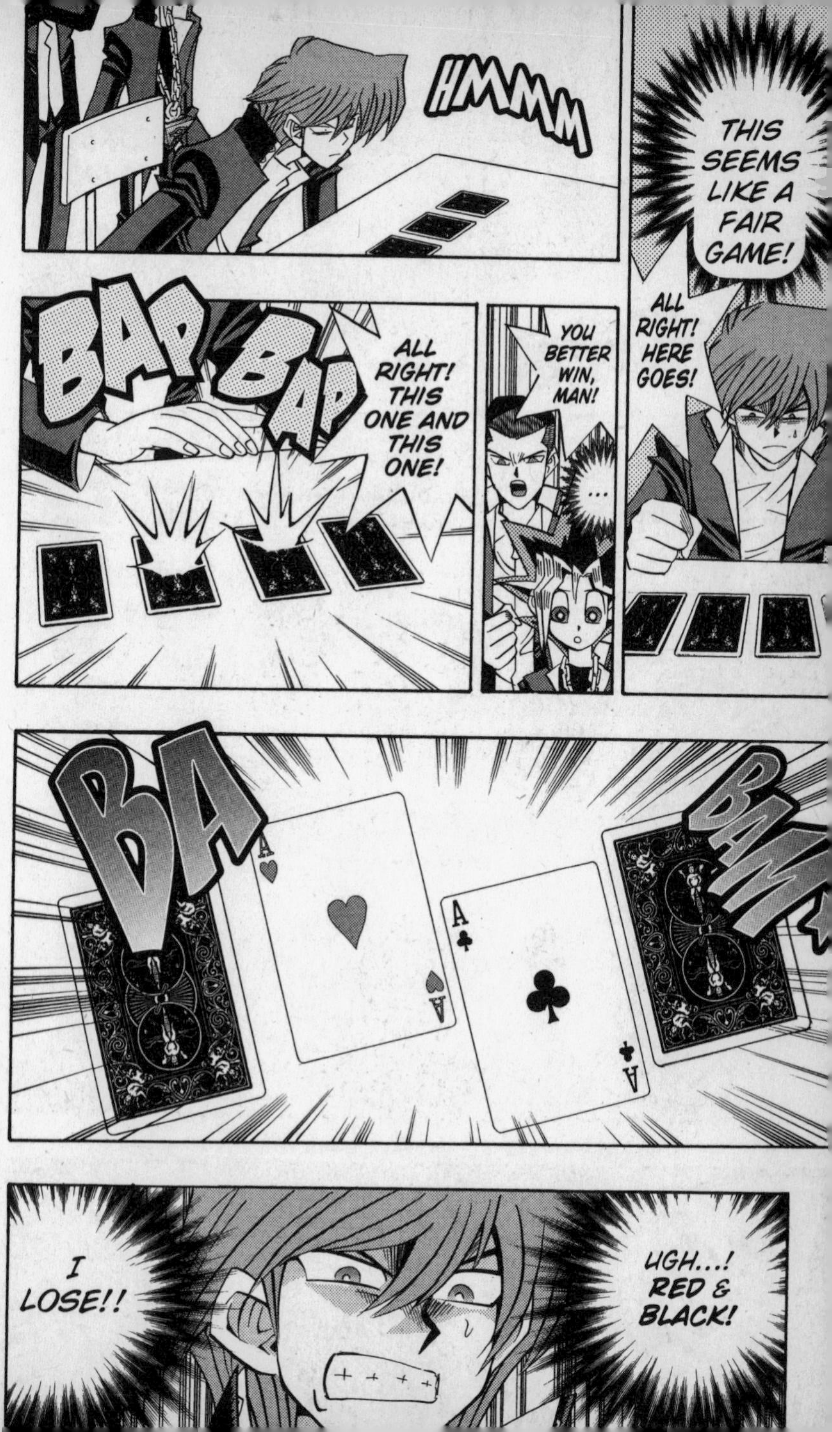
THIS SEEMS LIKE A FAIR GAME!
ALL RIGHT! HERE GOES!
HMMM
YOU BETTER WIN, MAN!
...
BAP BAP
ALL RIGHT! THIS ONE AND THIS ONE!
BAM
BA
UGH...! RED & BLACK!
I LOSE!!

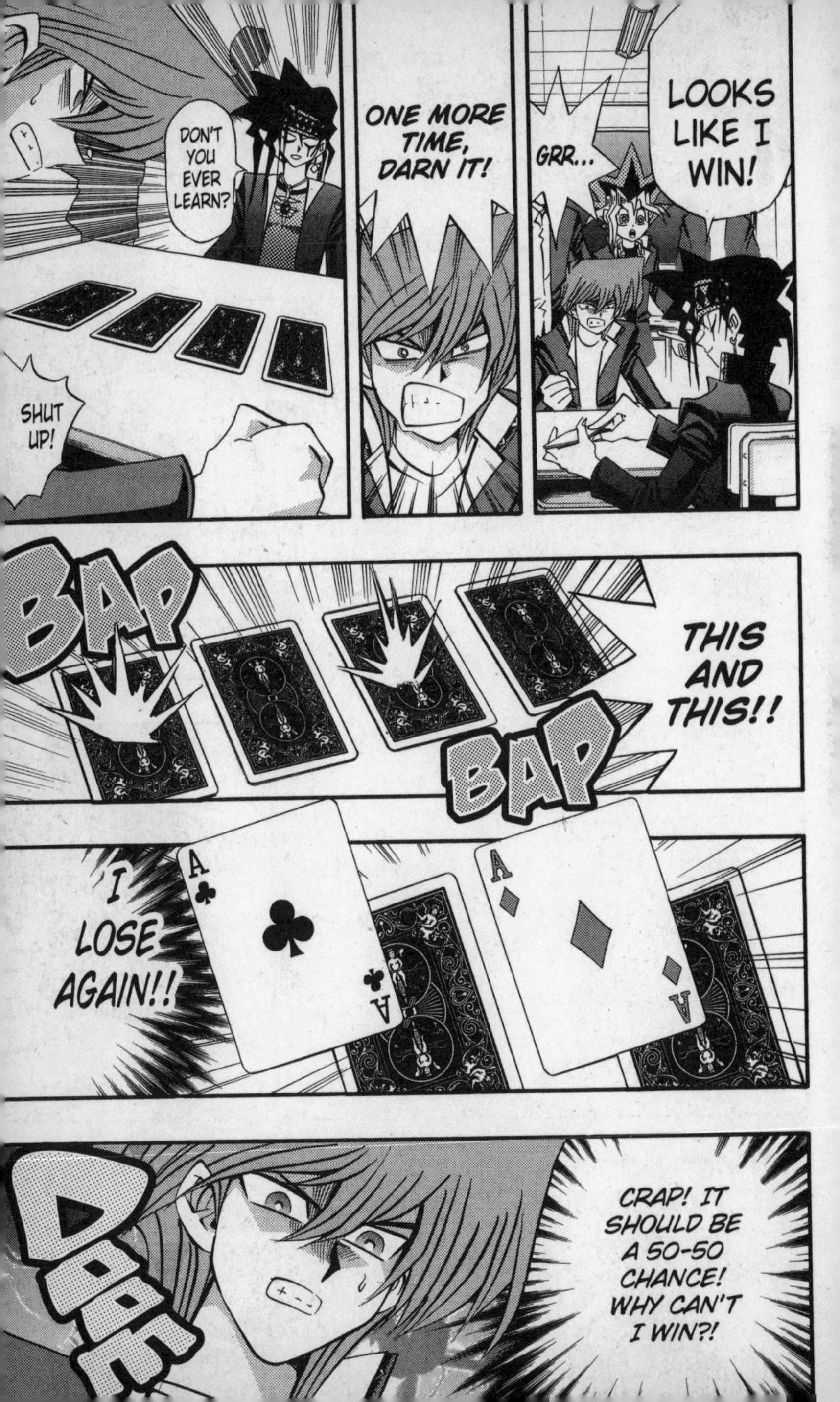
LOOKS LIKE I WIN!
GRR...
ONE MORE TIME, DARN IT!
DON'T YOU EVER LEARN?
SHUT UP!
THIS AND THIS!!
BAP
BAP
I LOSE AGAIN!!
CRAP! IT SHOULD BE A 50-50 CHANCE! WHY CAN'T I WIN?!

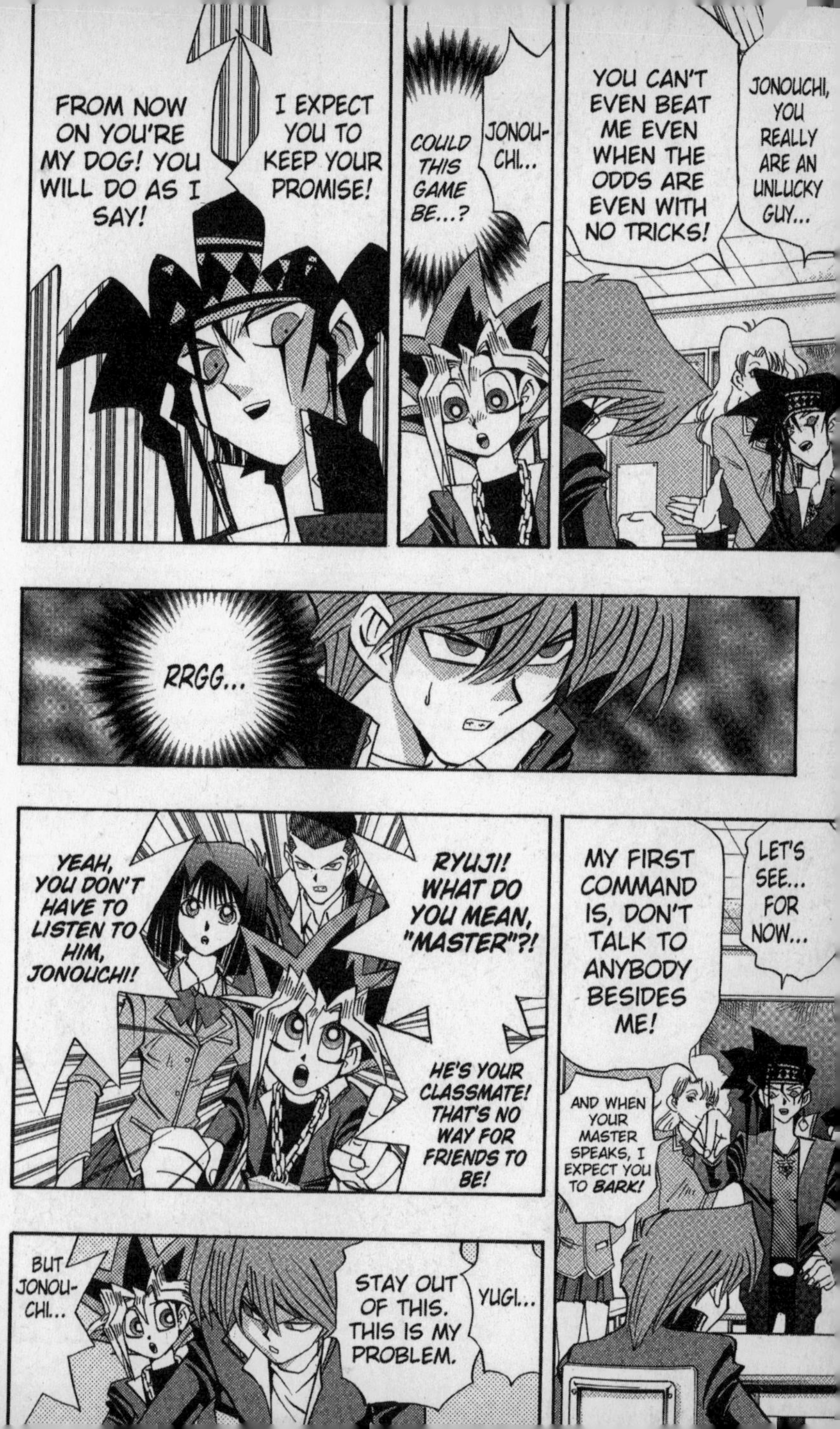
JONOUCHI, YOU REALLY ARE AN UNLUCKY GUY...
YOU CAN'T EVEN BEAT ME EVEN WHEN THE ODDS ARE EVEN WITH NO TRICKS!
JONOU-CHI...
COULD THIS GAME BE...?
I EXPECT YOU TO KEEP YOUR PROMISE!
FROM NOW ON YOU'RE MY DOG! YOU WILL DO AS I SAY!
RRGG...
LET'S SEE... FOR NOW...
MY FIRST COMMAND IS, DON'T TALK TO ANYBODY BESIDES ME!
AND WHEN YOUR MASTER SPEAKS, I EXPECT YOU TO BARK!
RYUJI! WHAT DO YOU MEAN, "MASTER"?!
HE'S YOUR CLASSMATE! THAT'S NO WAY FOR FRIENDS TO BE!
YEAH, YOU DON'T HAVE TO LISTEN TO HIM, JONOUCHI!
YUGI...
STAY OUT OF THIS. THIS IS MY PROBLEM.
BUT JONOU-CHI...

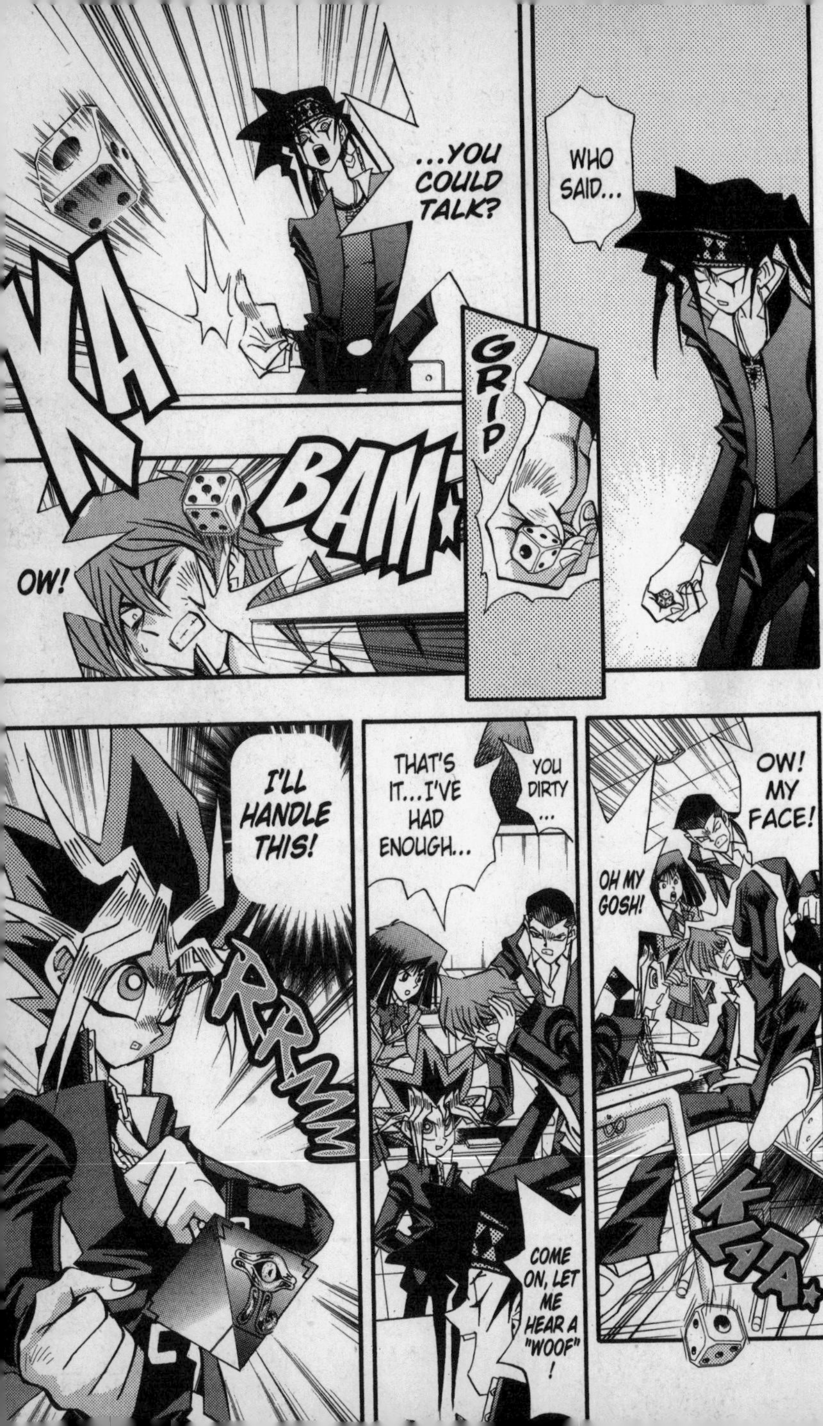
WHO SAID...
GRIP
...YOU COULD TALK?
KA
BAM
OW!
OW! MY FACE!
OH MY GOSH!
KATA
YOU DIRTY ...
THAT'S IT...I'VE HAD ENOUGH...
COME ON, LET ME HEAR A "WOOF"!
I'LL HANDLE THIS!
RRMM

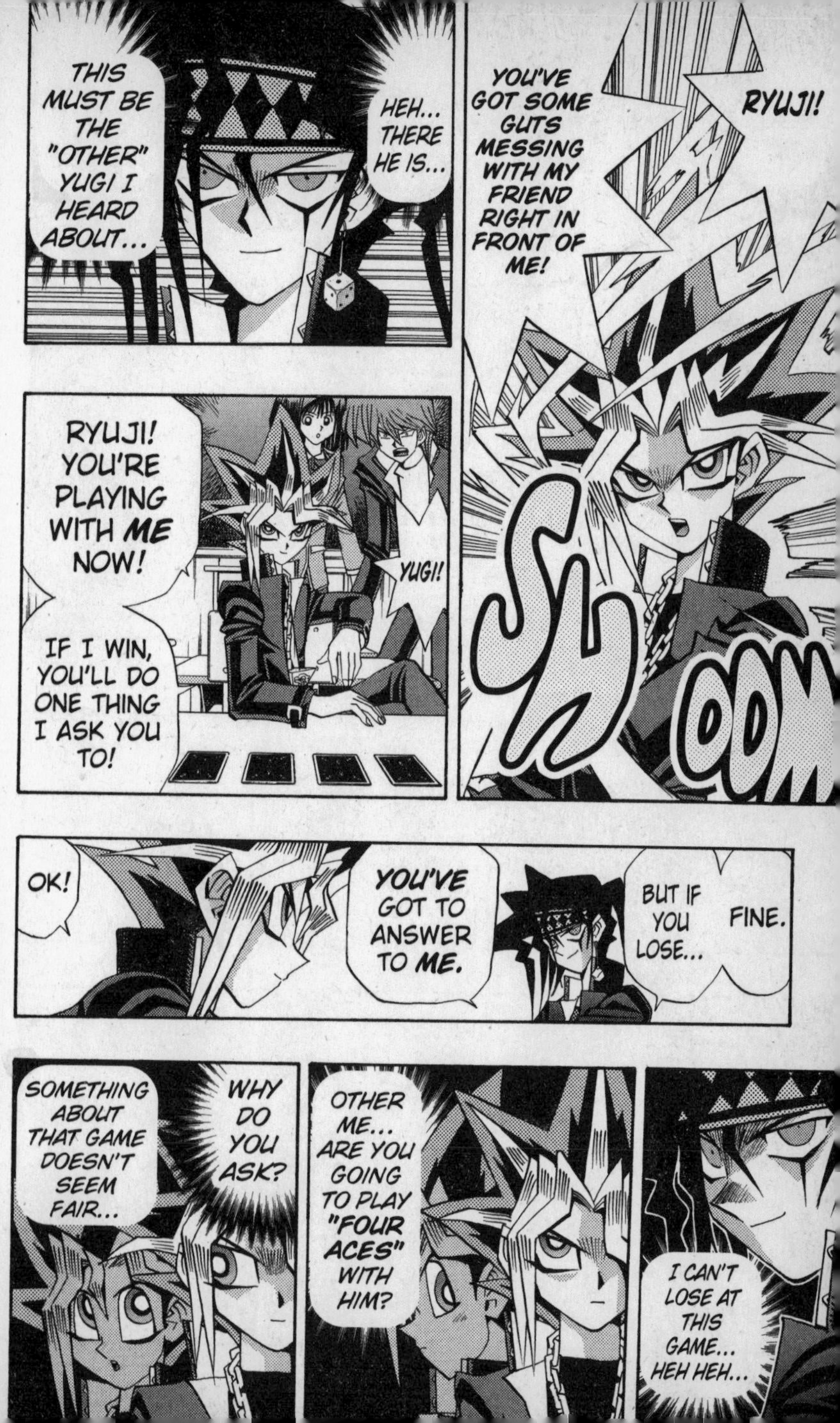
RYUJI!
YOU'VE GOT SOME GUTS MESSING WITH MY FRIEND RIGHT IN FRONT OF ME!
SHOOM
HEH... THERE HE IS...
THIS MUST BE THE "OTHER" YUGI I HEARD ABOUT...
RYUJI! YOU'RE PLAYING WITH ME NOW!
YUGI!
IF I WIN, YOU'LL DO ONE THING I ASK YOU TO!
FINE.
BUT IF YOU LOSE...
YOU'VE GOT TO ANSWER TO ME.
OK!
I CAN'T LOSE AT THIS GAME... HEH HEH...
OTHER ME... ARE YOU GOING TO PLAY "FOUR ACES" WITH HIM?
WHY DO YOU ASK?
SOMETHING ABOUT THAT GAME DOESN'T SEEM FAIR...

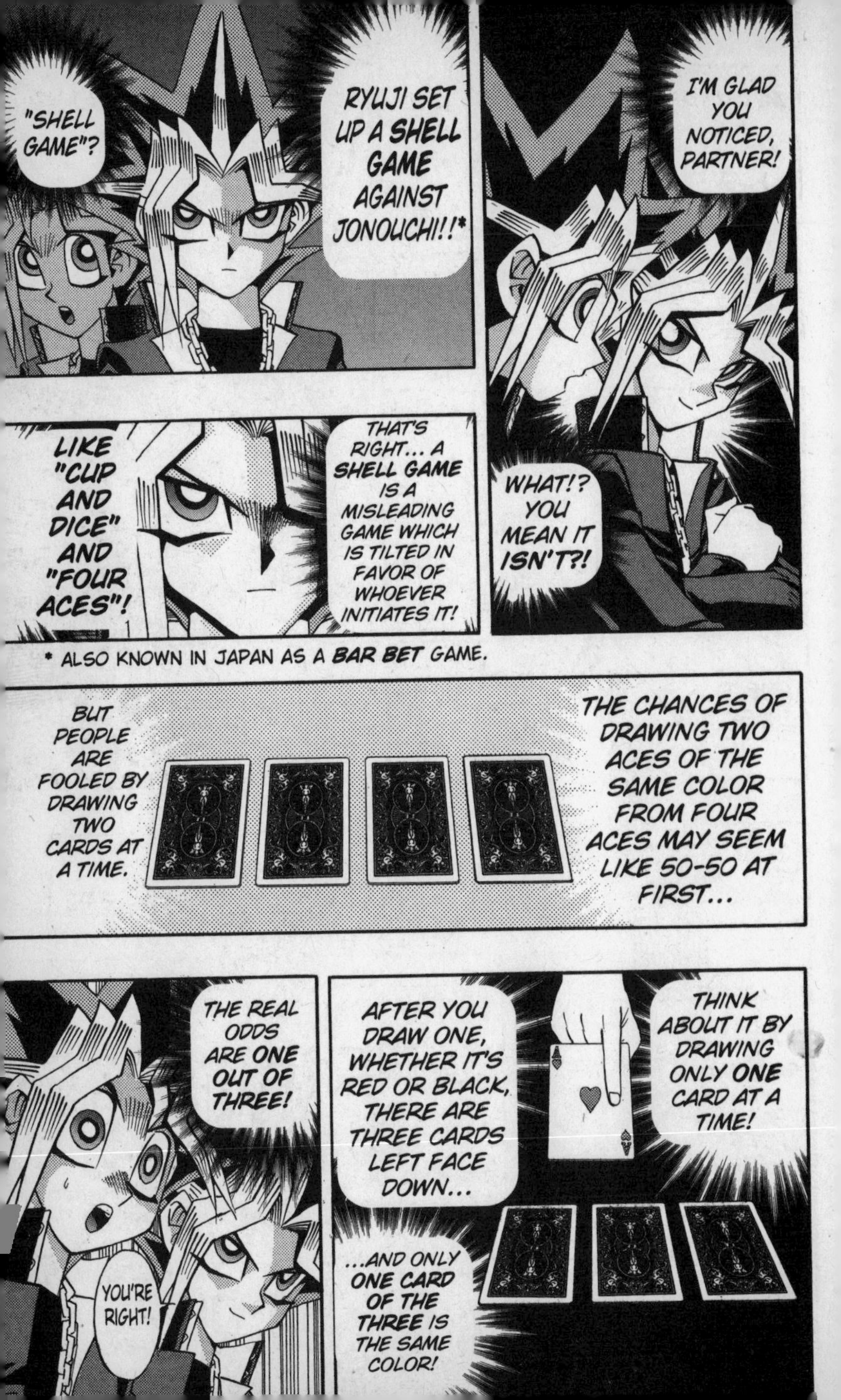
I'M GLAD YOU NOTICED, PARTNER!
WHAT!? YOU MEAN IT ISN'T?!
RYUJI SET UP A SHELL GAME AGAINST JONOUCHI!!*
"SHELL GAME"?
THAT'S RIGHT... A SHELL GAME IS A MISLEADING GAME WHICH IS TILTED IN FAVOR OF WHOEVER INITIATES IT!
LIKE "CUP AND DICE" AND "FOUR ACES"!
* ALSO KNOWN IN JAPAN AS A BAR BET GAME.
THE CHANCES OF DRAWING TWO ACES OF THE SAME COLOR FROM FOUR ACES MAY SEEM LIKE 50-50 AT FIRST...
BUT PEOPLE ARE FOOLED BY DRAWING TWO CARDS AT A TIME.
THINK ABOUT IT BY DRAWING ONLY ONE CARD AT A TIME!
AFTER YOU DRAW ONE, WHETHER IT'S RED OR BLACK, THERE ARE THREE CARDS LEFT FACE DOWN...
...AND ONLY ONE CARD OF THE THREE IS THE SAME COLOR!
THE REAL ODDS ARE ONE OUT OF THREE!
YOU'RE RIGHT!

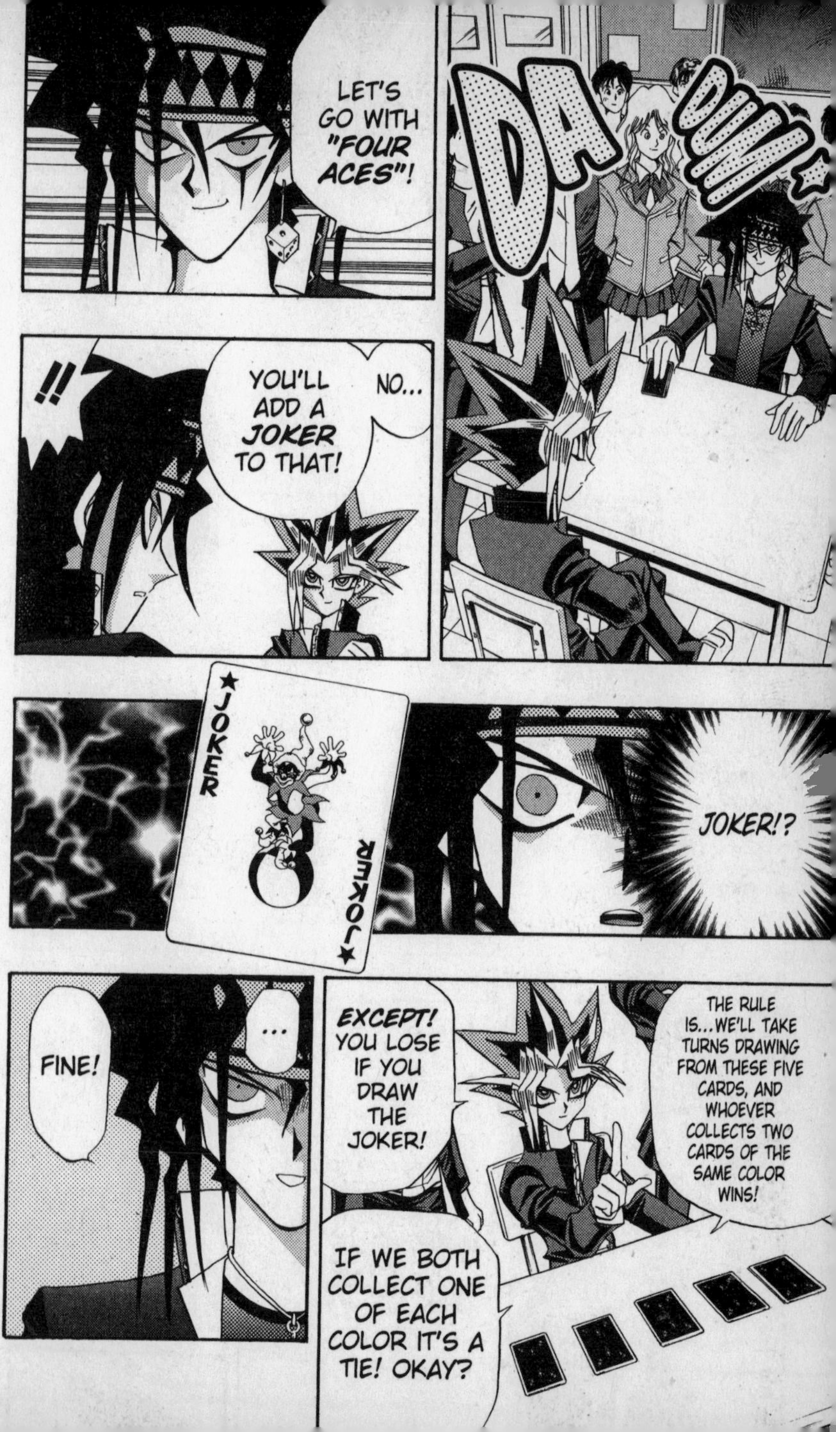
DA DUM
LET'S GO WITH "FOUR ACES"!
NO...
YOU'LL ADD A JOKER TO THAT!
!!
JOKER!?
JOKER
JOKER
THE RULE IS...WE'LL TAKE TURNS DRAWING FROM THESE FIVE CARDS, AND WHOEVER COLLECTS TWO CARDS OF THE SAME COLOR WINS!
EXCEPT! YOU LOSE IF YOU DRAW THE JOKER!
IF WE BOTH COLLECT ONE OF EACH COLOR IT'S A TIE! OKAY?
...
FINE!

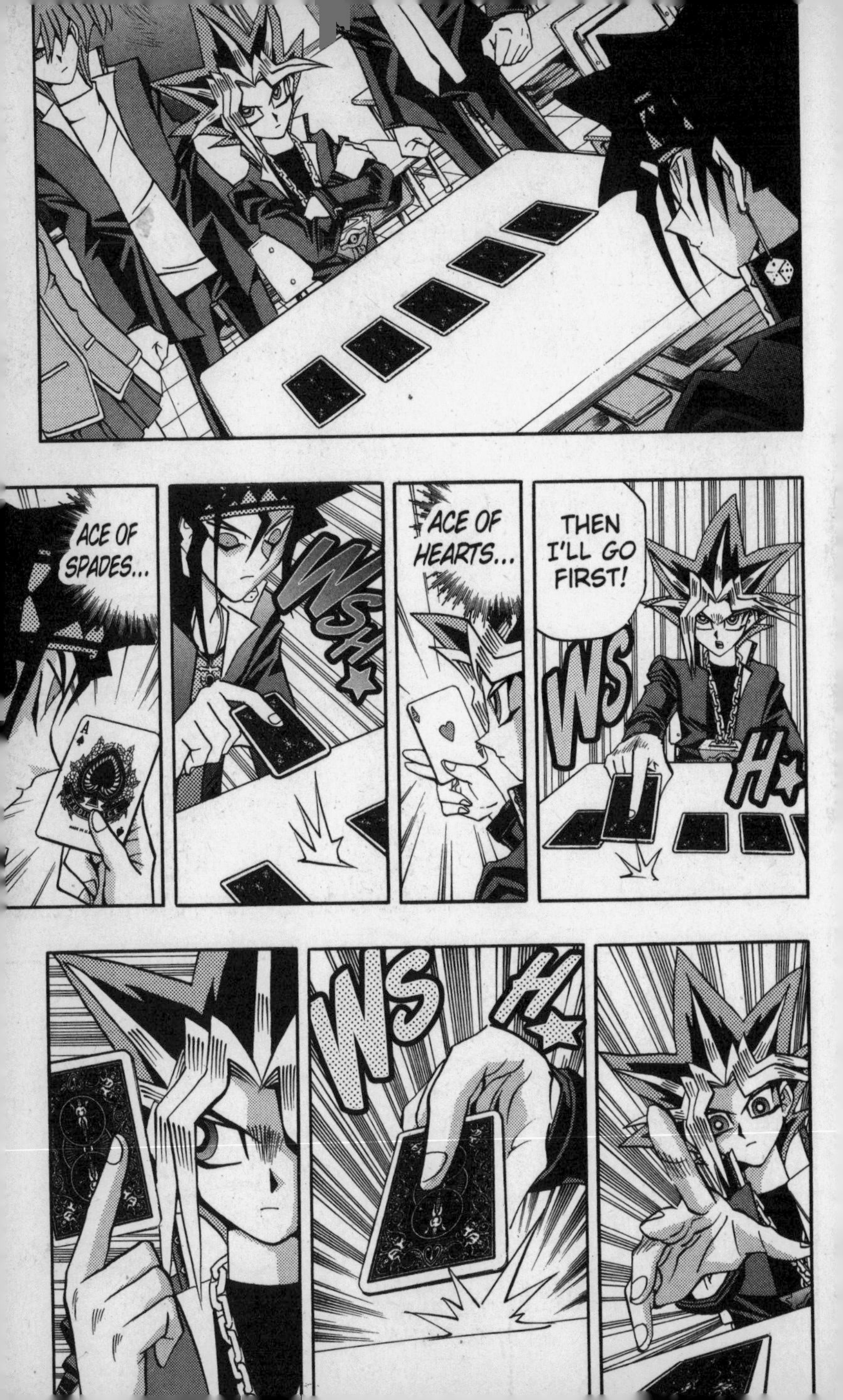
THEN I'LL GO FIRST!
WSH★
ACE OF HEARTS...
WSH★
ACE OF SPADES...
WSH★

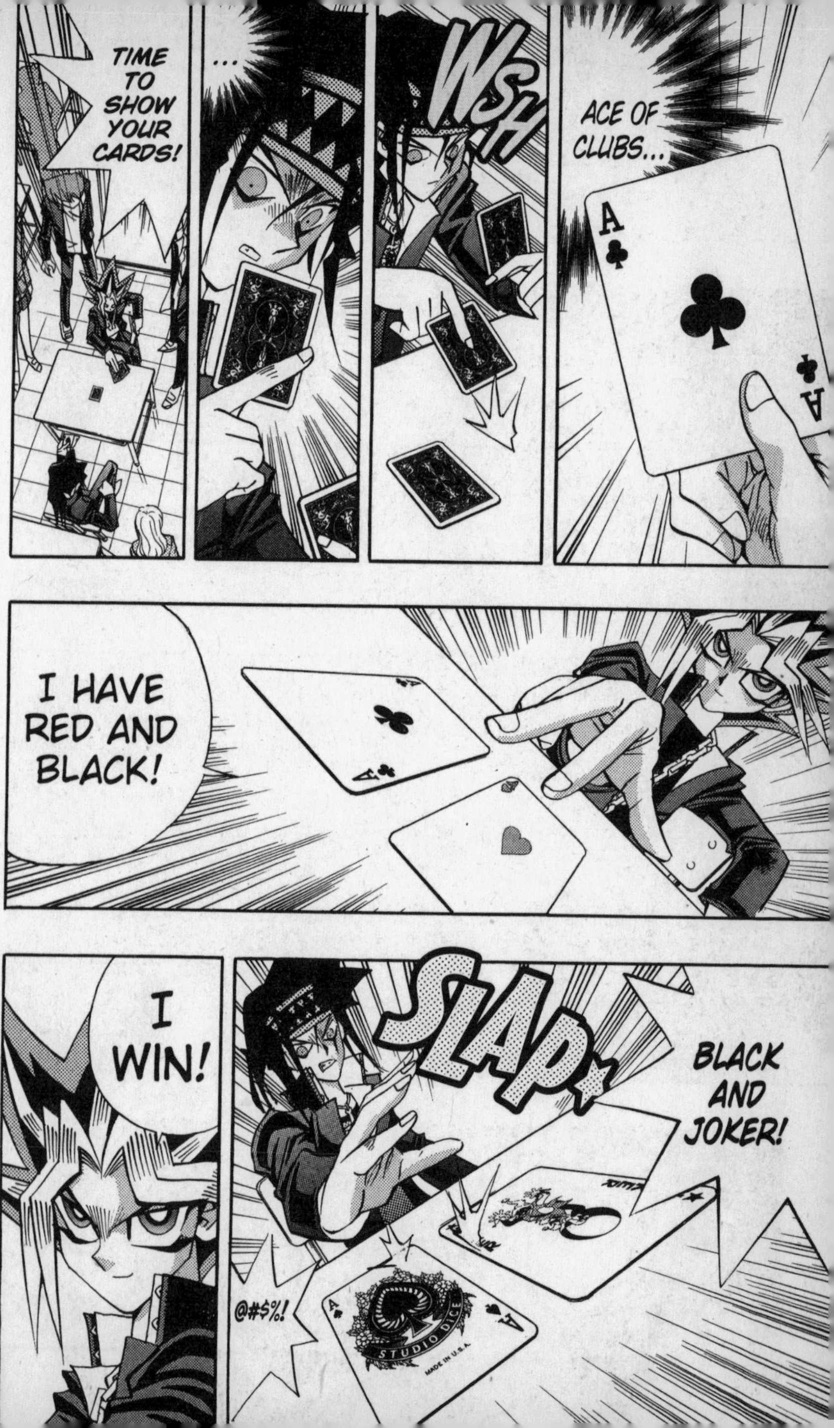
ACE OF CLUBS...
WSH
...
TIME TO SHOW YOUR CARDS!
I HAVE RED AND BLACK!
SLAP
BLACK AND JOKER!
@#$%!
I WIN!

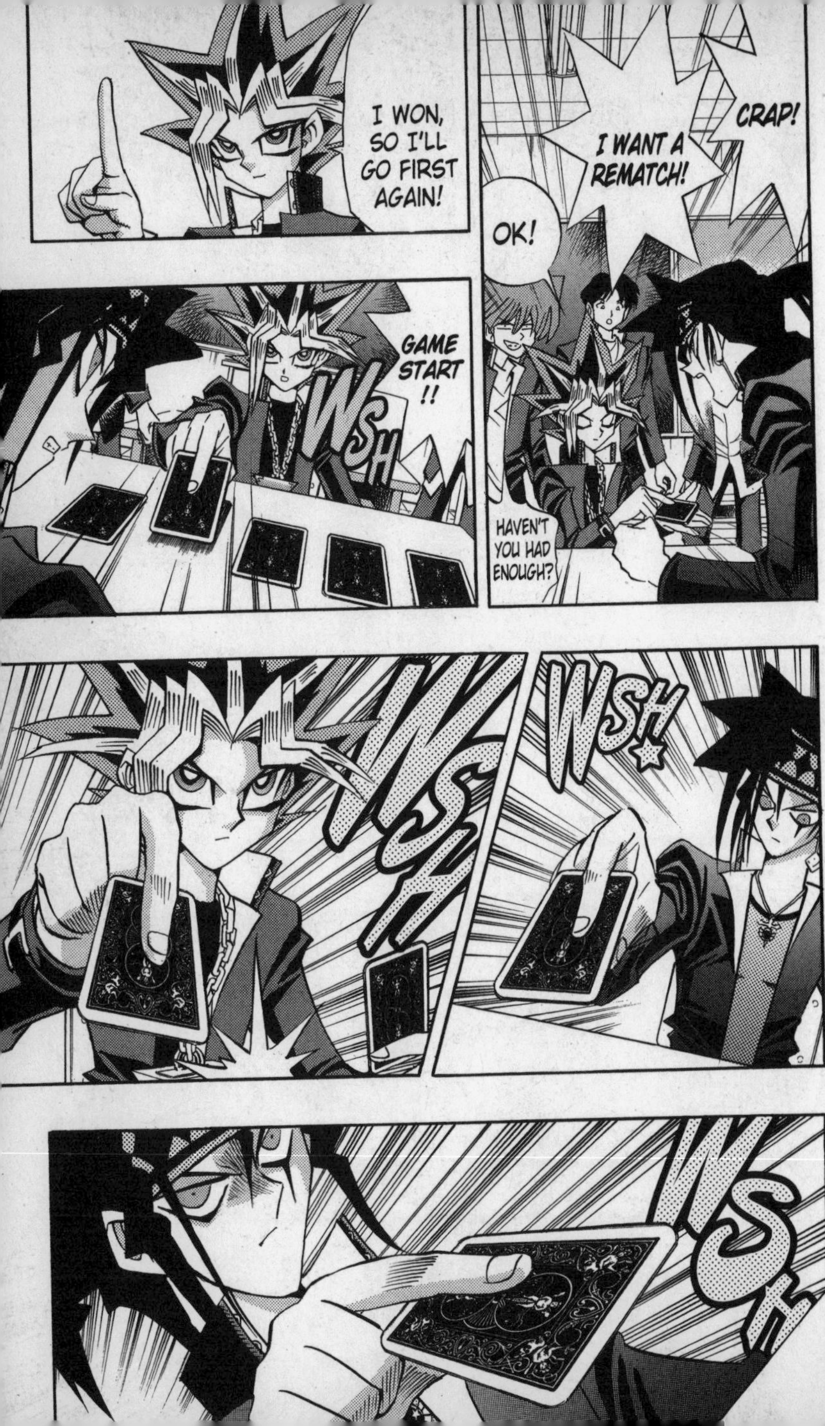
CRAP!
I WANT A REMATCH!
OK!
HAVEN'T YOU HAD ENOUGH?
I WON, SO I'LL GO FIRST AGAIN!
GAME START !!
WSH
WSH!
WSH
WSH

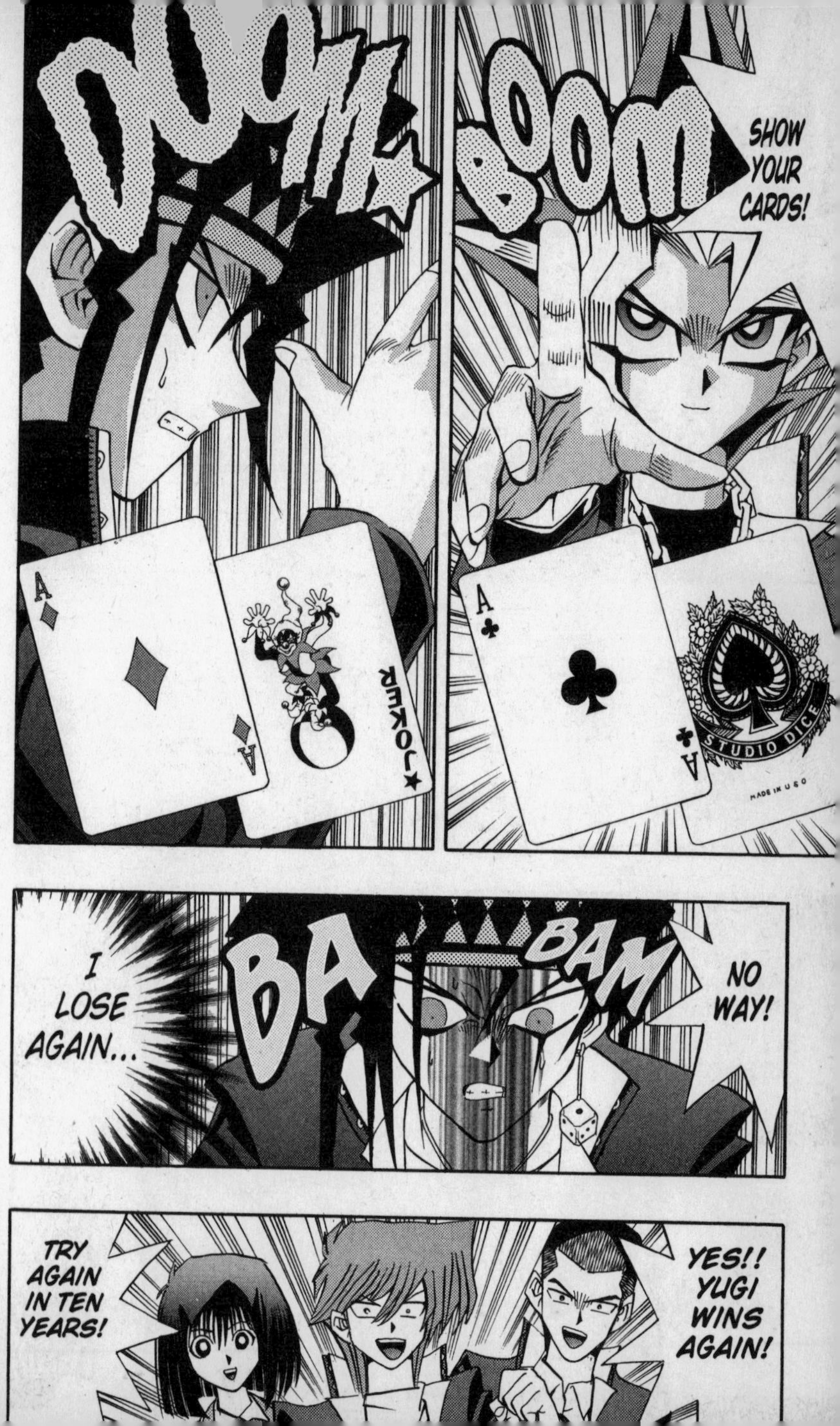
BOOM
SHOW YOUR CARDS!
STUDIO DICE
JOKER
NO WAY!
BAM
BA
I LOSE AGAIN...
YES!! YUGI WINS AGAIN!
TRY AGAIN IN TEN YEARS!

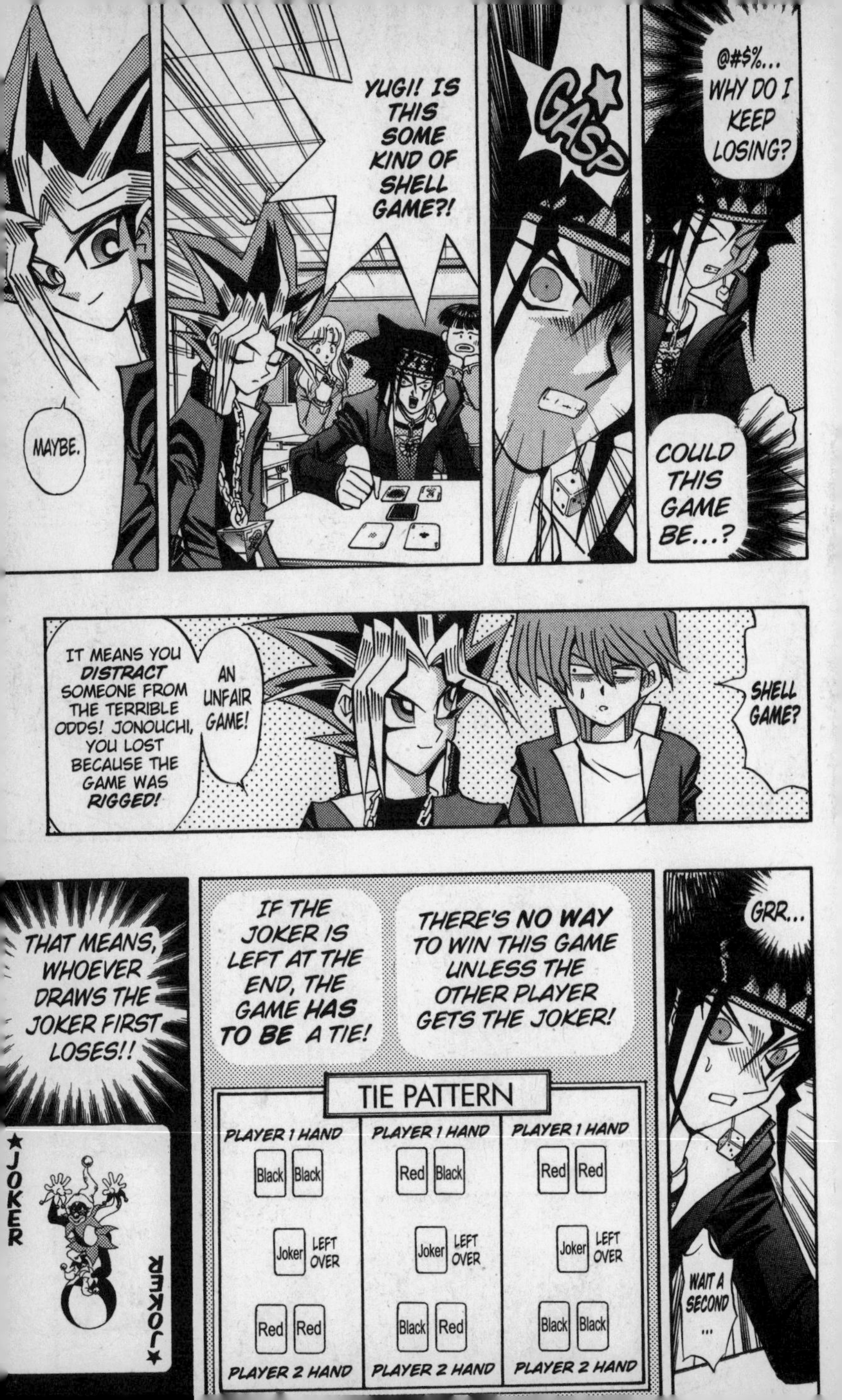
@#$%... WHY DO I KEEP LOSING?
COULD THIS GAME BE...?
GASP
YUGI! IS THIS SOME KIND OF SHELL GAME?!
MAYBE.
SHELL GAME?
AN UNFAIR GAME!
IT MEANS YOU DISTRACT SOMEONE FROM THE TERRIBLE ODDS! JONOUCHI, YOU LOST BECAUSE THE GAME WAS RIGGED!
GRR...
WAIT A SECOND ...
THERE'S NO WAY TO WIN THIS GAME UNLESS THE OTHER PLAYER GETS THE JOKER!
IF THE JOKER IS LEFT AT THE END, THE GAME HAS TO BE A TIE!
TIE PATTERN
PLAYER 1 HAND
Black Black
Joker LEFT OVER
Red Red
PLAYER 2 HAND
PLAYER 1 HAND
Red Black
Joker LEFT OVER
Black Red
PLAYER 2 HAND
PLAYER 1 HAND
Red Red
Joker LEFT OVER
Black Black
PLAYER 2 HAND
THAT MEANS, WHOEVER DRAWS THE JOKER FIRST LOSES!!
★JOKER
JOKER★

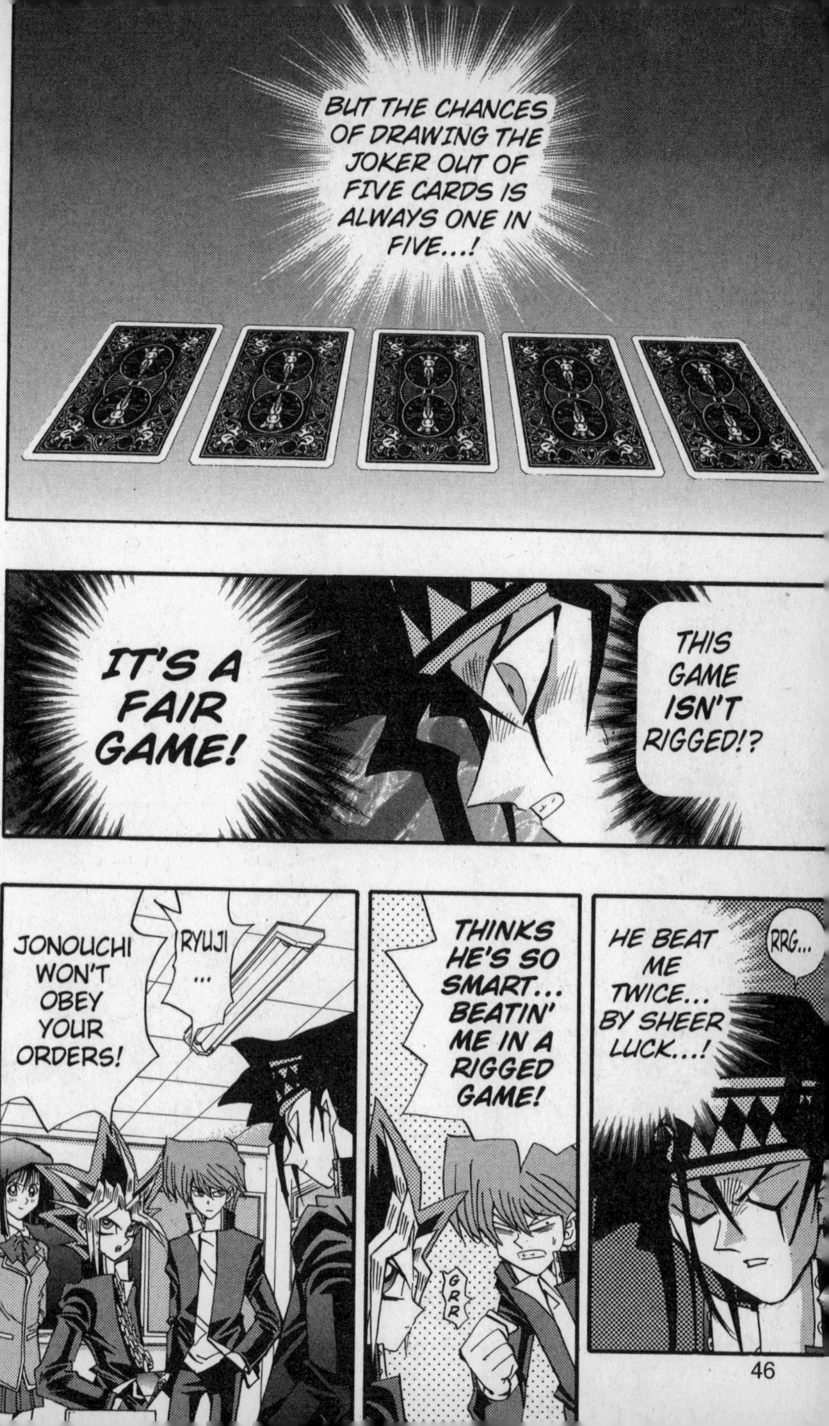
BUT THE CHANCES OF DRAWING THE JOKER OUT OF FIVE CARDS IS ALWAYS ONE IN FIVE...!
THIS GAME ISN'T RIGGED!?
IT'S A FAIR GAME!
RRG...
HE BEAT ME TWICE... BY SHEER LUCK...!
THINKS HE'S SO SMART... BEATIN' ME IN A RIGGED GAME!
GRR
RYUJI ...
JONOUCHI WON'T OBEY YOUR ORDERS!

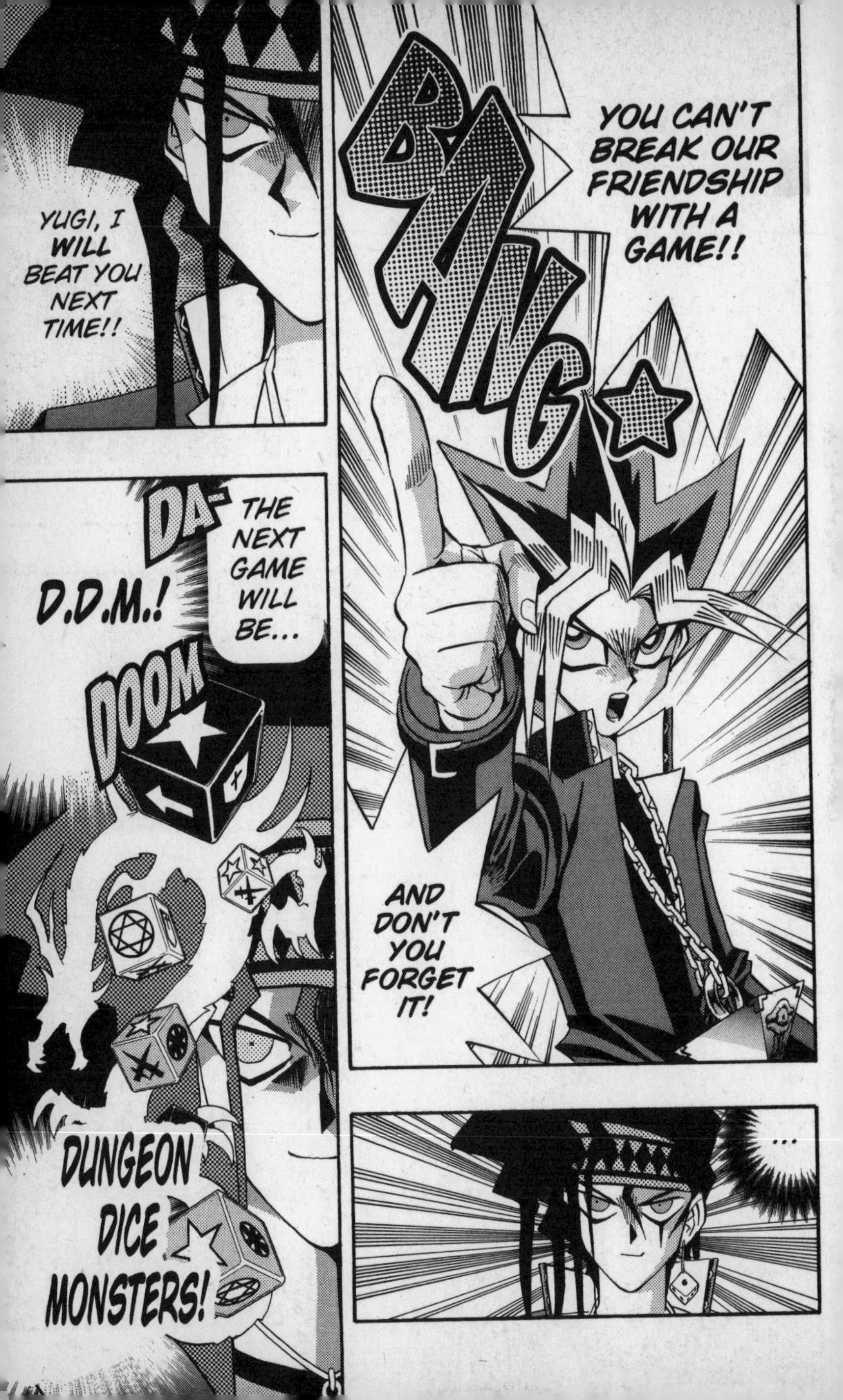
BANG
YOU CAN'T BREAK OUR FRIENDSHIP WITH A GAME!!
AND DON'T YOU FORGET IT!
...
YUGI, I WILL BEAT YOU NEXT TIME!!
DA-
THE NEXT GAME WILL BE...
D.D.M.!
DOOM
DUNGEON DICE MONSTERS!

APOLOGY AND CORRECTION

When the previous chapter was published in Japan in **Weekly Shonen Jump** magazine, we received word from readers regarding a serious error in the explanation of the probability of the game.

We apologize for the corrections which were made for the graphic novel version.

Below are the corrected portions:

The probability of drawing a joker (one card) from five cards

Yugi's first turn — $\frac{1}{5}$

Ryuji's next turn--The probability of drawing the joker from four cards ***if Yugi did not draw the joker***

$$(1 - \tfrac{1}{5}) \times \tfrac{1}{4} = \tfrac{4}{5} \times \tfrac{1}{4} = \tfrac{1}{5}$$

Yugi's next turn--The probability of drawing the joker from the three remaining cards

$$(1 - \tfrac{1}{5} \times 2) \times \tfrac{1}{3} = \tfrac{3}{5} \times \tfrac{1}{3} = \tfrac{1}{5}$$

(And so on)

The probability of drawing the joker in this game is constantly $\frac{1}{5}$, making the rules fair.

H- HEH HEH!

STUPID AUTHOR!

Duel 77: D.D.M.!!

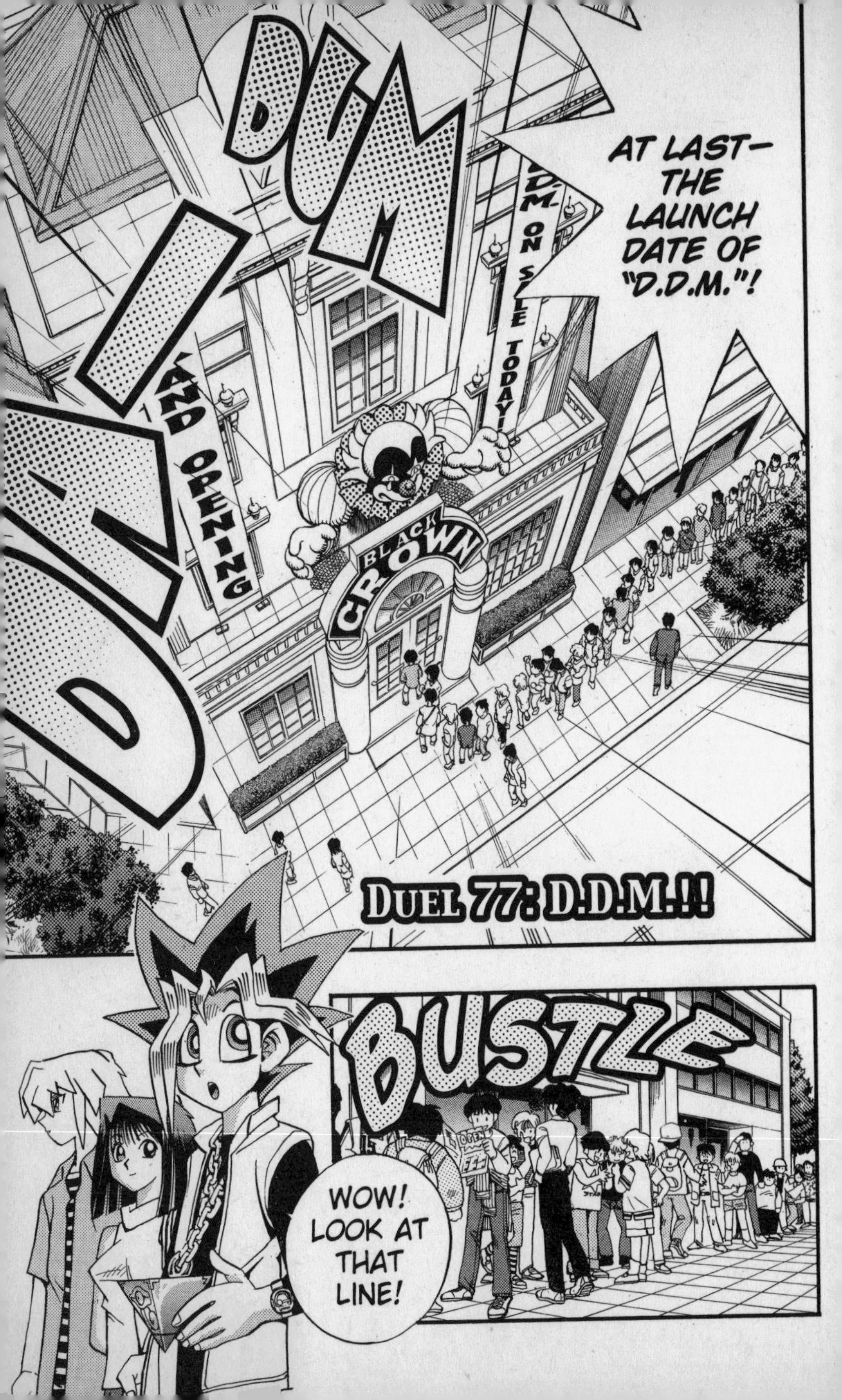
DUM
D.D.M. ON SALE TODAY!
AND OPENING
BLACK CROWN
AT LAST— THE LAUNCH DATE OF "D.D.M."!
BUSTLE
WOW! LOOK AT THAT LINE!

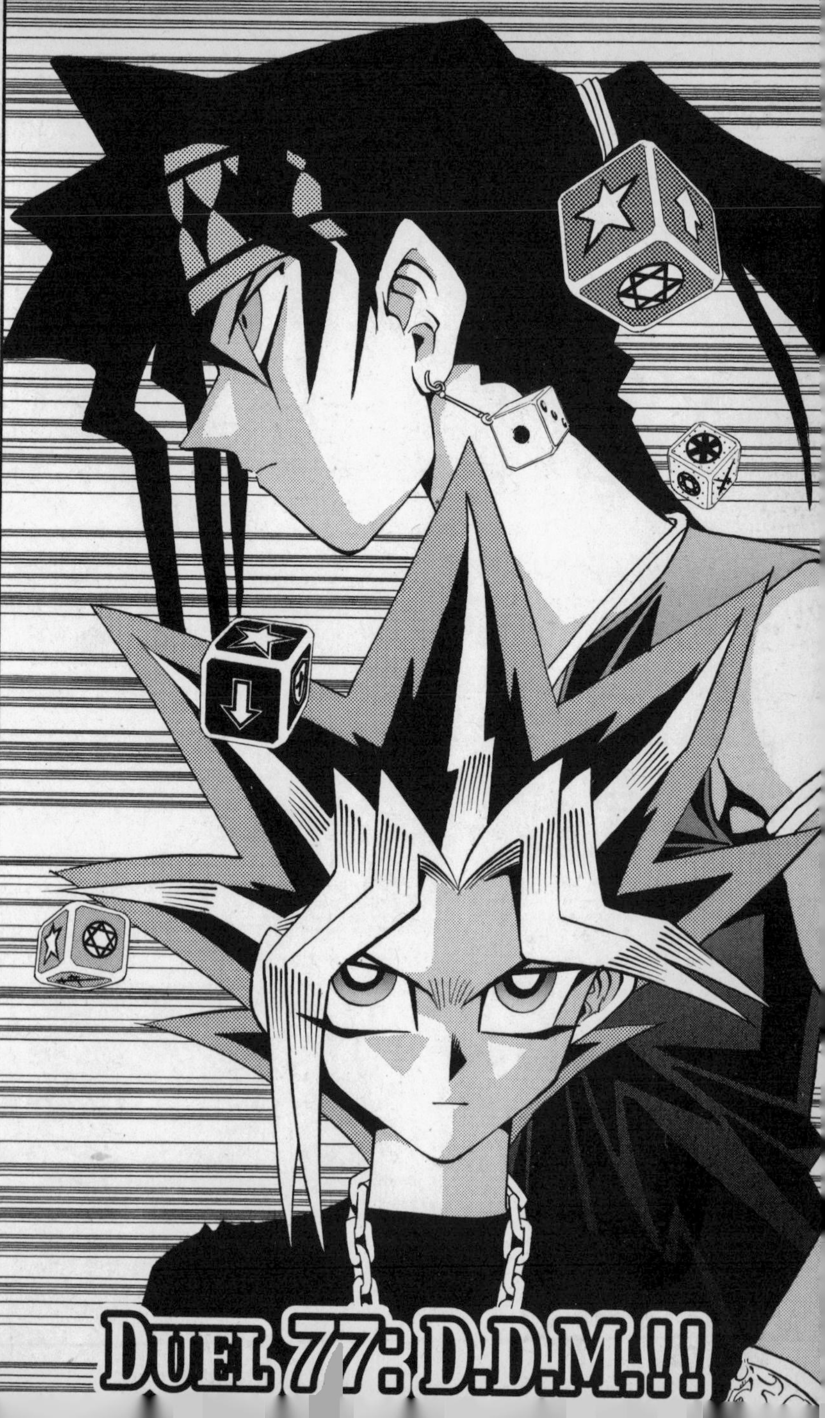
DUEL 77: D.D.M.!!

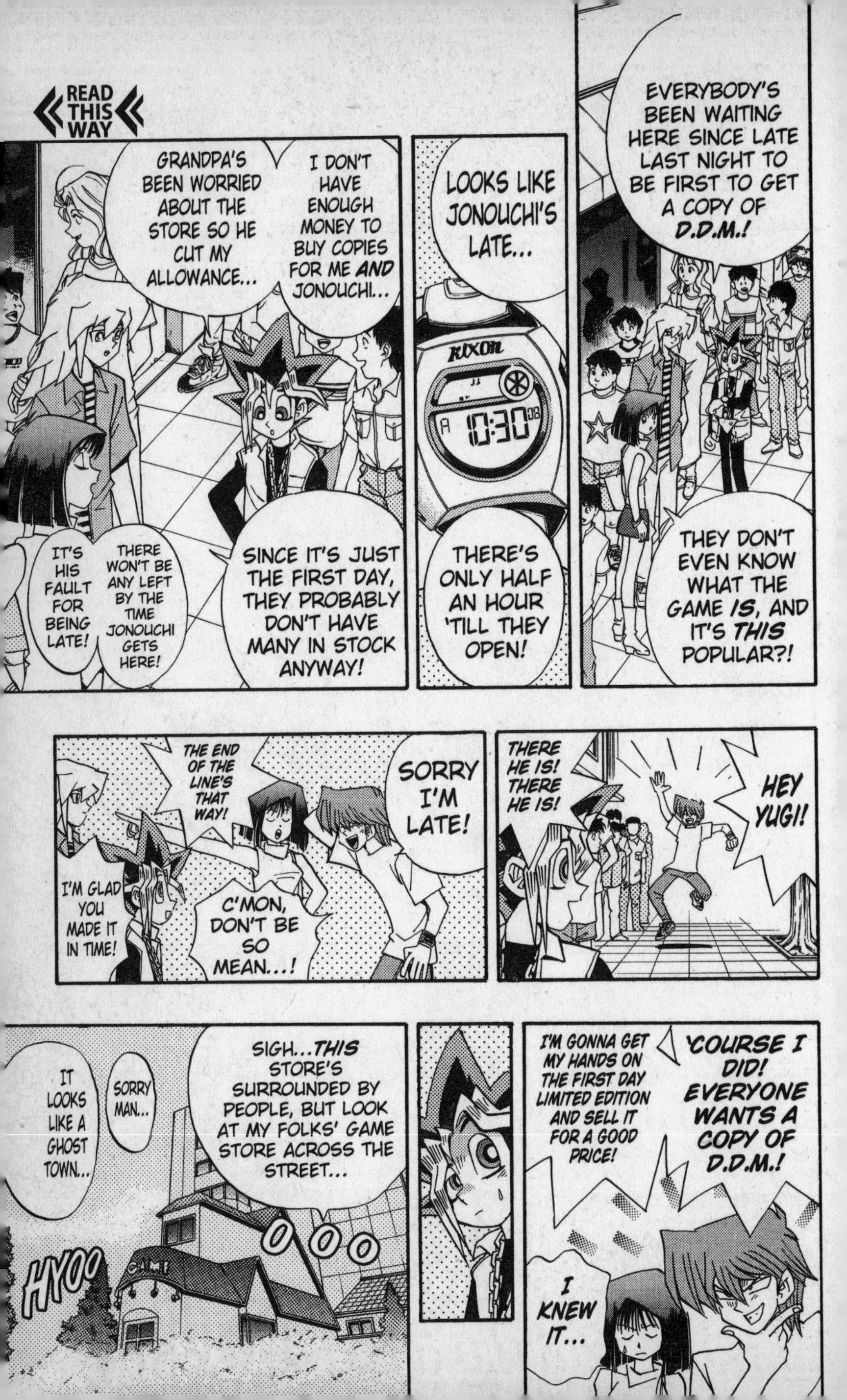
READ THIS WAY
EVERYBODY'S BEEN WAITING HERE SINCE LATE LAST NIGHT TO BE FIRST TO GET A COPY OF *D.D.M.!*
THEY DON'T EVEN KNOW WHAT THE GAME *IS*, AND IT'S *THIS* POPULAR?!
LOOKS LIKE JONOUCHI'S LATE...
RIXON
10:30
THERE'S ONLY HALF AN HOUR 'TILL THEY OPEN!
I DON'T HAVE ENOUGH MONEY TO BUY COPIES FOR ME *AND* JONOUCHI...
GRANDPA'S BEEN WORRIED ABOUT THE STORE SO HE CUT MY ALLOWANCE...
SINCE IT'S JUST THE FIRST DAY, THEY PROBABLY DON'T HAVE MANY IN STOCK ANYWAY!
THERE WON'T BE ANY LEFT BY THE TIME JONOUCHI GETS HERE!
IT'S HIS FAULT FOR BEING LATE!
HEY YUGI!
THERE HE IS! THERE HE IS!
SORRY I'M LATE!
THE END OF THE LINE'S THAT WAY!
C'MON, DON'T BE SO MEAN...!
I'M GLAD YOU MADE IT IN TIME!
'COURSE I DID! EVERYONE WANTS A COPY OF D.D.M.!
I'M GONNA GET MY HANDS ON THE FIRST DAY LIMITED EDITION AND SELL IT FOR A GOOD PRICE!
I KNEW IT...
SIGH...*THIS* STORE'S SURROUNDED BY PEOPLE, BUT LOOK AT MY FOLKS' GAME STORE ACROSS THE STREET...
SORRY MAN...
IT LOOKS LIKE A GHOST TOWN...
OOO
HYOO

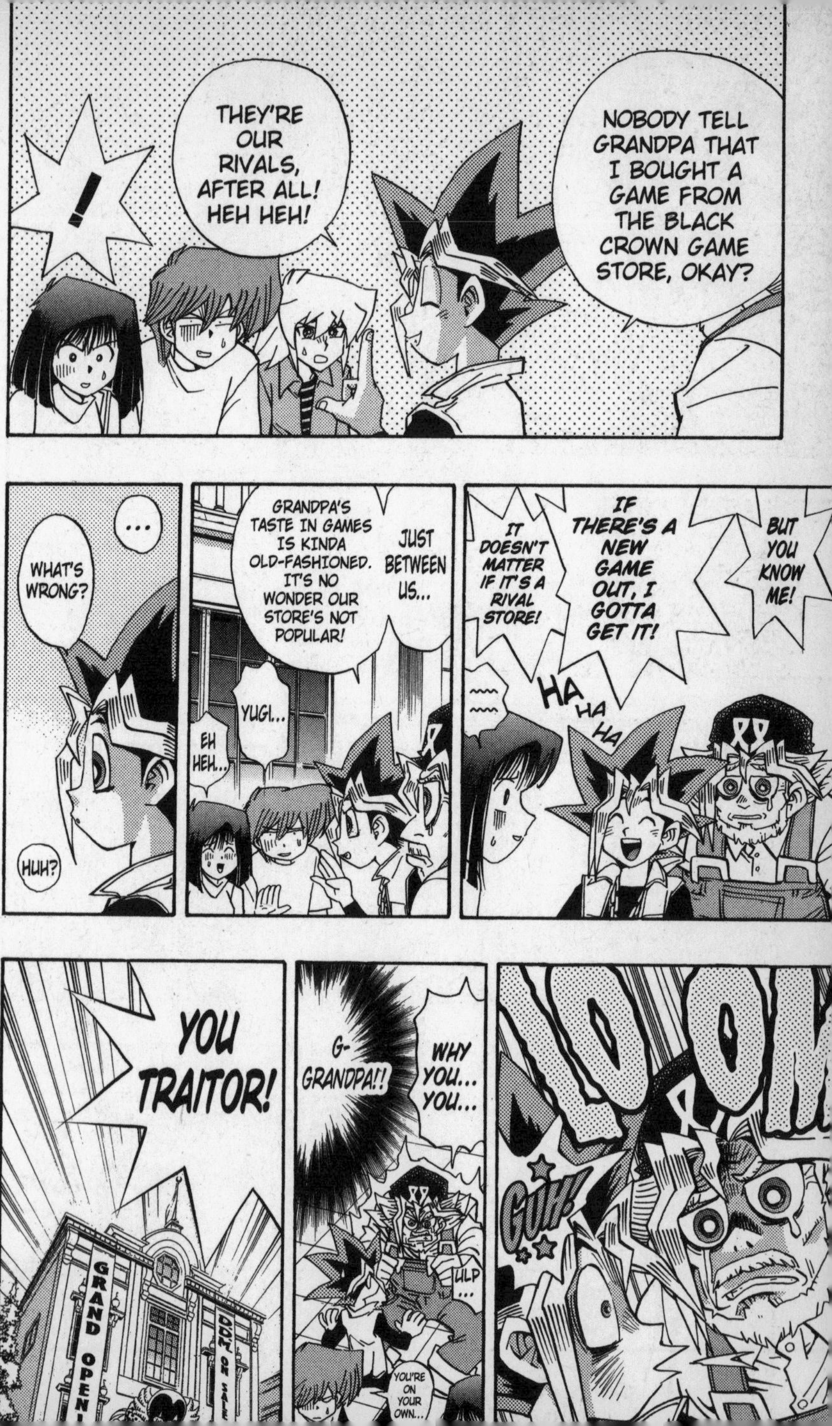
NOBODY TELL GRANDPA THAT I BOUGHT A GAME FROM THE BLACK CROWN GAME STORE, OKAY?
THEY'RE OUR RIVALS, AFTER ALL! HEH HEH!
!
BUT YOU KNOW ME!
IF THERE'S A NEW GAME OUT, I GOTTA GET IT!
IT DOESN'T MATTER IF IT'S A RIVAL STORE!
HA HA HA
~~ ~~
JUST BETWEEN US...
GRANDPA'S TASTE IN GAMES IS KINDA OLD-FASHIONED. IT'S NO WONDER OUR STORE'S NOT POPULAR!
YUGI...
EH HEH...
...
WHAT'S WRONG?
HUH?
GUH!
WHY YOU... YOU...
G-GRANDPA!!
ULP...
YOU'RE ON YOUR OWN...
YOU TRAITOR!

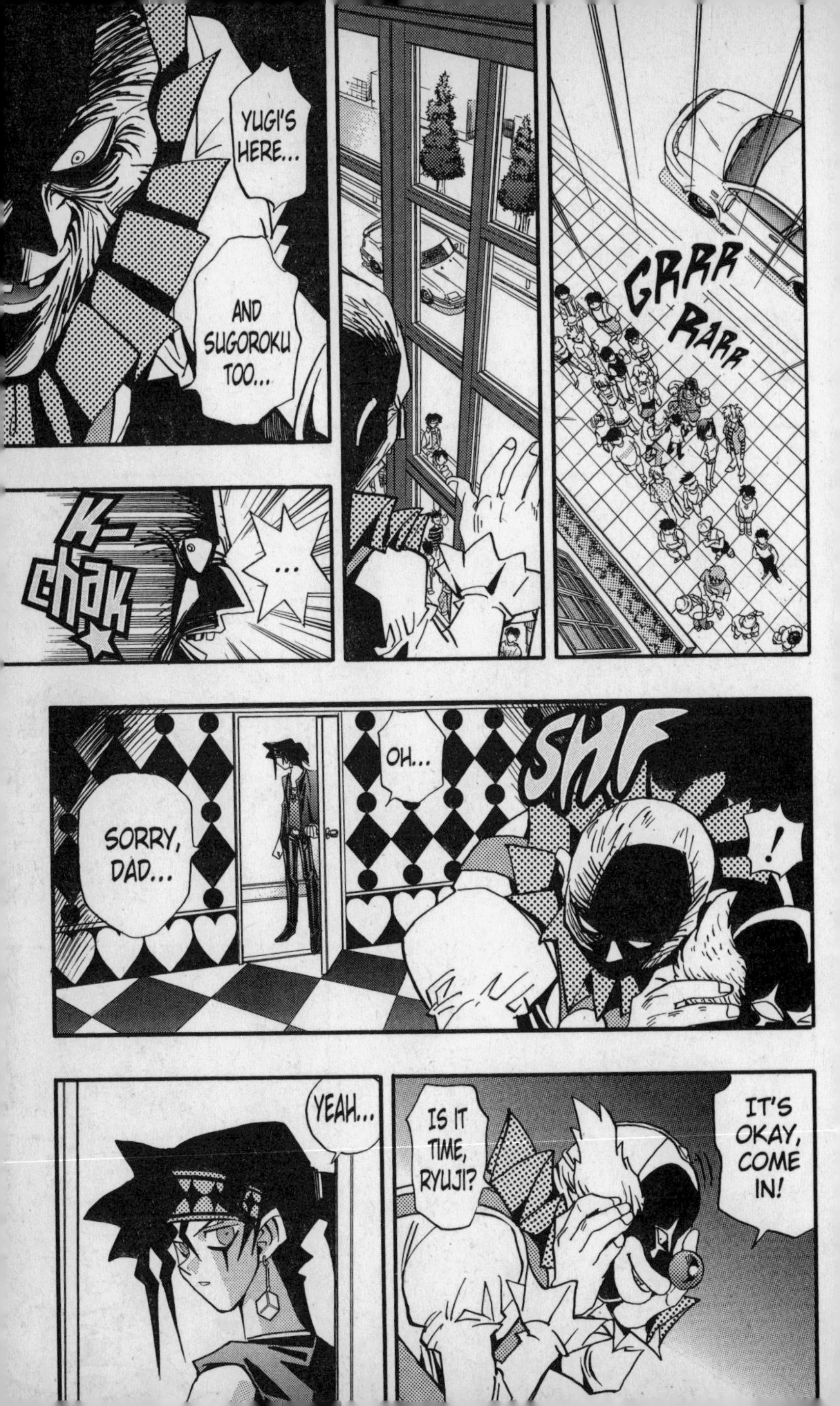
GRRR
RARR
YUGI'S HERE...
AND SUGOROKU TOO...
K-CHAK
...
SHF
!
OH...
SORRY, DAD...
IT'S OKAY, COME IN!
IS IT TIME, RYUJI?
YEAH...

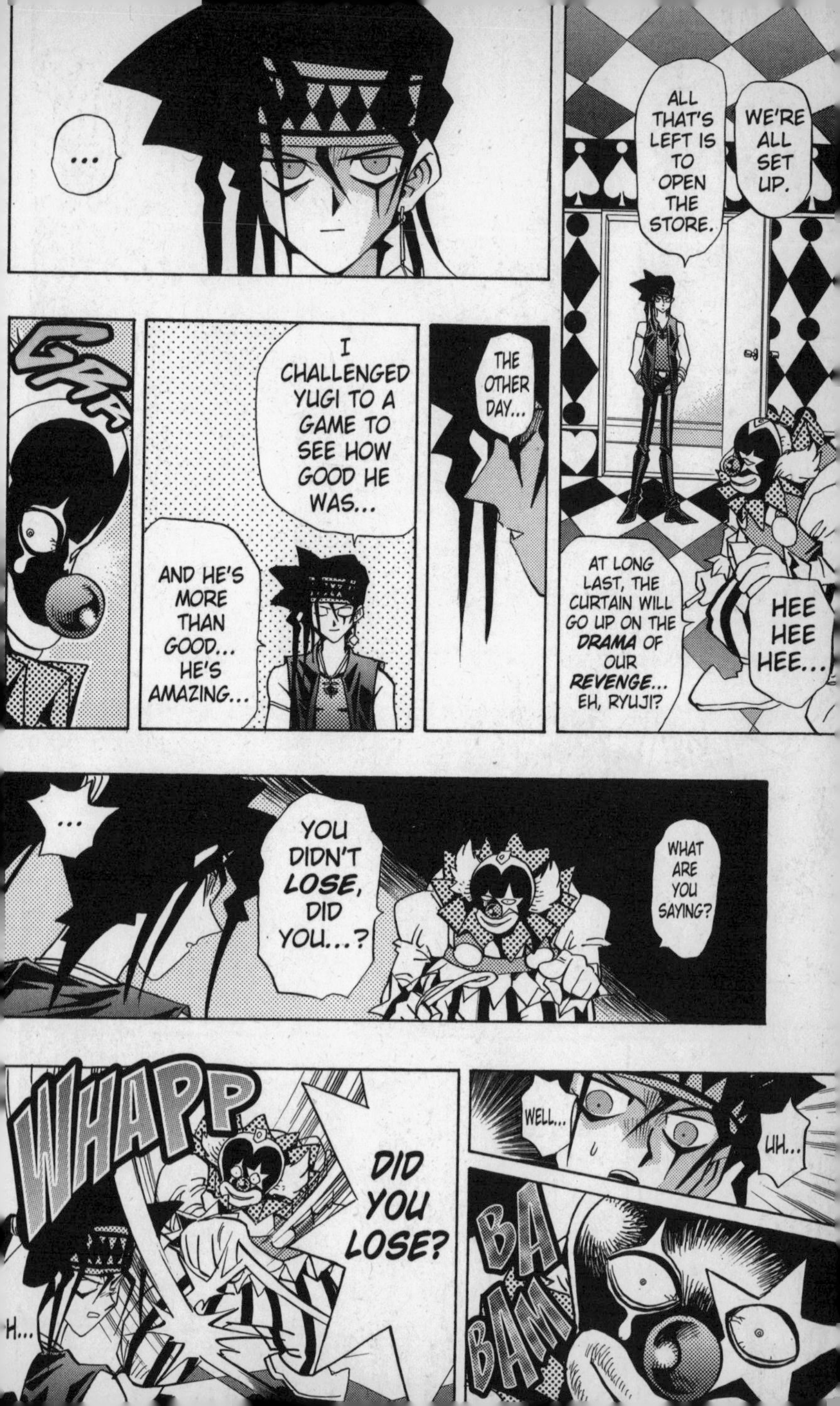
WE'RE ALL SET UP.
ALL THAT'S LEFT IS TO OPEN THE STORE.
HEE HEE HEE...
AT LONG LAST, THE CURTAIN WILL GO UP ON THE *DRAMA* OF OUR *REVENGE*... EH, RYUJI?
...
THE OTHER DAY...
I CHALLENGED YUGI TO A GAME TO SEE HOW GOOD HE WAS...
AND HE'S MORE THAN GOOD... HE'S AMAZING...
GAR
WHAT ARE YOU SAYING?
YOU DIDN'T *LOSE*, DID YOU...?
...
UH...
WELL...
BA BAM
DID YOU LOSE?
WHAPP
H...

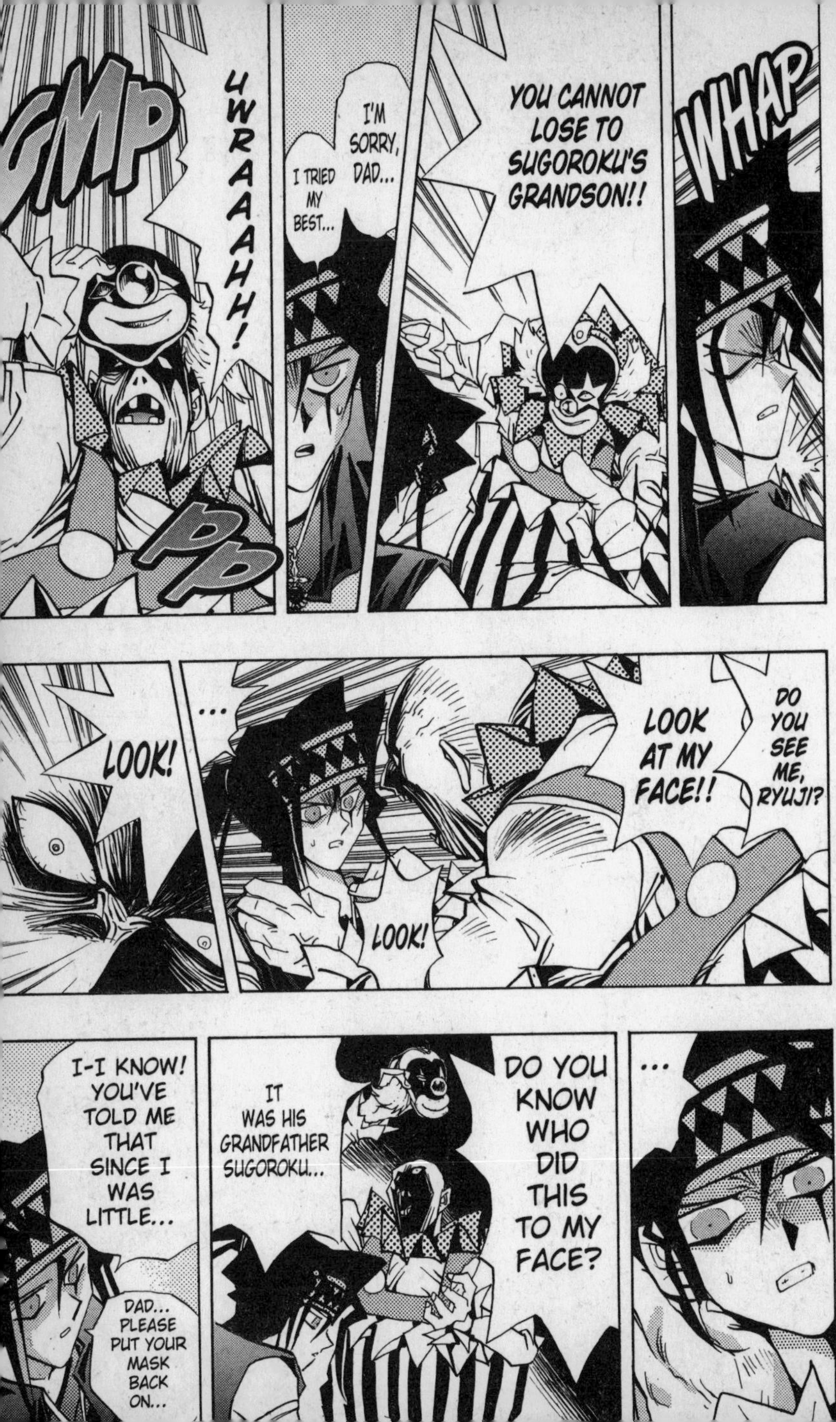
WHAP
YOU CANNOT LOSE TO SUGOROKU'S GRANDSON!!
I'M SORRY, DAD...
I TRIED MY BEST...
UWRAAAAHH!
GMP
PP
DO YOU SEE ME, RYUJI?
LOOK AT MY FACE!!
...
LOOK!
LOOK!
...
DO YOU KNOW WHO DID THIS TO MY FACE?
IT WAS HIS GRANDFATHER SUGOROKU...
I-I KNOW! YOU'VE TOLD ME THAT SINCE I WAS LITTLE...
DAD... PLEASE PUT YOUR MASK BACK ON...

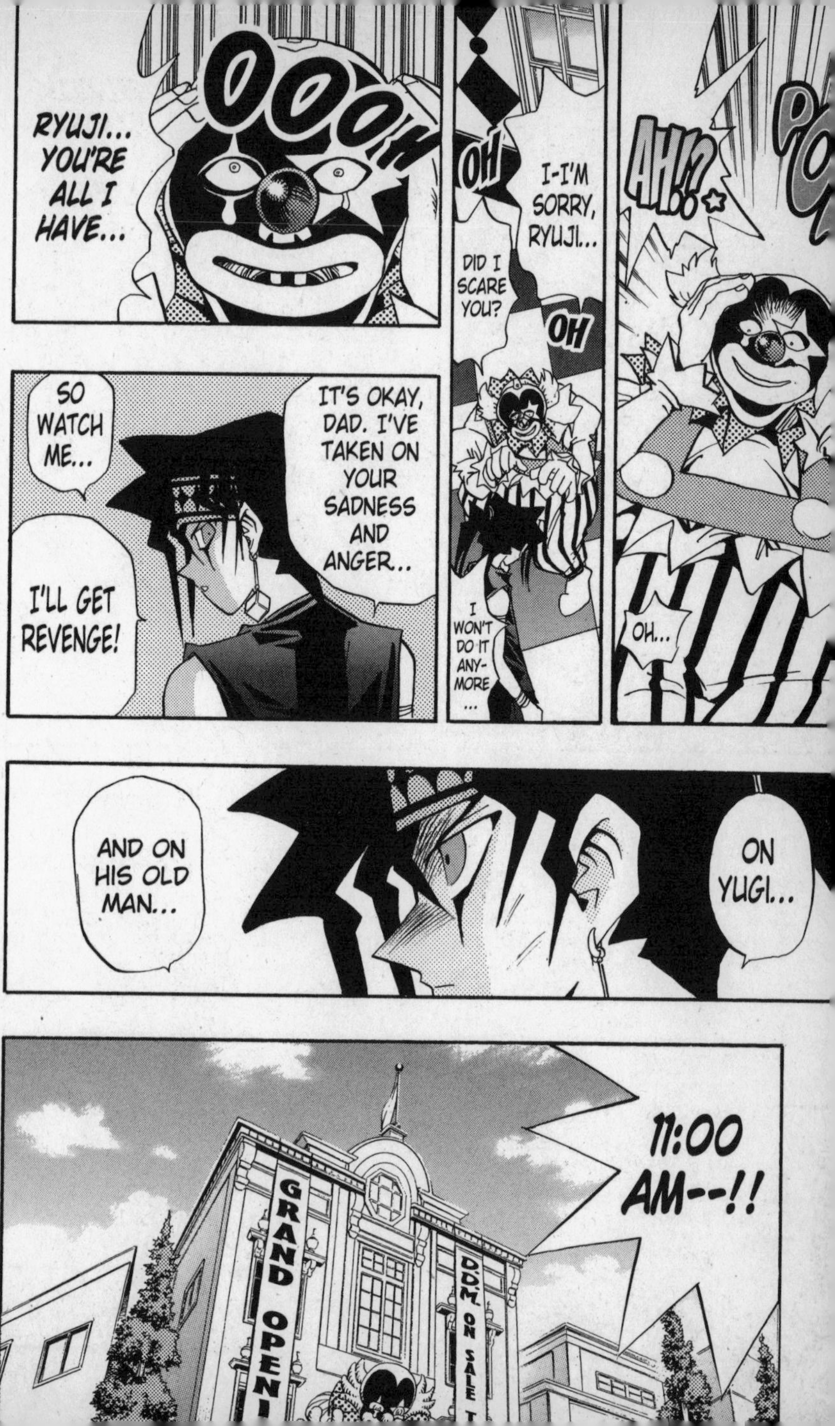
AH!?
OH...
OH
I-I'M SORRY, RYUJI...
DID I SCARE YOU?
OH
I WON'T DO IT ANYMORE...
OOOOH
RYUJI... YOU'RE ALL I HAVE...
IT'S OKAY, DAD. I'VE TAKEN ON YOUR SADNESS AND ANGER...
SO WATCH ME...
I'LL GET REVENGE!
ON YUGI...
AND ON HIS OLD MAN...
11:00 AM--!!
GRAND OPENI
D.D.M. ON SALE

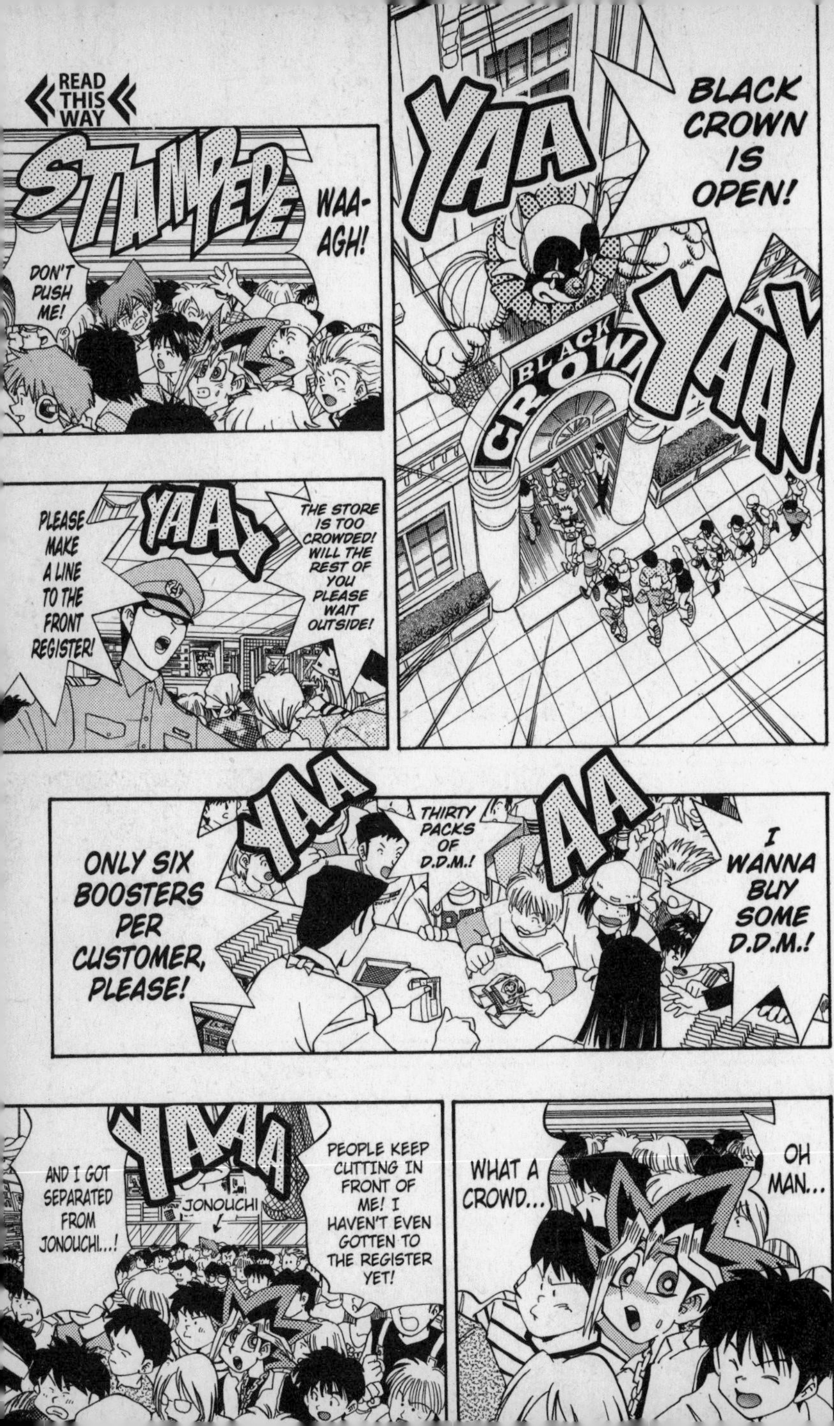
READ THIS WAY
YAA
BLACK CROWN IS OPEN!
BLACK CROWN
YAAY
STAMPEDE
WAA-AGH!
DON'T PUSH ME!
YAAY
THE STORE IS TOO CROWDED! WILL THE REST OF YOU PLEASE WAIT OUTSIDE!
PLEASE MAKE A LINE TO THE FRONT REGISTER!
I WANNA BUY SOME D.D.M.!
AA
THIRTY PACKS OF D.D.M.!
YAA
ONLY SIX BOOSTERS PER CUSTOMER, PLEASE!
OH MAN...
WHAT A CROWD...
PEOPLE KEEP CUTTING IN FRONT OF ME! I HAVEN'T EVEN GOTTEN TO THE REGISTER YET!
YAAA
JONOUCHI
AND I GOT SEPARATED FROM JONOUCHI...!

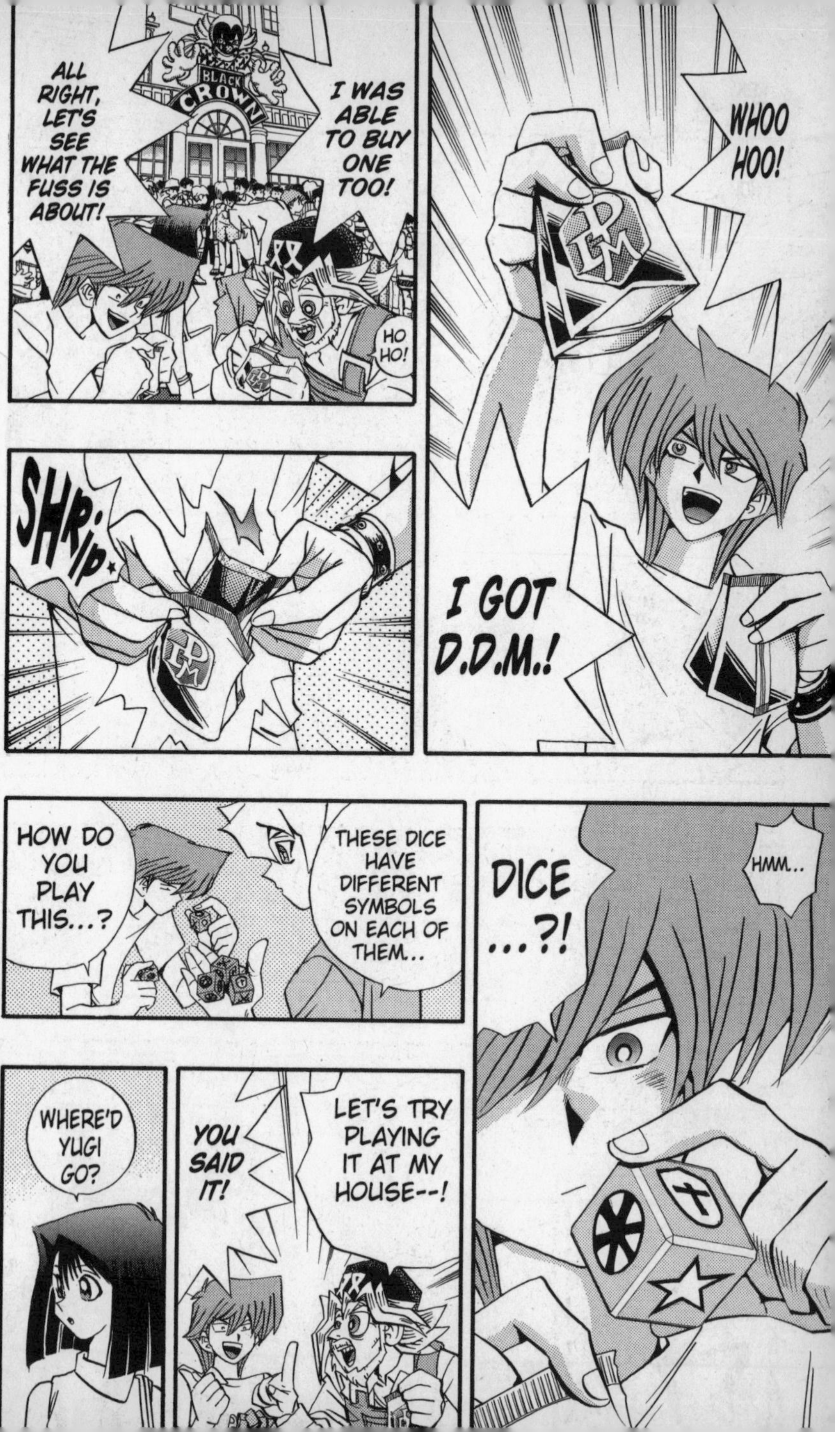
BLACK CROWN
ALL RIGHT, LET'S SEE WHAT THE FUSS IS ABOUT!
I WAS ABLE TO BUY ONE TOO!
HO HO!
SHRIP
WHOO HOO!
I GOT D.D.M.!
HOW DO YOU PLAY THIS...?
THESE DICE HAVE DIFFERENT SYMBOLS ON EACH OF THEM...
DICE ...?!
HMM...
WHERE'D YUGI GO?
YOU SAID IT!
LET'S TRY PLAYING IT AT MY HOUSE--!

READ THIS WAY

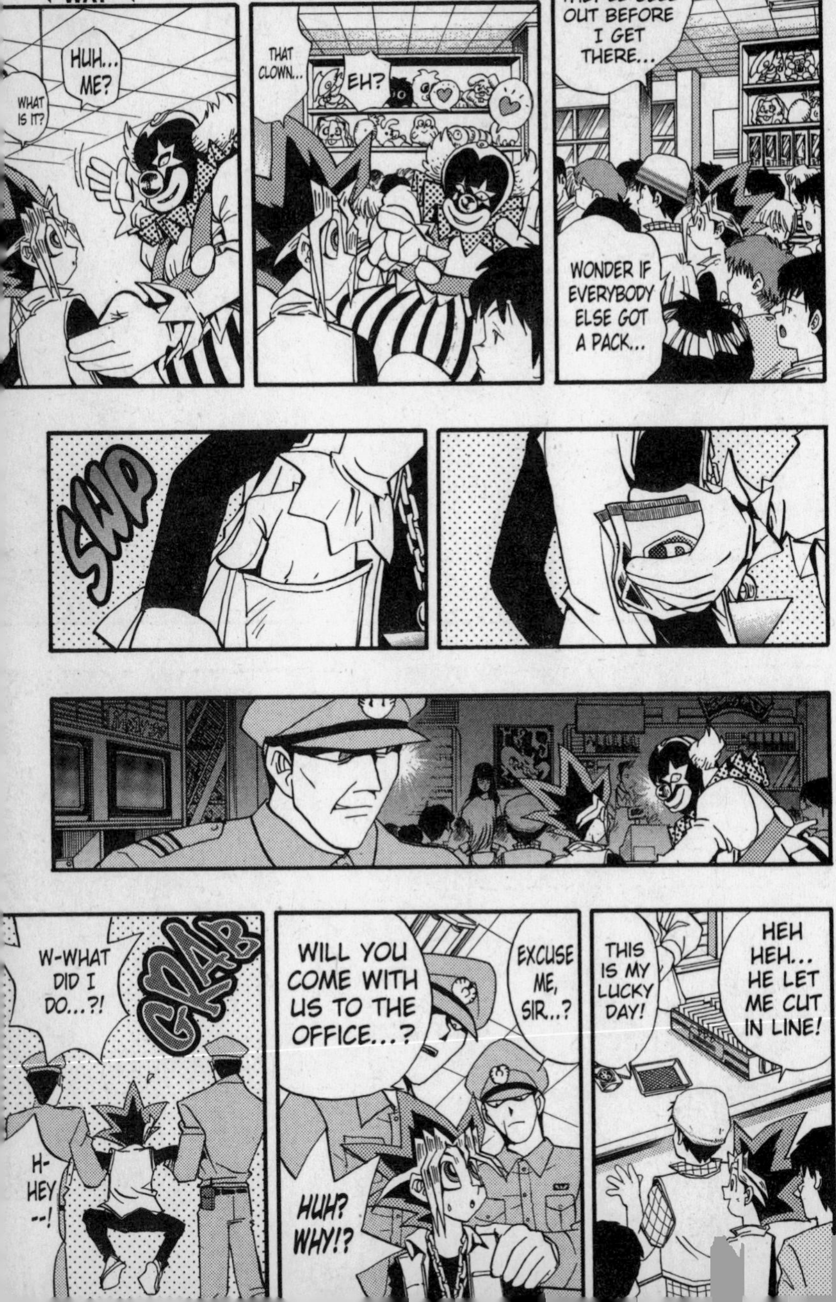
OH NO...I WONDER IF THEY'LL SELL OUT BEFORE I GET THERE...
WONDER IF EVERYBODY ELSE GOT A PACK...
THAT CLOWN...
EH?
HUH... ME?
WHAT IS IT?
SWP
HEH HEH... HE LET ME CUT IN LINE!
THIS IS MY LUCKY DAY!
EXCUSE ME, SIR..?
WILL YOU COME WITH US TO THE OFFICE...?
HUH? WHY!?
GRAB
W-WHAT DID I DO...?!
H-HEY --!

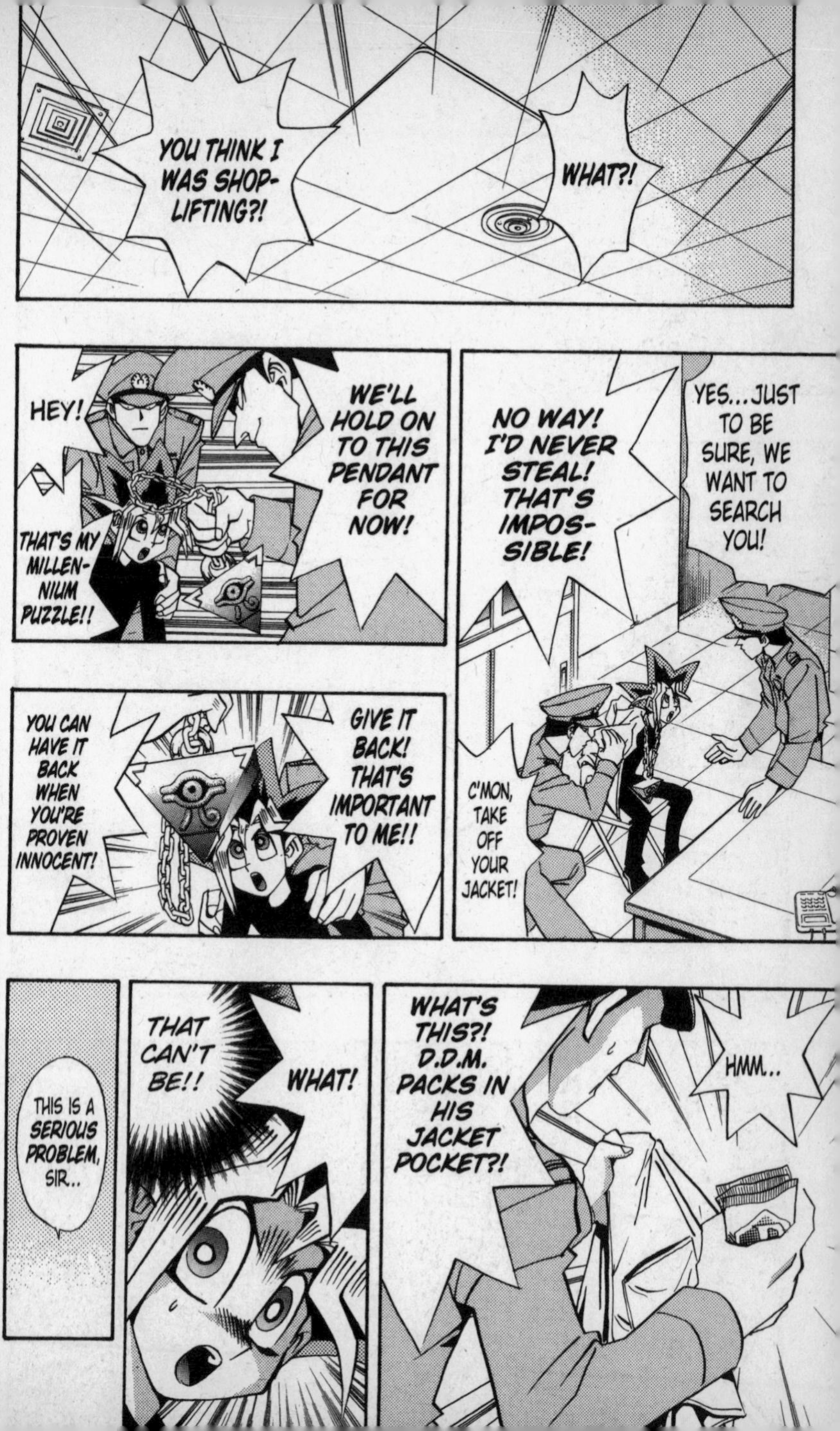
WHAT?!
YOU THINK I WAS SHOP-LIFTING?!
YES...JUST TO BE SURE, WE WANT TO SEARCH YOU!
NO WAY! I'D NEVER STEAL! THAT'S IMPOSSIBLE!
C'MON, TAKE OFF YOUR JACKET!
WE'LL HOLD ON TO THIS PENDANT FOR NOW!
HEY!
THAT'S MY MILLENNIUM PUZZLE!!
GIVE IT BACK! THAT'S IMPORTANT TO ME!!
YOU CAN HAVE IT BACK WHEN YOU'RE PROVEN INNOCENT!
HMM...
WHAT'S THIS?! D.D.M. PACKS IN HIS JACKET POCKET?!
WHAT!
THAT CAN'T BE!!
THIS IS A SERIOUS PROBLEM, SIR...

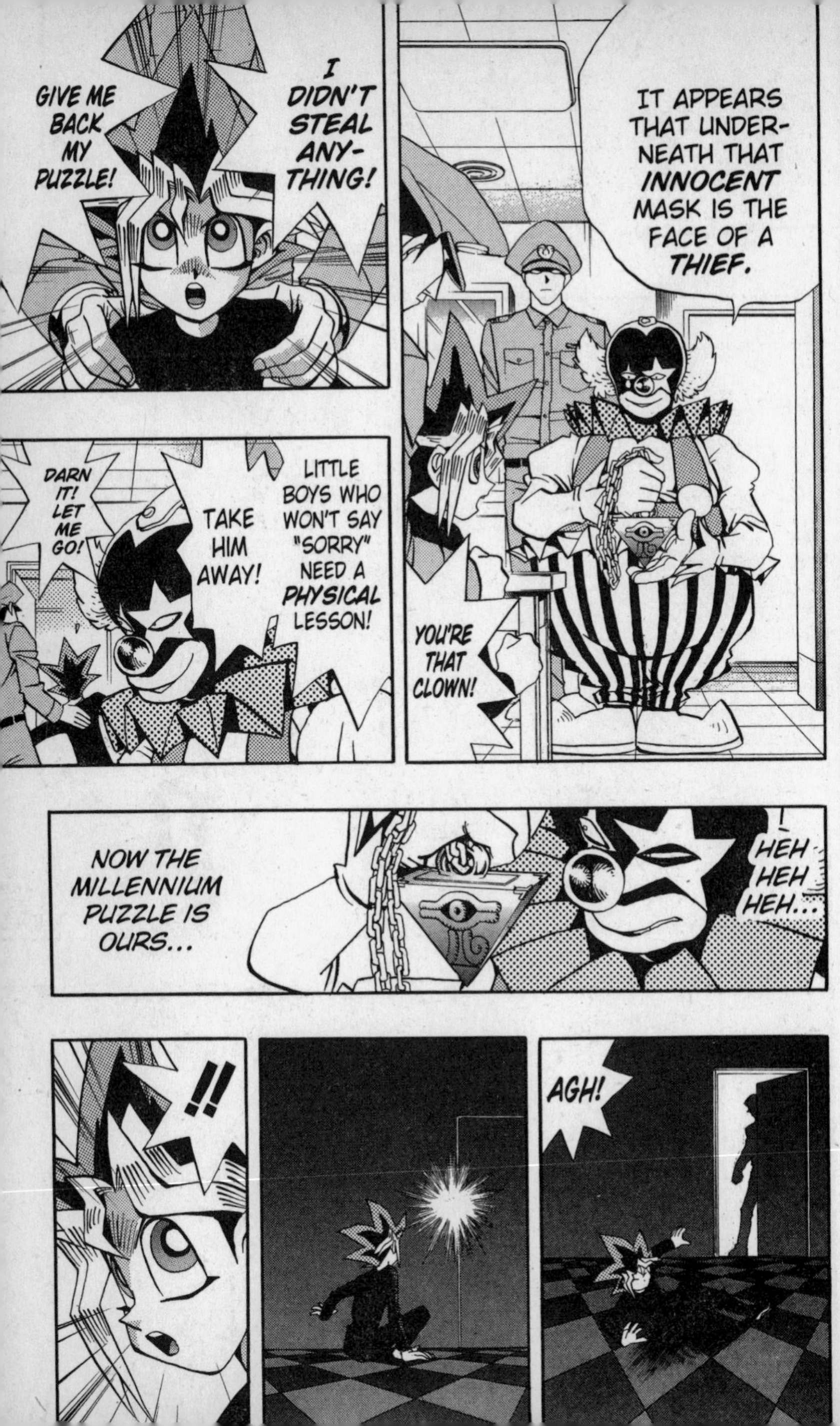
IT APPEARS THAT UNDERNEATH THAT INNOCENT MASK IS THE FACE OF A THIEF.
YOU'RE THAT CLOWN!
I DIDN'T STEAL ANYTHING!
GIVE ME BACK MY PUZZLE!
LITTLE BOYS WHO WON'T SAY "SORRY" NEED A PHYSICAL LESSON!
TAKE HIM AWAY!
DARN IT! LET ME GO!
!
HEH HEH HEH...
NOW THE MILLENNIUM PUZZLE IS OURS...
AGH!
!!

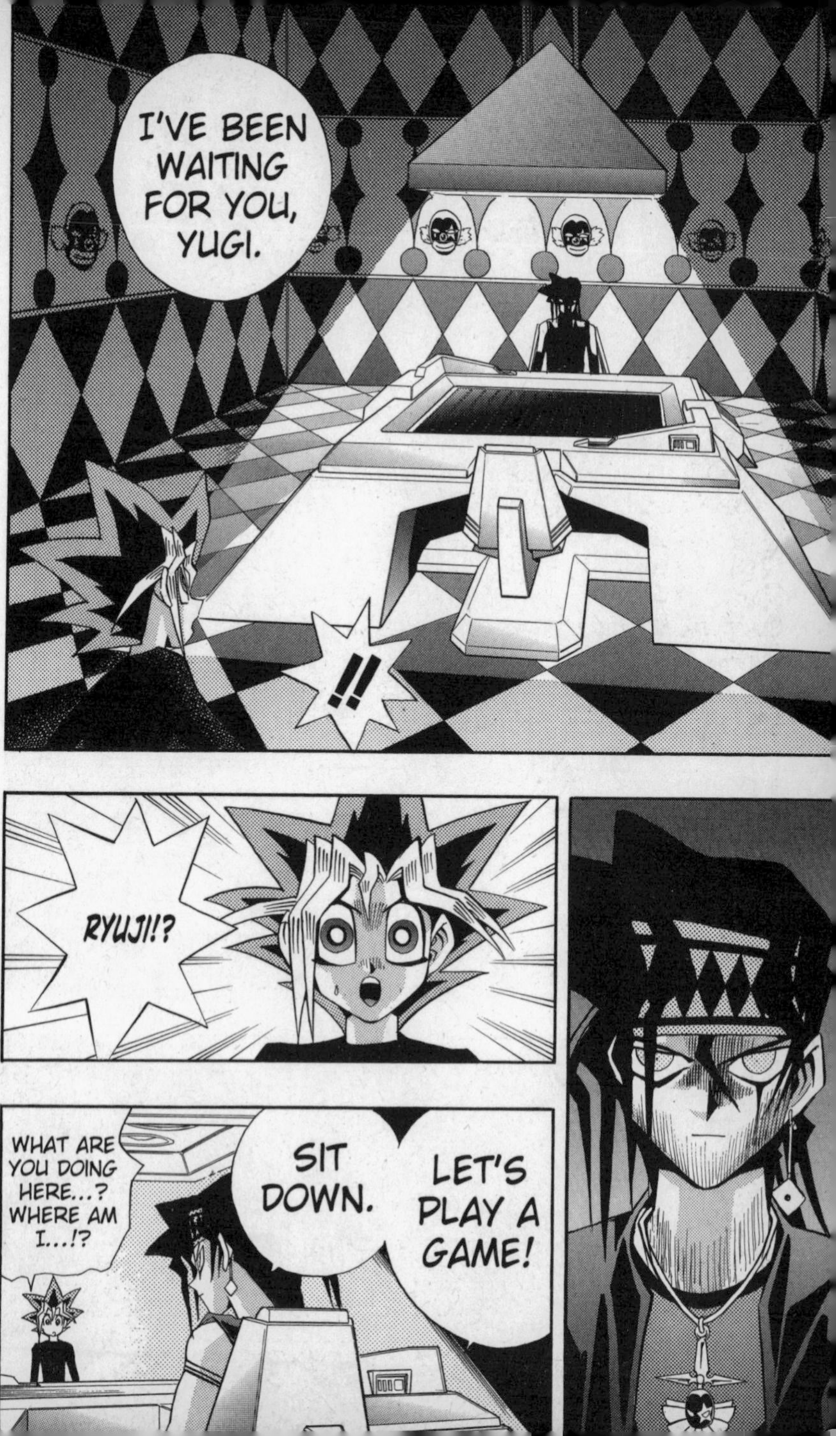
I'VE BEEN WAITING FOR YOU, YUGI.
!!
RYUJI!?
WHAT ARE YOU DOING HERE...? WHERE AM I...!?
SIT DOWN.
LET'S PLAY A GAME!

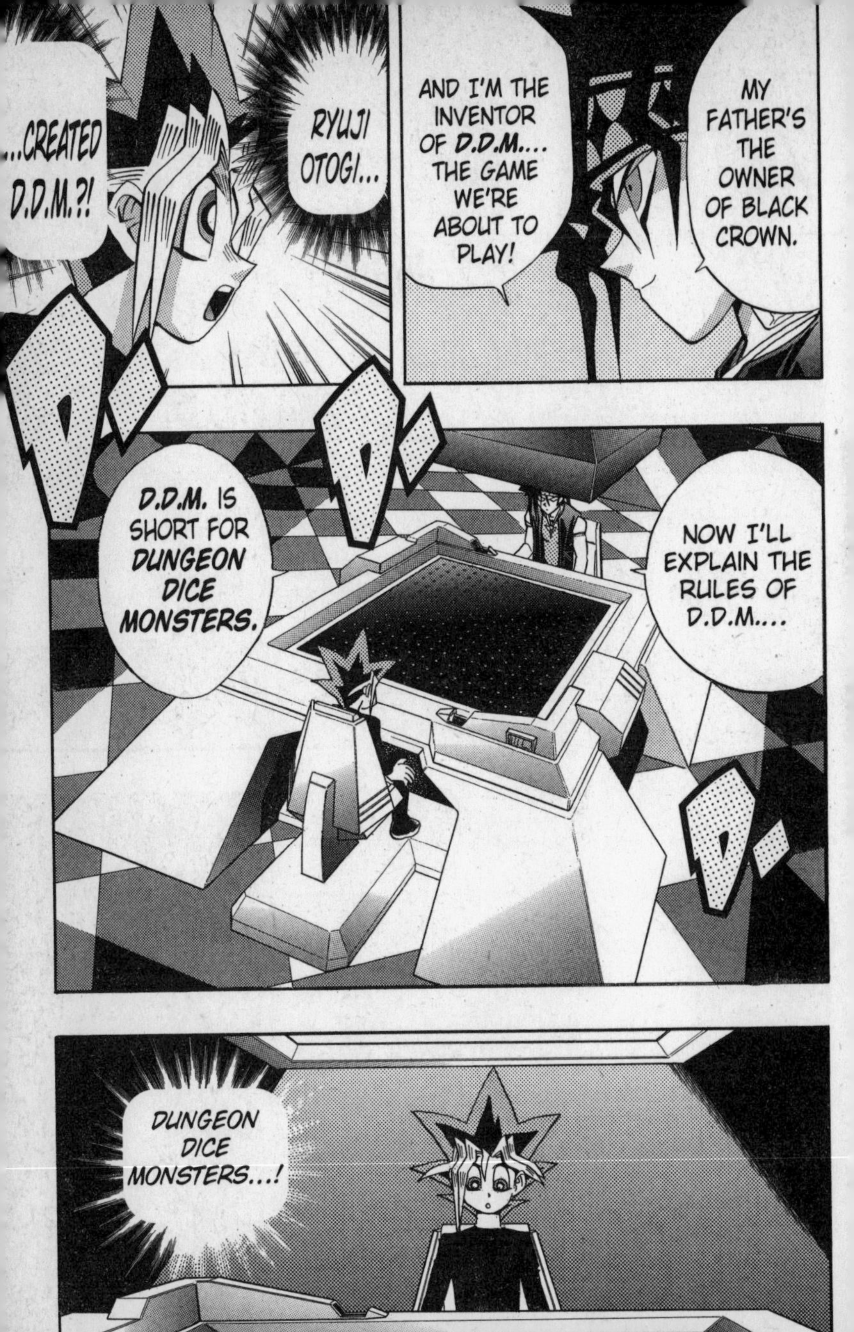
MY FATHER'S THE OWNER OF BLACK CROWN.
AND I'M THE INVENTOR OF D.D.M.... THE GAME WE'RE ABOUT TO PLAY!
RYUJI OTOGI...
...CREATED D.D.M.?!
NOW I'LL EXPLAIN THE RULES OF D.D.M....
D.D.M. IS SHORT FOR DUNGEON DICE MONSTERS.
DUNGEON DICE MONSTERS...!

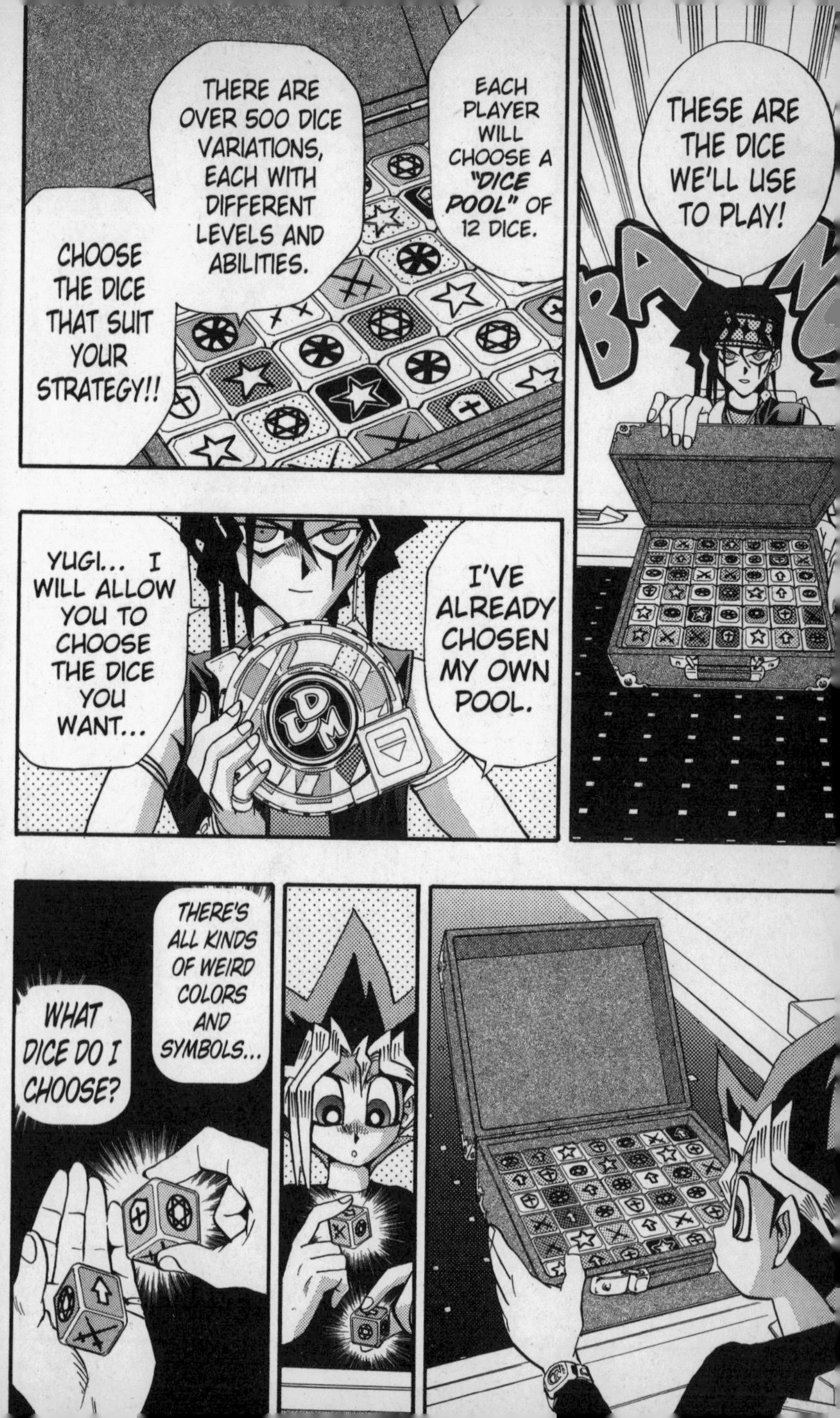
THESE ARE THE DICE WE'LL USE TO PLAY!
EACH PLAYER WILL CHOOSE A "DICE POOL" OF 12 DICE.
THERE ARE OVER 500 DICE VARIATIONS, EACH WITH DIFFERENT LEVELS AND ABILITIES.
CHOOSE THE DICE THAT SUIT YOUR STRATEGY!!
I'VE ALREADY CHOSEN MY OWN POOL.
YUGI... I WILL ALLOW YOU TO CHOOSE THE DICE YOU WANT...
THERE'S ALL KINDS OF WEIRD COLORS AND SYMBOLS...
WHAT DICE DO I CHOOSE?

THE COLOR OF THE DICE INDICATES THE *TYPE* OF CREATURE.

RED	GREEN	YELLOW	BLUE	WHITE
DRAGON	BEAST	UNDEAD	WARRIOR	SPELLCASTER

OKAY...I'LL CHOOSE THE BLUE, WHITE, AND BLACK DICE.

THE ONE EXCEPTION IS THE *BLACK* DICE. THEY CONTAIN SPECIAL ABILITIES AND MAGICAL POWERS...

CREATURE!?!?!......

THE STAGE FOR OUR GAME IS THE *"DARK FIELD."*

A LAND OF *PERPETUAL DARKNESS,* DEEP UNDERGROUND!

PLACE ALL YOUR DICE IN THE SHOOTER...

THE GAME IS READY!

TUMBLE

GA

TMP

HEY... A HOLE OPENED UP!

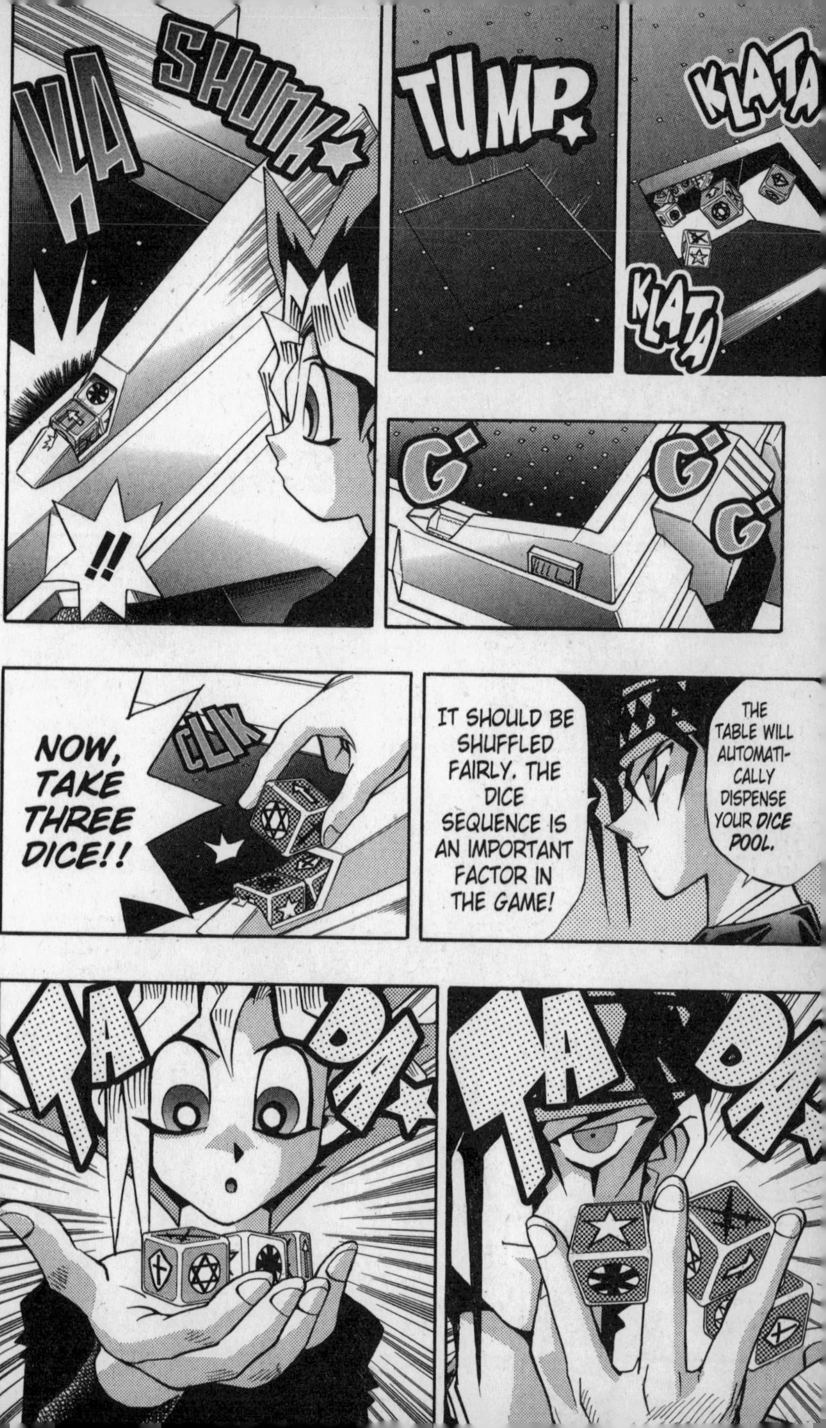
KLATA
KLATA
TUMP
G
G
G
KA SHUNK
!!
THE TABLE WILL AUTOMATICALLY DISPENSE YOUR DICE POOL.
IT SHOULD BE SHUFFLED FAIRLY. THE DICE SEQUENCE IS AN IMPORTANT FACTOR IN THE GAME!
CLIK
NOW, TAKE THREE DICE!!
TA DA
TA DA

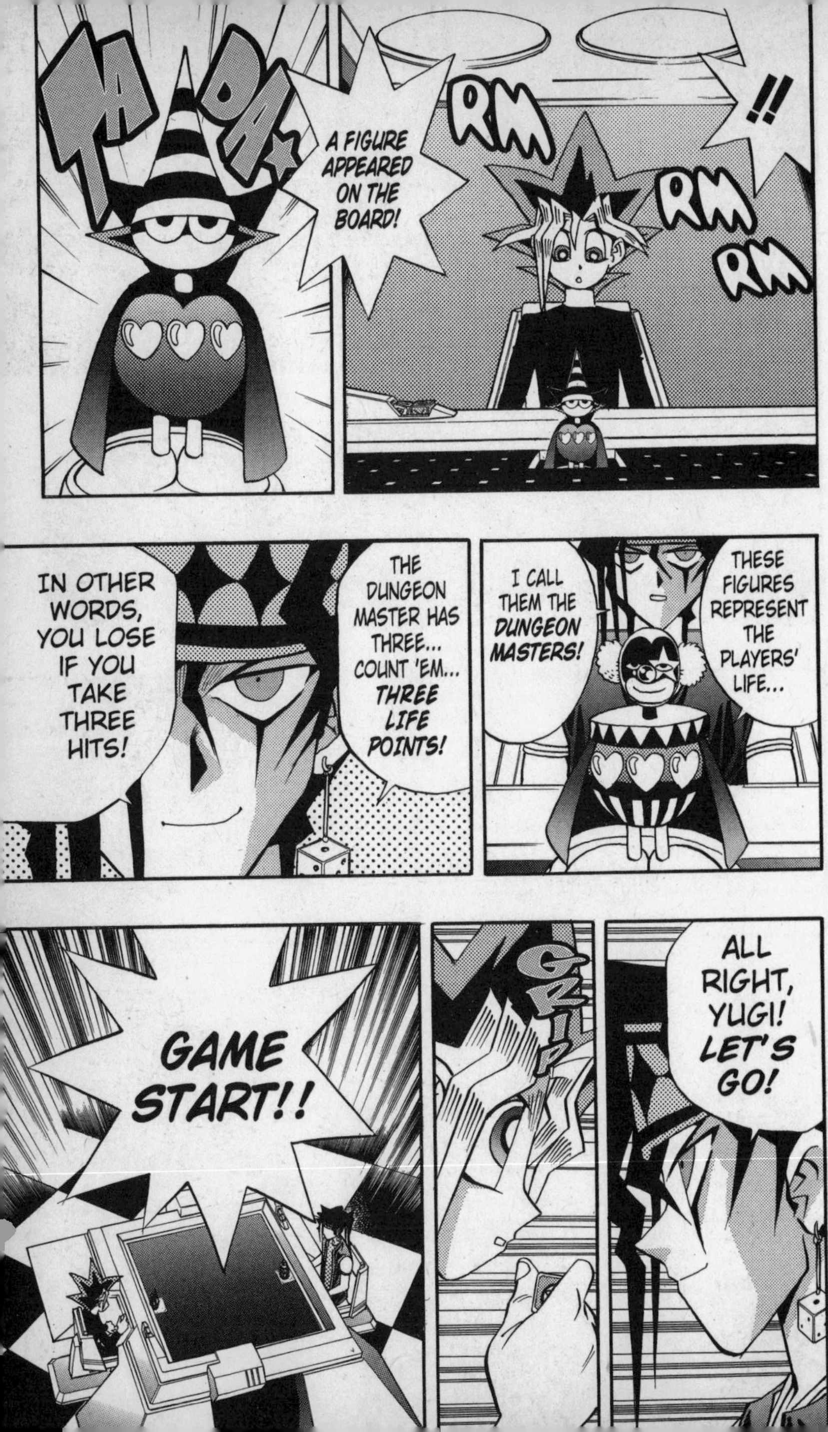
!!
RM
RM
RM
A FIGURE APPEARED ON THE BOARD!
TA DA
THESE FIGURES REPRESENT THE PLAYERS' LIFE...
I CALL THEM THE DUNGEON MASTERS!
THE DUNGEON MASTER HAS THREE... COUNT 'EM... THREE LIFE POINTS!
IN OTHER WORDS, YOU LOSE IF YOU TAKE THREE HITS!
ALL RIGHT, YUGI! LET'S GO!
GRIP
GAME START!!

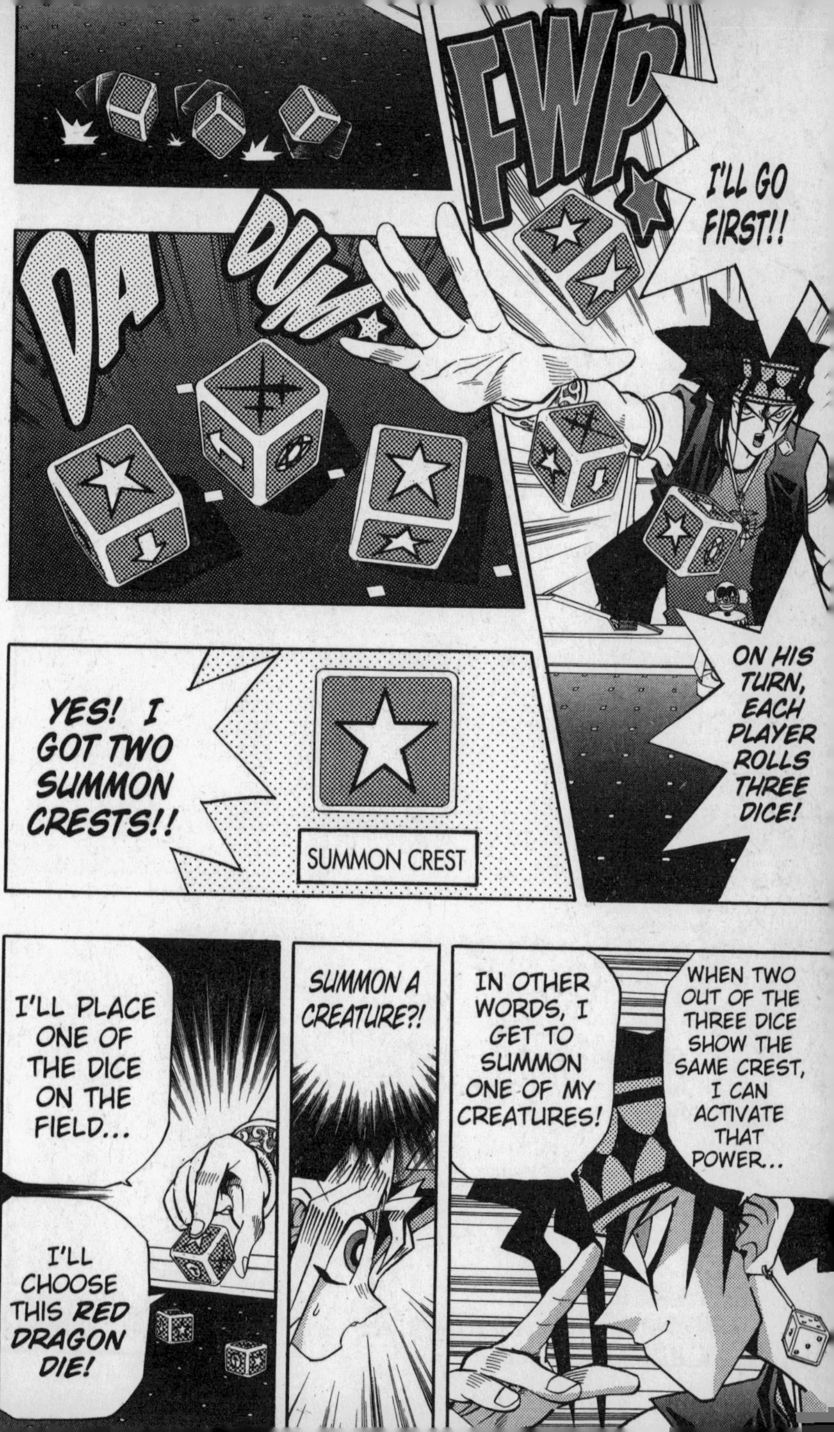
FWP
I'LL GO FIRST!!
ON HIS TURN, EACH PLAYER ROLLS THREE DICE!
DA DUN
YES! I GOT TWO SUMMON CRESTS!!
SUMMON CREST
WHEN TWO OUT OF THE THREE DICE SHOW THE SAME CREST, I CAN ACTIVATE THAT POWER...
IN OTHER WORDS, I GET TO SUMMON ONE OF MY CREATURES!
SUMMON A CREATURE?!
I'LL PLACE ONE OF THE DICE ON THE FIELD...
I'LL CHOOSE THIS RED DRAGON DIE!

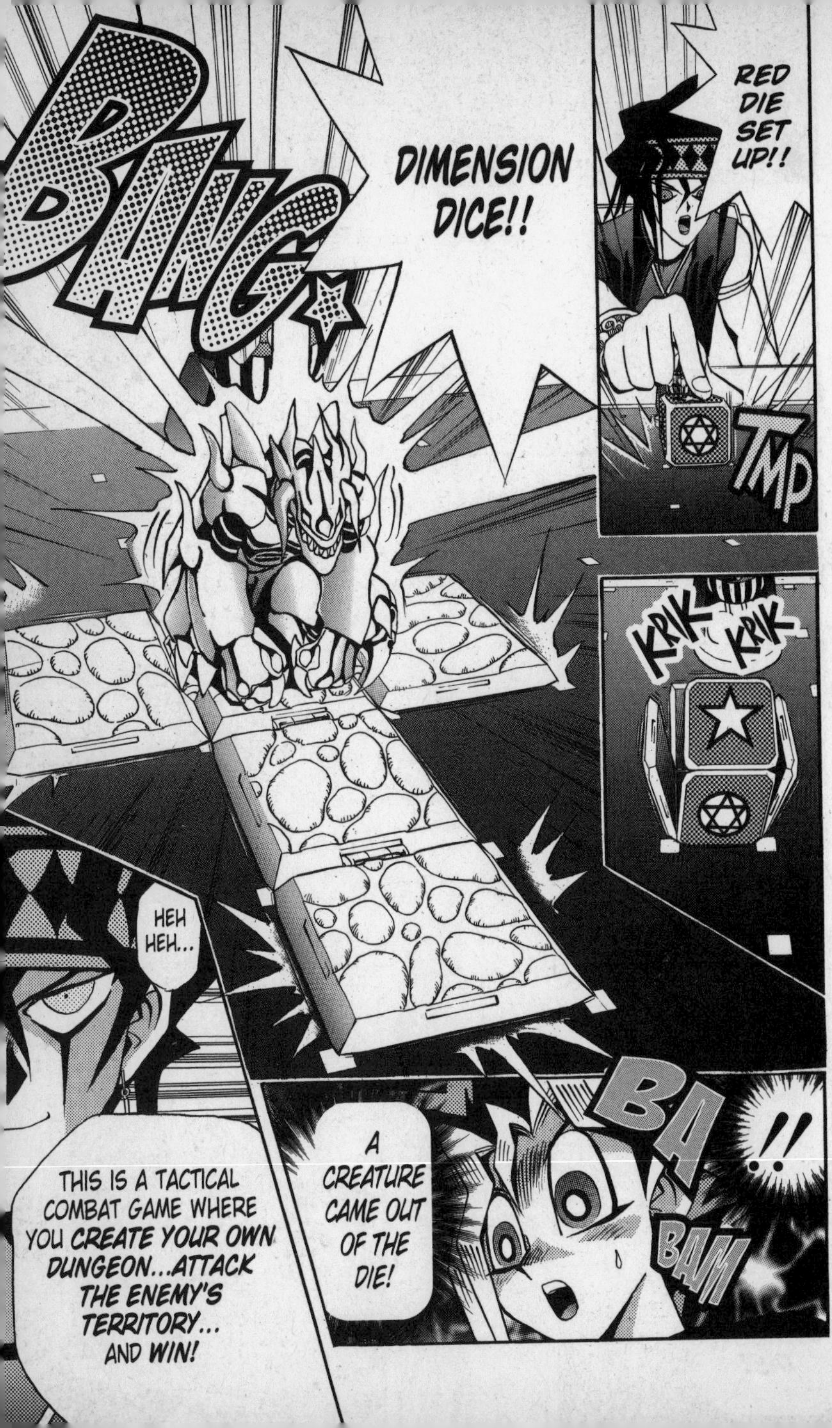
RED DIE SET UP!!
TMP
KRIK KRIK
BANG
DIMENSION DICE!!
BA!!
BAM
A CREATURE CAME OUT OF THE DIE!
HEH HEH...
THIS IS A TACTICAL COMBAT GAME WHERE YOU CREATE YOUR OWN DUNGEON...ATTACK THE ENEMY'S TERRITORY... AND WIN!

Duel 78: The Path of Darkness!

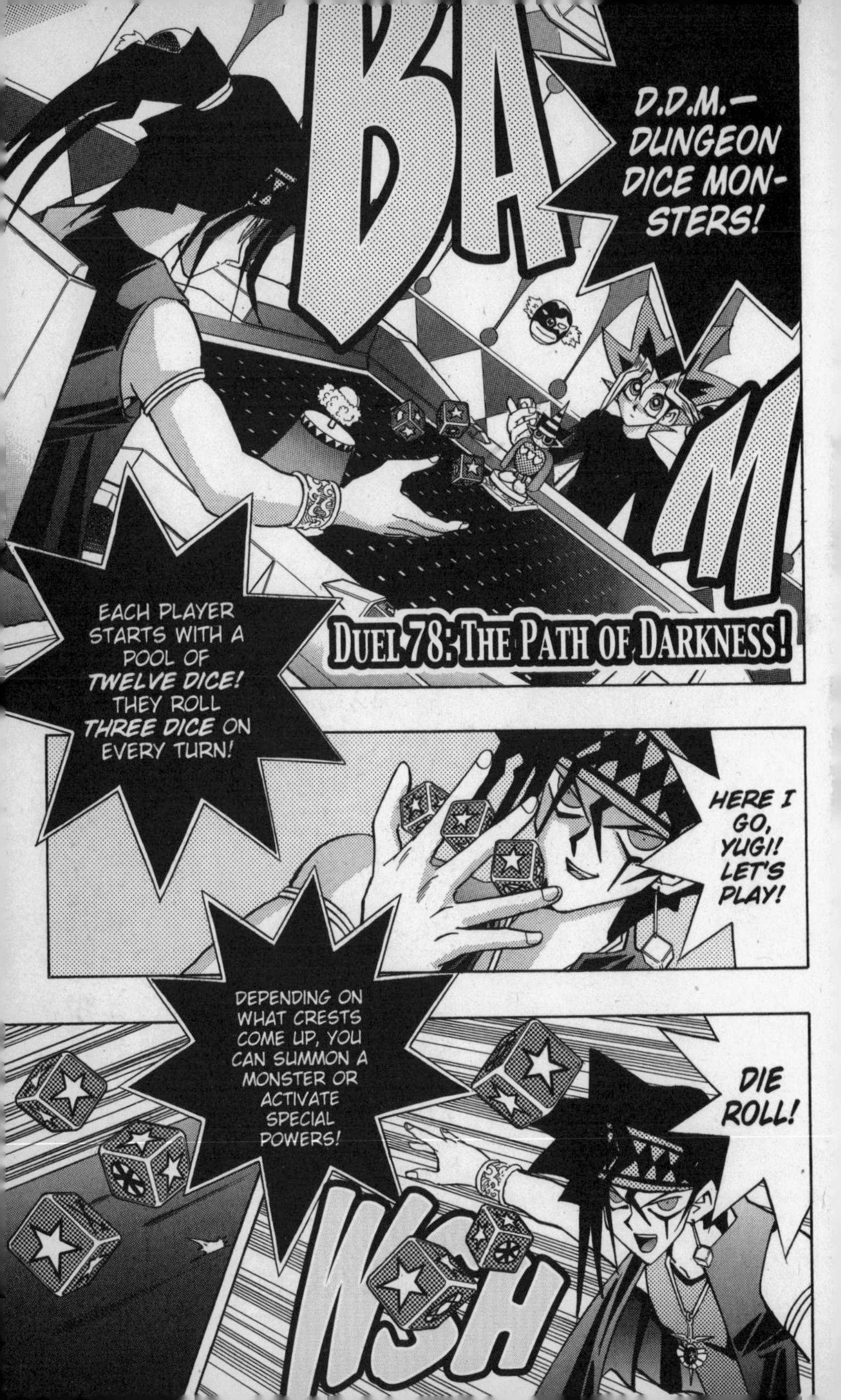
D.D.M.—DUNGEON DICE MONSTERS!
BAM
EACH PLAYER STARTS WITH A POOL OF TWELVE DICE! THEY ROLL THREE DICE ON EVERY TURN!
HERE I GO, YUGI! LET'S PLAY!
DIE ROLL!
DEPENDING ON WHAT CRESTS COME UP, YOU CAN SUMMON A MONSTER OR ACTIVATE SPECIAL POWERS!

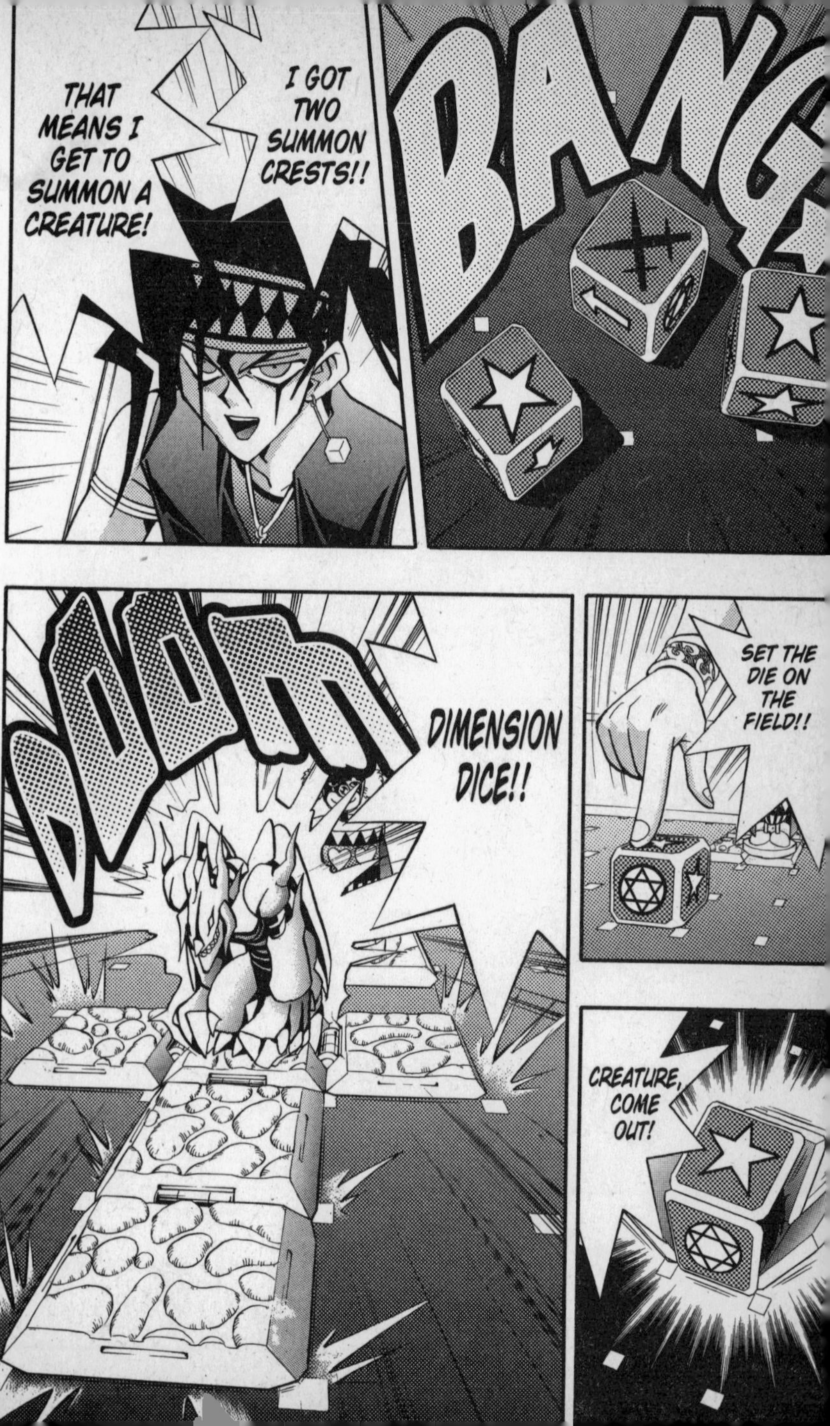
BANG
I GOT TWO SUMMON CRESTS!!
THAT MEANS I GET TO SUMMON A CREATURE!
SET THE DIE ON THE FIELD!!
CREATURE, COME OUT!
DOOM
DIMENSION DICE!!

DUEL 78: THE PATH OF DARKNESS!

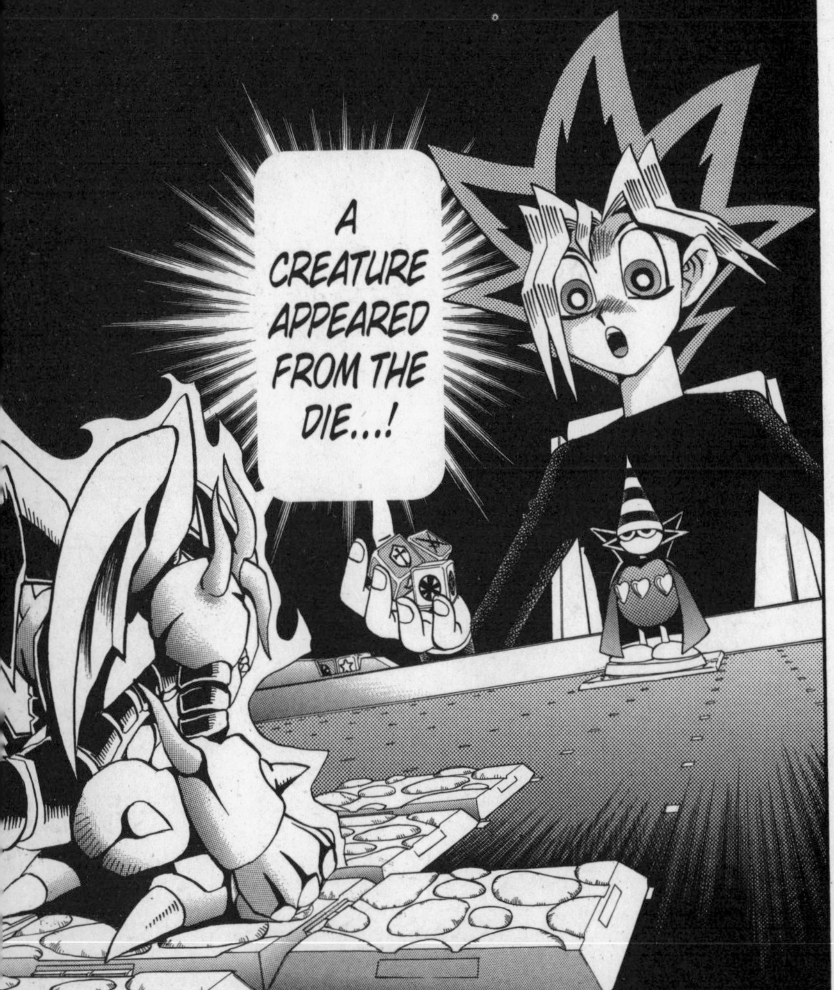
A CREATURE APPEARED FROM THE DIE...!

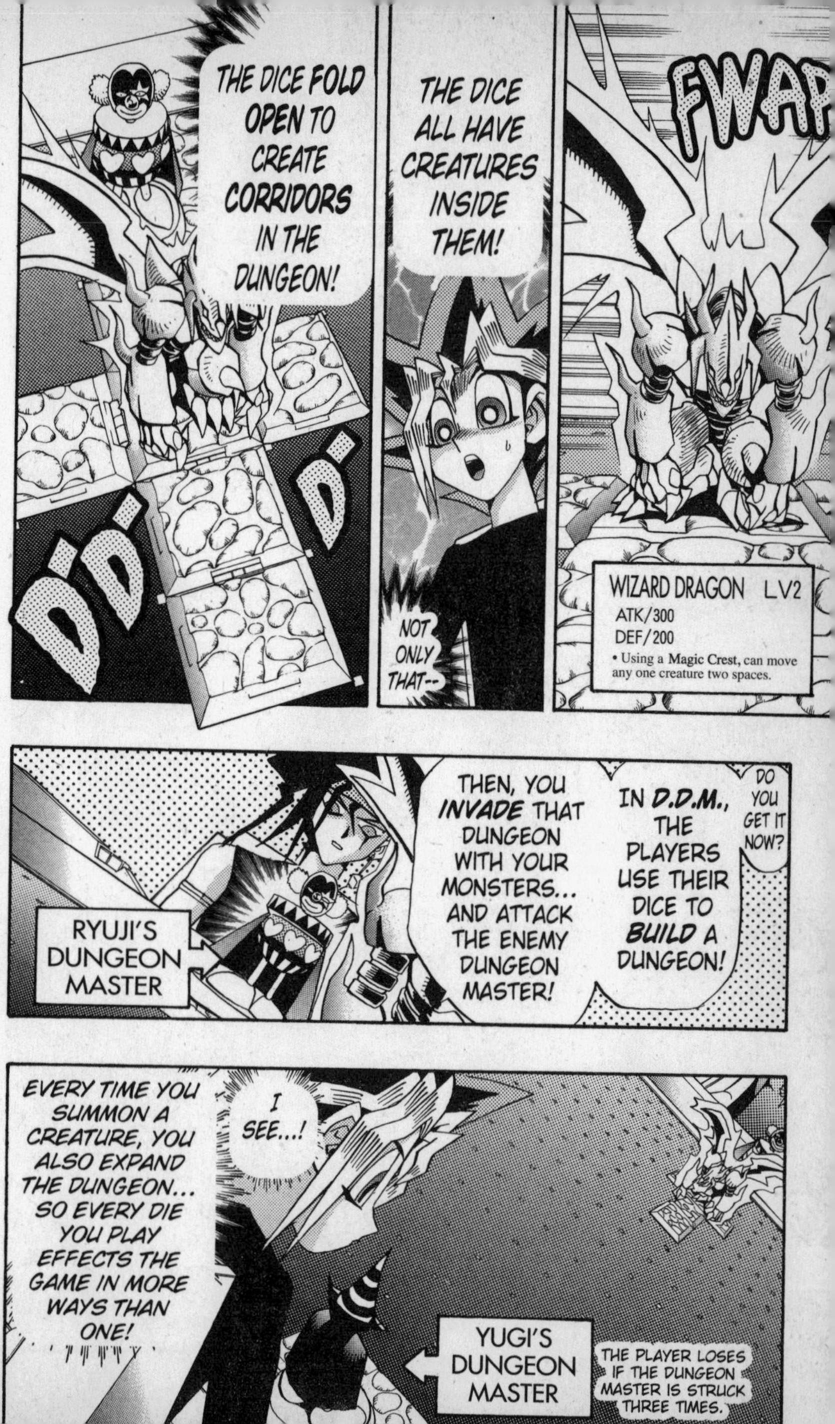
FWAP
WIZARD DRAGON LV2
ATK/300
DEF/200
• Using a Magic Crest, can move any one creature two spaces.
THE DICE ALL HAVE CREATURES INSIDE THEM!
NOT ONLY THAT--
THE DICE FOLD OPEN TO CREATE CORRIDORS IN THE DUNGEON!
DDD
DO YOU GET IT NOW?
IN D.D.M., THE PLAYERS USE THEIR DICE TO BUILD A DUNGEON!
THEN, YOU INVADE THAT DUNGEON WITH YOUR MONSTERS... AND ATTACK THE ENEMY DUNGEON MASTER!
RYUJI'S DUNGEON MASTER
THE PLAYER LOSES IF THE DUNGEON MASTER IS STRUCK THREE TIMES.
YUGI'S DUNGEON MASTER
I SEE...!
EVERY TIME YOU SUMMON A CREATURE, YOU ALSO EXPAND THE DUNGEON... SO EVERY DIE YOU PLAY EFFECTS THE GAME IN MORE WAYS THAN ONE!

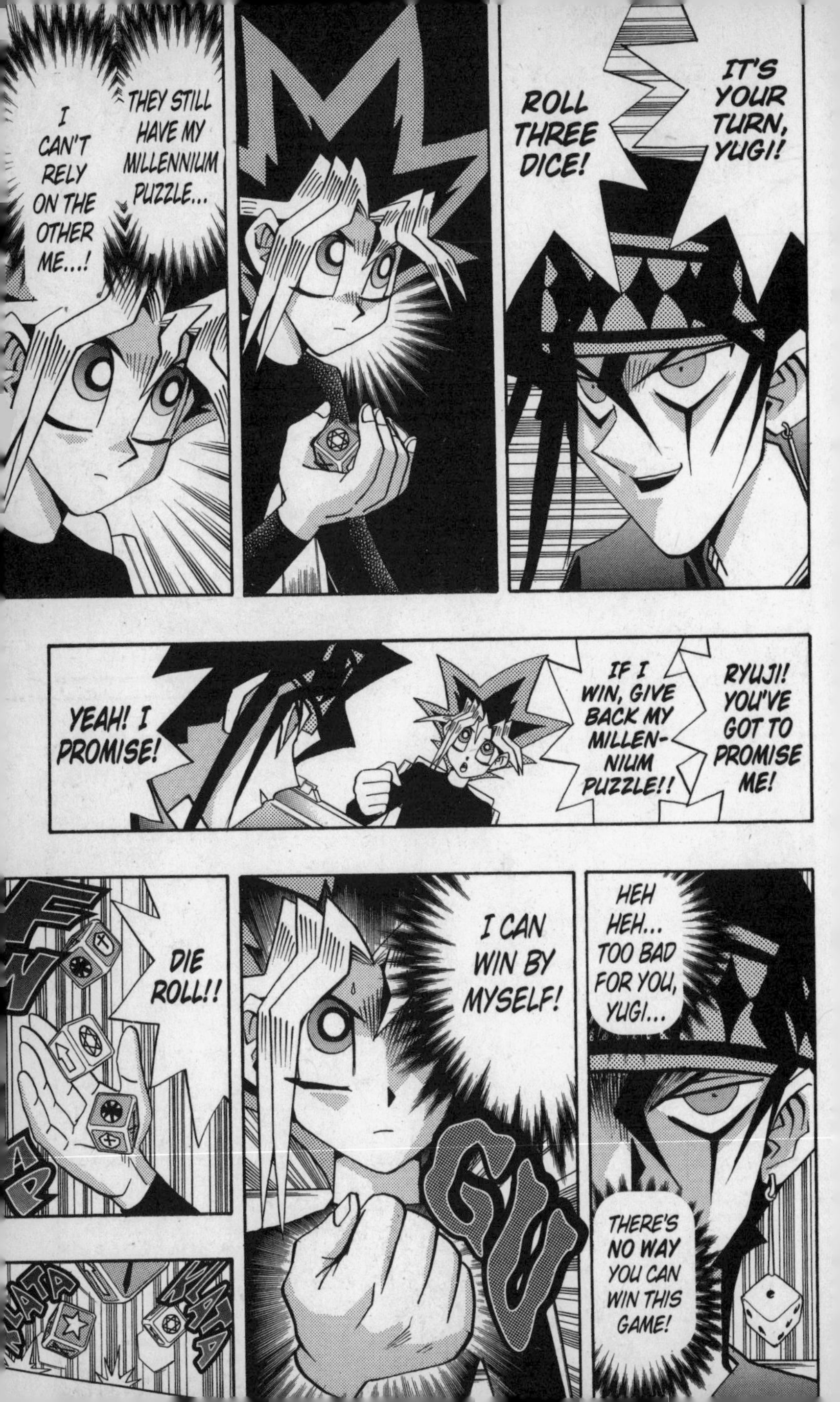
IT'S YOUR TURN, YUGI!
ROLL THREE DICE!
THEY STILL HAVE MY MILLENNIUM PUZZLE...
I CAN'T RELY ON THE OTHER ME...!
RYUJI! YOU'VE GOT TO PROMISE ME!
IF I WIN, GIVE BACK MY MILLENNIUM PUZZLE!!
YEAH! I PROMISE!
HEH HEH... TOO BAD FOR YOU, YUGI...
THERE'S NO WAY YOU CAN WIN THIS GAME!
I CAN WIN BY MYSELF!
GU
DIE ROLL!!
KATA
KATA

THE CRESTS ARE ALL DIFFERENT!

!!

DO

OM...

TOO BAD, YUGI! **SUMMON FAILED!**

HEH HEH...

☆	Summon
⬆	Movement
✴	Magic
✕	Attack
✝	Defense
✳	Trap

THERE ARE SIX DIFFERENT CRESTS...

YOU CAN SEE THEM ON THE DICE...

"HIGH LEVEL"?!

THE DICE YOU CHOSE WERE HIGH LEVEL, MEANING THEY'RE DIFFICULT TO SUMMON!

LEVEL IS A MEASURE OF POWER, OF COURSE. BUT WHAT DO THE **LEVELS** HAVE TO DO WITH THE **CRESTS**, YOU ASK...?

ZM

ZM

FOR EXAMPLE, MY MONSTER ON THE FIELD, **WIZARD DRAGON**, IS LEVEL 2!

AND THEN THERE'S **LEVELS.**

IT'S DETERMINED BY THE NUMBER OF SUMMON CRESTS ON THE CREATURE DICE!

⁉

BUT, TAKE A LOOK AT *YOUR* DICE!

!

ALL OF THEM ONLY HAVE ONE SUMMON CREST...!

FOR EXAMPLE, ON *WIZARD DRAGON'S* DICE, THERE ARE *THREE* SUMMON CRESTS. IN OTHER WORDS, THE CHANCES OF SUMMONING HIM ARE ONE IN TWO!

WIZARD DRAGON IS EASY TO SUMMON, BUT IN RETURN, ITS LEVEL IS LOW!

THAT'S RIGHT!

THE LESS SUMMON CRESTS THERE ARE, THE LOWER THE CHANCES OF SUMMMONING!

YOU TAKE A GREATER RISK TO SUMMON A TOUGHER MONSTER!

OH NO...! I DIDN'T REALIZE THE RULES WHEN I CHOSE THEM! THE LEVELS OF THESE DICE ARE TOO HIGH...!

DICE CREATURE LEVEL SET UP

★	★★	★★★	★★★★	NUMBER OF SUMMON CRESTS (OUT OF SIX)
/6	/6	/6	/6	
LV4	LV3	LV2	LV1	CREATURE LEVEL

ATTACK POWER

Strong ⟷ Weak

THE OUTCOME OF THIS GAME WILL BE DECIDED BY HOW MANY CREATURES YOU CAN BRING TO THE FIELD.

IF YOU ONLY CHOOSE HIGH LEVEL DICE, YOU'LL HAVE NO CHANCE OF WINNING...

UNLESS YOU'VE GOT GREAT LUCK...

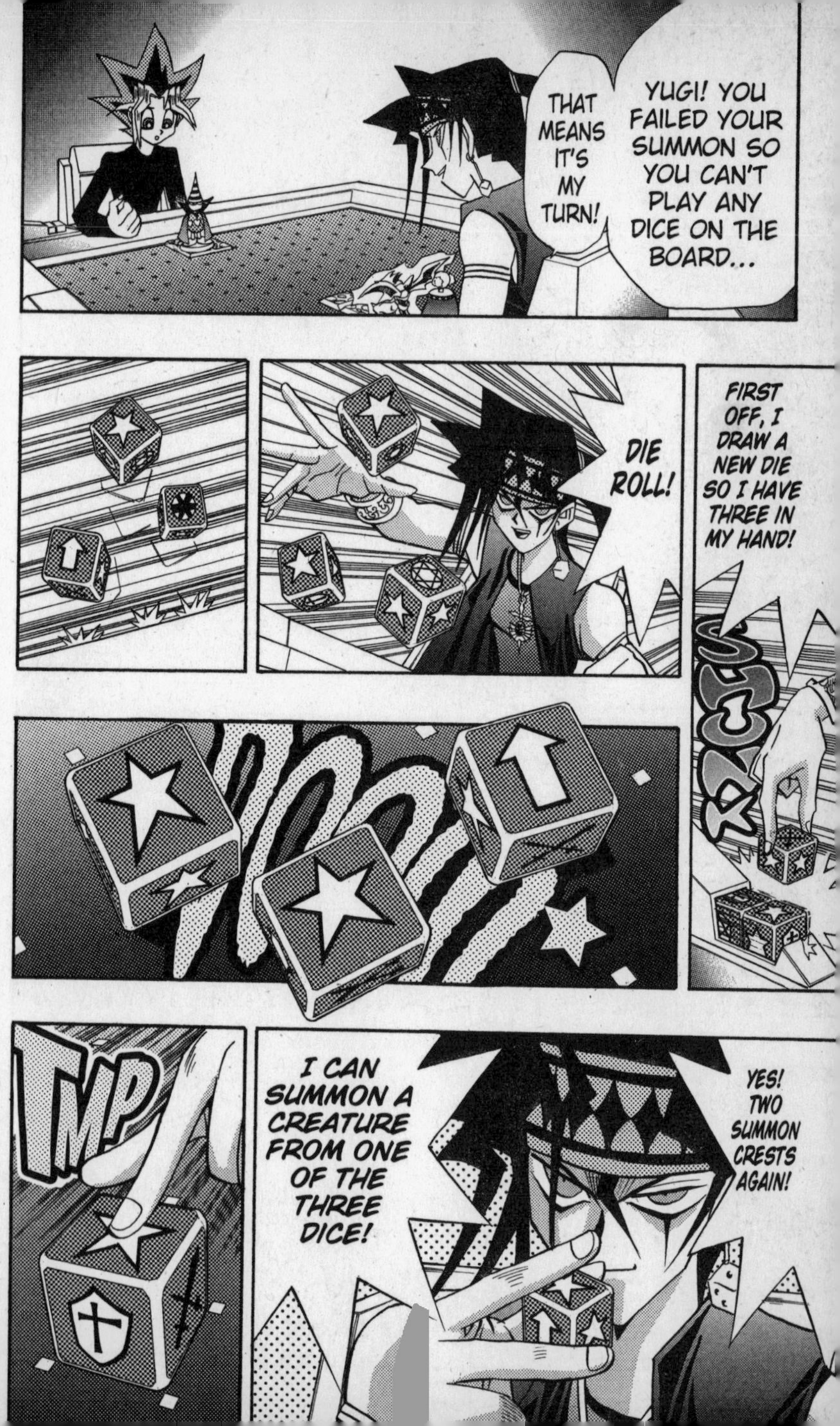
YUGI! YOU FAILED YOUR SUMMON SO YOU CAN'T PLAY ANY DICE ON THE BOARD...
THAT MEANS IT'S MY TURN!
FIRST OFF, I DRAW A NEW DIE SO I HAVE THREE IN MY HAND!
DIE ROLL!
YES! TWO SUMMON CRESTS AGAIN!
I CAN SUMMON A CREATURE FROM ONE OF THE THREE DICE!
TMP

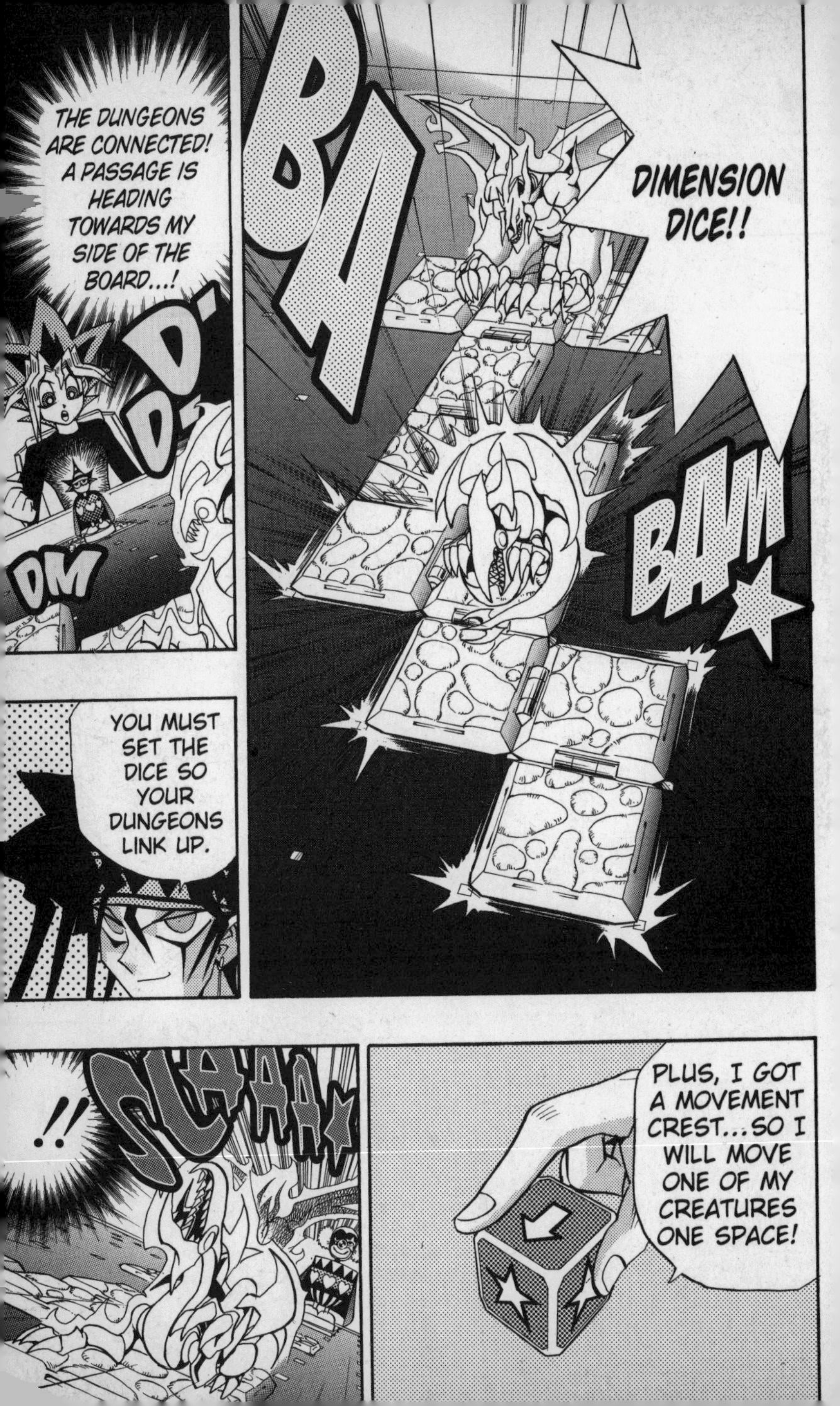
BA
DIMENSION DICE!!
BAM
THE DUNGEONS ARE CONNECTED! A PASSAGE IS HEADING TOWARDS MY SIDE OF THE BOARD...!
DOM
YOU MUST SET THE DICE SO YOUR DUNGEONS LINK UP.
PLUS, I GOT A MOVEMENT CREST...SO I WILL MOVE ONE OF MY CREATURES ONE SPACE!
!!

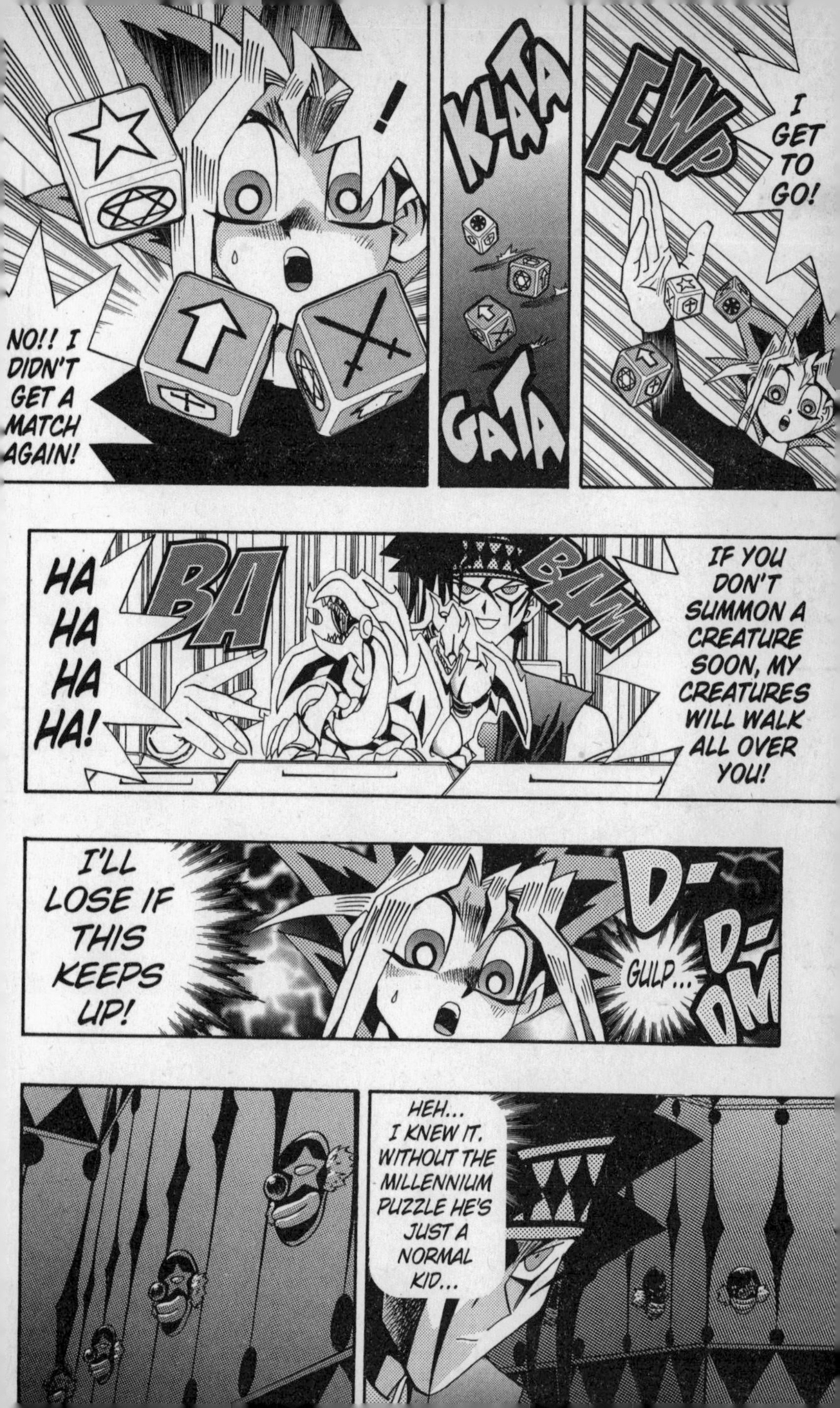
FWP
I GET TO GO!
KLATA
GATA
!
NO!! I DIDN'T GET A MATCH AGAIN!
BAM
IF YOU DON'T SUMMON A CREATURE SOON, MY CREATURES WILL WALK ALL OVER YOU!
BA
HA HA HA HA HA!
D-D-DOM
GULP...
I'LL LOSE IF THIS KEEPS UP!
HEH... I KNEW IT. WITHOUT THE MILLENNIUM PUZZLE HE'S JUST A NORMAL KID...

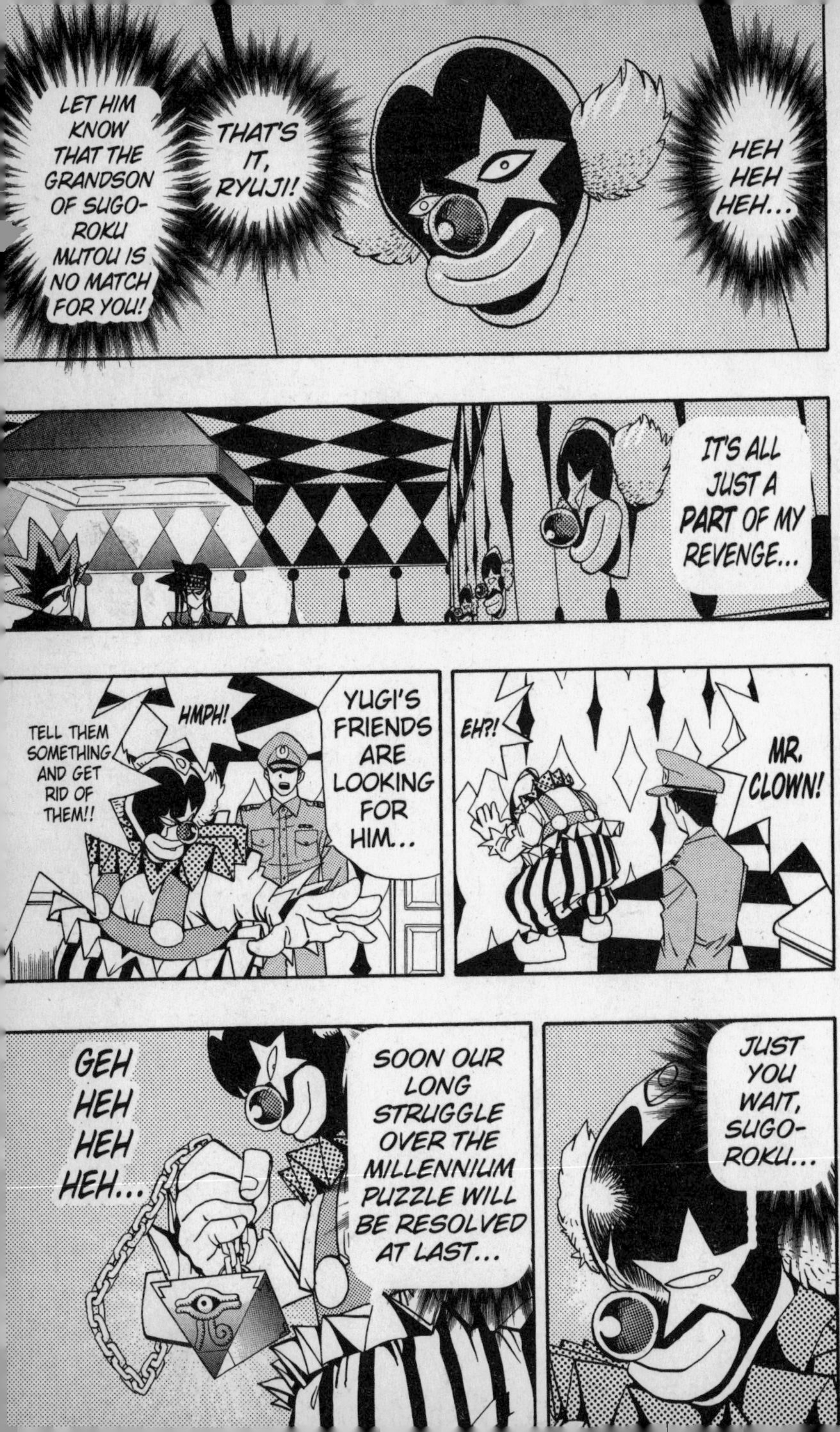
HEH HEH HEH...
THAT'S IT, RYUJI!
LET HIM KNOW THAT THE GRANDSON OF SUGO-ROKU MUTOU IS NO MATCH FOR YOU!
IT'S ALL JUST A PART OF MY REVENGE...
MR. CLOWN!
EH?!
YUGI'S FRIENDS ARE LOOKING FOR HIM...
HMPH!
TELL THEM SOMETHING AND GET RID OF THEM!!
JUST YOU WAIT, SUGO-ROKU...
SOON OUR LONG STRUGGLE OVER THE MILLENNIUM PUZZLE WILL BE RESOLVED AT LAST...
GEH HEH HEH HEH...

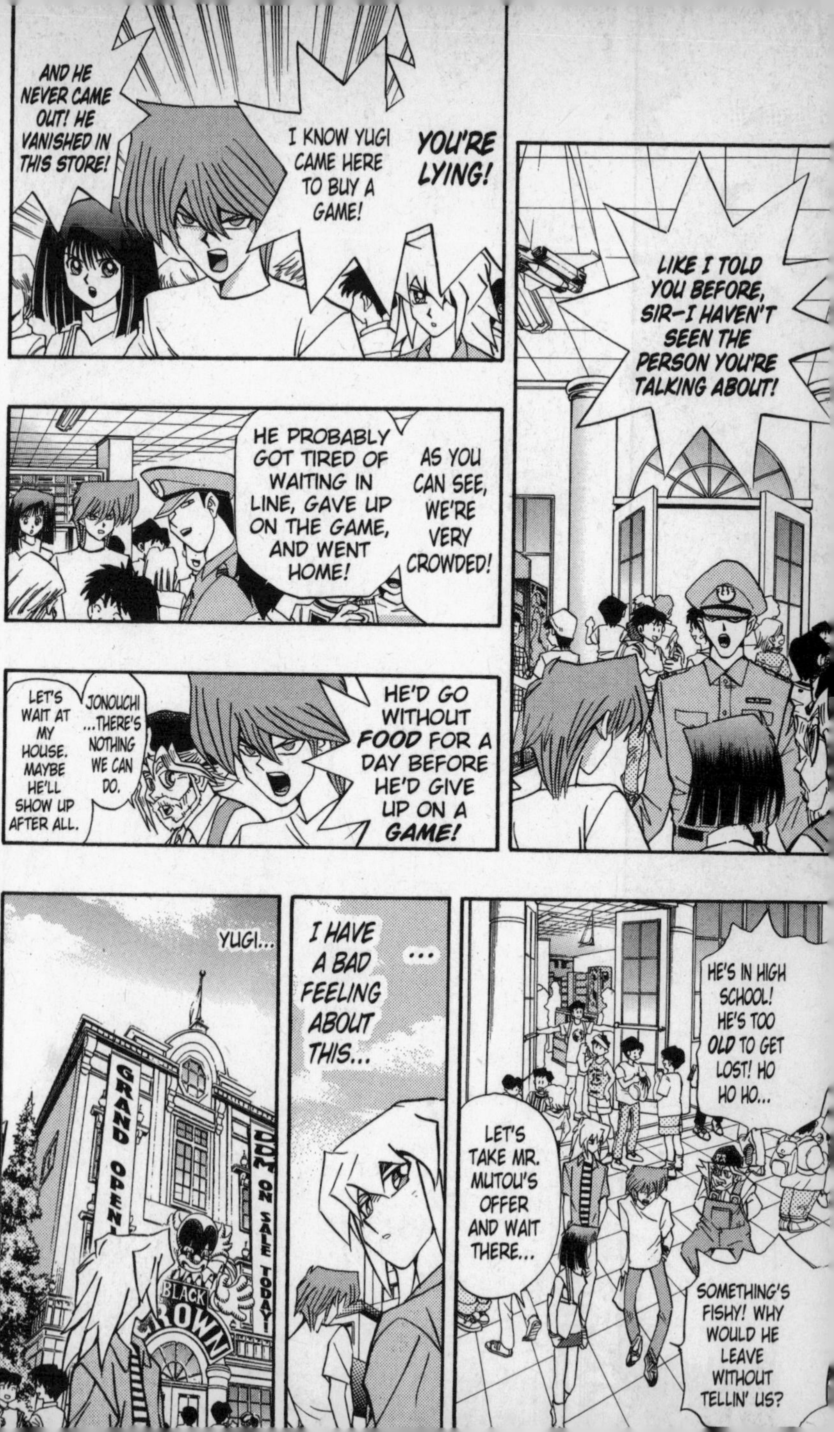
YOU'RE LYING!
I KNOW YUGI CAME HERE TO BUY A GAME!
AND HE NEVER CAME OUT! HE VANISHED IN THIS STORE!
LIKE I TOLD YOU BEFORE, SIR—I HAVEN'T SEEN THE PERSON YOU'RE TALKING ABOUT!
AS YOU CAN SEE, WE'RE VERY CROWDED!
HE PROBABLY GOT TIRED OF WAITING IN LINE, GAVE UP ON THE GAME, AND WENT HOME!
HE'D GO WITHOUT FOOD FOR A DAY BEFORE HE'D GIVE UP ON A GAME!
JONOUCHI ...THERE'S NOTHING WE CAN DO.
LET'S WAIT AT MY HOUSE. MAYBE HE'LL SHOW UP AFTER ALL.
HE'S IN HIGH SCHOOL! HE'S TOO OLD TO GET LOST! HO HO HO...
SOMETHING'S FISHY! WHY WOULD HE LEAVE WITHOUT TELLIN' US?
LET'S TAKE MR. MUTOU'S OFFER AND WAIT THERE...
...
I HAVE A BAD FEELING ABOUT THIS...
YUGI...
GRAND OPEN
ON SALE TODAY!
BLACK CROWN

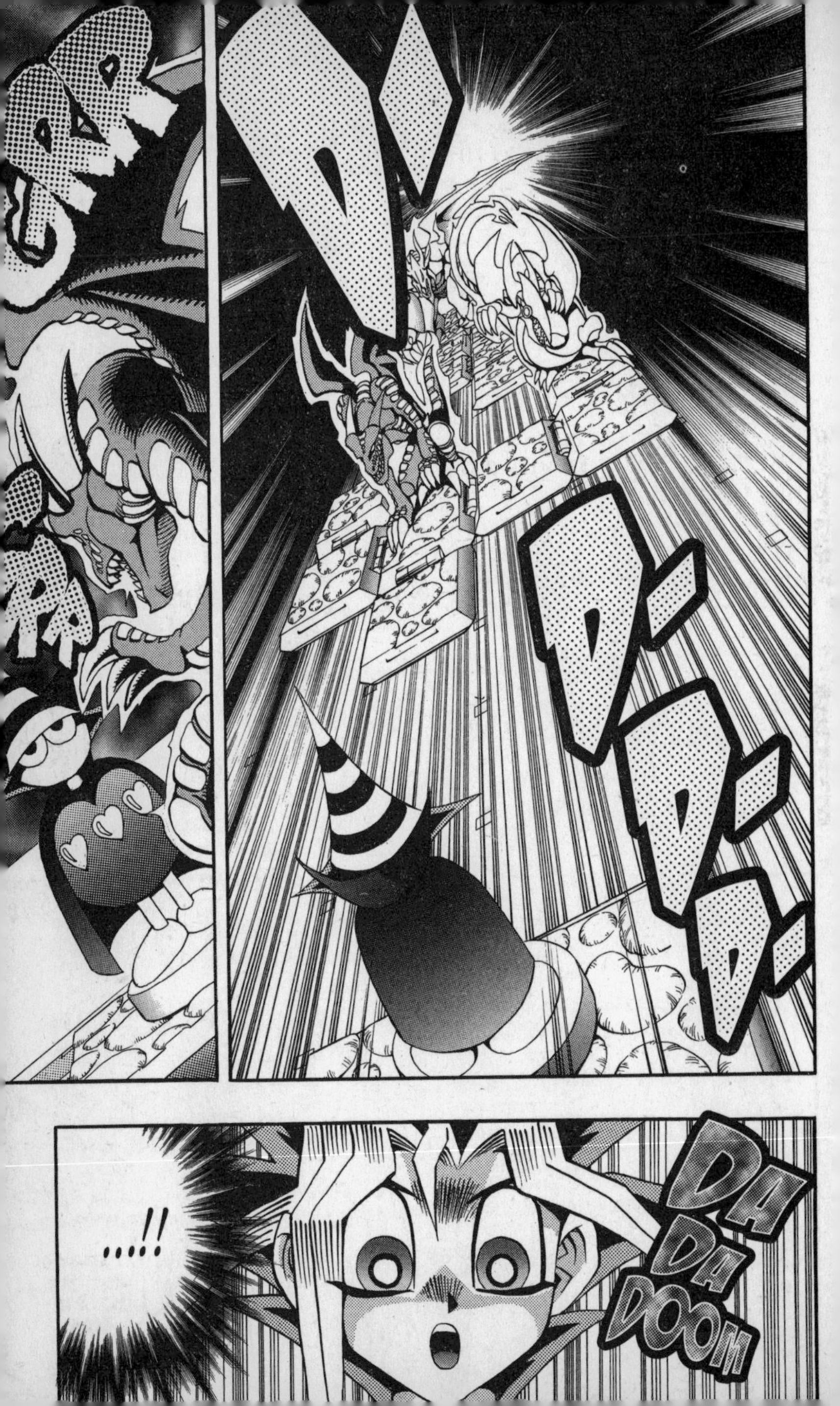
DA DA DOOM
....!!

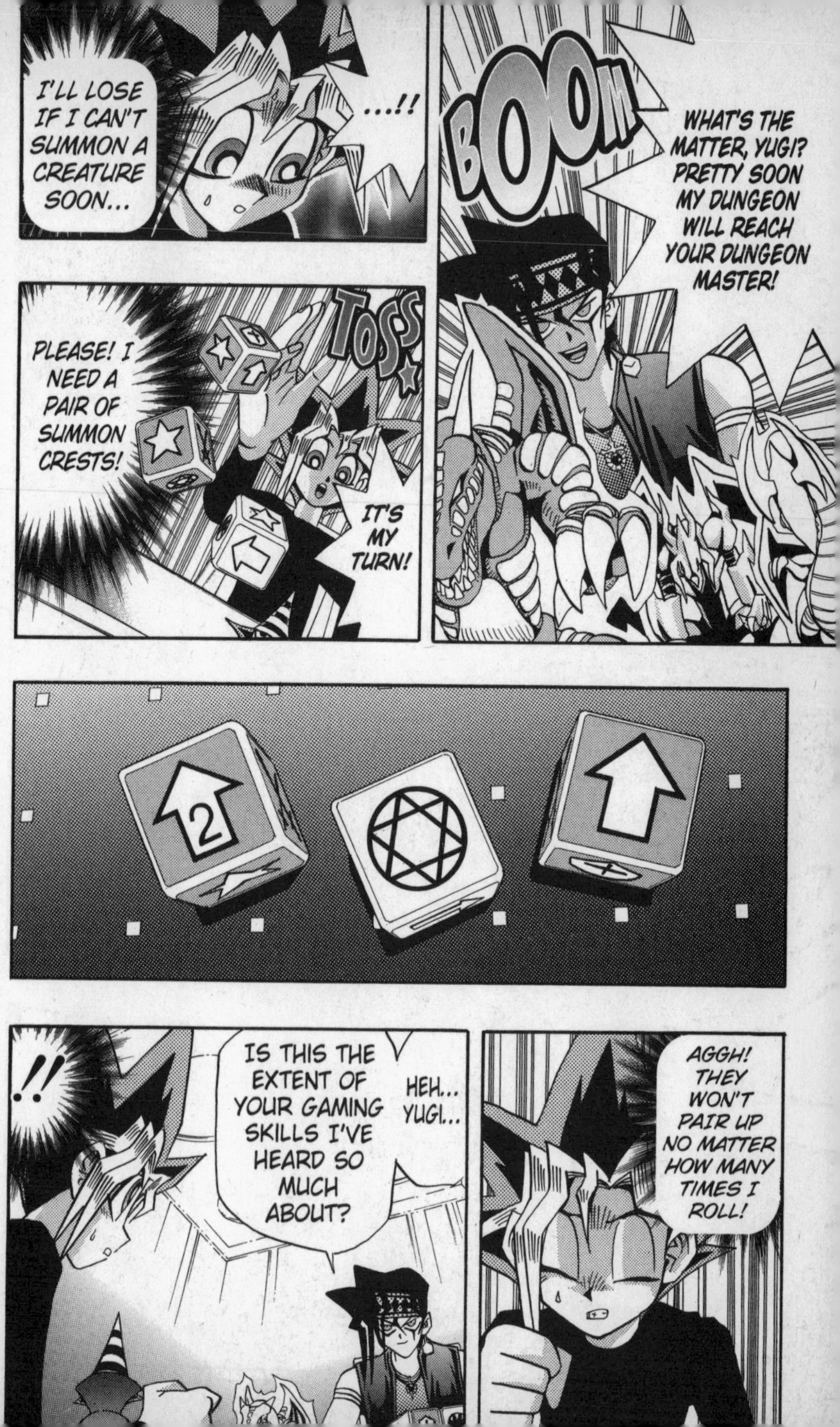
BOOM
WHAT'S THE MATTER, YUGI? PRETTY SOON MY DUNGEON WILL REACH YOUR DUNGEON MASTER!
...!!
I'LL LOSE IF I CAN'T SUMMON A CREATURE SOON...
TOSS
IT'S MY TURN!
PLEASE! I NEED A PAIR OF SUMMON CRESTS!
2
AGGH! THEY WON'T PAIR UP NO MATTER HOW MANY TIMES I ROLL!
HEH... YUGI...
IS THIS THE EXTENT OF YOUR GAMING SKILLS I'VE HEARD SO MUCH ABOUT?
!!

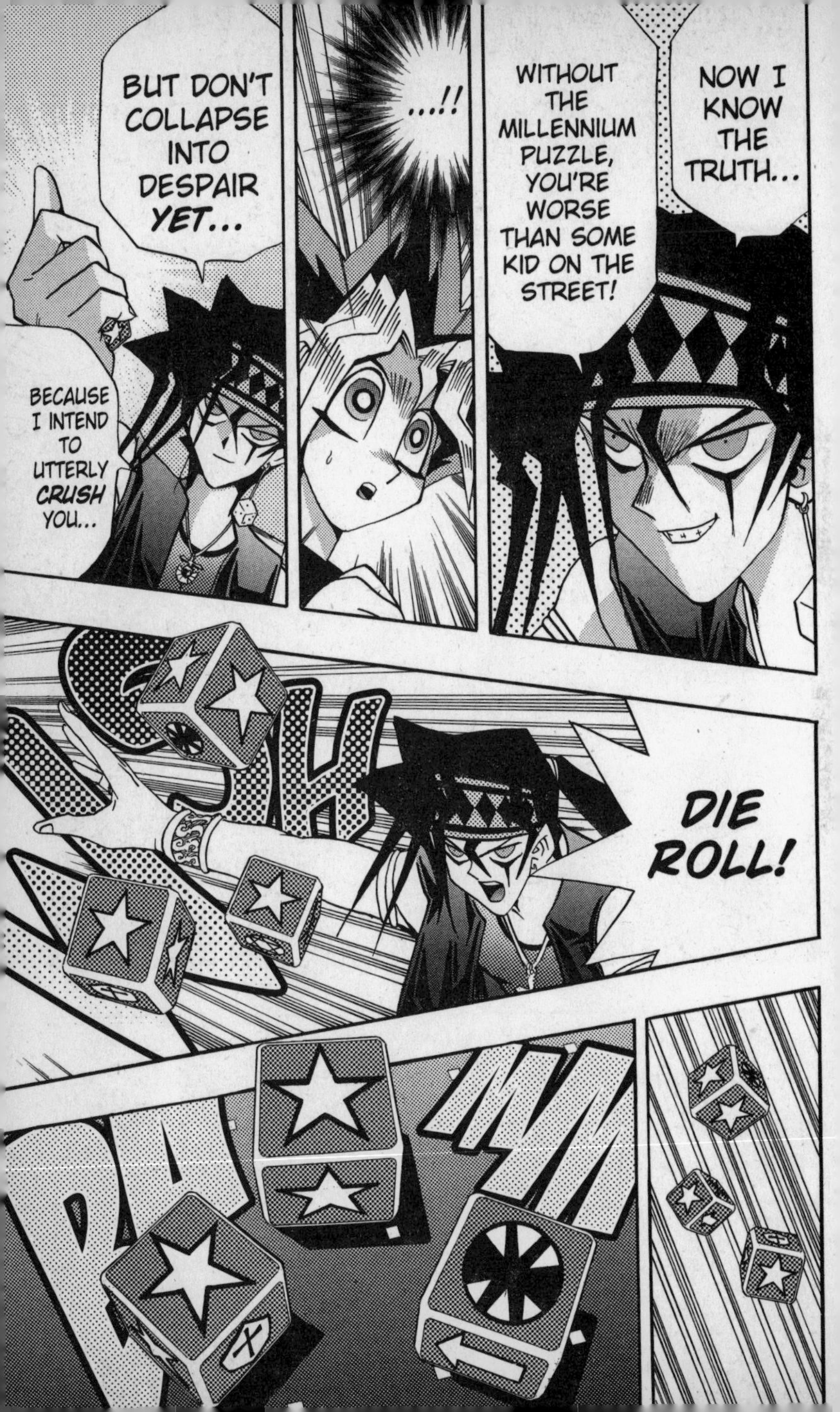
NOW I KNOW THE TRUTH...
WITHOUT THE MILLENNIUM PUZZLE, YOU'RE WORSE THAN SOME KID ON THE STREET!
...!!
BUT DON'T COLLAPSE INTO DESPAIR *YET*...
BECAUSE I INTEND TO UTTERLY *CRUSH* YOU...
DIE ROLL!

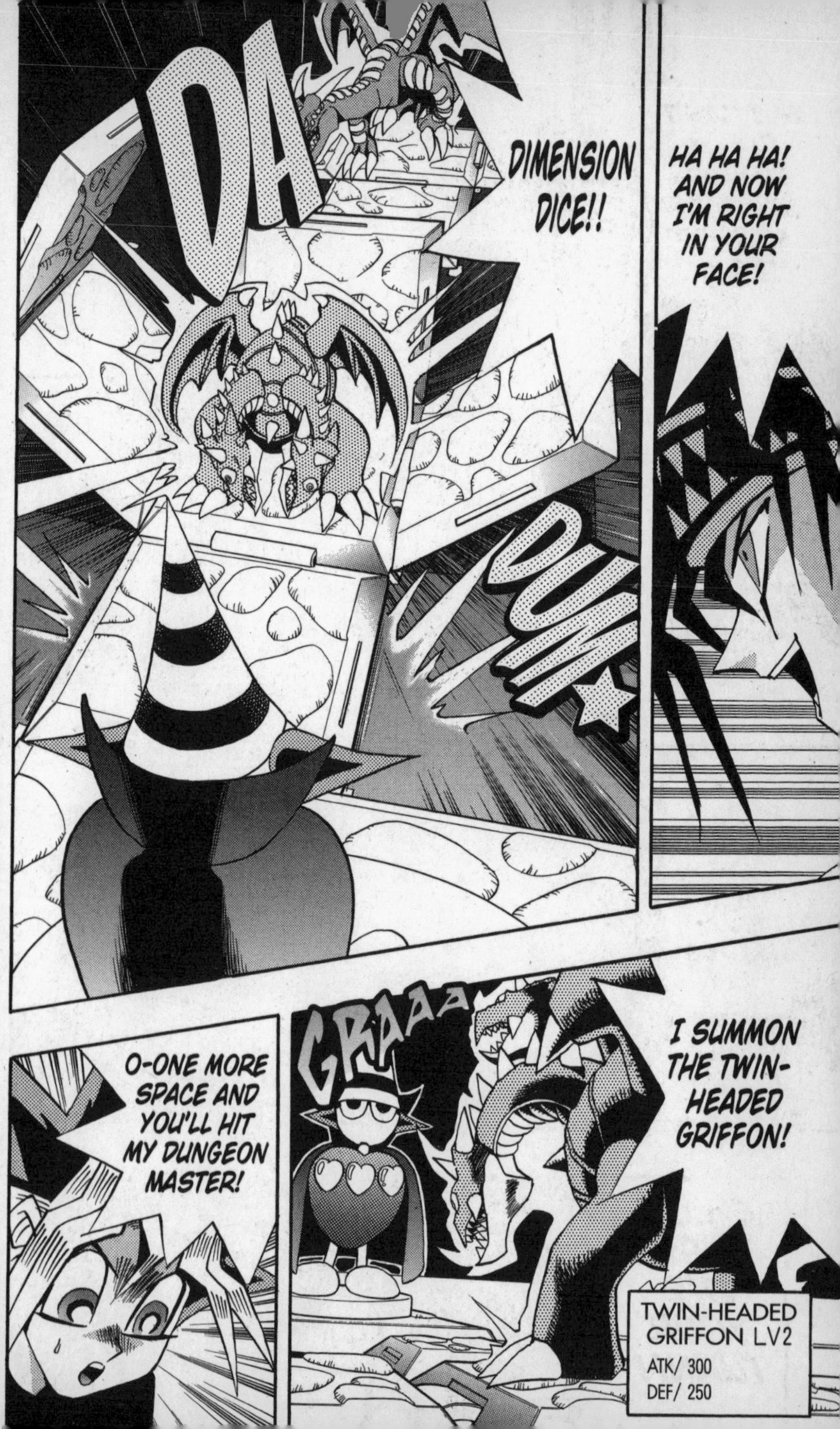
HA HA HA! AND NOW I'M RIGHT IN YOUR FACE!
DA
DIMENSION DICE!!
DUM
I SUMMON THE TWIN-HEADED GRIFFON!
GRAAA
TWIN-HEADED GRIFFON LV2
ATK/ 300
DEF/ 250
O-ONE MORE SPACE AND YOU'LL HIT MY DUNGEON MASTER!

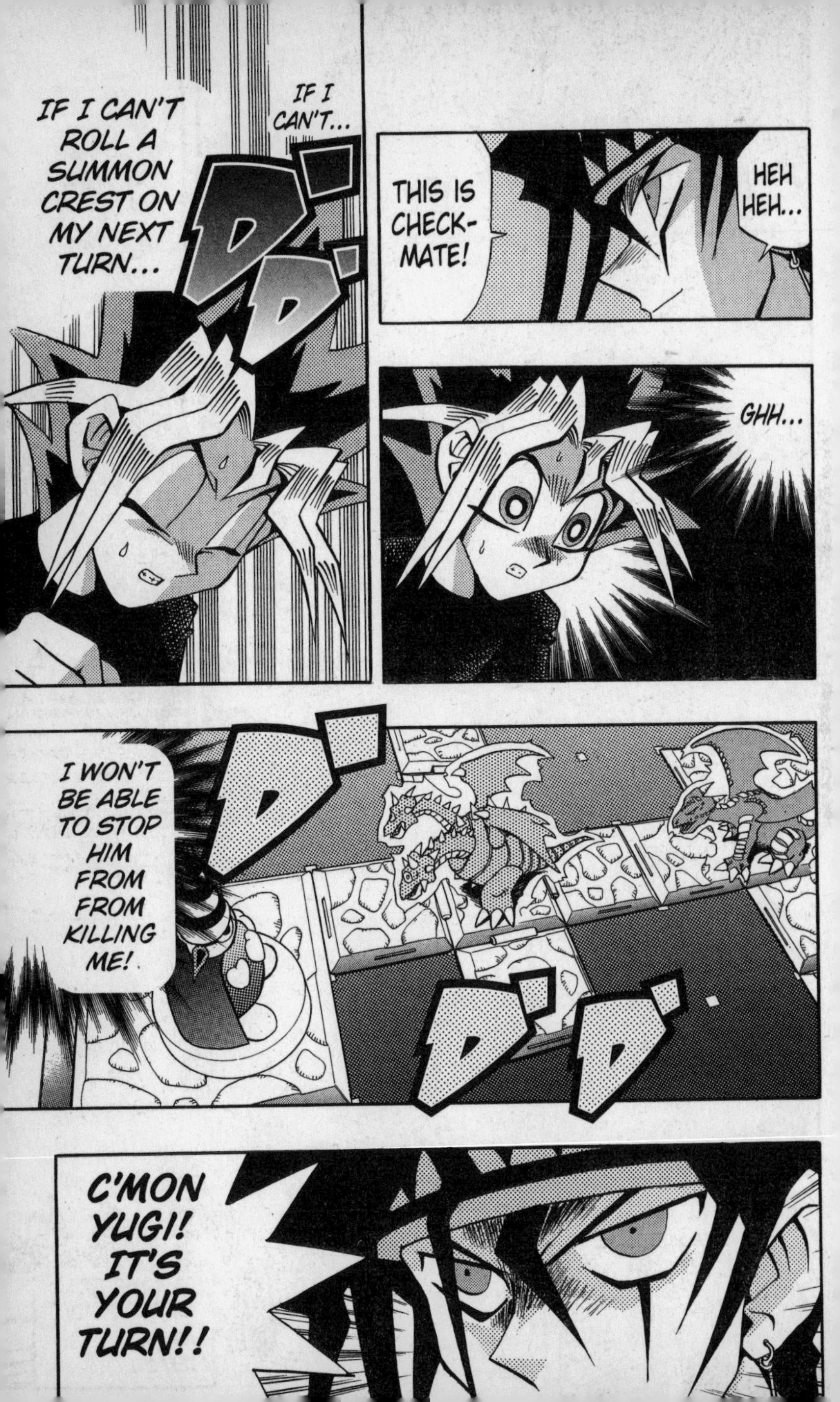
HEH HEH...
THIS IS CHECKMATE!
GHH...
IF I CAN'T...
IF I CAN'T ROLL A SUMMON CREST ON MY NEXT TURN...
I WON'T BE ABLE TO STOP HIM FROM FROM KILLING ME!
C'MON YUGI! IT'S YOUR TURN!!

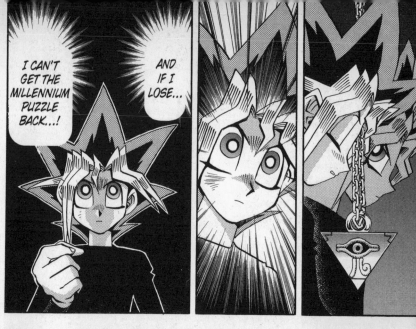

I CAN'T GET THE MILLENNIUM PUZZLE BACK...!

AND IF I LOSE...

OTHER ME...!!

I WILL GET YOU BACK!!

GRIP

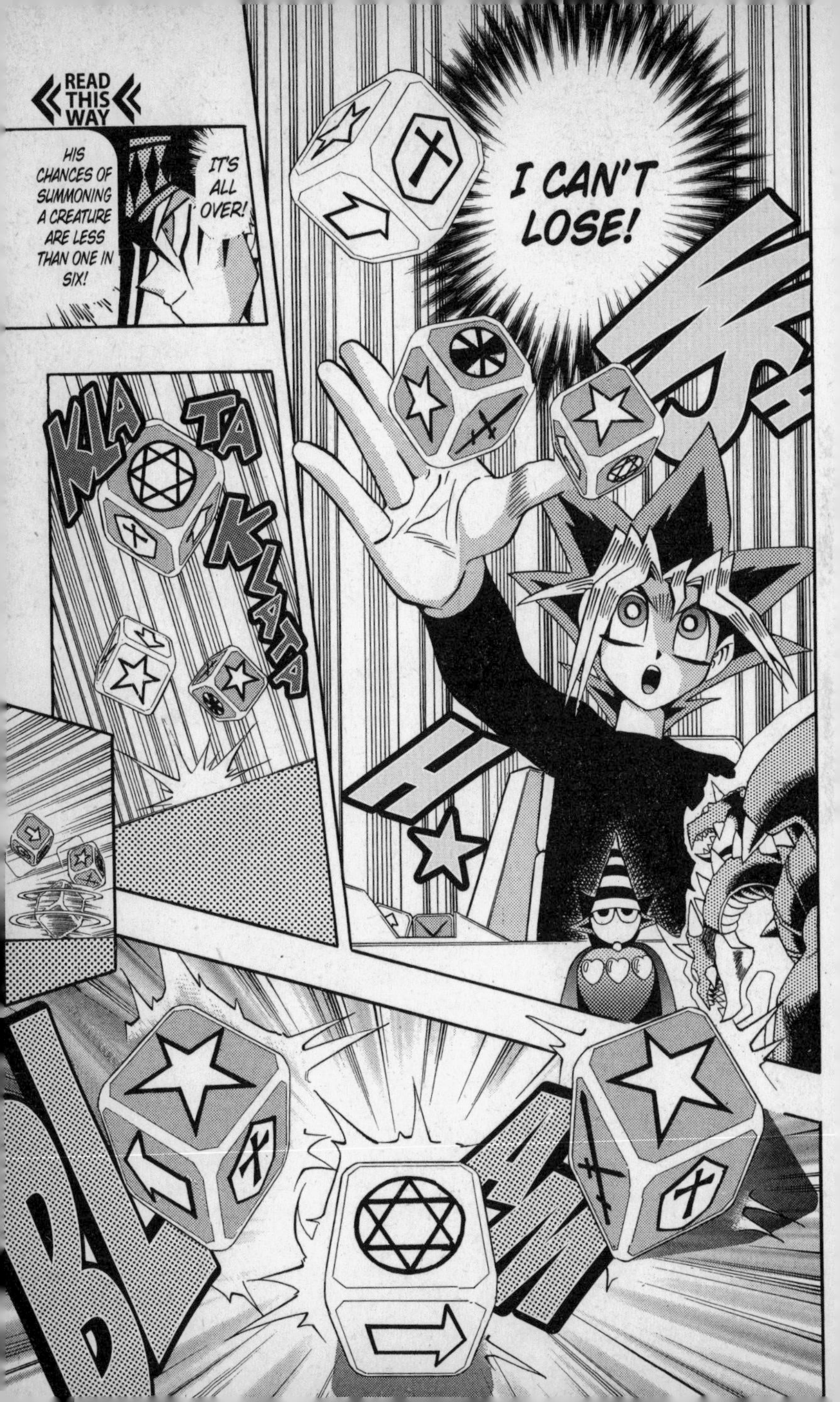
READ THIS WAY
I CAN'T LOSE!
IT'S ALL OVER!
HIS CHANCES OF SUMMONING A CREATURE ARE LESS THAN ONE IN SIX!
KLA TA KLATA KLATA

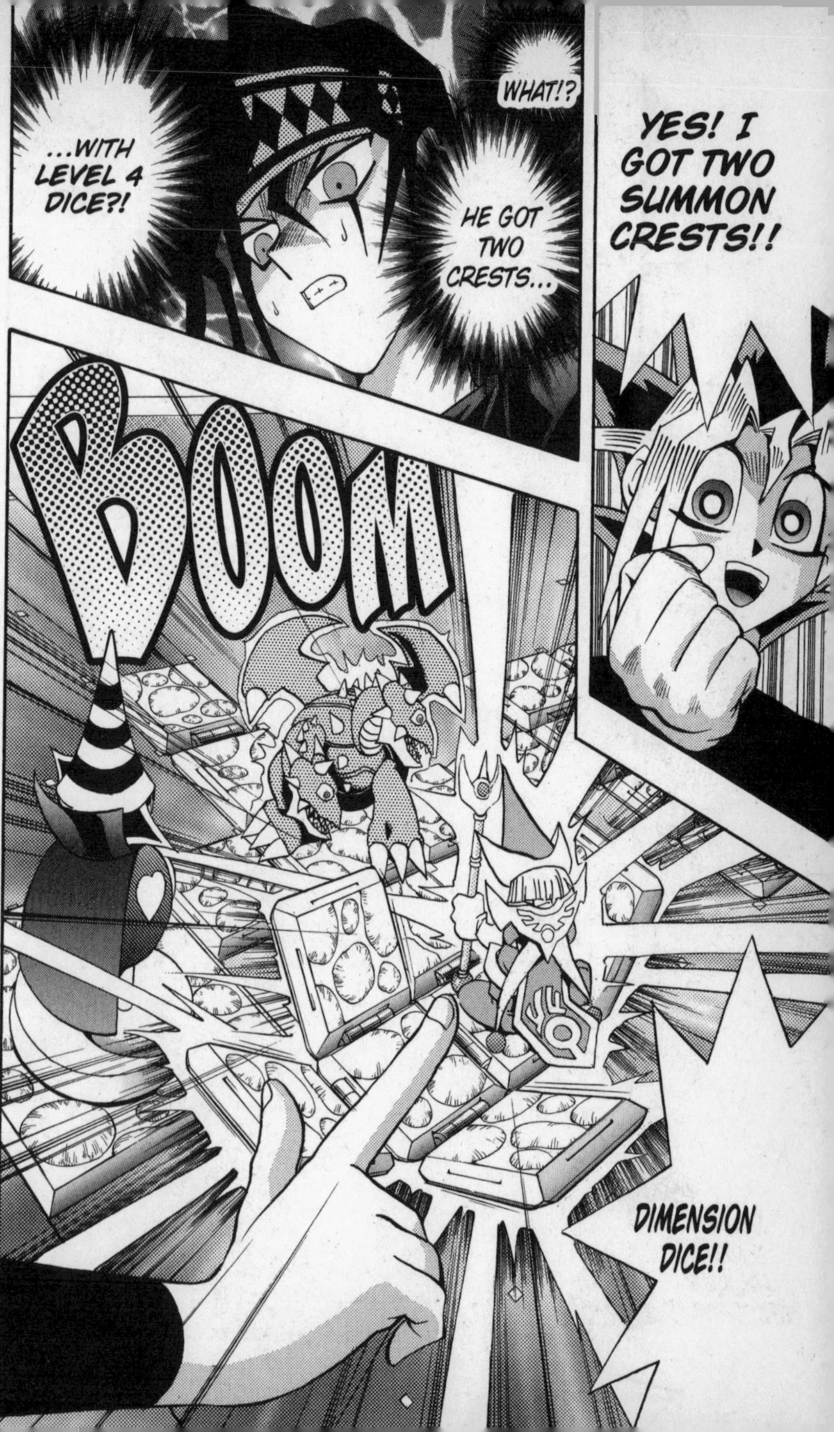
YES! I GOT TWO SUMMON CRESTS!!
WHAT!?
HE GOT TWO CRESTS...
...WITH LEVEL 4 DICE?!
DIMENSION DICE!!
BOOM

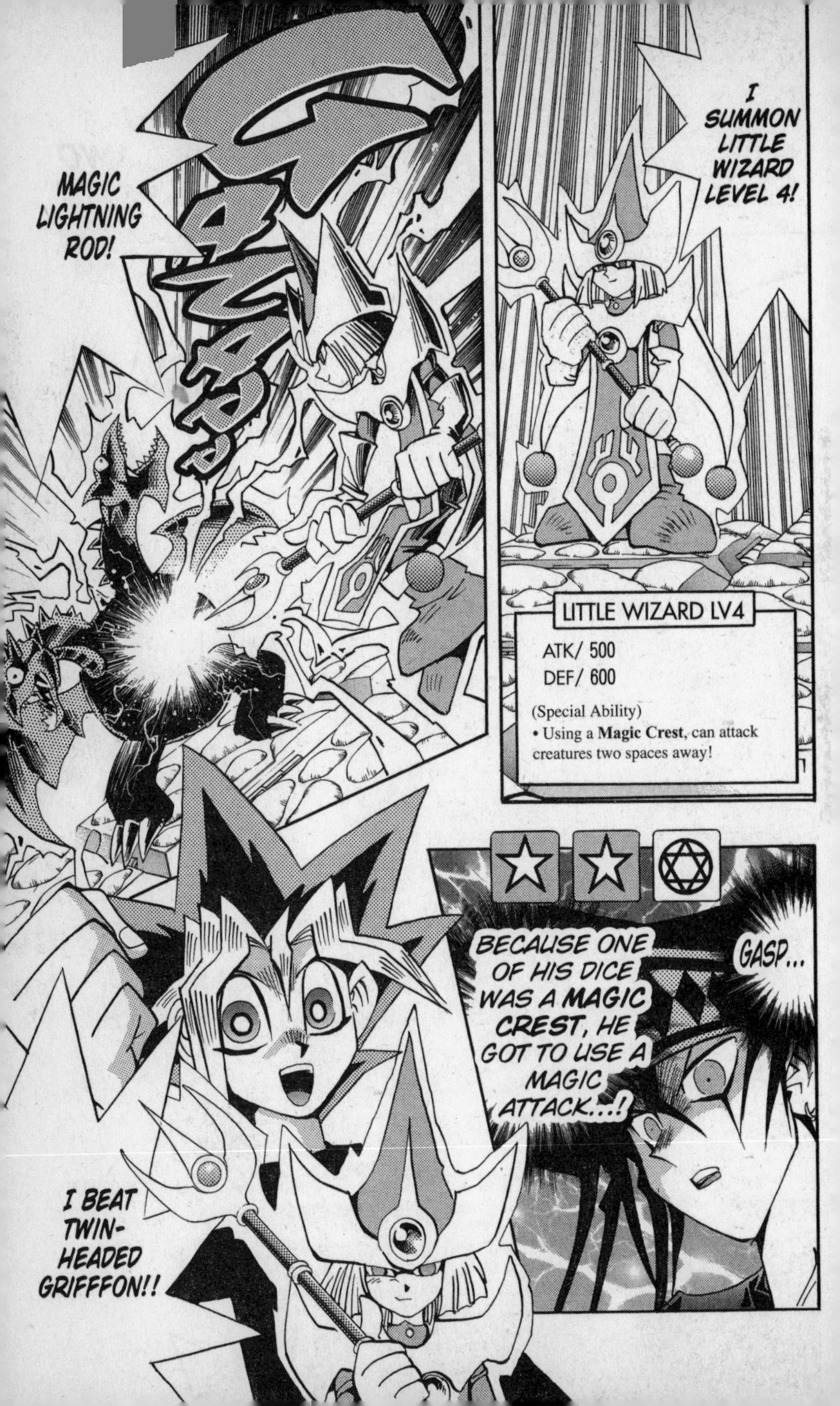
I SUMMON LITTLE WIZARD LEVEL 4!
LITTLE WIZARD LV4
ATK/ 500
DEF/ 600
(Special Ability)
• Using a Magic Crest, can attack creatures two spaces away!
MAGIC LIGHTNING ROD!
GASP...
BECAUSE ONE OF HIS DICE WAS A MAGIC CREST, HE GOT TO USE A MAGIC ATTACK...!
I BEAT TWIN-HEADED GRIFFFON!!

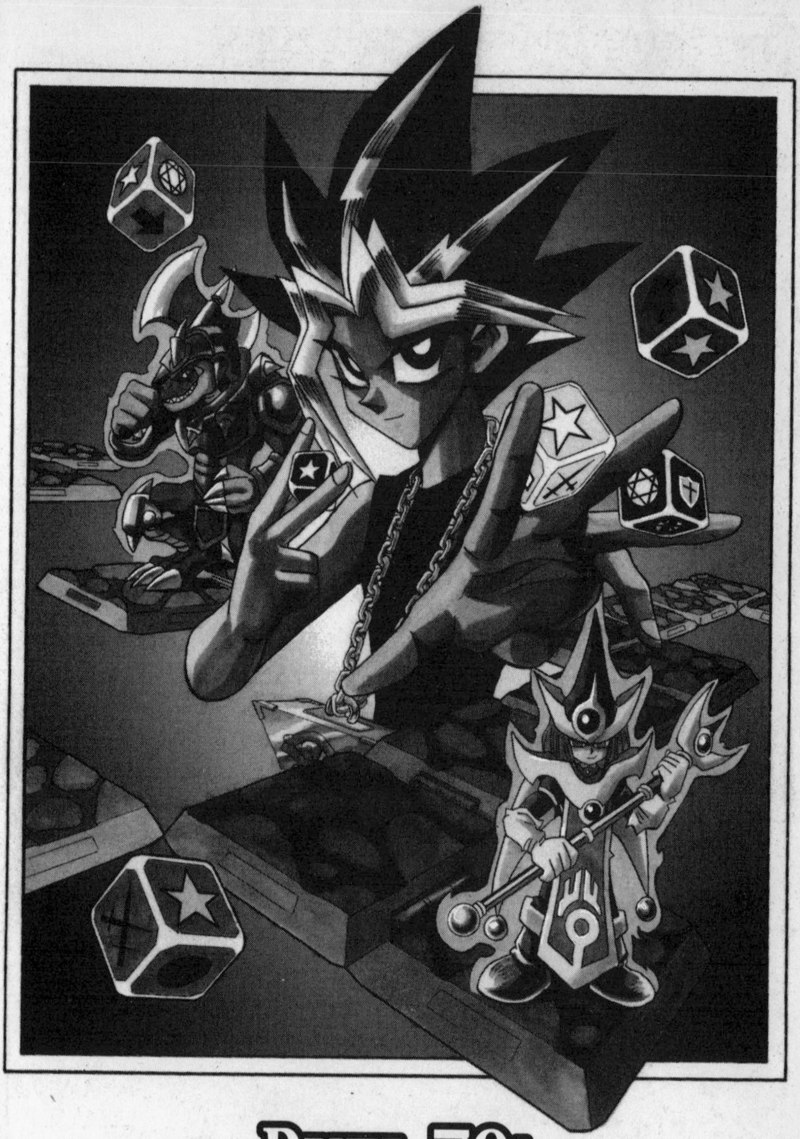

Duel 79: Dungeon Crisis!!

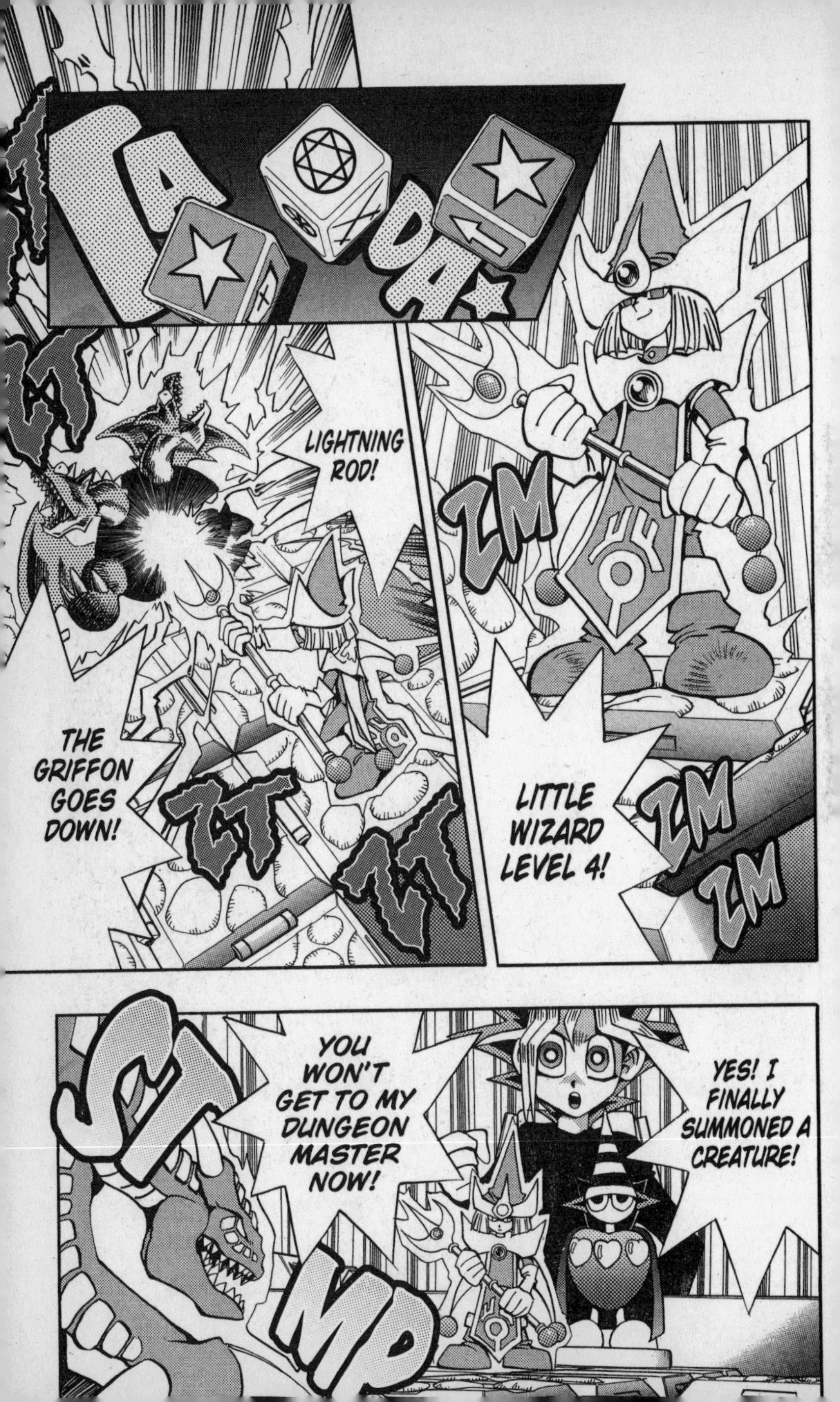
CA
DA
LIGHTNING ROD!
ZM
LITTLE WIZARD LEVEL 4!
ZM
ZM
THE GRIFFON GOES DOWN!
YES! I FINALLY SUMMONED A CREATURE!
YOU WON'T GET TO MY DUNGEON MASTER NOW!

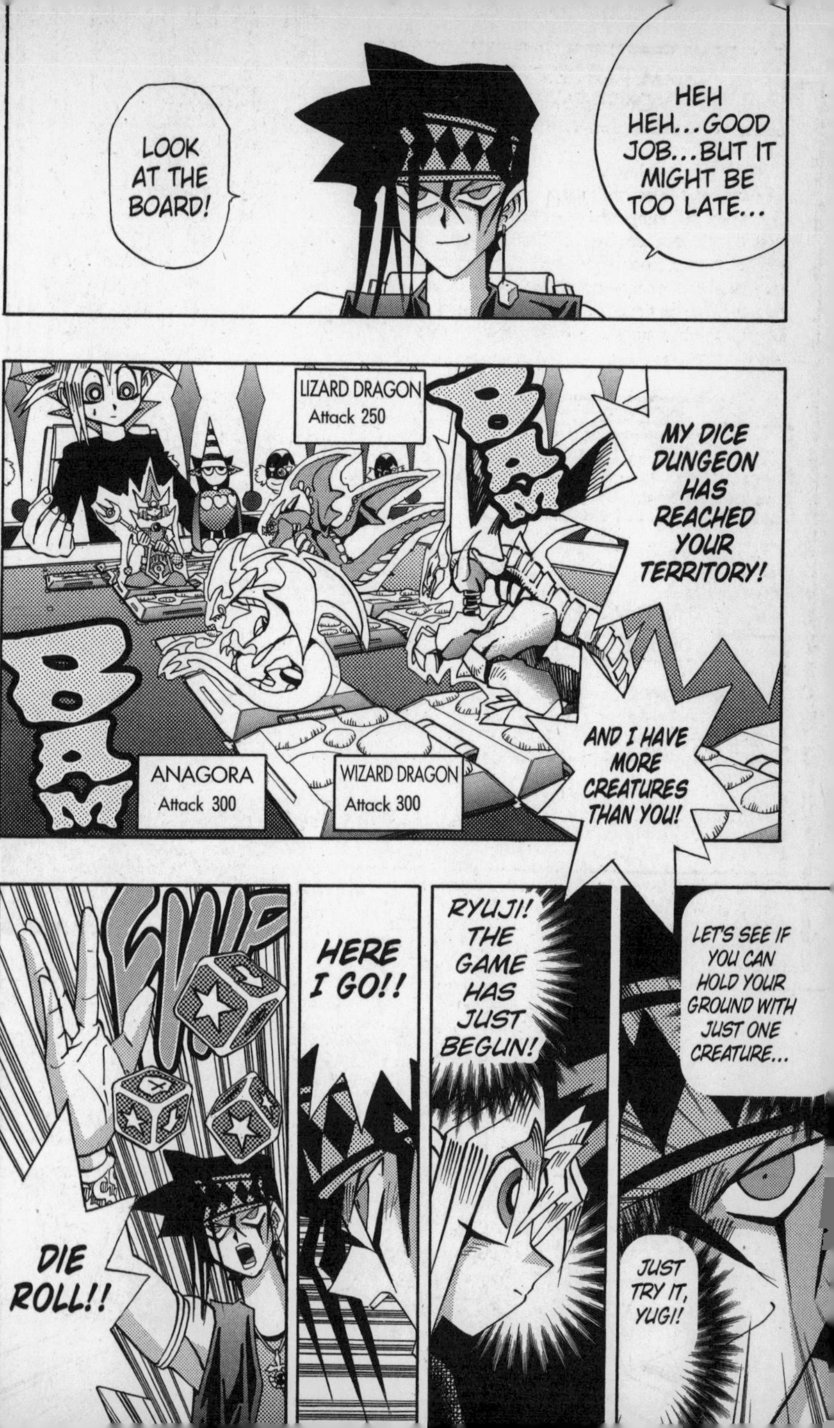
HEH HEH...GOOD JOB...BUT IT MIGHT BE TOO LATE...
LOOK AT THE BOARD!
MY DICE DUNGEON HAS REACHED YOUR TERRITORY!
LIZARD DRAGON
Attack 250
BAM
AND I HAVE MORE CREATURES THAN YOU!
WIZARD DRAGON
Attack 300
ANAGORA
Attack 300
BAM
LET'S SEE IF YOU CAN HOLD YOUR GROUND WITH JUST ONE CREATURE...
JUST TRY IT, YUGI!
RYUJI! THE GAME HAS JUST BEGUN!
HERE I GO!!
DIE ROLL!!

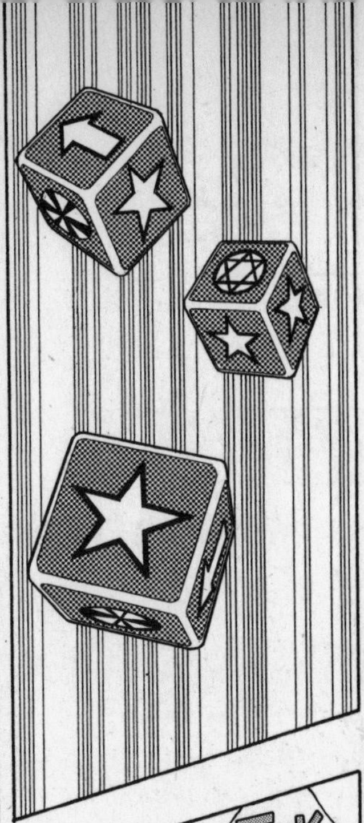

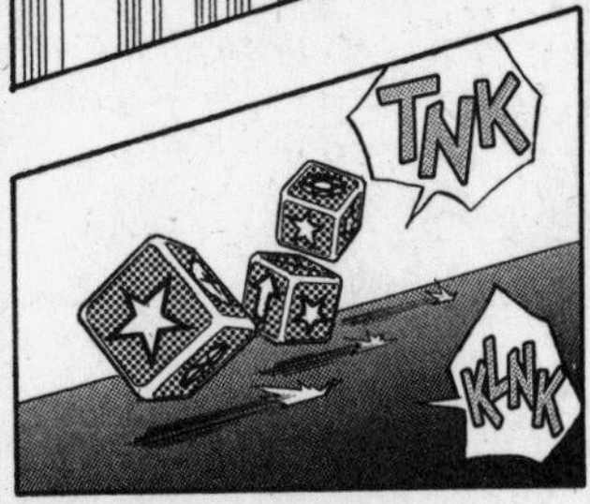
TNK
KLNK

D.D.M. (DUNGEON DICE MONSTERS) RULES

• 2-4 people can play.
• Each player selects a "dice pool" of twelve dice. Determine randomly who goes first, and then begin!
• On their turn, each player rolls three dice.
• When two or more Summon Crests appear, the dice may be placed on any space adjacent to the player's dungeon. When the player calls out "Dimension Dice!", the dice unfold, revealing a creature and six dungeon spaces.

DICE CREATURES: LEVEL

The more stars on a die, the lower the creature's level. Higher-level creatures have fewer stars and are harder to summon.

(How to Win)

• To win, the player must enter enemy territory and successfully attack the opponent's "Dungeon Master" three times.

DICE CREATURES: ATTACK, DEFENSE AND SPECIAL ABILITIES

Each creature has an ATK (attack) and DEF (defense) value. In addition, some creatures have special abilities. Attack, defense and magic powers are activated by the appropriate crests.

Crests earned by rolling the dice are stored in the "crest pool." Once they are stored, their effect can be used at any time by paying the appropriate cost in crests. (Summon Crests cannot be stored.)

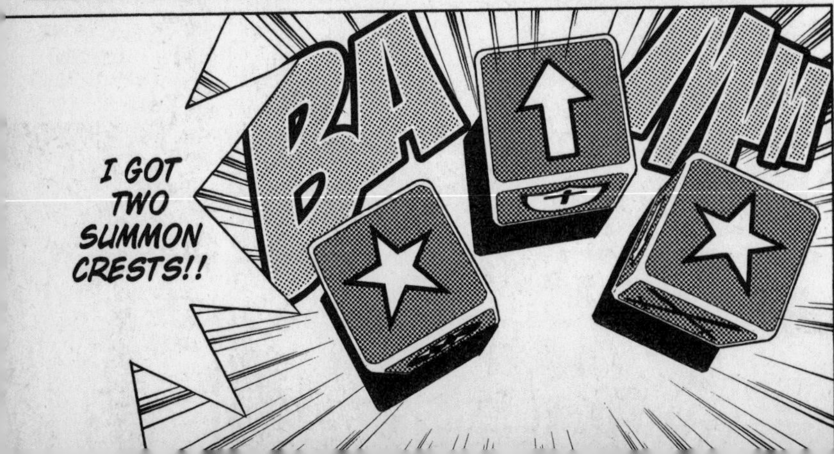
I GOT TWO SUMMON CRESTS!!

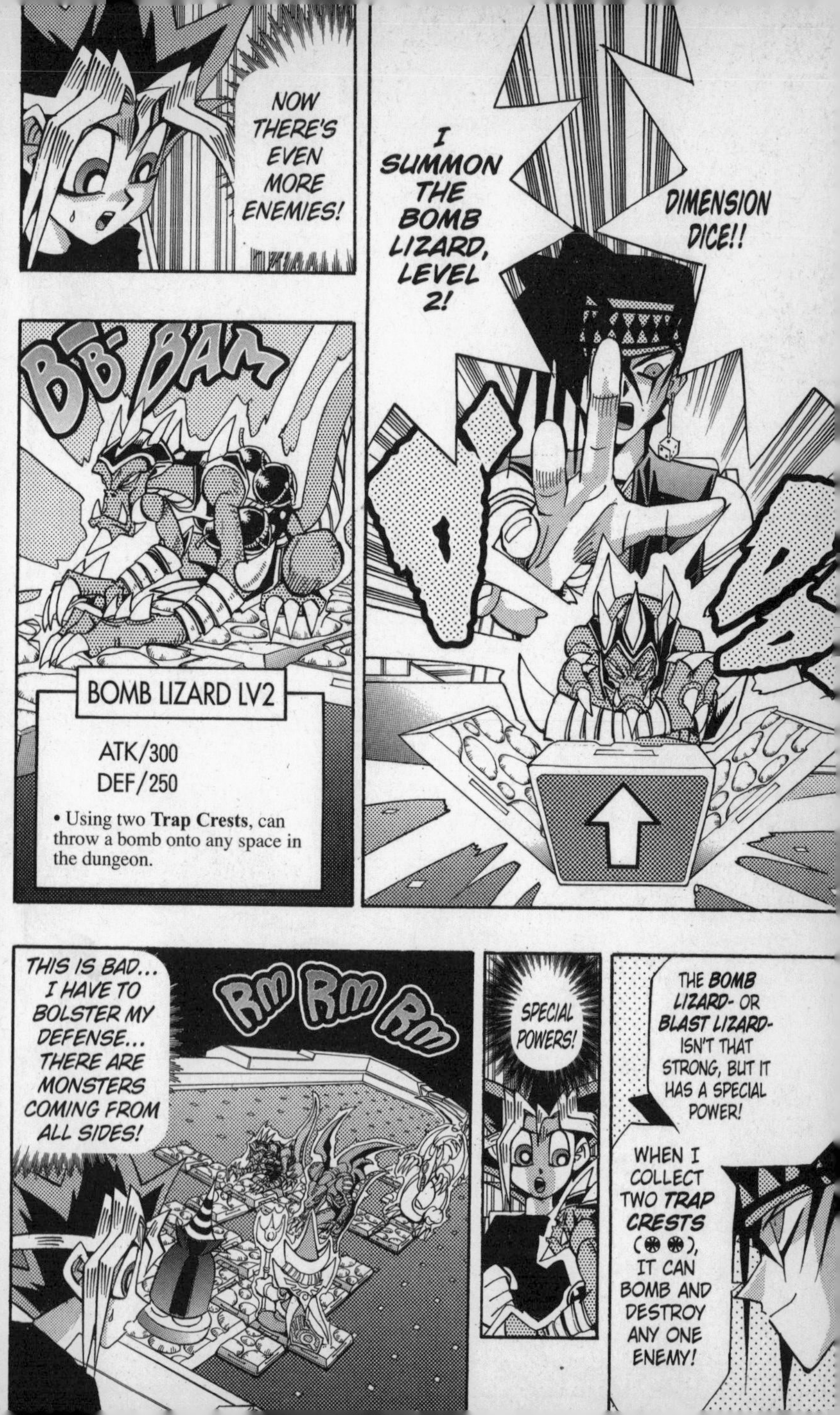
I SUMMON THE BOMB LIZARD, LEVEL 2!
DIMENSION DICE!!
NOW THERE'S EVEN MORE ENEMIES!
B-B-BAM
BOMB LIZARD LV2
ATK/300
DEF/250
• Using two **Trap Crests**, can throw a bomb onto any space in the dungeon.
THE BOMB LIZARD- OR BLAST LIZARD- ISN'T THAT STRONG, BUT IT HAS A SPECIAL POWER!
WHEN I COLLECT TWO TRAP CRESTS (✵ ✵), IT CAN BOMB AND DESTROY ANY ONE ENEMY!
SPECIAL POWERS!
THIS IS BAD... I HAVE TO BOLSTER MY DEFENSE... THERE ARE MONSTERS COMING FROM ALL SIDES!
RM RM RM

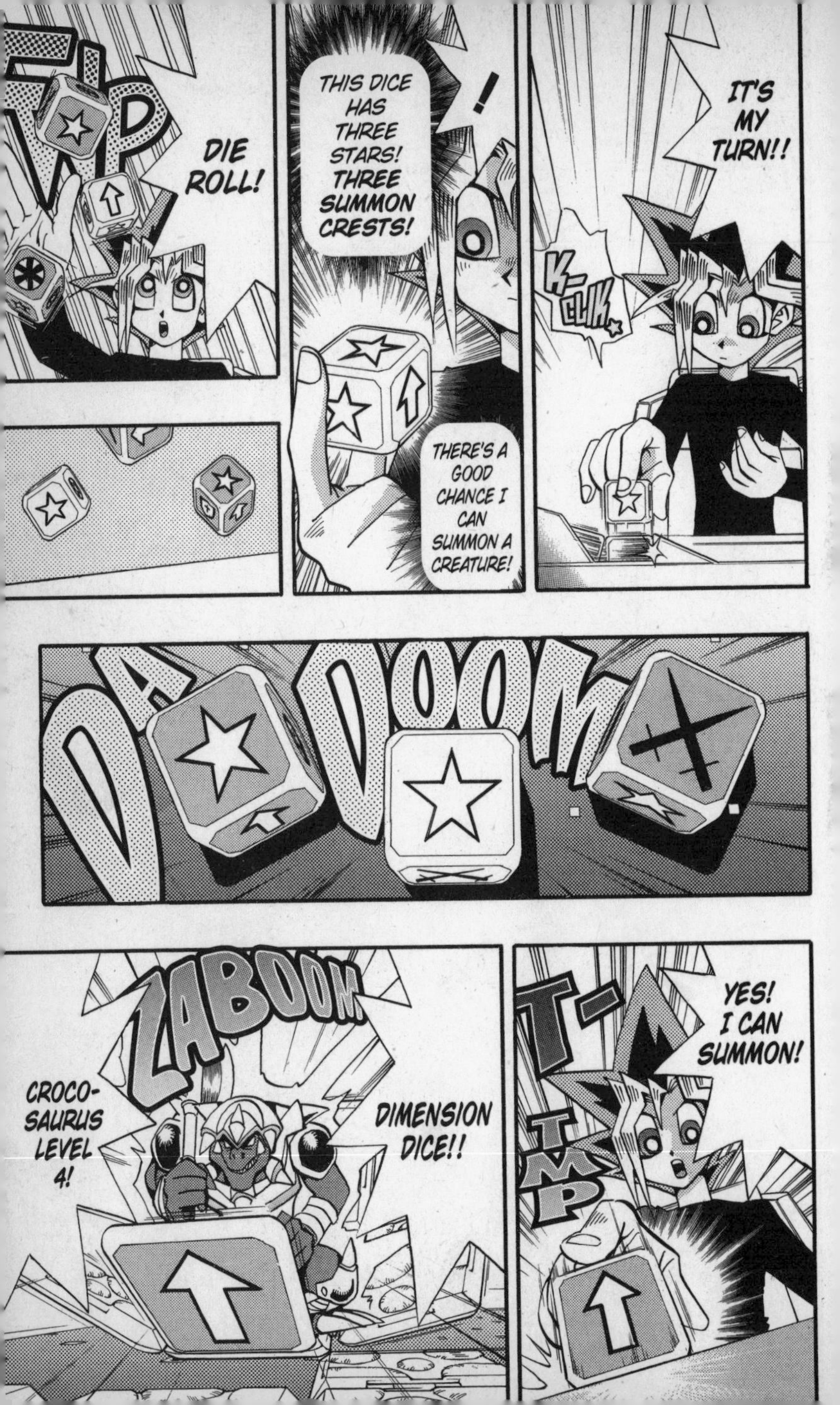
IT'S MY TURN!!
K-CLIK
THIS DICE HAS THREE STARS! THREE SUMMON CRESTS!
THERE'S A GOOD CHANCE I CAN SUMMON A CREATURE!
DIE ROLL!
DADOOM
YES! I CAN SUMMON!
TMP
DIMENSION DICE!!
CROCO-SAURUS LEVEL 4!
ZABOOM

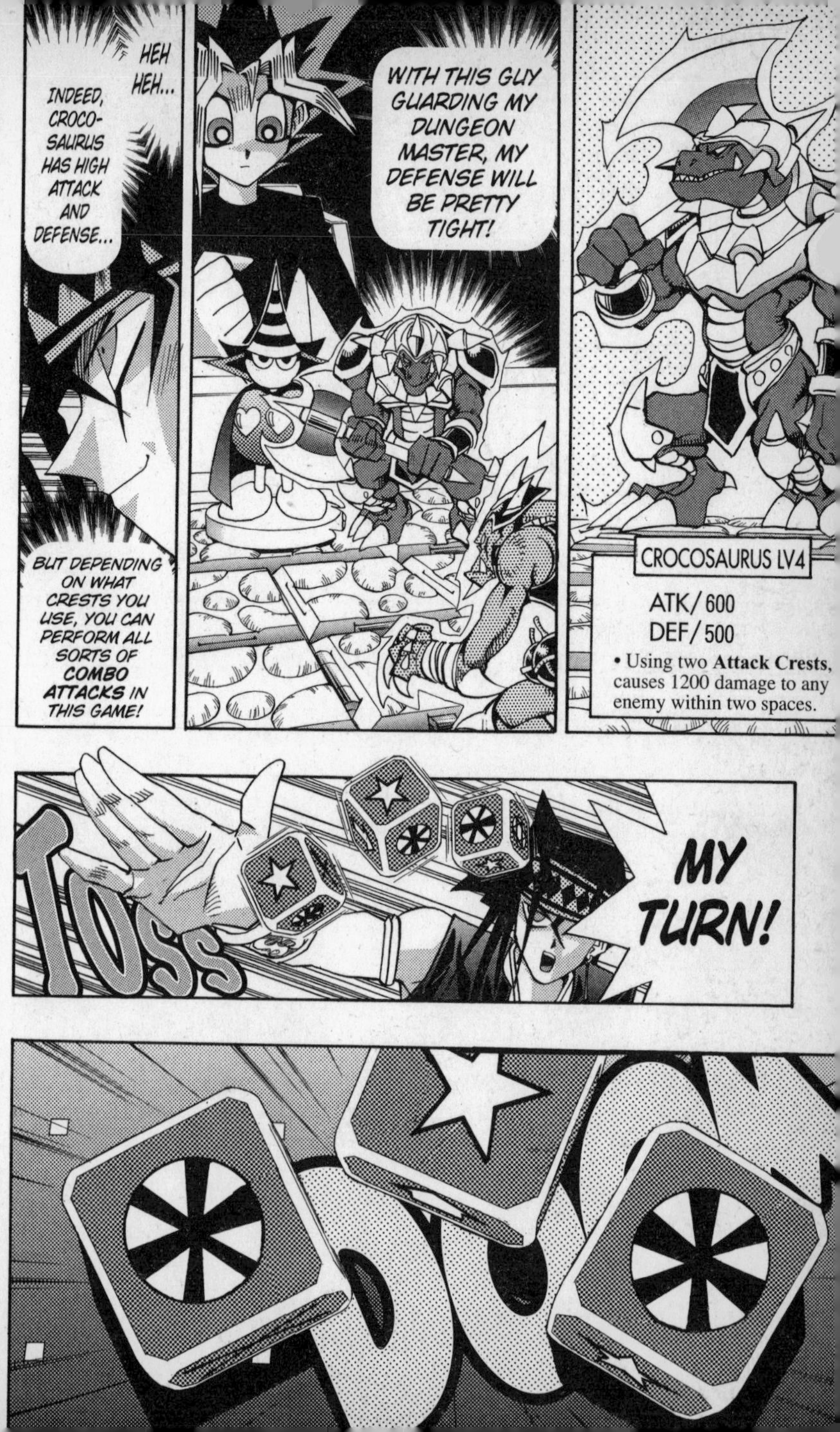
CROCOSAURUS LV4
ATK/ 600
DEF/ 500
• Using two **Attack Crests**, causes 1200 damage to any enemy within two spaces.
WITH THIS GUY GUARDING MY DUNGEON MASTER, MY DEFENSE WILL BE PRETTY TIGHT!
HEH HEH...
INDEED, CROCOSAURUS HAS HIGH ATTACK AND DEFENSE...
BUT DEPENDING ON WHAT CRESTS YOU USE, YOU CAN PERFORM ALL SORTS OF **COMBO ATTACKS** IN THIS GAME!
MY TURN!
TOSS

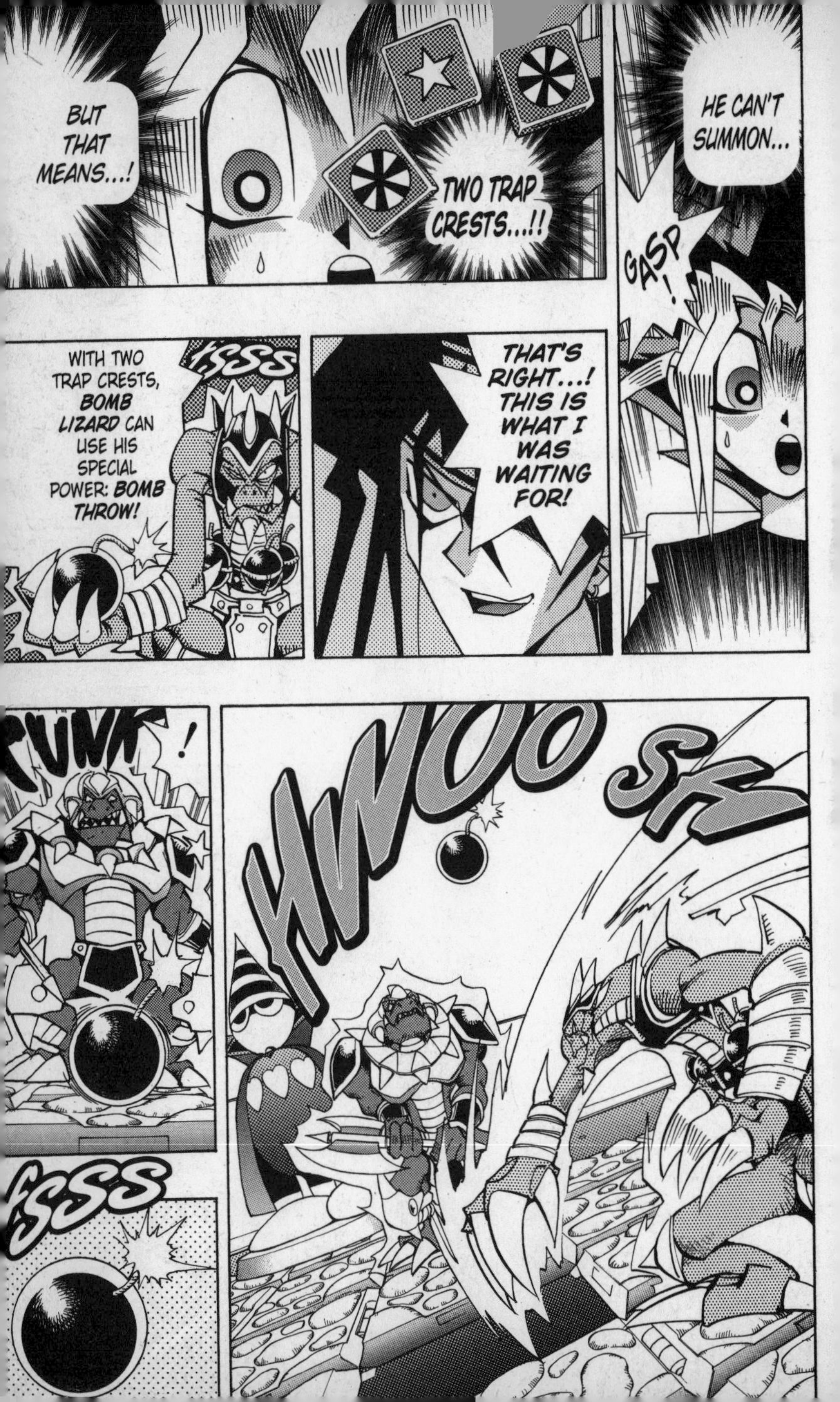
HE CAN'T SUMMON...
GASP!
BUT THAT MEANS...!
TWO TRAP CRESTS...!!
THAT'S RIGHT...! THIS IS WHAT I WAS WAITING FOR!
WITH TWO TRAP CRESTS, BOMB LIZARD CAN USE HIS SPECIAL POWER: BOMB THROW!
fSSS
WHOOSH
TUNK!
fSSS

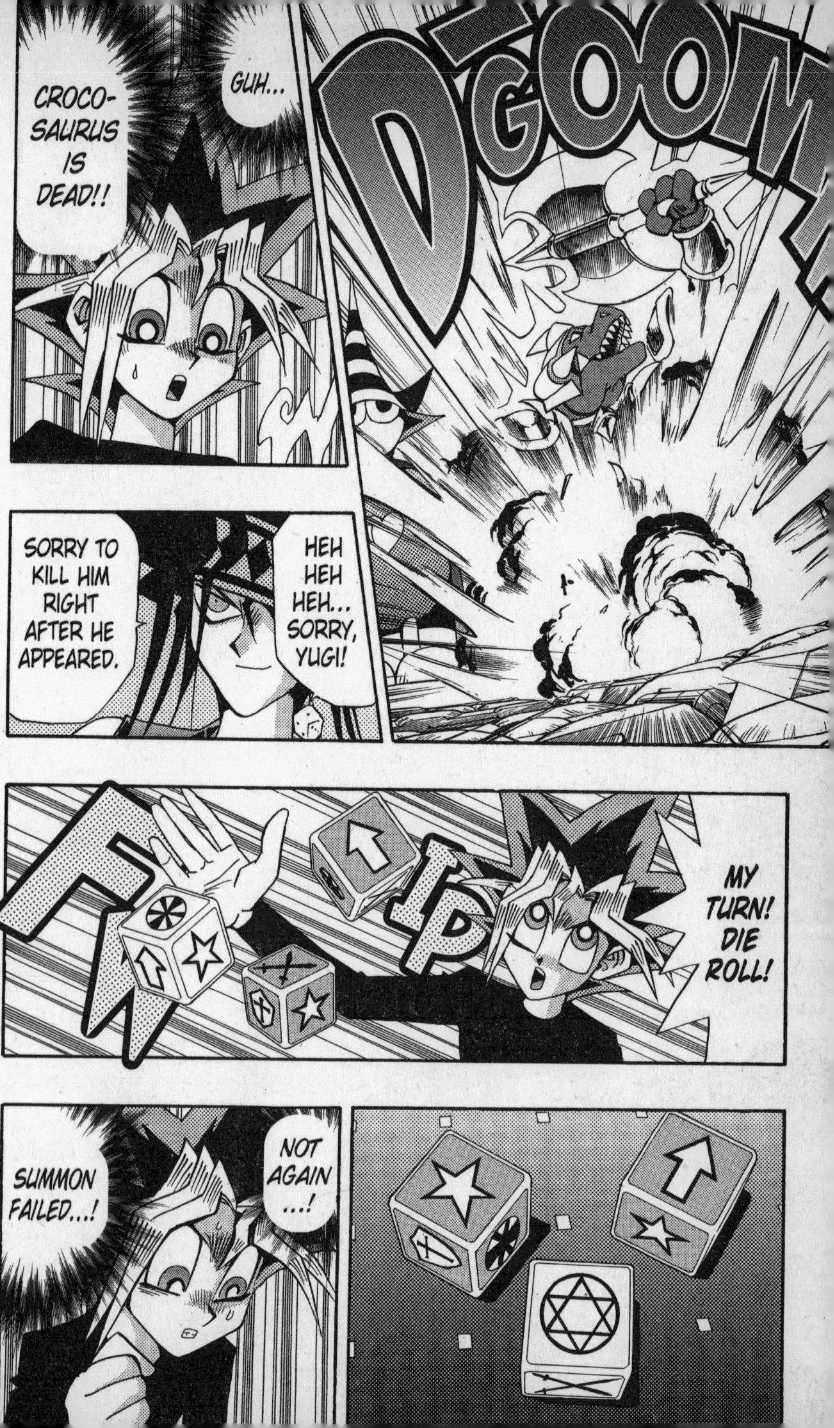
DGOOM
GUH...
CROCO-SAURUS IS DEAD!!
HEH HEH HEH... SORRY, YUGI!
SORRY TO KILL HIM RIGHT AFTER HE APPEARED.
MY TURN! DIE ROLL!
FLIP
NOT AGAIN...!
SUMMON FAILED...!

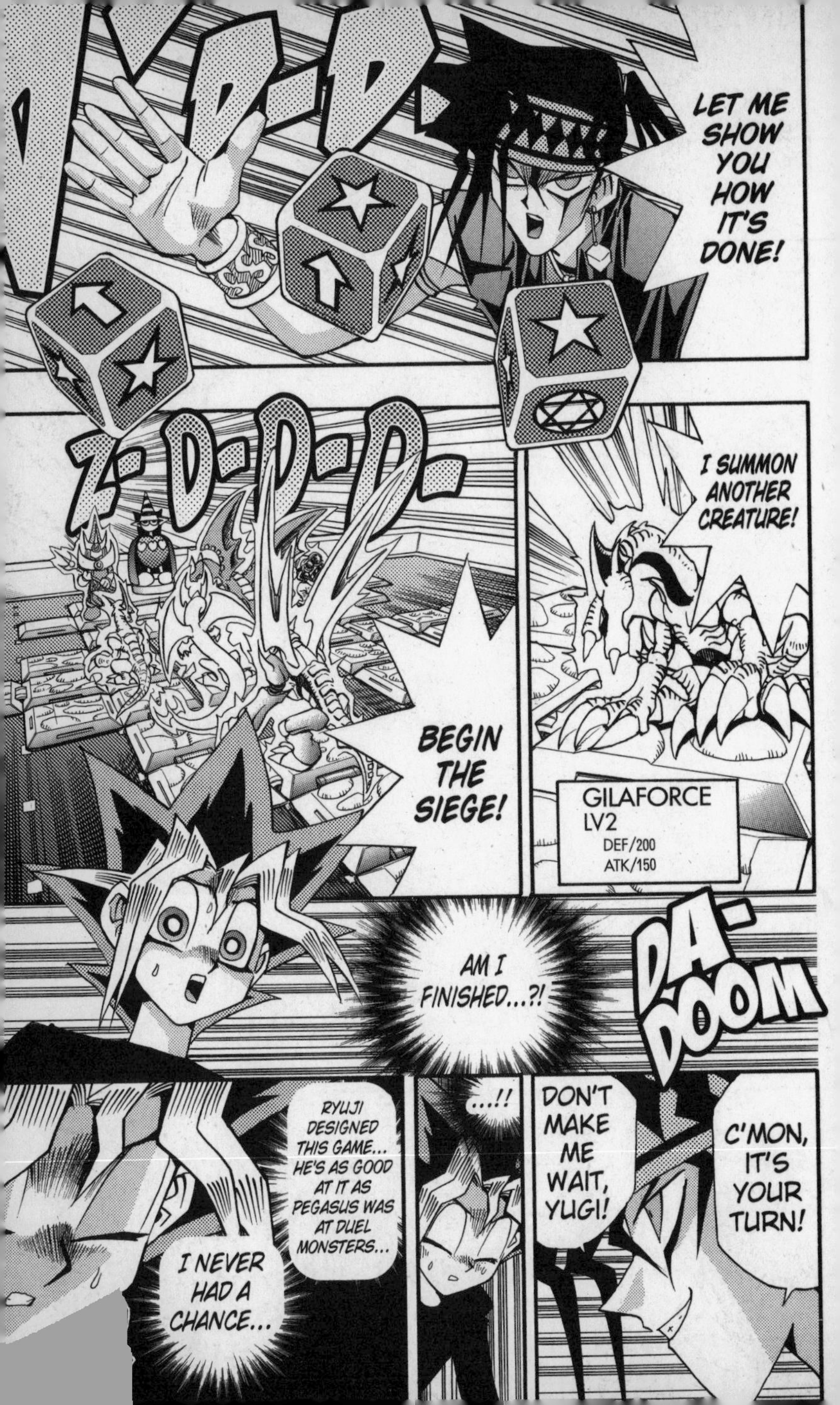
LET ME SHOW YOU HOW IT'S DONE!
I SUMMON ANOTHER CREATURE!
GILAFORCE
LV2
DEF/200
ATK/150
Z-D-D-D-
BEGIN THE SIEGE!
DA-DOOM
AM I FINISHED...?!
C'MON, IT'S YOUR TURN!
DON'T MAKE ME WAIT, YUGI!
...!!
RYUJI DESIGNED THIS GAME... HE'S AS GOOD AT IT AS PEGASUS WAS AT DUEL MONSTERS...
I NEVER HAD A CHANCE...

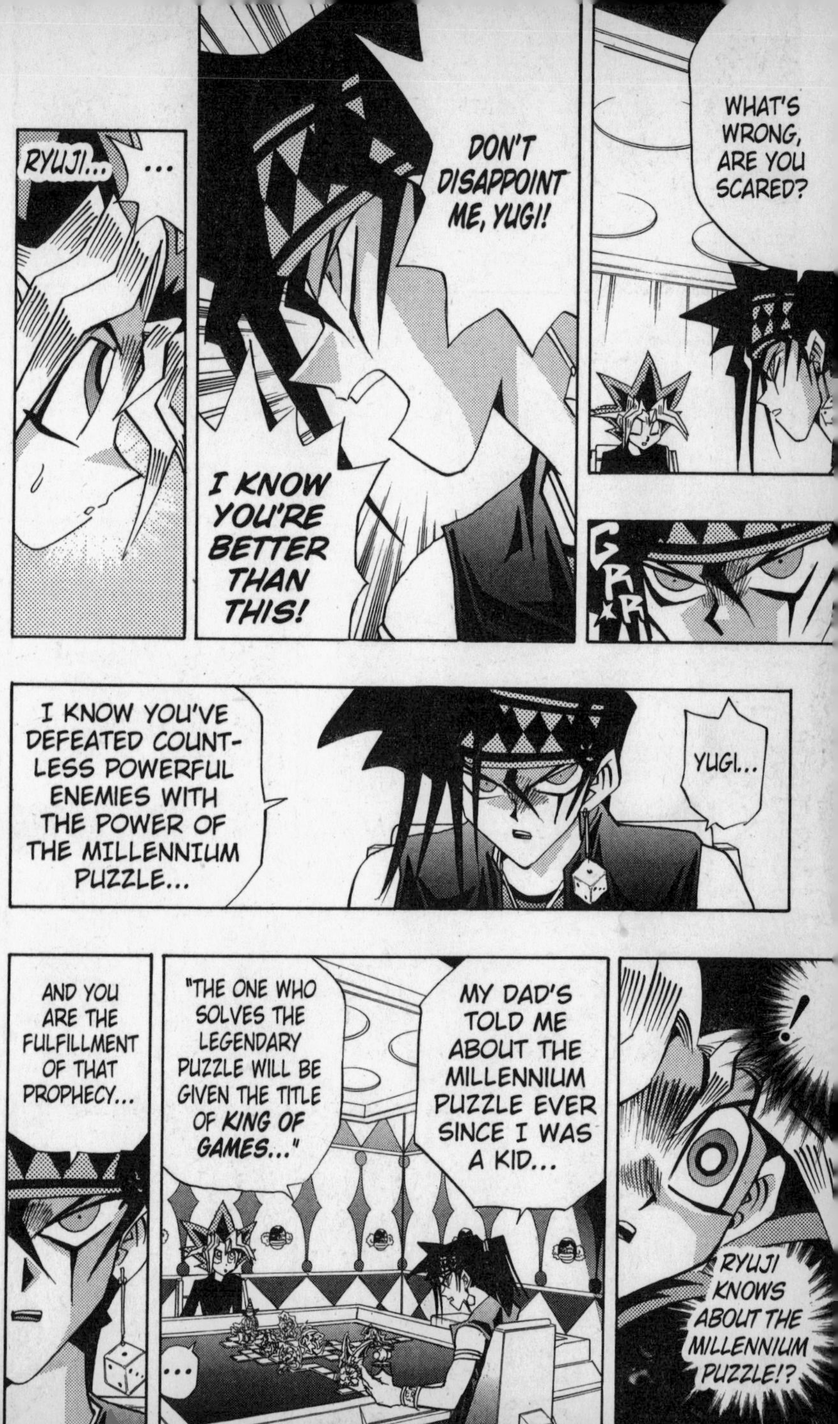
WHAT'S WRONG, ARE YOU SCARED?
GRR
DON'T DISAPPOINT ME, YUGI!
I KNOW YOU'RE BETTER THAN THIS!
...
RYUJI...
YUGI...
I KNOW YOU'VE DEFEATED COUNTLESS POWERFUL ENEMIES WITH THE POWER OF THE MILLENNIUM PUZZLE...
!
RYUJI KNOWS ABOUT THE MILLENNIUM PUZZLE!?
MY DAD'S TOLD ME ABOUT THE MILLENNIUM PUZZLE EVER SINCE I WAS A KID...
"THE ONE WHO SOLVES THE LEGENDARY PUZZLE WILL BE GIVEN THE TITLE OF *KING OF GAMES*..."
...
AND YOU ARE THE FULFILLMENT OF THAT PROPHECY...

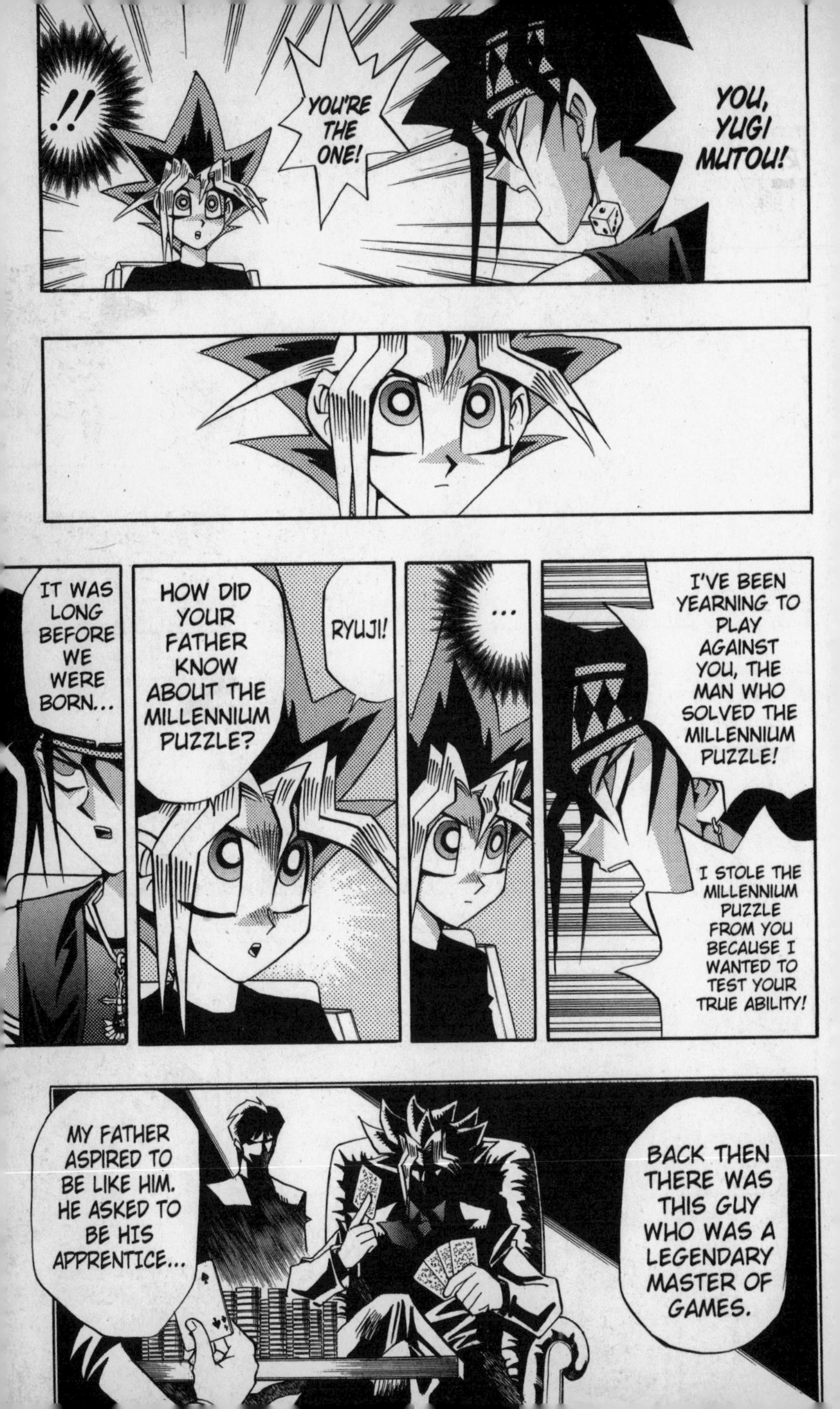
YOU, YUGI MUTOU!
YOU'RE THE ONE!
!!
I'VE BEEN YEARNING TO PLAY AGAINST YOU, THE MAN WHO SOLVED THE MILLENNIUM PUZZLE!
I STOLE THE MILLENNIUM PUZZLE FROM YOU BECAUSE I WANTED TO TEST YOUR TRUE ABILITY!
...
RYUJI!
HOW DID YOUR FATHER KNOW ABOUT THE MILLENNIUM PUZZLE?
IT WAS LONG BEFORE WE WERE BORN...
BACK THEN THERE WAS THIS GUY WHO WAS A LEGENDARY MASTER OF GAMES.
MY FATHER ASPIRED TO BE LIKE HIM. HE ASKED TO BE HIS APPRENTICE...

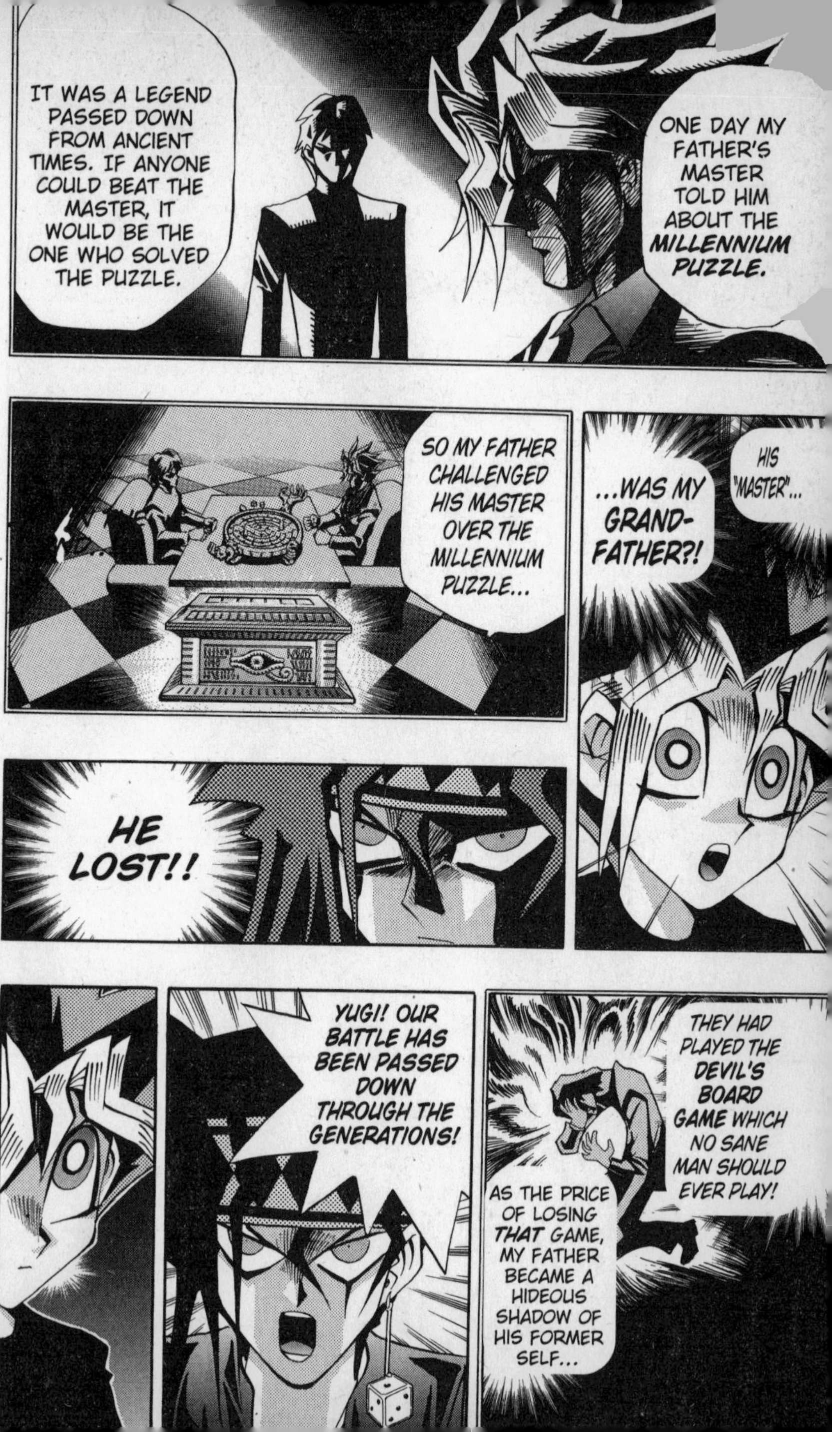
ONE DAY MY FATHER'S MASTER TOLD HIM ABOUT THE MILLENNIUM PUZZLE.
IT WAS A LEGEND PASSED DOWN FROM ANCIENT TIMES. IF ANYONE COULD BEAT THE MASTER, IT WOULD BE THE ONE WHO SOLVED THE PUZZLE.
HIS "MASTER"...
...WAS MY GRAND-FATHER?!
SO MY FATHER CHALLENGED HIS MASTER OVER THE MILLENNIUM PUZZLE...
HE LOST!!
THEY HAD PLAYED THE DEVIL'S BOARD GAME WHICH NO SANE MAN SHOULD EVER PLAY!
AS THE PRICE OF LOSING THAT GAME, MY FATHER BECAME A HIDEOUS SHADOW OF HIS FORMER SELF...
YUGI! OUR BATTLE HAS BEEN PASSED DOWN THROUGH THE GENERATIONS!

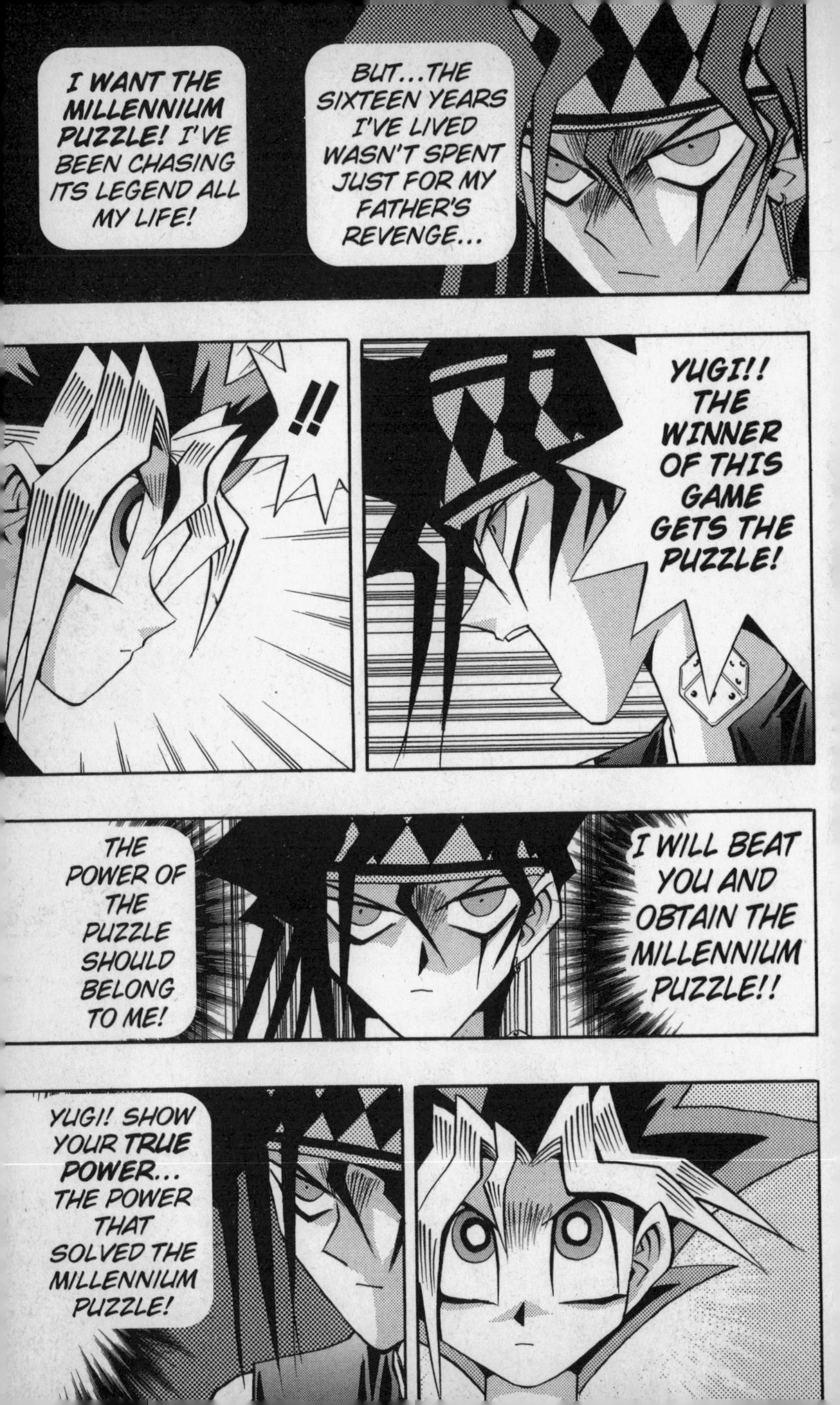
BUT...THE SIXTEEN YEARS I'VE LIVED WASN'T SPENT JUST FOR MY FATHER'S REVENGE...
I WANT THE MILLENNIUM PUZZLE! I'VE BEEN CHASING ITS LEGEND ALL MY LIFE!
YUGI!! THE WINNER OF THIS GAME GETS THE PUZZLE!
!!
I WILL BEAT YOU AND OBTAIN THE MILLENNIUM PUZZLE!!
THE POWER OF THE PUZZLE SHOULD BELONG TO ME!
YUGI! SHOW YOUR TRUE POWER... THE POWER THAT SOLVED THE MILLENNIUM PUZZLE!

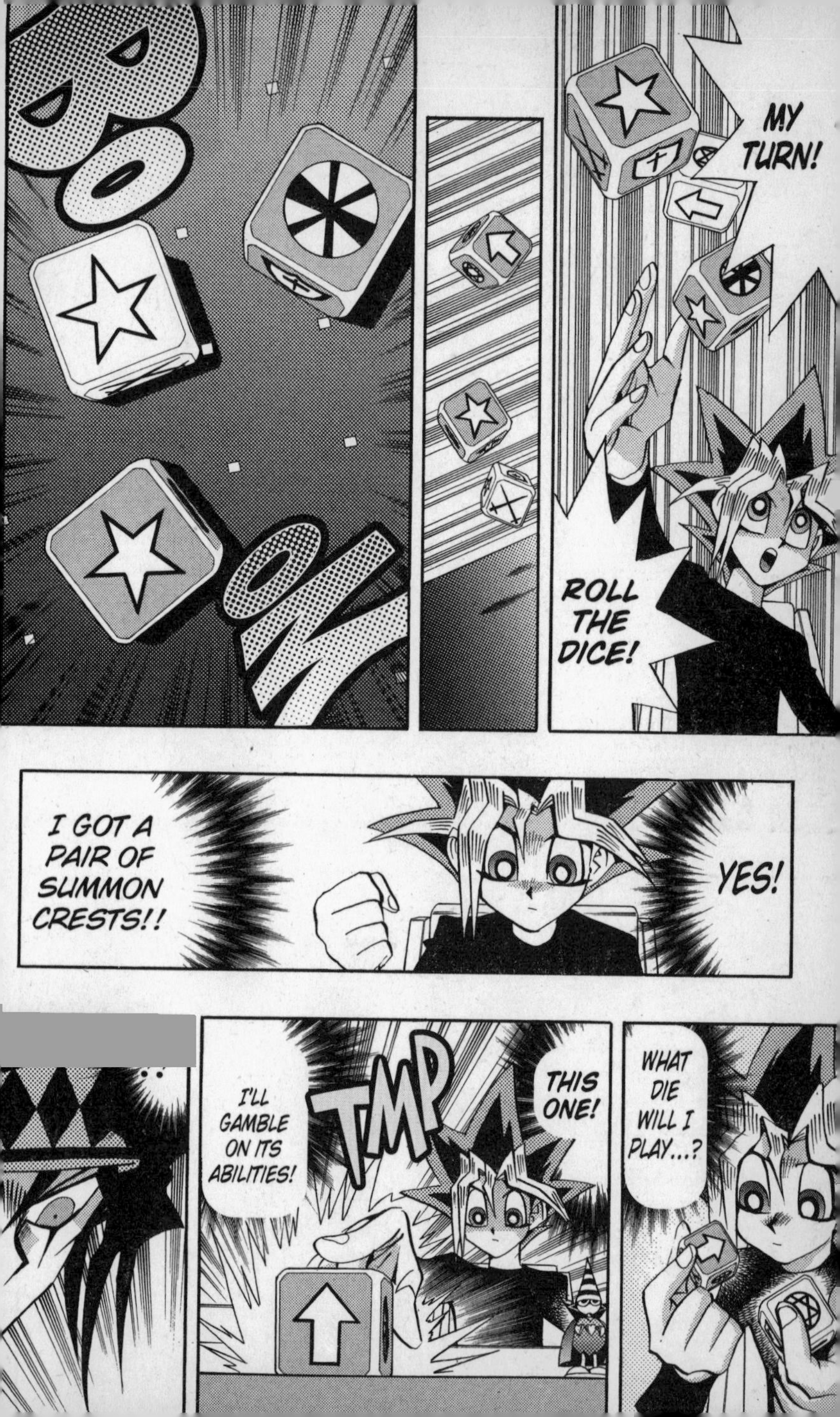
MY TURN!
ROLL THE DICE!
YES!
I GOT A PAIR OF SUMMON CRESTS!!
WHAT DIE WILL I PLAY...?
THIS ONE!
TMP
I'LL GAMBLE ON ITS ABILITIES!

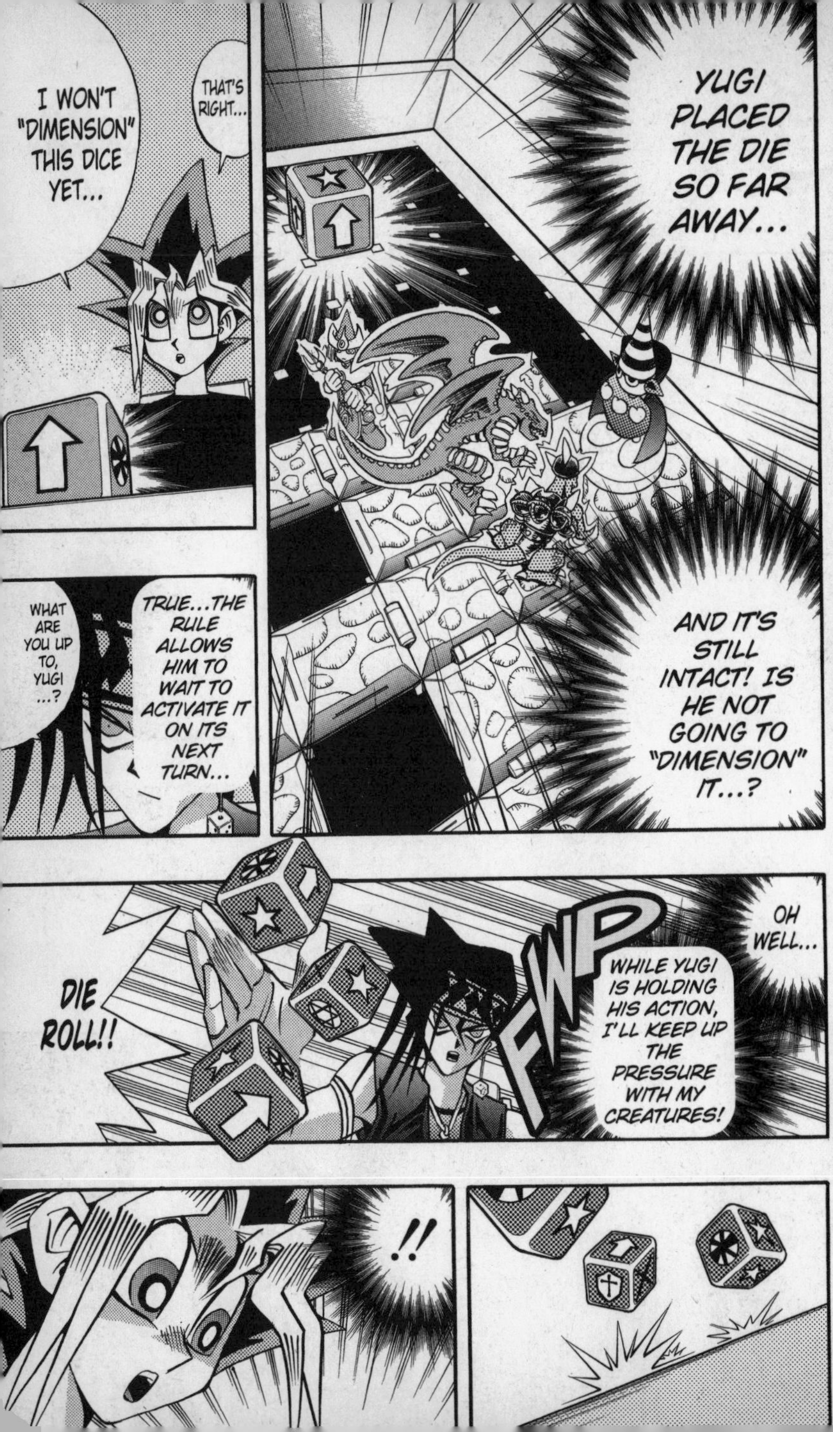
YUGI PLACED THE DIE SO FAR AWAY...
AND IT'S STILL INTACT! IS HE NOT GOING TO "DIMENSION" IT...?
THAT'S RIGHT...
I WON'T "DIMENSION" THIS DICE YET...
TRUE...THE RULE ALLOWS HIM TO WAIT TO ACTIVATE IT ON ITS NEXT TURN...
WHAT ARE YOU UP TO, YUGI ...?
OH WELL...
WHILE YUGI IS HOLDING HIS ACTION, I'LL KEEP UP THE PRESSURE WITH MY CREATURES!
FWP
DIE ROLL!!
!!

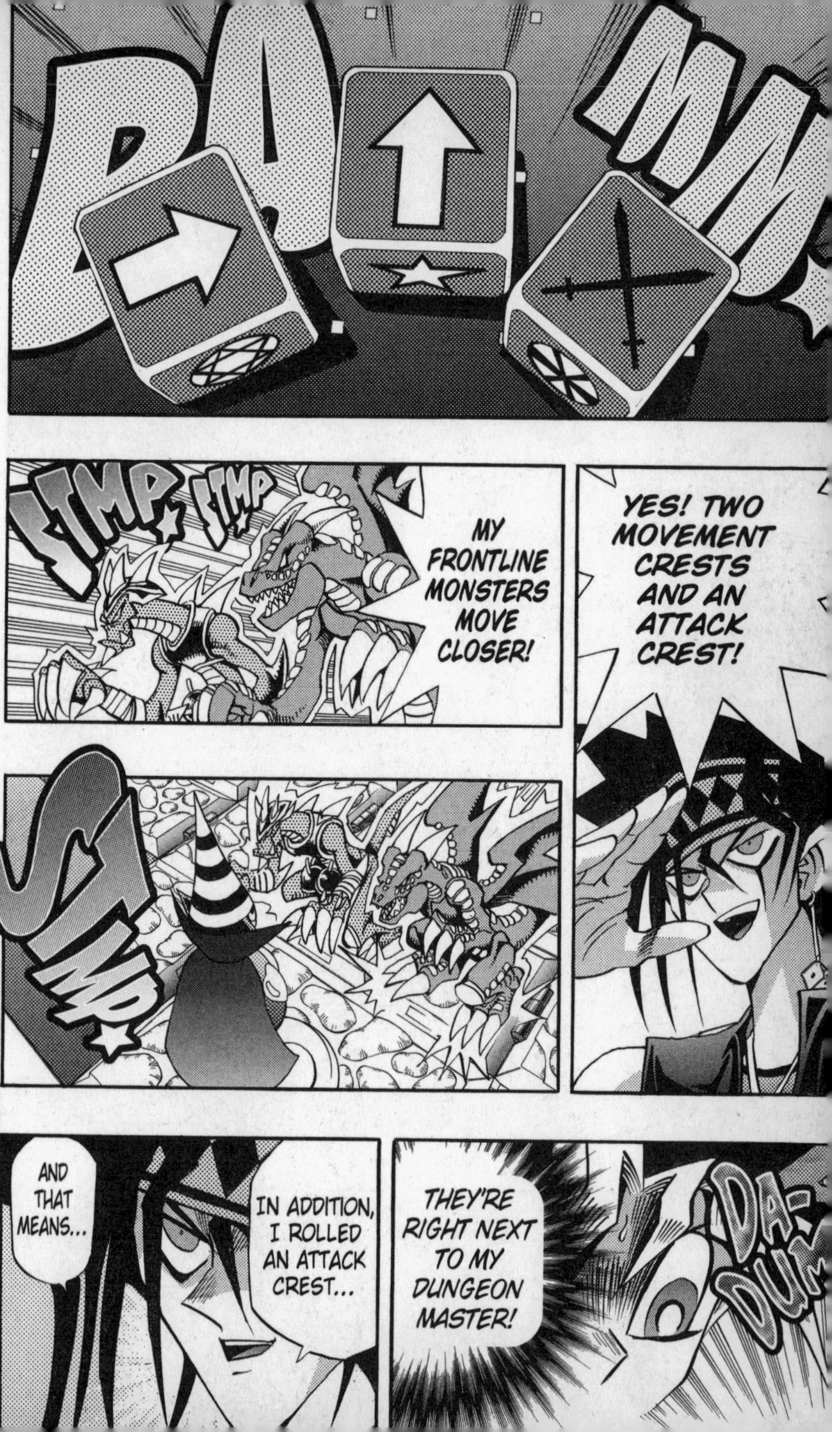

BAMM
YES! TWO MOVEMENT CRESTS AND AN ATTACK CREST!
STMP, STMP
MY FRONTLINE MONSTERS MOVE CLOSER!
STMP
DA-DUM
THEY'RE RIGHT NEXT TO MY DUNGEON MASTER!
IN ADDITION, I ROLLED AN ATTACK CREST...
AND THAT MEANS...

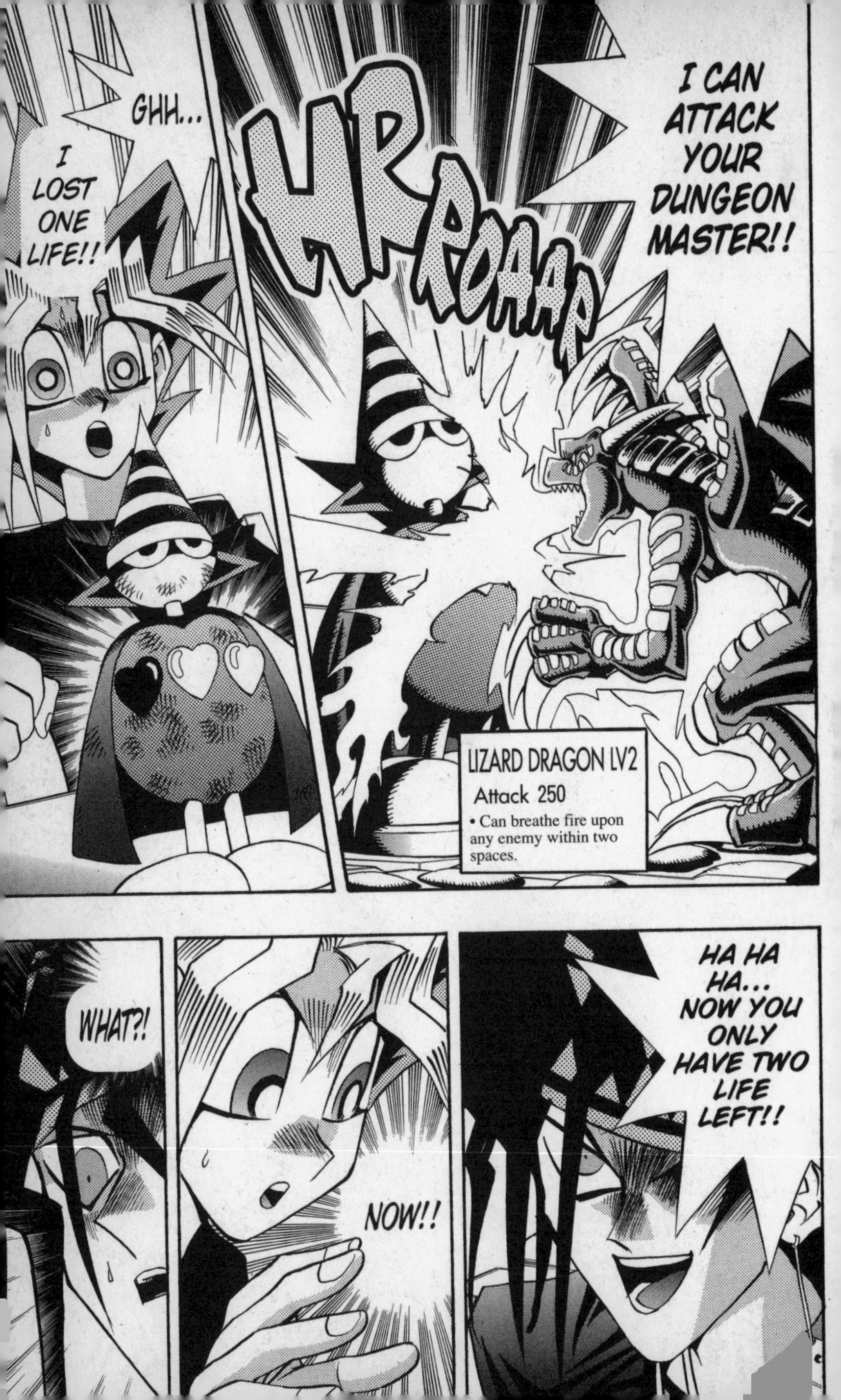
I CAN ATTACK YOUR DUNGEON MASTER!!
HRROAAR
LIZARD DRAGON LV2
Attack 250
• Can breathe fire upon any enemy within two spaces.
GHH...
I LOST ONE LIFE!!
HA HA HA... NOW YOU ONLY HAVE TWO LIFE LEFT!!
NOW!!
WHAT?!

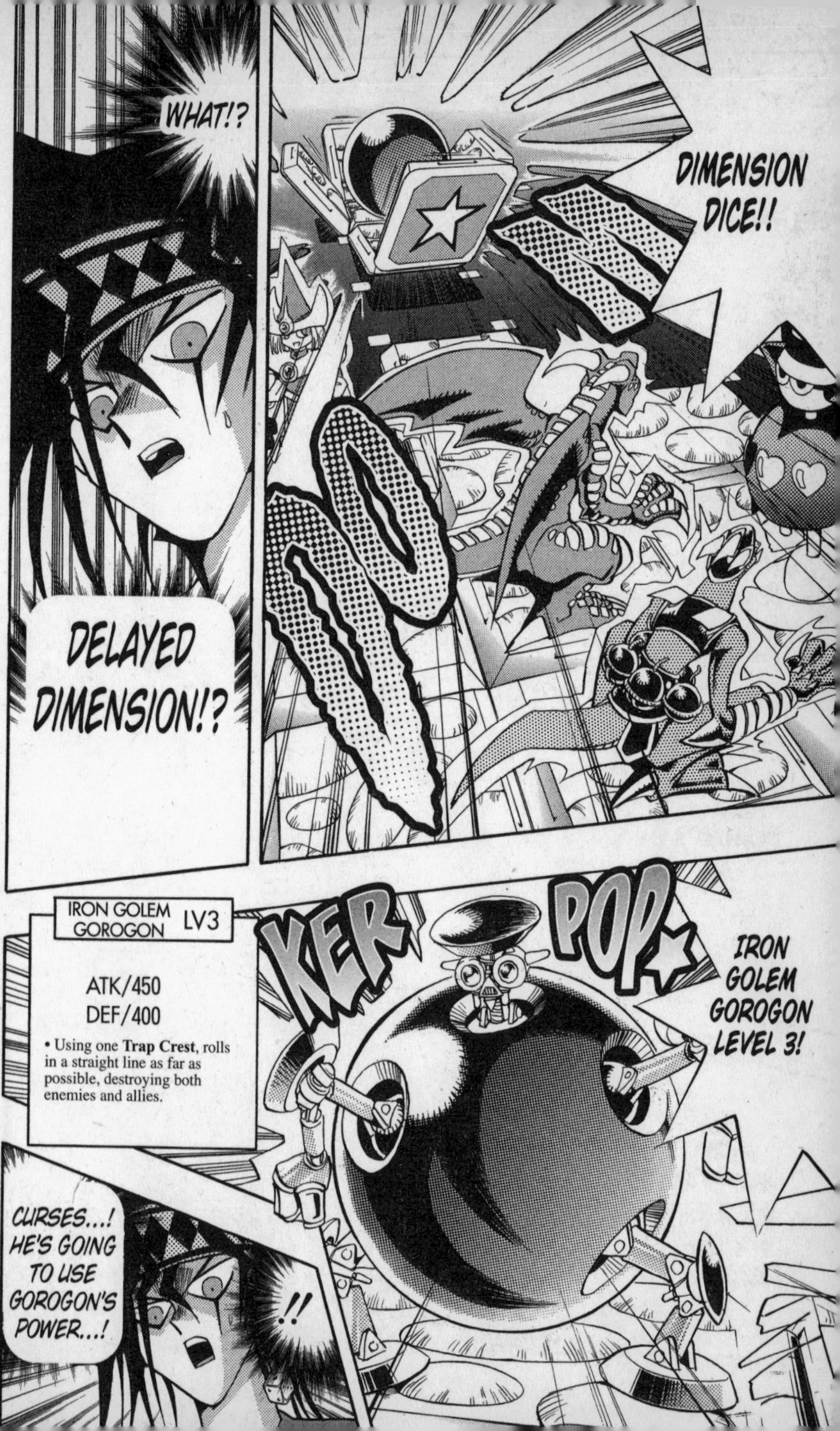
DIMENSION DICE!!
WHAT!?
DELAYED DIMENSION!?
KER POP
IRON GOLEM GOROGON LEVEL 3!
IRON GOLEM GOROGON LV3
ATK/450
DEF/400
• Using one **Trap Crest**, rolls in a straight line as far as possible, destroying both enemies and allies.
!!
CURSES...! HE'S GOING TO USE GOROGON'S POWER...!

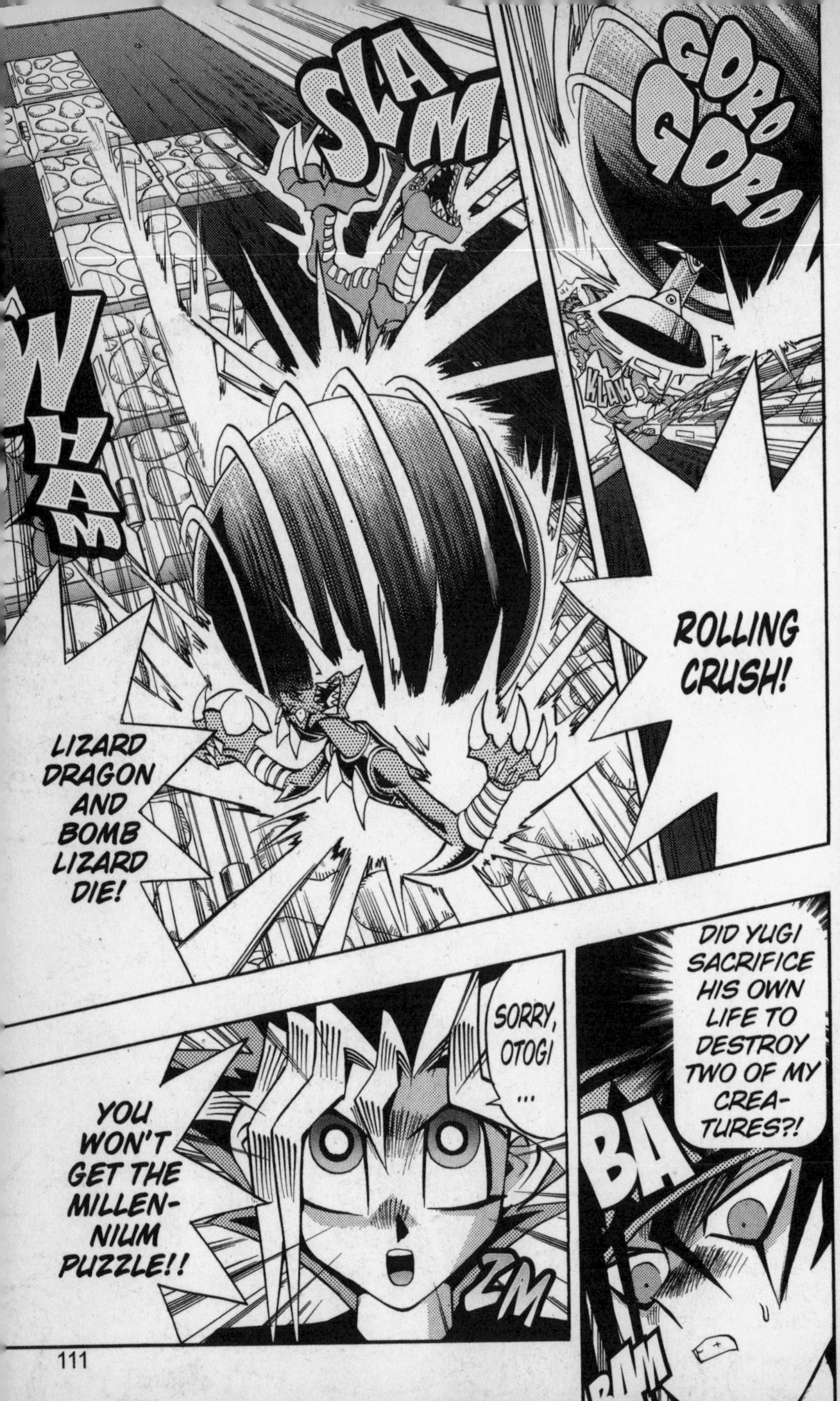
GORO GORO
KLAM
SLAM
WHAM
ROLLING CRUSH!
LIZARD DRAGON AND BOMB LIZARD DIE!
DID YUGI SACRIFICE HIS OWN LIFE TO DESTROY TWO OF MY CREA-TURES?!
BA
BAM
SORRY, OTOGI ...
YOU WON'T GET THE MILLEN-NIUM PUZZLE!!
ZM

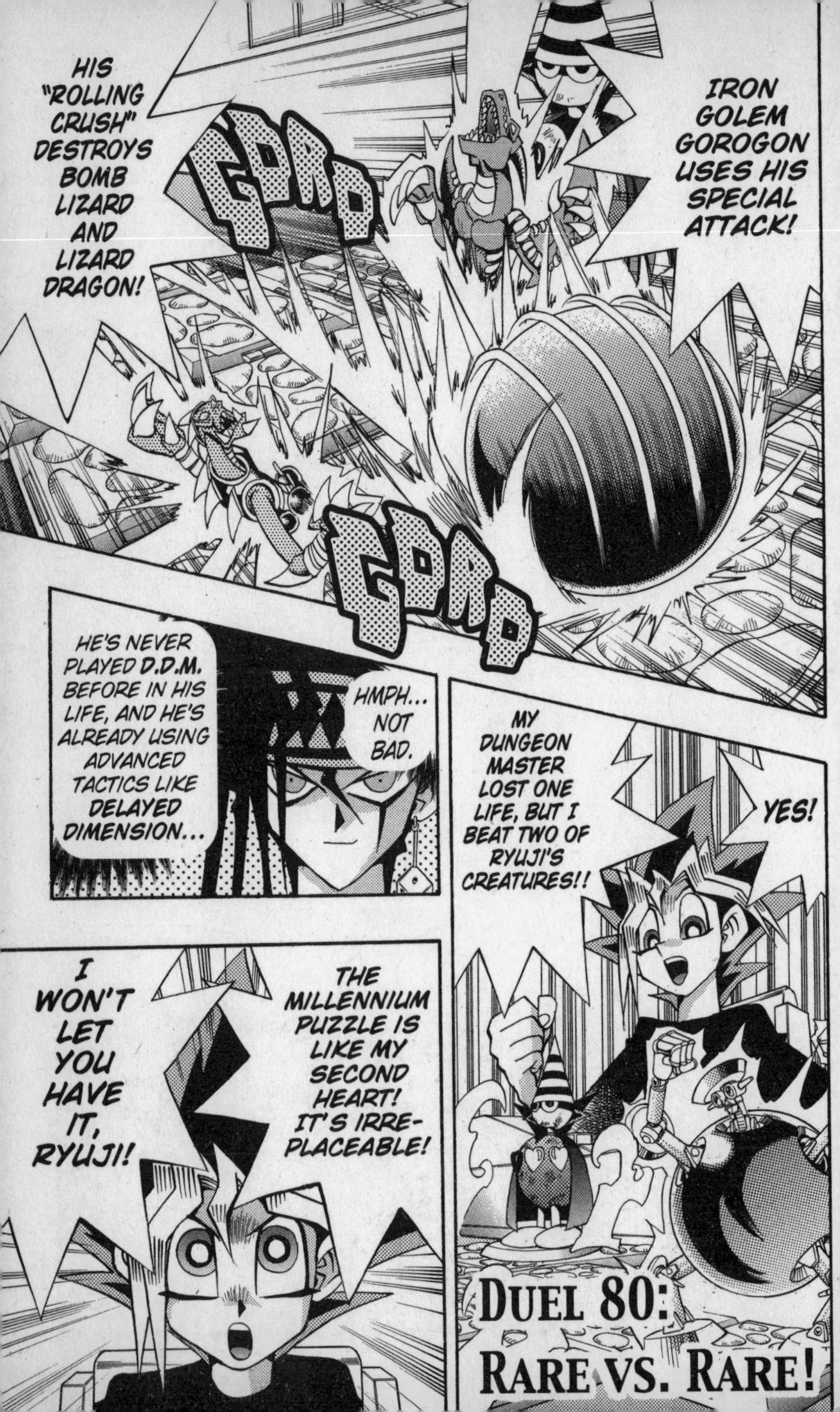
IRON GOLEM GOROGON USES HIS SPECIAL ATTACK!
GORO
HIS "ROLLING CRUSH" DESTROYS BOMB LIZARD AND LIZARD DRAGON!
GORO
MY DUNGEON MASTER LOST ONE LIFE, BUT I BEAT TWO OF RYUJI'S CREATURES!!
YES!
DUEL 80: RARE VS. RARE!
HMPH... NOT BAD.
HE'S NEVER PLAYED D.D.M. BEFORE IN HIS LIFE, AND HE'S ALREADY USING ADVANCED TACTICS LIKE DELAYED DIMENSION...
THE MILLENNIUM PUZZLE IS LIKE MY SECOND HEART! IT'S IRRE-PLACEABLE!
I WON'T LET YOU HAVE IT, RYUJI!

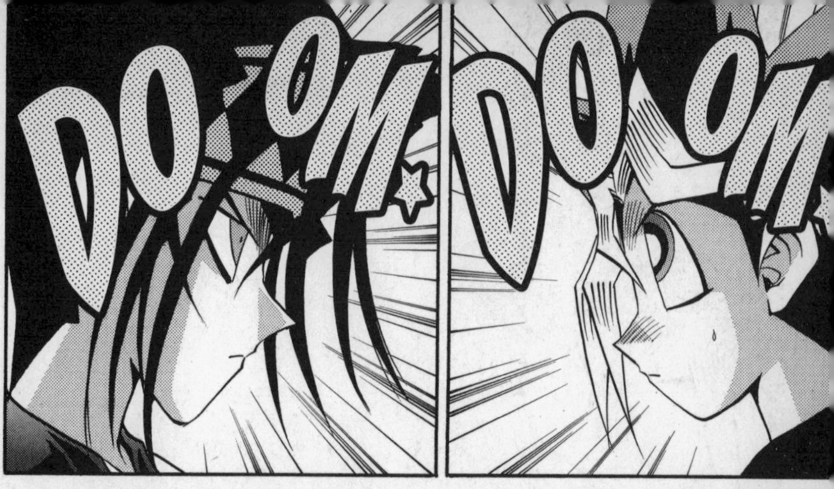
DO-OM
DO-OM

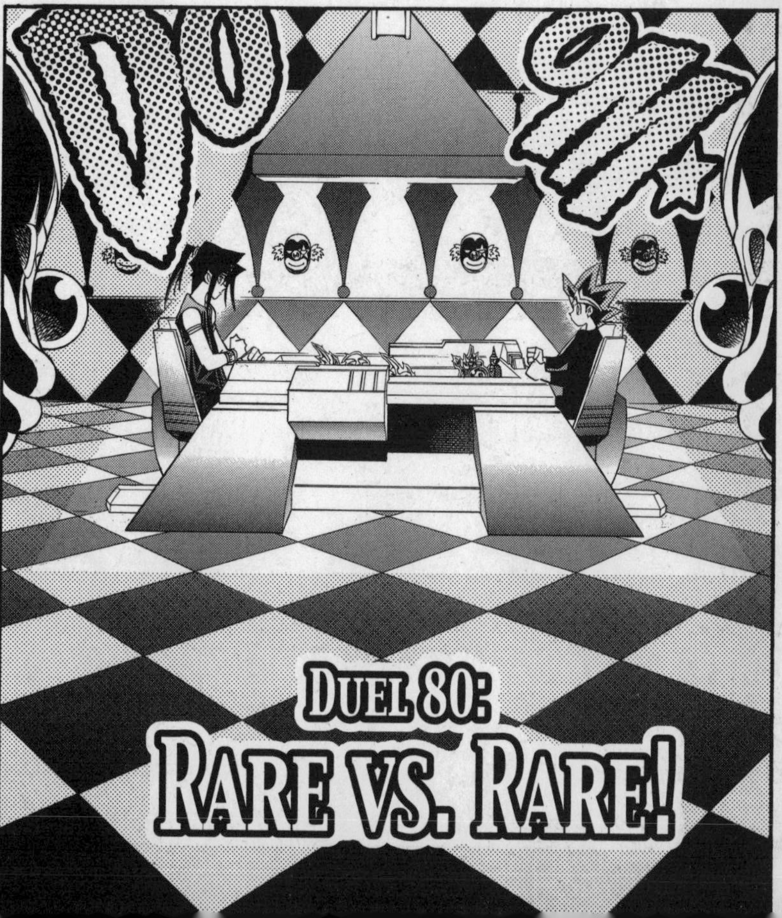
DO-OM
DUEL 80:
RARE VS. RARE!

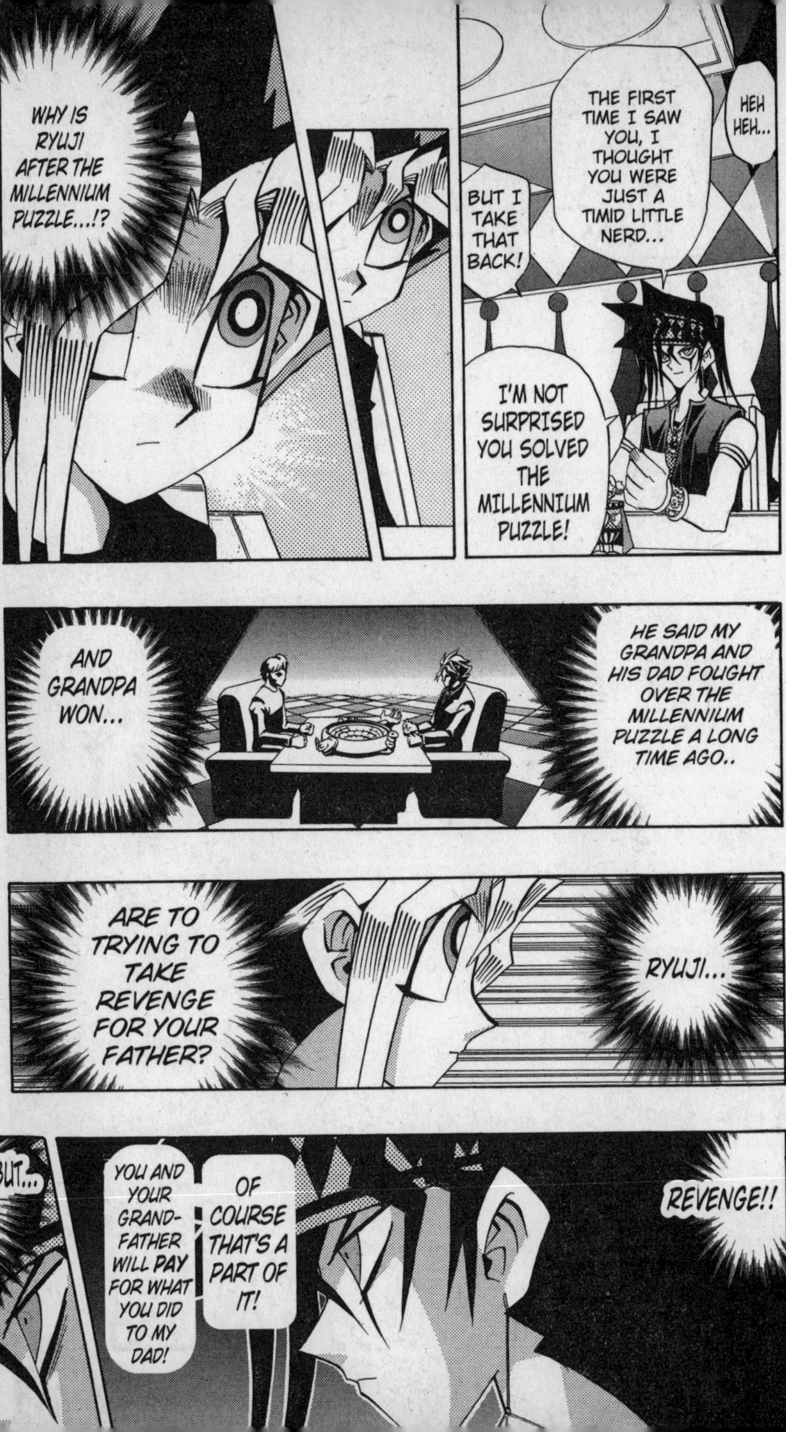
HEH HEH...
THE FIRST TIME I SAW YOU, I THOUGHT YOU WERE JUST A TIMID LITTLE NERD...
BUT I TAKE THAT BACK!
I'M NOT SURPRISED YOU SOLVED THE MILLENNIUM PUZZLE!
WHY IS RYUJI AFTER THE MILLENNIUM PUZZLE...!?
HE SAID MY GRANDPA AND HIS DAD FOUGHT OVER THE MILLENNIUM PUZZLE A LONG TIME AGO..
AND GRANDPA WON...
RYUJI...
ARE TO TRYING TO TAKE REVENGE FOR YOUR FATHER?
REVENGE!!
OF COURSE THAT'S A PART OF IT!
YOU AND YOUR GRAND-FATHER WILL PAY FOR WHAT YOU DID TO MY DAD!
BUT...

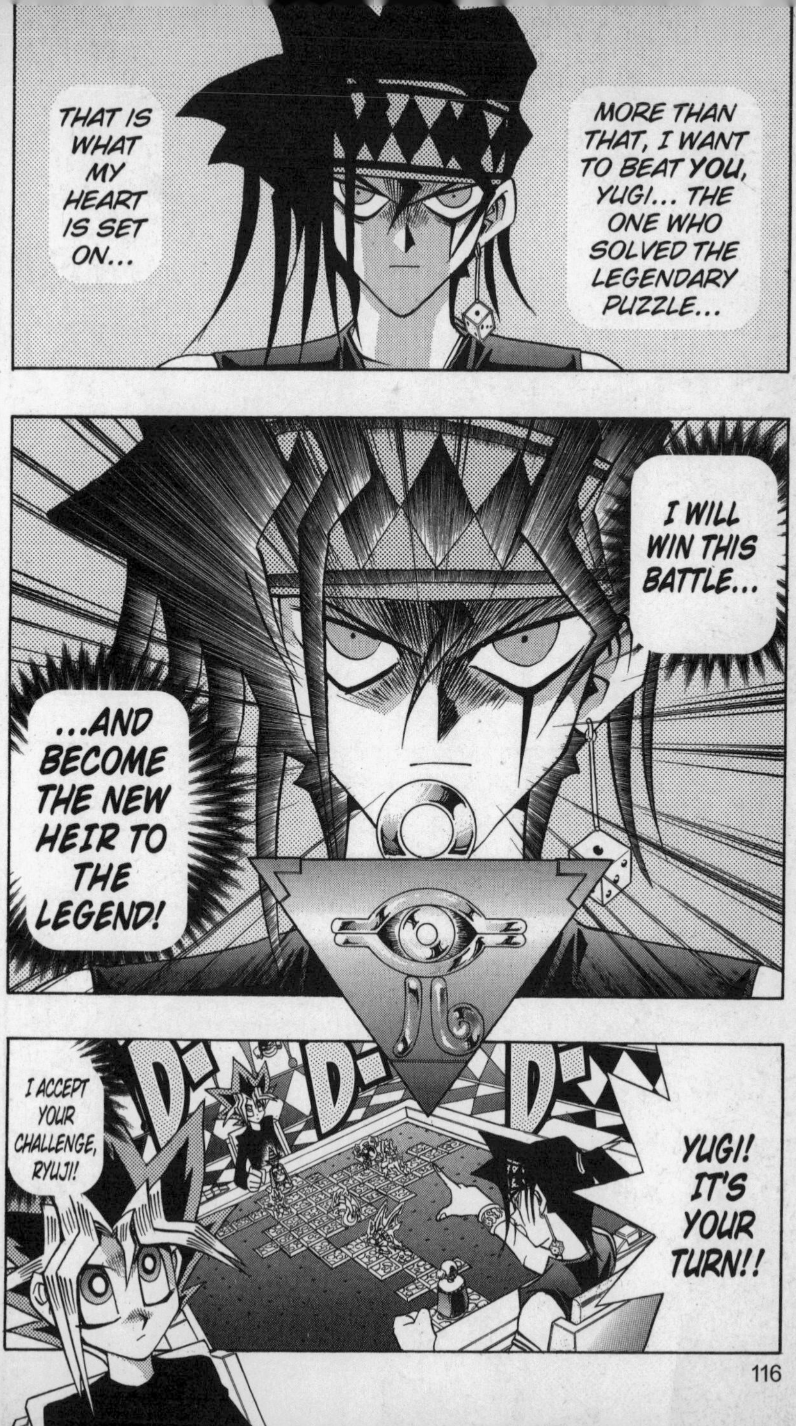
MORE THAN THAT, I WANT TO BEAT YOU, YUGI... THE ONE WHO SOLVED THE LEGENDARY PUZZLE...
THAT IS WHAT MY HEART IS SET ON...
I WILL WIN THIS BATTLE...
...AND BECOME THE NEW HEIR TO THE LEGEND!
YUGI! IT'S YOUR TURN!!
I ACCEPT YOUR CHALLENGE, RYUJI!

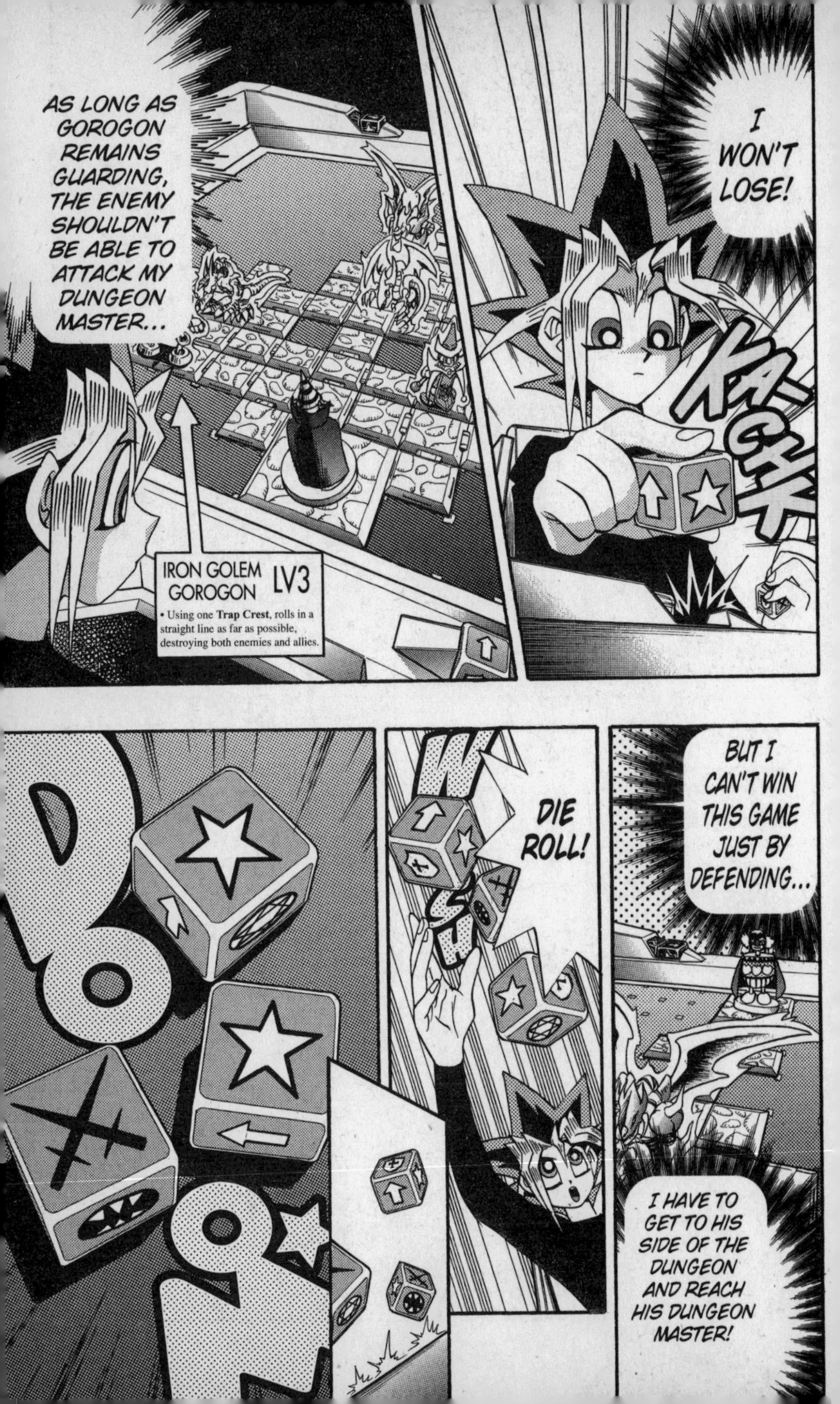
I WON'T LOSE!
KA-CHK
AS LONG AS GOROGON REMAINS GUARDING, THE ENEMY SHOULDN'T BE ABLE TO ATTACK MY DUNGEON MASTER...
IRON GOLEM GOROGON LV3
• Using one Trap Crest, rolls in a straight line as far as possible, destroying both enemies and allies.
BUT I CAN'T WIN THIS GAME JUST BY DEFENDING...
I HAVE TO GET TO HIS SIDE OF THE DUNGEON AND REACH HIS DUNGEON MASTER!
DIE ROLL!

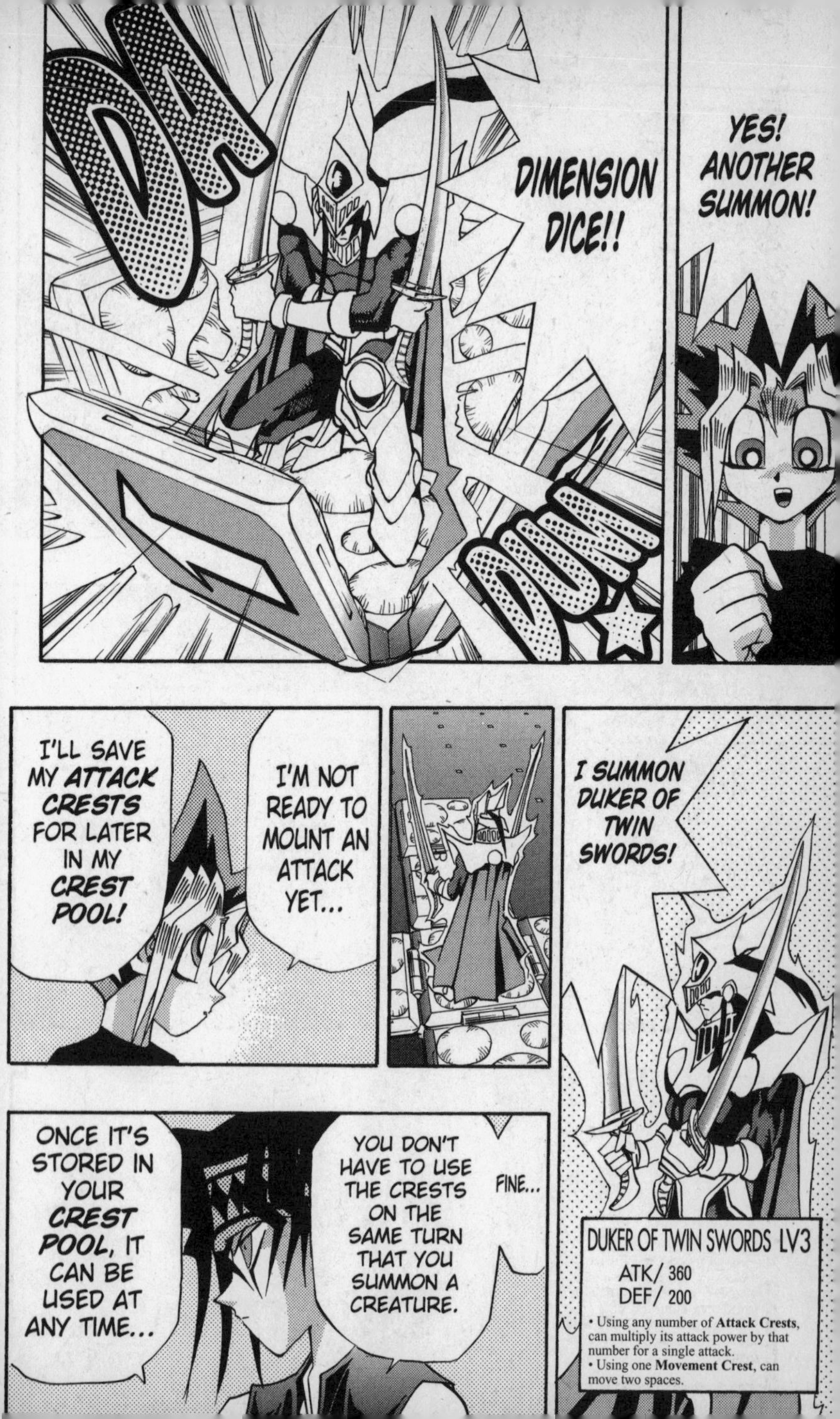
YES! ANOTHER SUMMON!
DIMENSION DICE!!
I SUMMON DUKER OF TWIN SWORDS!
I'M NOT READY TO MOUNT AN ATTACK YET...
I'LL SAVE MY ATTACK CRESTS FOR LATER IN MY CREST POOL!
DUKER OF TWIN SWORDS LV3
ATK/ 360
DEF/ 200
• Using any number of Attack Crests, can multiply its attack power by that number for a single attack.
• Using one Movement Crest, can move two spaces.
FINE...
YOU DON'T HAVE TO USE THE CRESTS ON THE SAME TURN THAT YOU SUMMON A CREATURE.
ONCE IT'S STORED IN YOUR CREST POOL, IT CAN BE USED AT ANY TIME...

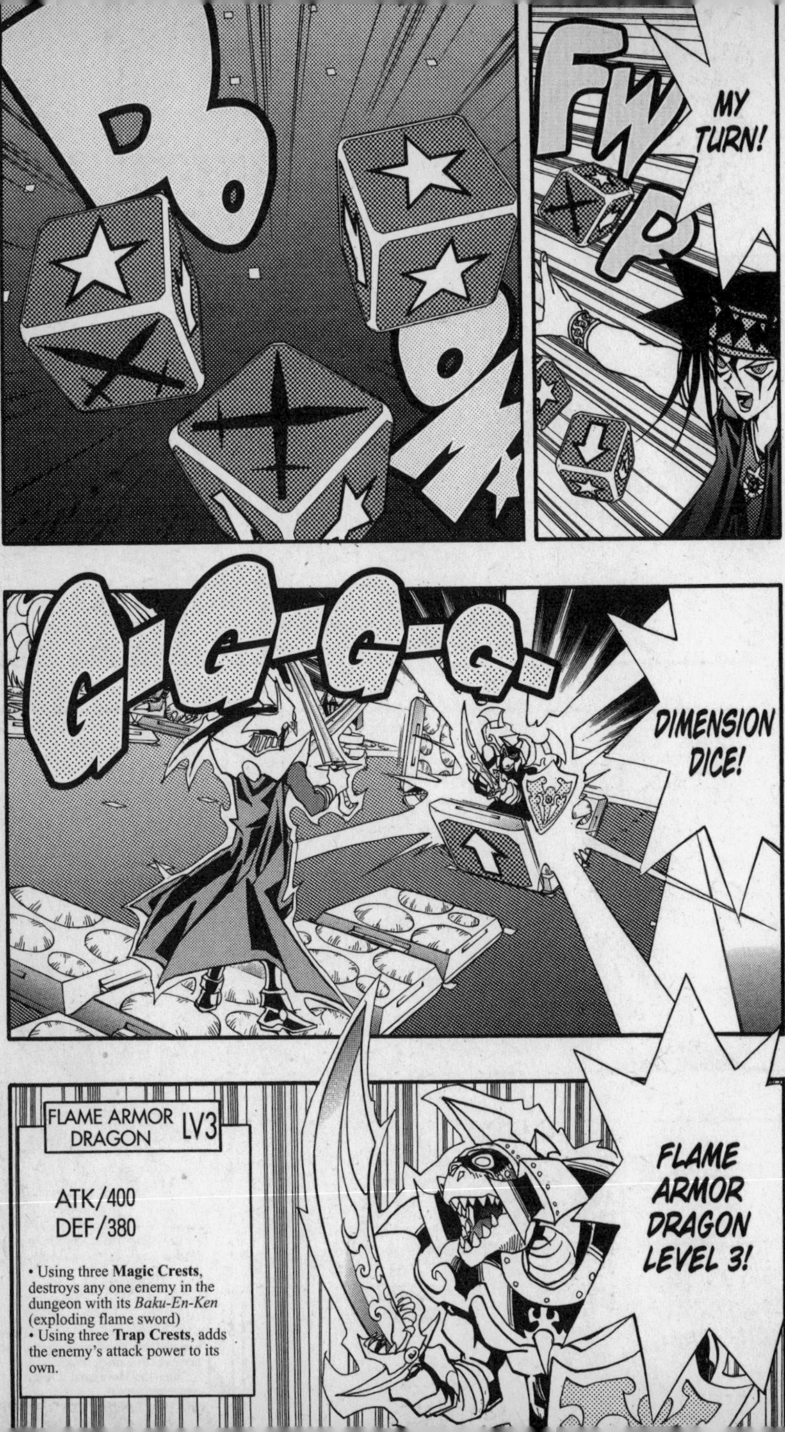
FWP
MY TURN!
DOOM
G-G-G-G-
DIMENSION DICE!
FLAME ARMOR DRAGON LEVEL 3!
FLAME ARMOR DRAGON LV3
ATK/400
DEF/380
• Using three **Magic Crests**, destroys any one enemy in the dungeon with its *Baku-En-Ken* (exploding flame sword)
• Using three **Trap Crests**, adds the enemy's attack power to its own.

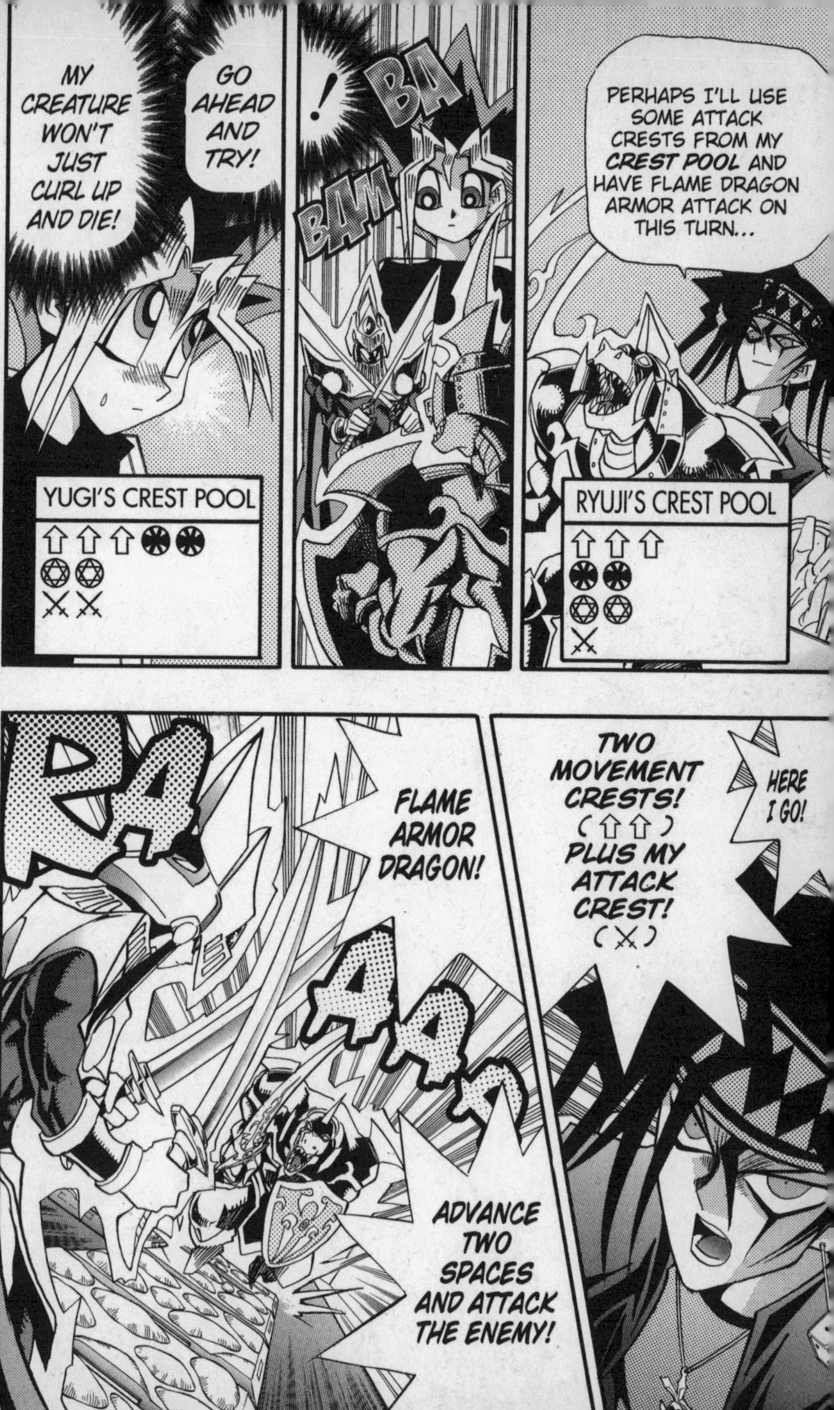
PERHAPS I'LL USE SOME ATTACK CRESTS FROM MY CREST POOL AND HAVE FLAME DRAGON ARMOR ATTACK ON THIS TURN...
RYUJI'S CREST POOL
BA
!
BAM
GO AHEAD AND TRY!
MY CREATURE WON'T JUST CURL UP AND DIE!
YUGI'S CREST POOL
HERE I GO!
TWO MOVEMENT CRESTS!
PLUS MY ATTACK CREST!
FLAME ARMOR DRAGON!
RA
AA
ADVANCE TWO SPACES AND ATTACK THE ENEMY!

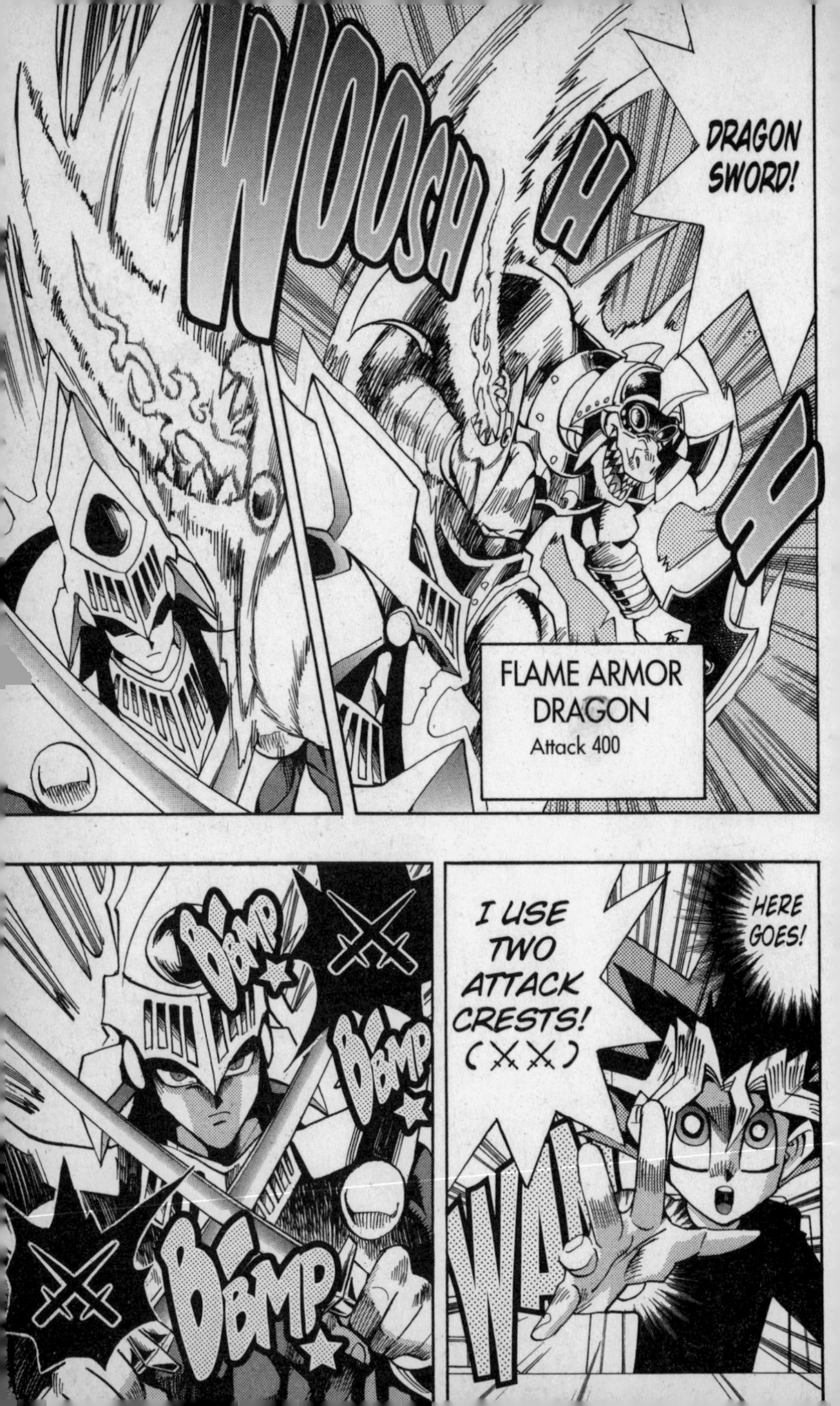
DRAGON SWORD!
WHOOSH
H
H
FLAME ARMOR DRAGON
Attack 400
HERE GOES!
I USE TWO ATTACK CRESTS! (✕✕)
WA!
BOMP
BOMP
BOMP

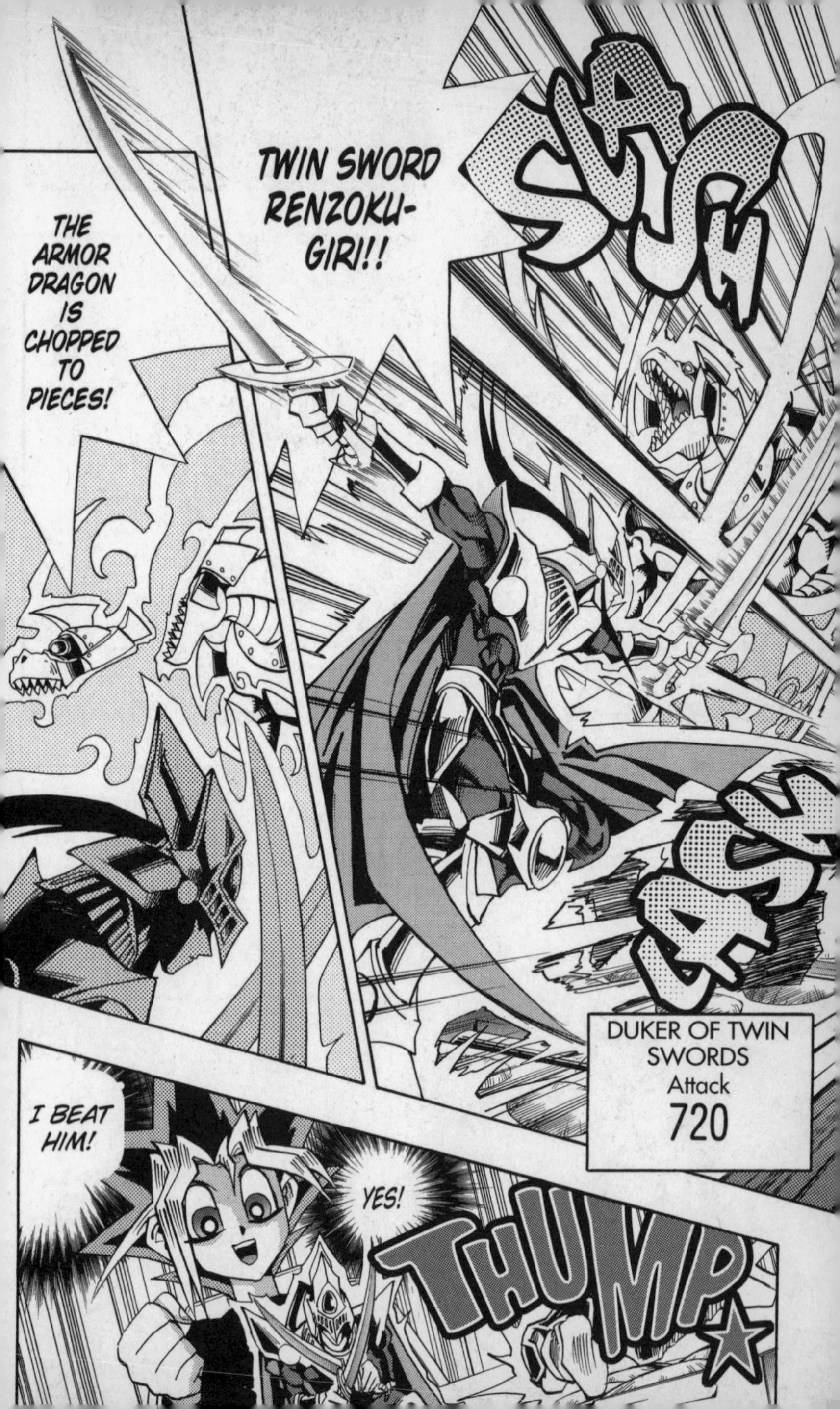
SLASH
TWIN SWORD RENZOKU-GIRI!!
THE ARMOR DRAGON IS CHOPPED TO PIECES!
DUKER OF TWIN SWORDS
Attack
720
THUMP
YES!
I BEAT HIM!

READ THIS WAY

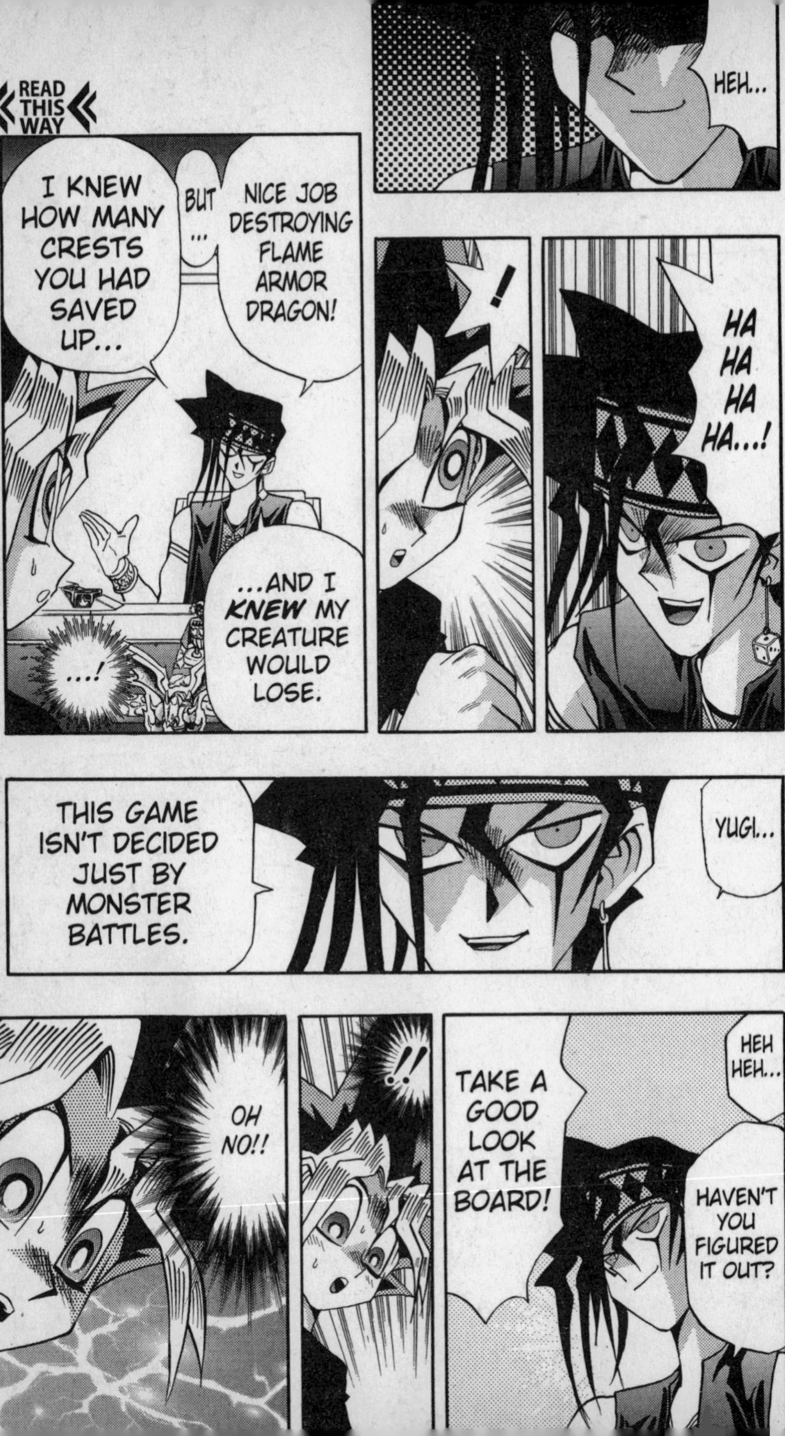
HEH...
NICE JOB DESTROYING FLAME ARMOR DRAGON!
BUT ...
I KNEW HOW MANY CRESTS YOU HAD SAVED UP...
...AND I KNEW MY CREATURE WOULD LOSE.
...!
HA HA HA HA...!
!
YUGI...
THIS GAME ISN'T DECIDED JUST BY MONSTER BATTLES.
HEH HEH...
HAVEN'T YOU FIGURED IT OUT?
TAKE A GOOD LOOK AT THE BOARD!
!!
OH NO!!

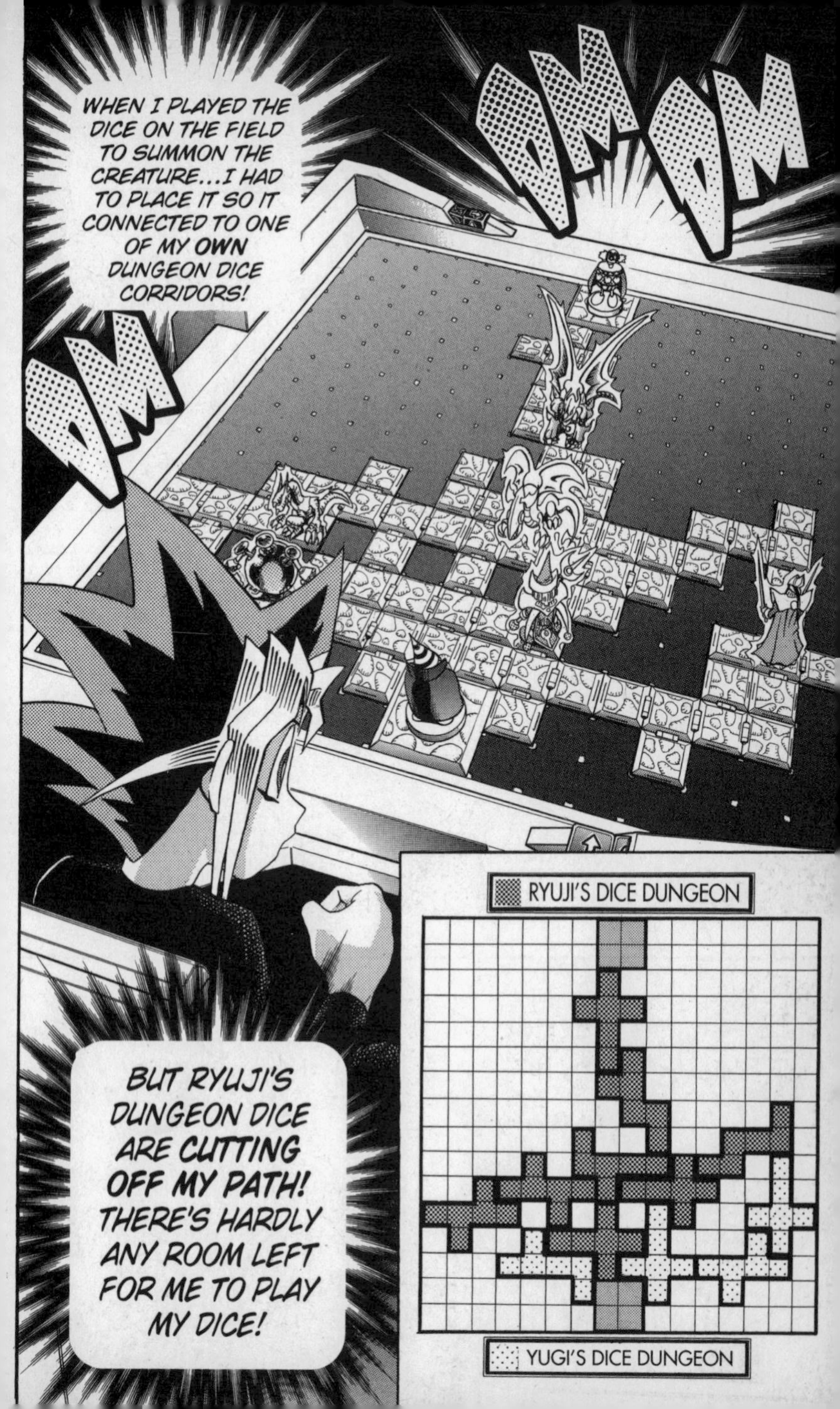
WHEN I PLAYED THE DICE ON THE FIELD TO SUMMON THE CREATURE...I HAD TO PLACE IT SO IT CONNECTED TO ONE OF MY **OWN** DUNGEON DICE CORRIDORS!
RYUJI'S DICE DUNGEON
YUGI'S DICE DUNGEON
BUT RYUJI'S DUNGEON DICE ARE CUTTING OFF MY PATH! THERE'S HARDLY ANY ROOM LEFT FOR ME TO PLAY MY DICE!

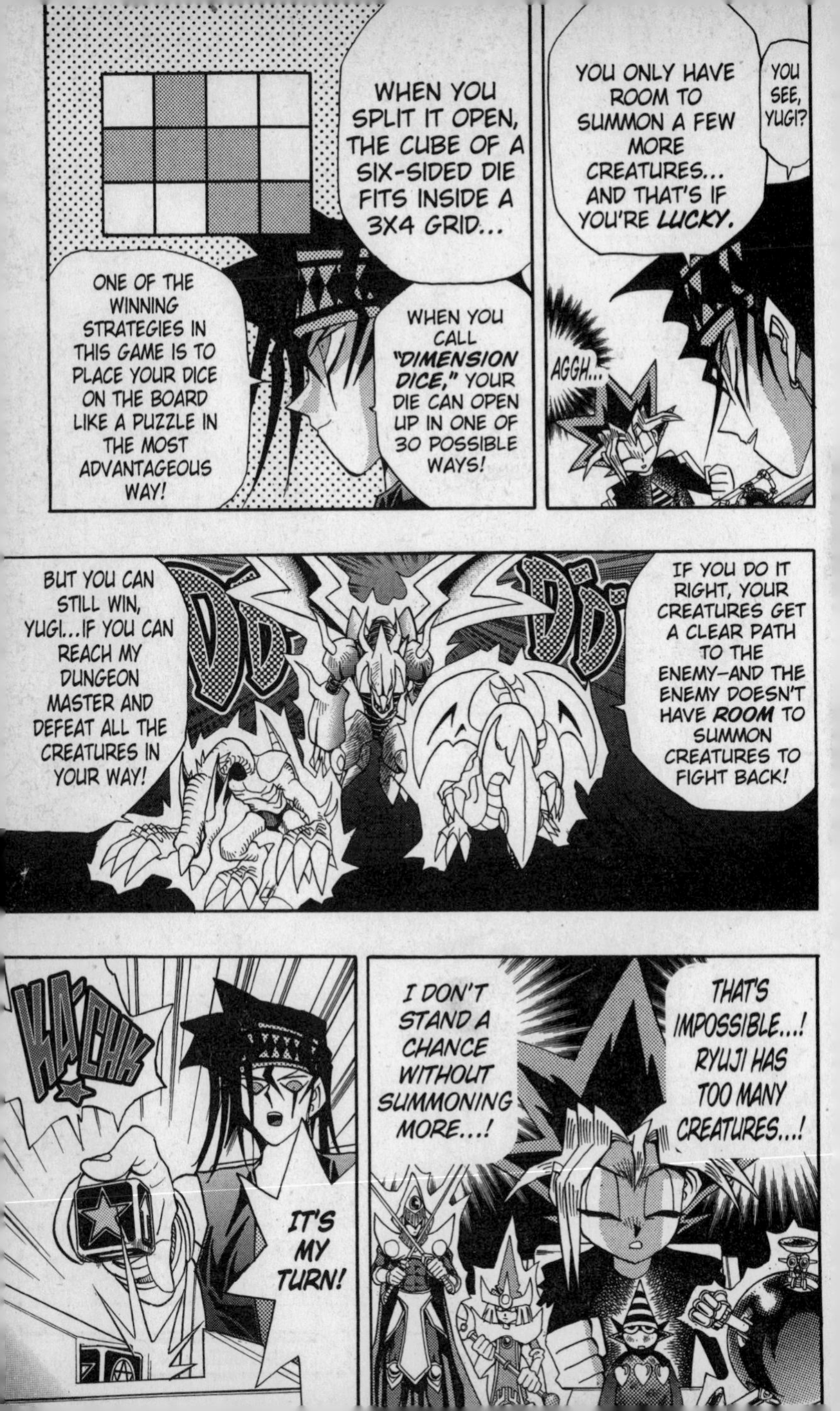
YOU SEE, YUGI?
YOU ONLY HAVE ROOM TO SUMMON A FEW MORE CREATURES... AND THAT'S IF YOU'RE LUCKY.
AGGH...
WHEN YOU SPLIT IT OPEN, THE CUBE OF A SIX-SIDED DIE FITS INSIDE A 3X4 GRID...
WHEN YOU CALL "DIMENSION DICE," YOUR DIE CAN OPEN UP IN ONE OF 30 POSSIBLE WAYS!
ONE OF THE WINNING STRATEGIES IN THIS GAME IS TO PLACE YOUR DICE ON THE BOARD LIKE A PUZZLE IN THE MOST ADVANTAGEOUS WAY!
IF YOU DO IT RIGHT, YOUR CREATURES GET A CLEAR PATH TO THE ENEMY—AND THE ENEMY DOESN'T HAVE ROOM TO SUMMON CREATURES TO FIGHT BACK!
BUT YOU CAN STILL WIN, YUGI...IF YOU CAN REACH MY DUNGEON MASTER AND DEFEAT ALL THE CREATURES IN YOUR WAY!
THAT'S IMPOSSIBLE...! RYUJI HAS TOO MANY CREATURES...!
I DON'T STAND A CHANCE WITHOUT SUMMONING MORE...!
KA-CHK
IT'S MY TURN!

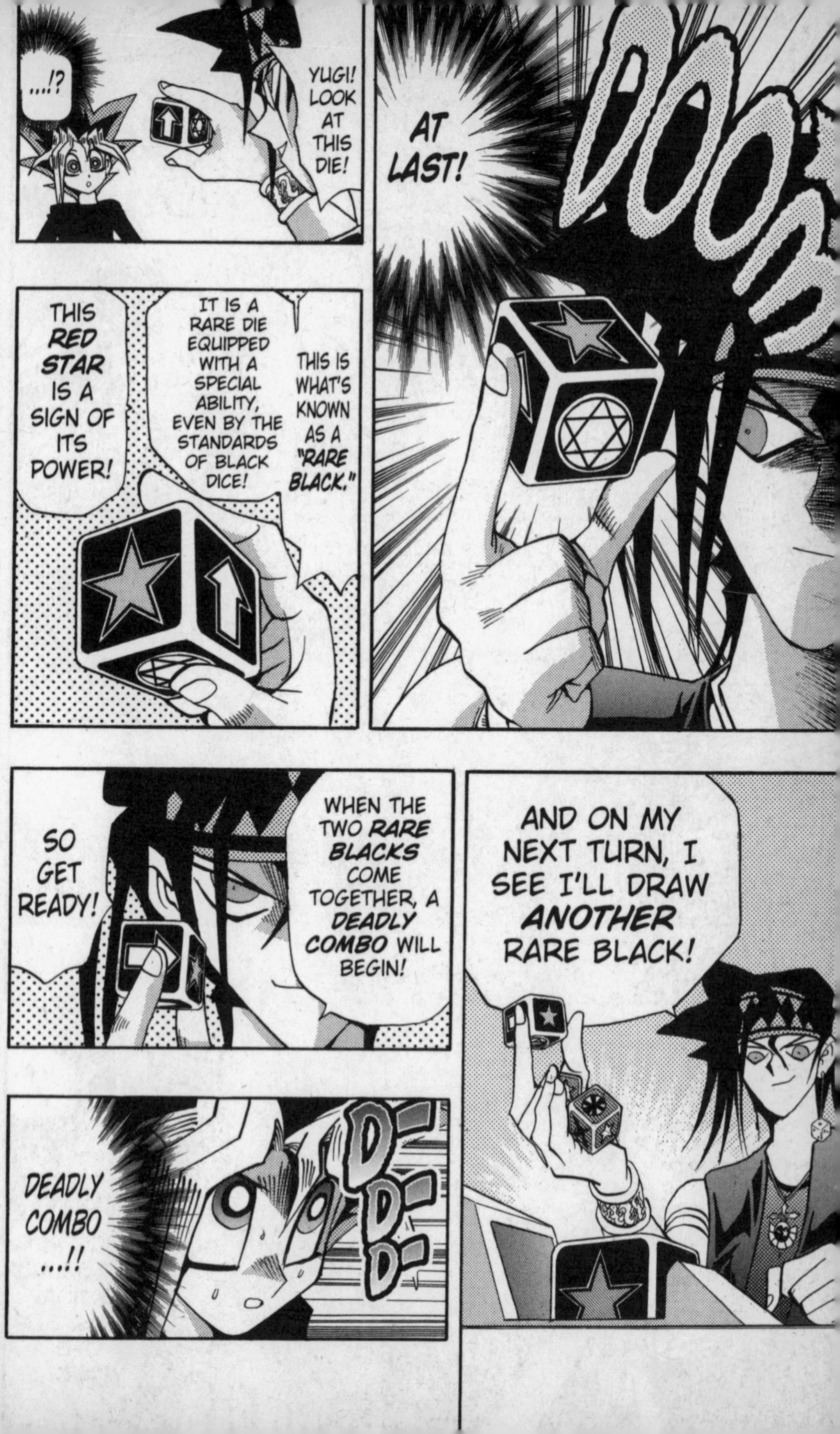
AT LAST!
YUGI! LOOK AT THIS DIE!
...!?
THIS IS WHAT'S KNOWN AS A "RARE BLACK."
IT IS A RARE DIE EQUIPPED WITH A SPECIAL ABILITY, EVEN BY THE STANDARDS OF BLACK DICE!
THIS RED STAR IS A SIGN OF ITS POWER!
AND ON MY NEXT TURN, I SEE I'LL DRAW ANOTHER RARE BLACK!
WHEN THE TWO RARE BLACKS COME TOGETHER, A DEADLY COMBO WILL BEGIN!
SO GET READY!
D- D- D-
DEADLY COMBO ...!!

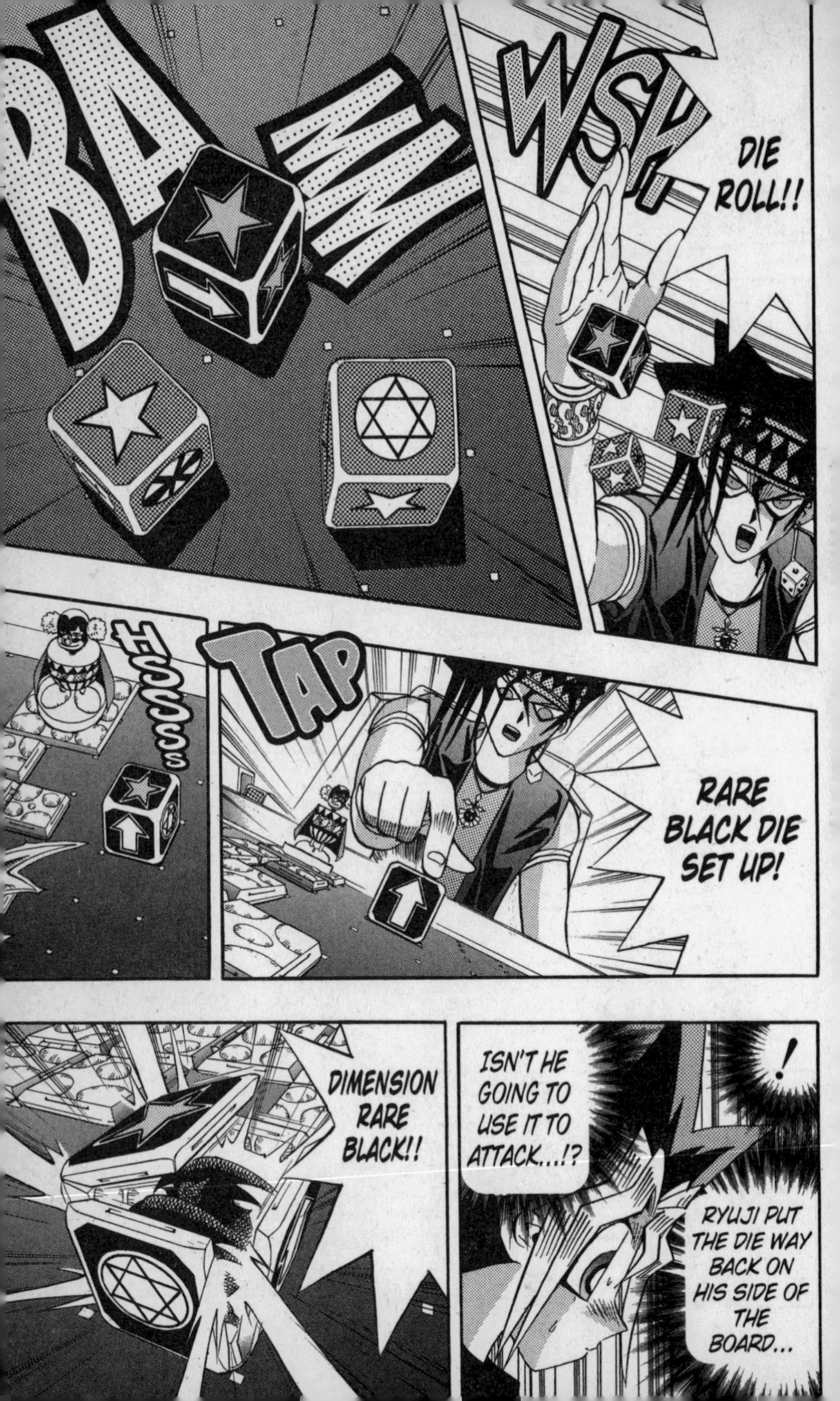
WSH
DIE ROLL!!
BAMM
TAP
RARE BLACK DIE SET UP!
FSSSS
!
ISN'T HE GOING TO USE IT TO ATTACK...!?
RYUJI PUT THE DIE WAY BACK ON HIS SIDE OF THE BOARD...
DIMENSION RARE BLACK!!

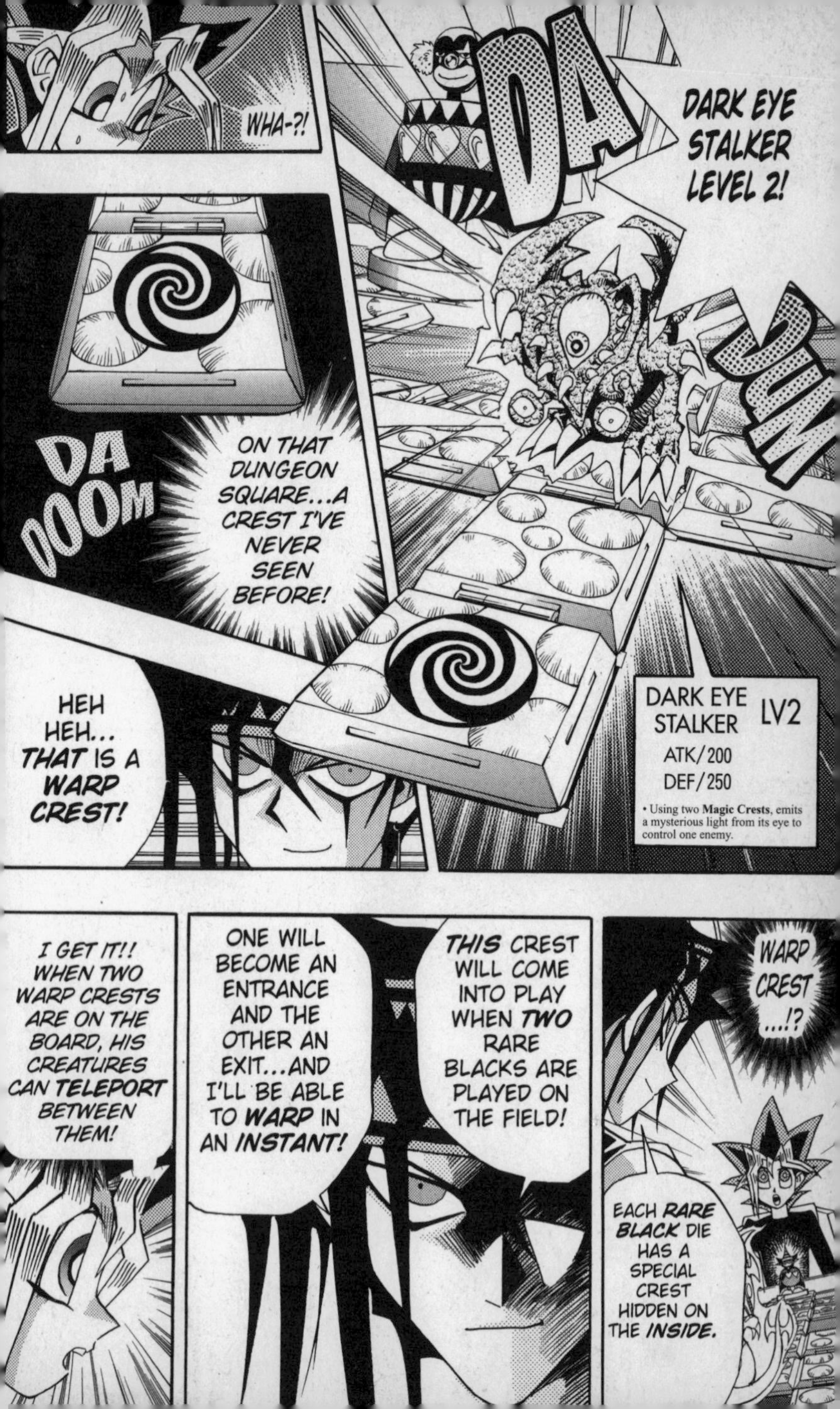
DA
DA
DARK EYE STALKER LEVEL 2!
DUN
DARK EYE STALKER LV2
ATK/200
DEF/250
• Using two Magic Crests, emits a mysterious light from its eye to control one enemy.
WHA-?!
DA DOOM
ON THAT DUNGEON SQUARE...A CREST I'VE NEVER SEEN BEFORE!
HEH HEH... THAT IS A WARP CREST!
WARP CREST ...!?
EACH RARE BLACK DIE HAS A SPECIAL CREST HIDDEN ON THE INSIDE.
THIS CREST WILL COME INTO PLAY WHEN TWO RARE BLACKS ARE PLAYED ON THE FIELD!
ONE WILL BECOME AN ENTRANCE AND THE OTHER AN EXIT...AND I'LL BE ABLE TO WARP IN AN INSTANT!
I GET IT!! WHEN TWO WARP CRESTS ARE ON THE BOARD, HIS CREATURES CAN TELEPORT BETWEEN THEM!

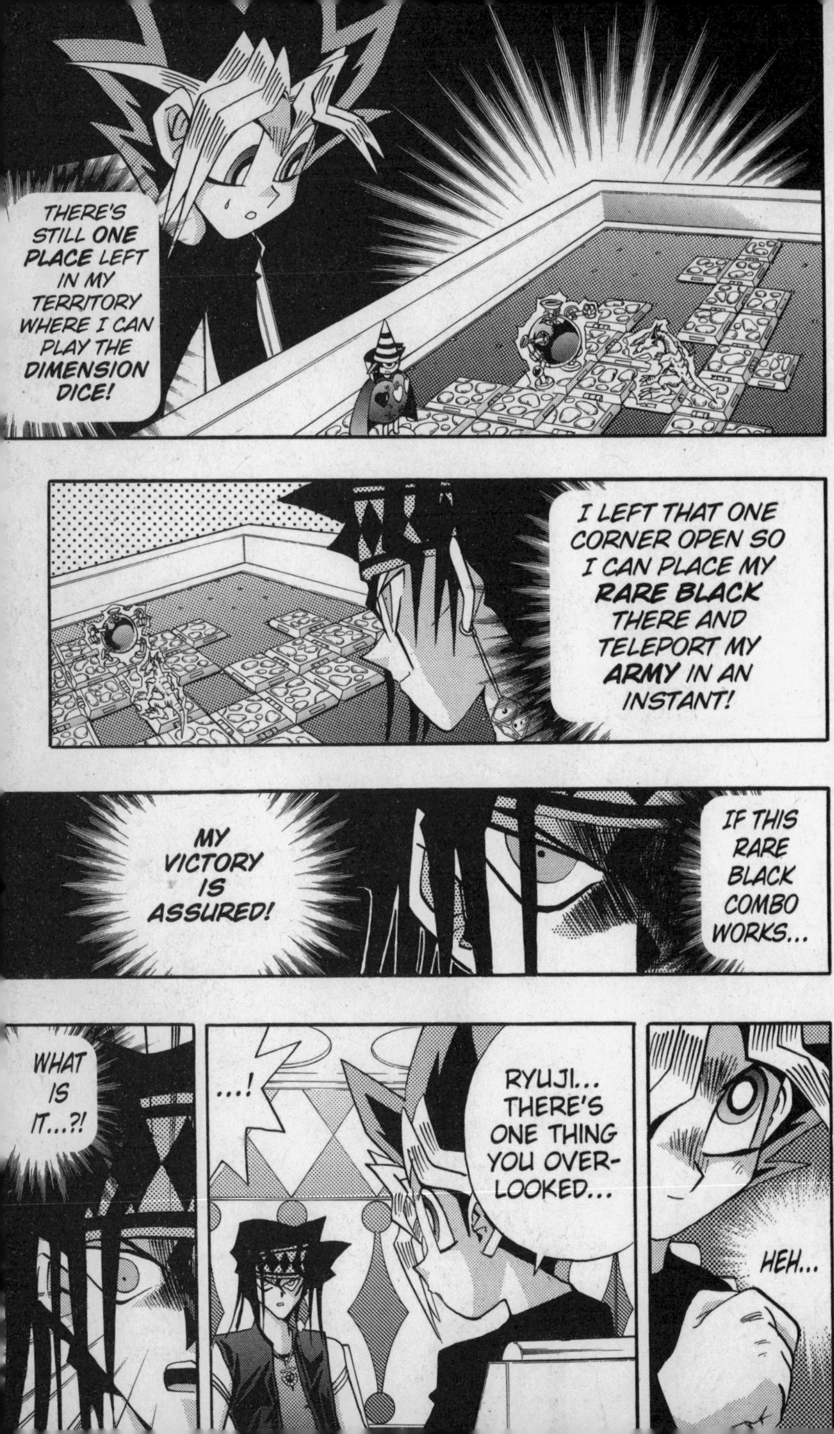
THERE'S STILL ONE PLACE LEFT IN MY TERRITORY WHERE I CAN PLAY THE DIMENSION DICE!
I LEFT THAT ONE CORNER OPEN SO I CAN PLACE MY RARE BLACK THERE AND TELEPORT MY ARMY IN AN INSTANT!
IF THIS RARE BLACK COMBO WORKS...
MY VICTORY IS ASSURED!
HEH...
RYUJI... THERE'S ONE THING YOU OVERLOOKED...
...!
WHAT IS IT...?!

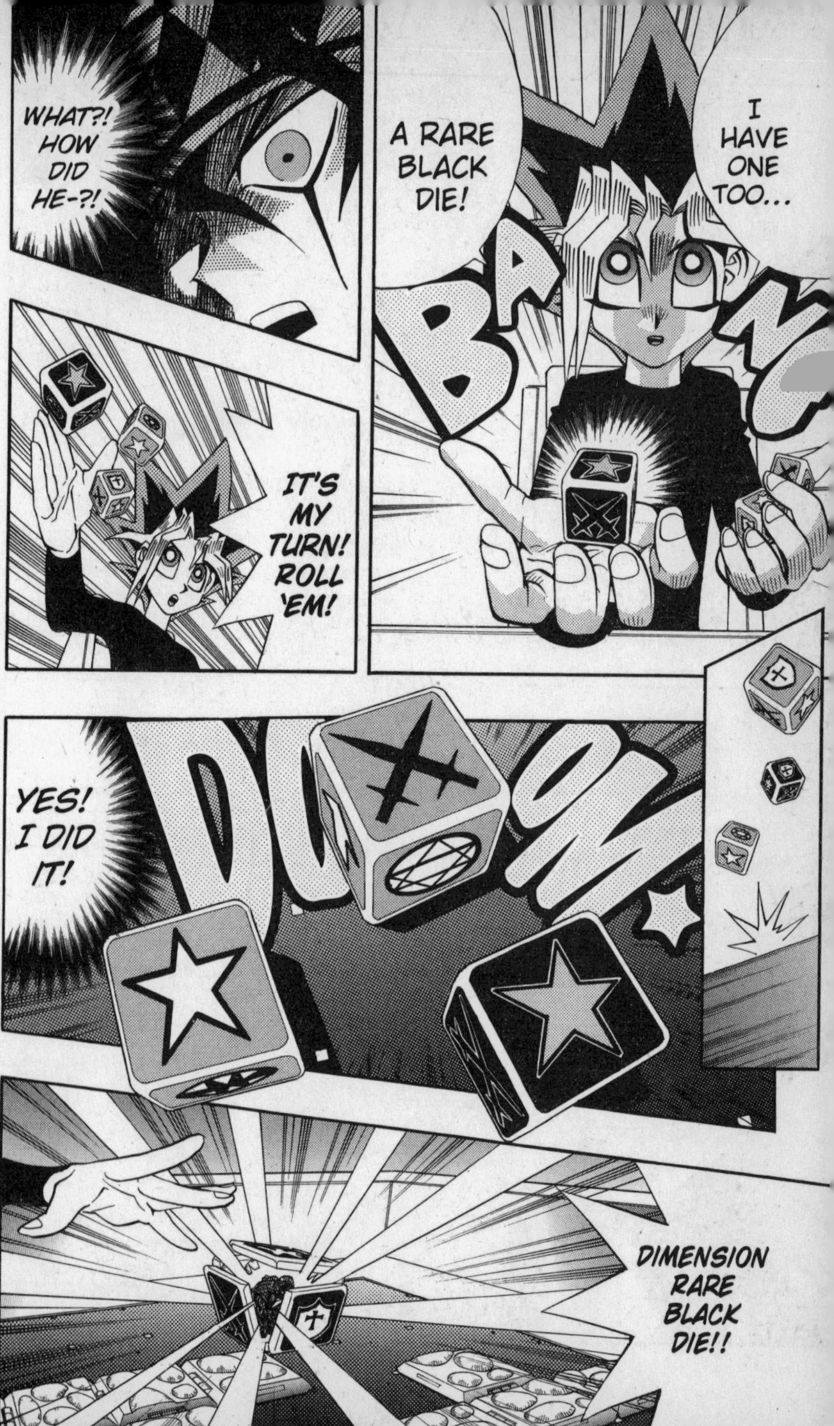
I HAVE ONE TOO...
A RARE BLACK DIE!
WHAT?! HOW DID HE-?!
IT'S MY TURN! ROLL 'EM!
YES! I DID IT!
DIMENSION RARE BLACK DIE!!

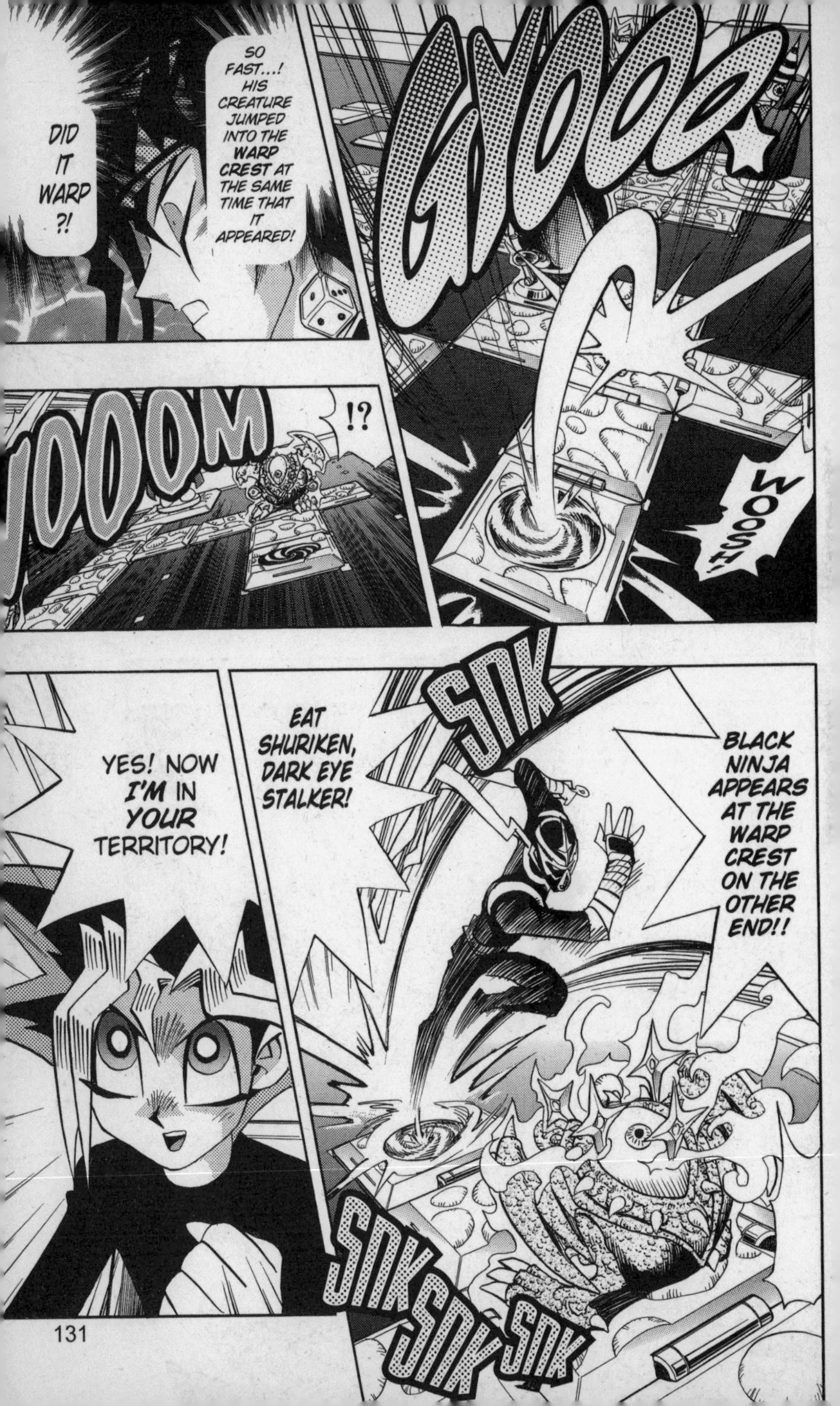
WOOSH!
SO FAST...! HIS CREATURE JUMPED INTO THE WARP CREST AT THE SAME TIME THAT IT APPEARED!
DID IT WARP?!
OOOM
!?
BLACK NINJA APPEARS AT THE WARP CREST ON THE OTHER END!!
SDK
EAT SHURIKEN, DARK EYE STALKER!
SDK SDK SDK
YES! NOW I'M IN YOUR TERRITORY!

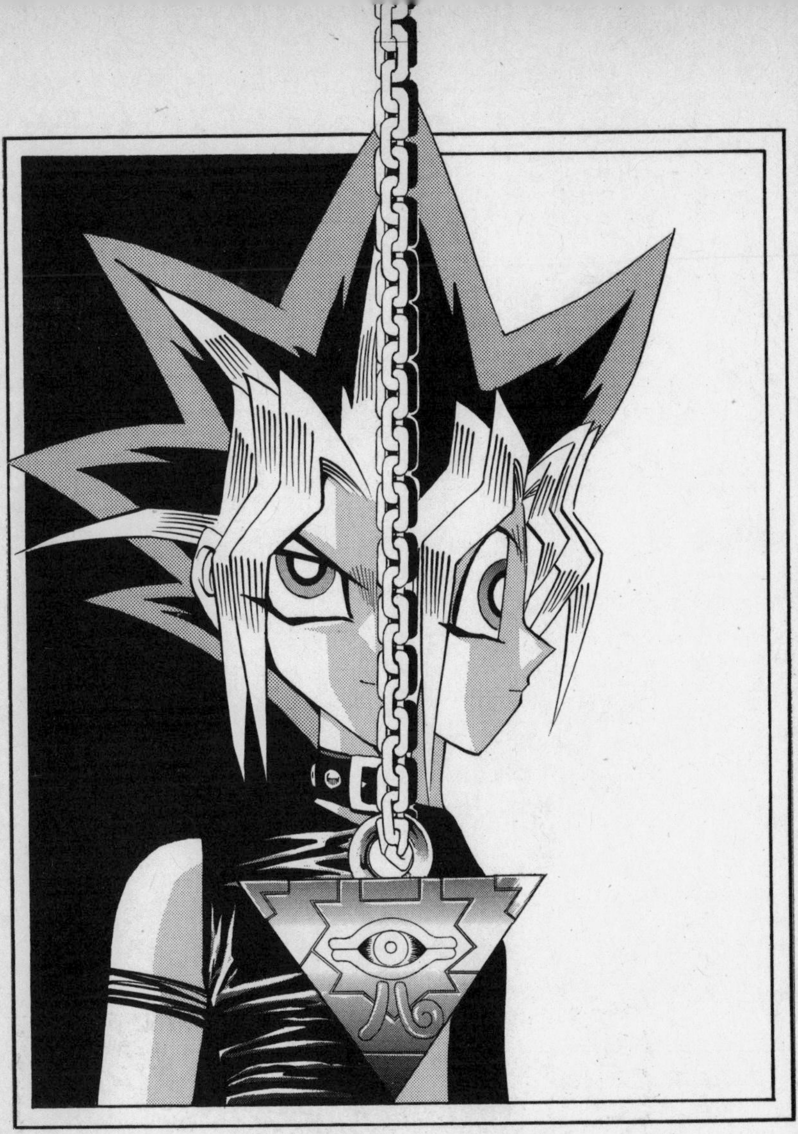

Duel 81: The Broken Bond

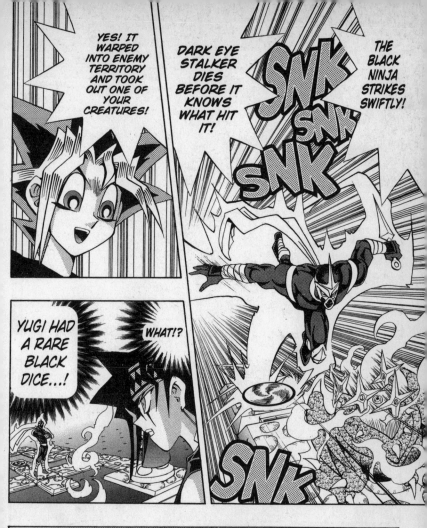

THE BLACK NINJA STRIKES SWIFTLY!
SNK
SNK
SNK
DARK EYE STALKER DIES BEFORE IT KNOWS WHAT HIT IT!
SNK
YES! IT WARPED INTO ENEMY TERRITORY AND TOOK OUT ONE OF YOUR CREATURES!
WHAT!?
YUGI HAD A RARE BLACK DICE...!

RARE BLACK DICE

IN ***DUNGEON DICE MONSTERS,*** BLACK DICE HAVE SPECIAL POWERS...BUT ***RARE BLACK DICE*** ARE THE MOST SOUGHT AFTER OF THEM ALL!

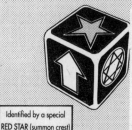

Identified by a special RED STAR (summon crest)

RARE BLACK DICE HAVE A SPECIAL CREST ON THE INSIDE, WHICH BECOMES VISIBLE WHEN THE DICE ARE PLAYED ON THE BOARD. THESE INCLUDE ***WARP CRESTS, TREASURE CRESTS*** AND MORE...

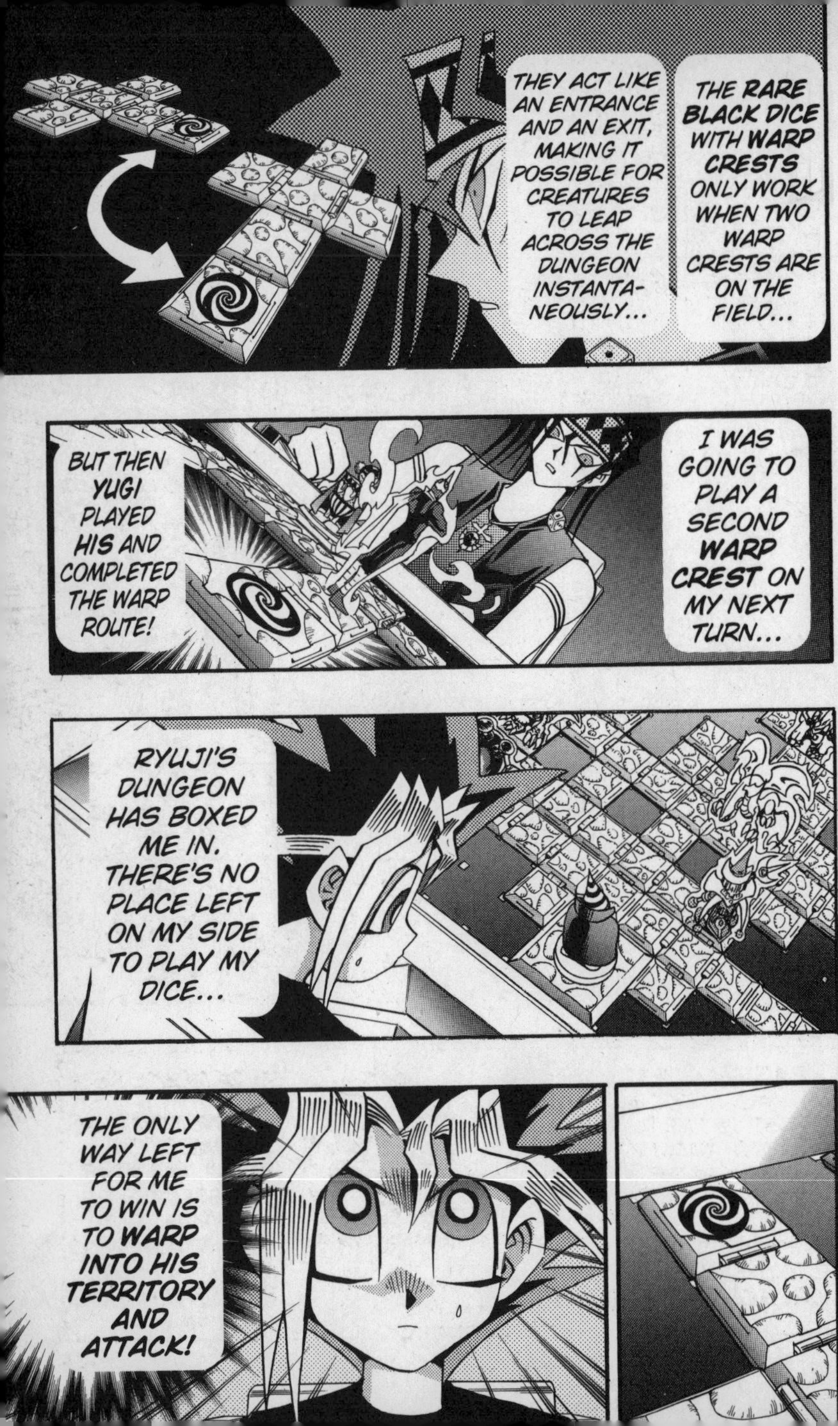
THE RARE BLACK DICE WITH WARP CRESTS ONLY WORK WHEN TWO WARP CRESTS ARE ON THE FIELD...
THEY ACT LIKE AN ENTRANCE AND AN EXIT, MAKING IT POSSIBLE FOR CREATURES TO LEAP ACROSS THE DUNGEON INSTANTA-NEOUSLY...
I WAS GOING TO PLAY A SECOND WARP CREST ON MY NEXT TURN...
BUT THEN YUGI PLAYED HIS AND COMPLETED THE WARP ROUTE!
RYUJI'S DUNGEON HAS BOXED ME IN. THERE'S NO PLACE LEFT ON MY SIDE TO PLAY MY DICE...
THE ONLY WAY LEFT FOR ME TO WIN IS TO WARP INTO HIS TERRITORY AND ATTACK!

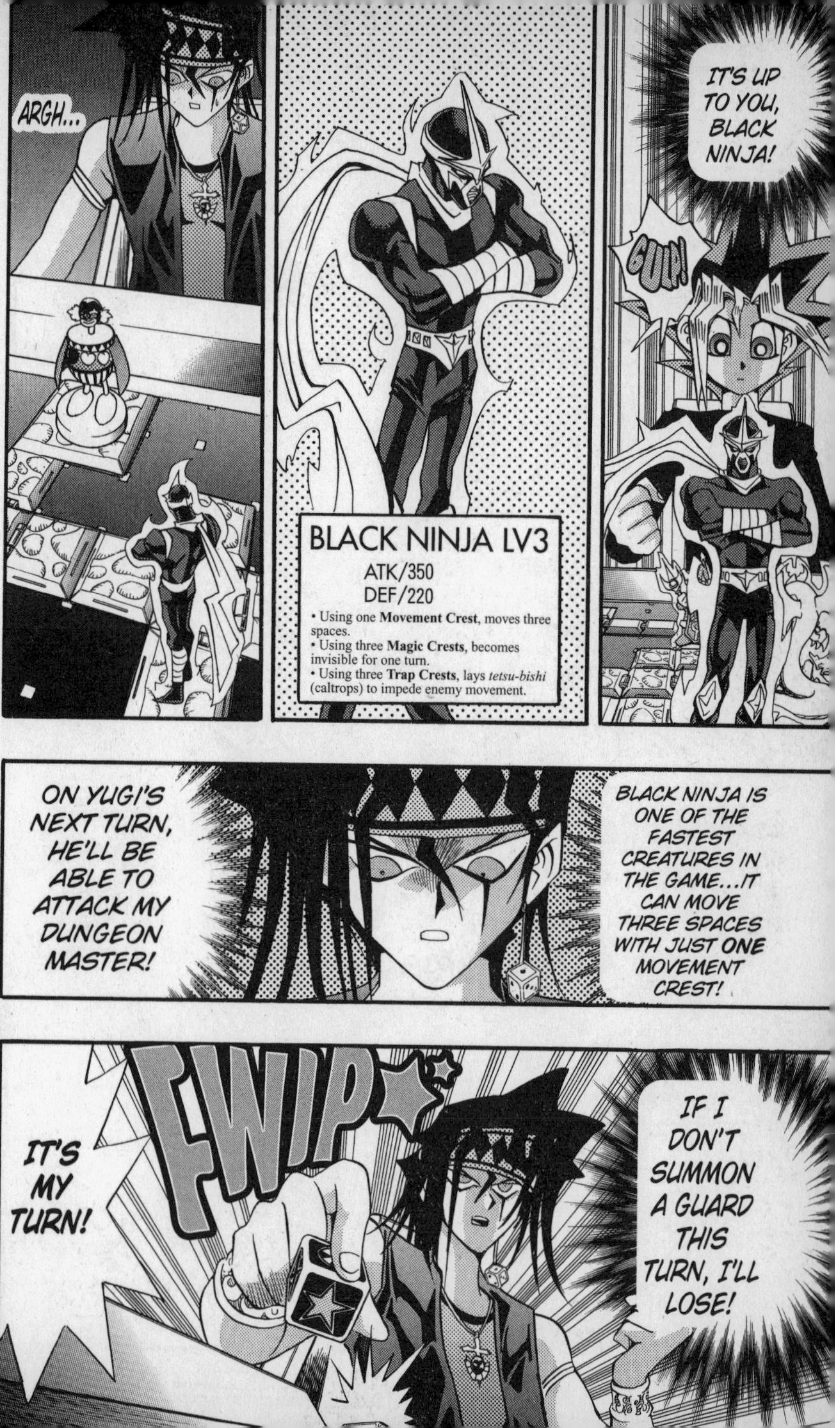
IT'S UP TO YOU, BLACK NINJA!
GULP!
BLACK NINJA LV3
ATK/350
DEF/220
• Using one **Movement Crest**, moves three spaces.
• Using three **Magic Crests**, becomes invisible for one turn.
• Using three **Trap Crests**, lays *tetsu-bishi* (caltrops) to impede enemy movement.
ARGH...
BLACK NINJA IS ONE OF THE FASTEST CREATURES IN THE GAME...IT CAN MOVE THREE SPACES WITH JUST ONE MOVEMENT CREST!
ON YUGI'S NEXT TURN, HE'LL BE ABLE TO ATTACK MY DUNGEON MASTER!
IF I DON'T SUMMON A GUARD THIS TURN, I'LL LOSE!
FWIP
IT'S MY TURN!

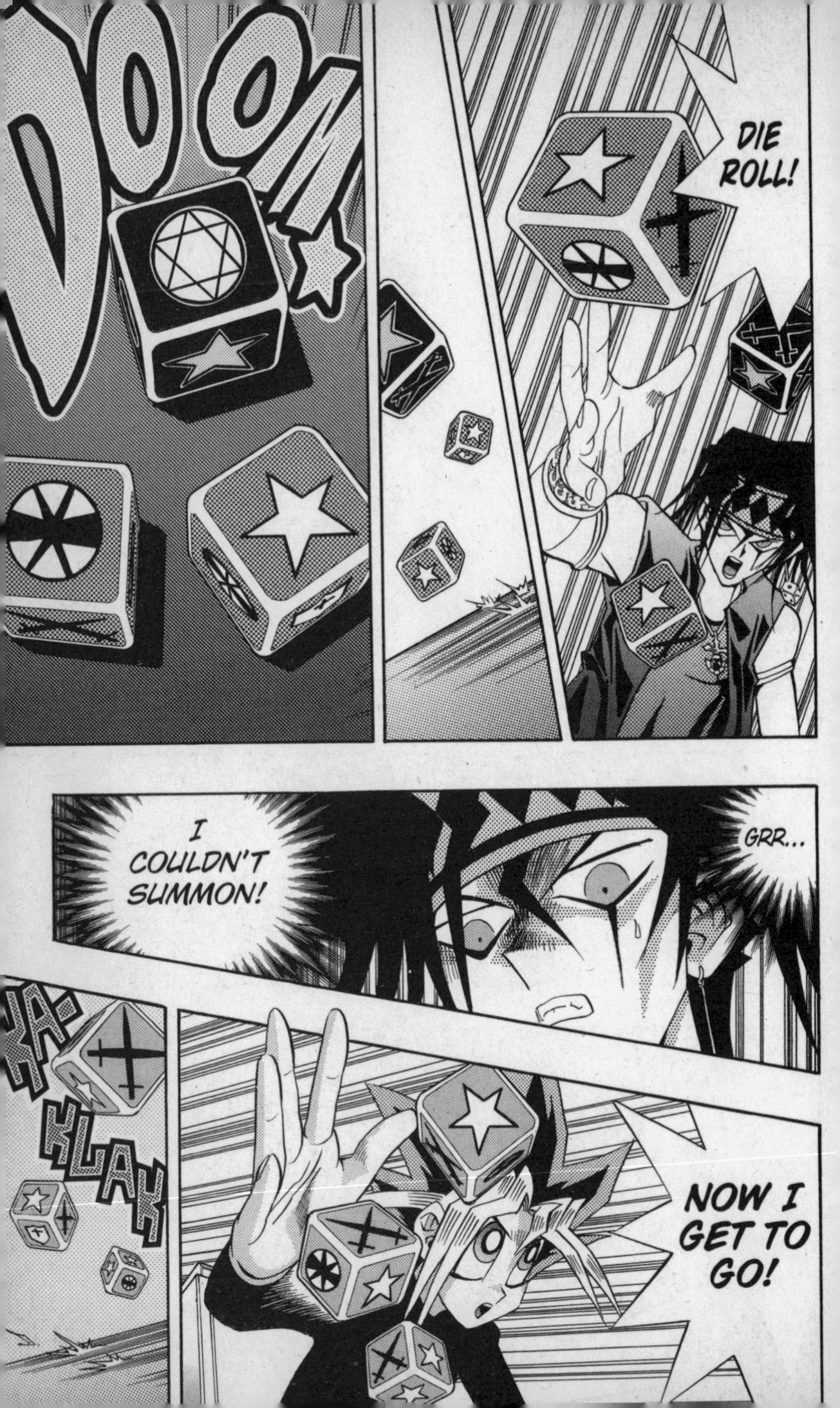
DIE ROLL!
GRR...
I COULDN'T SUMMON!
NOW I GET TO GO!
KA-KLAK

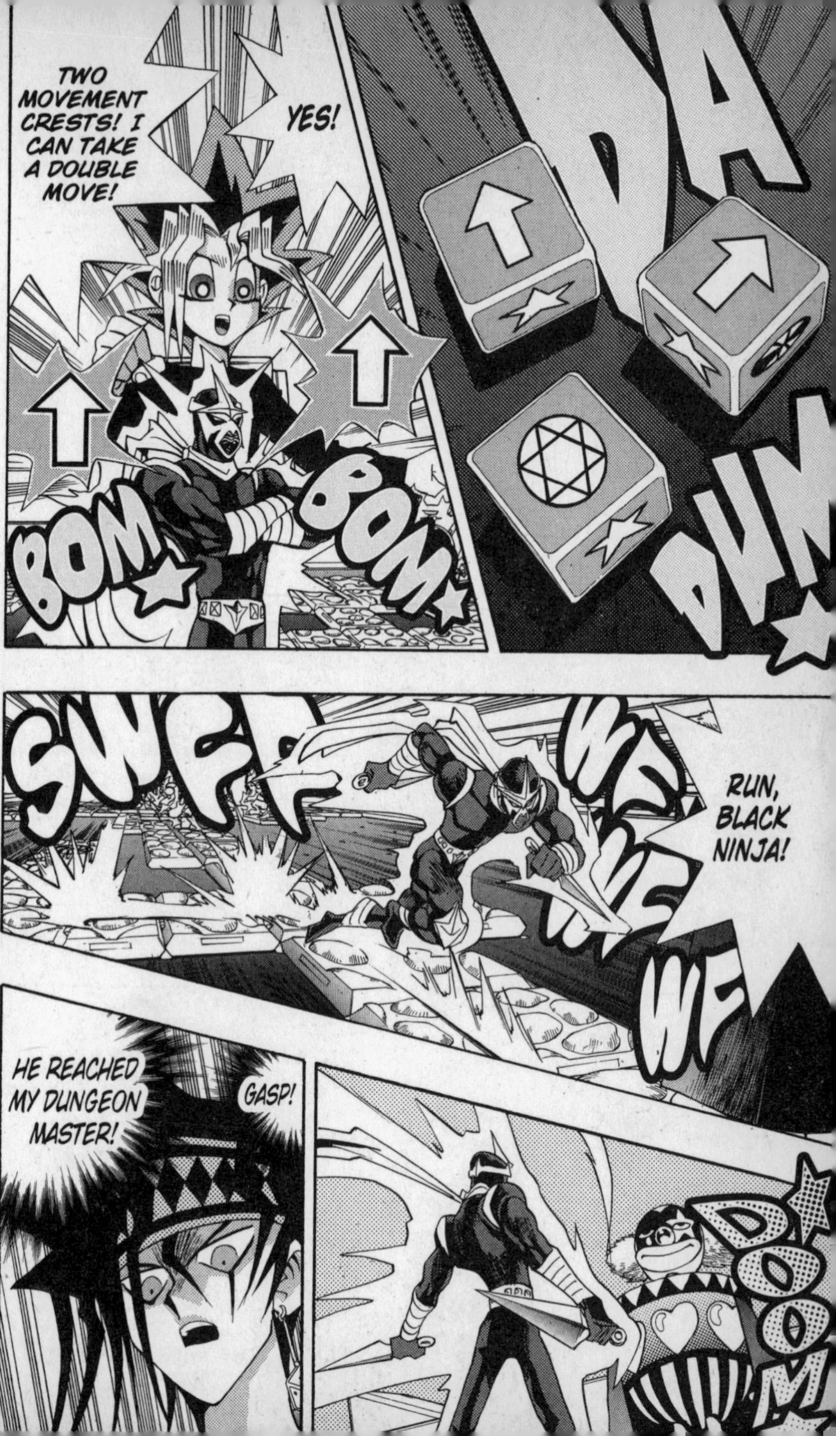
YES!
TWO MOVEMENT CRESTS! I CAN TAKE A DOUBLE MOVE!
BOM
BOM
RUN, BLACK NINJA!
GASP!
HE REACHED MY DUNGEON MASTER!

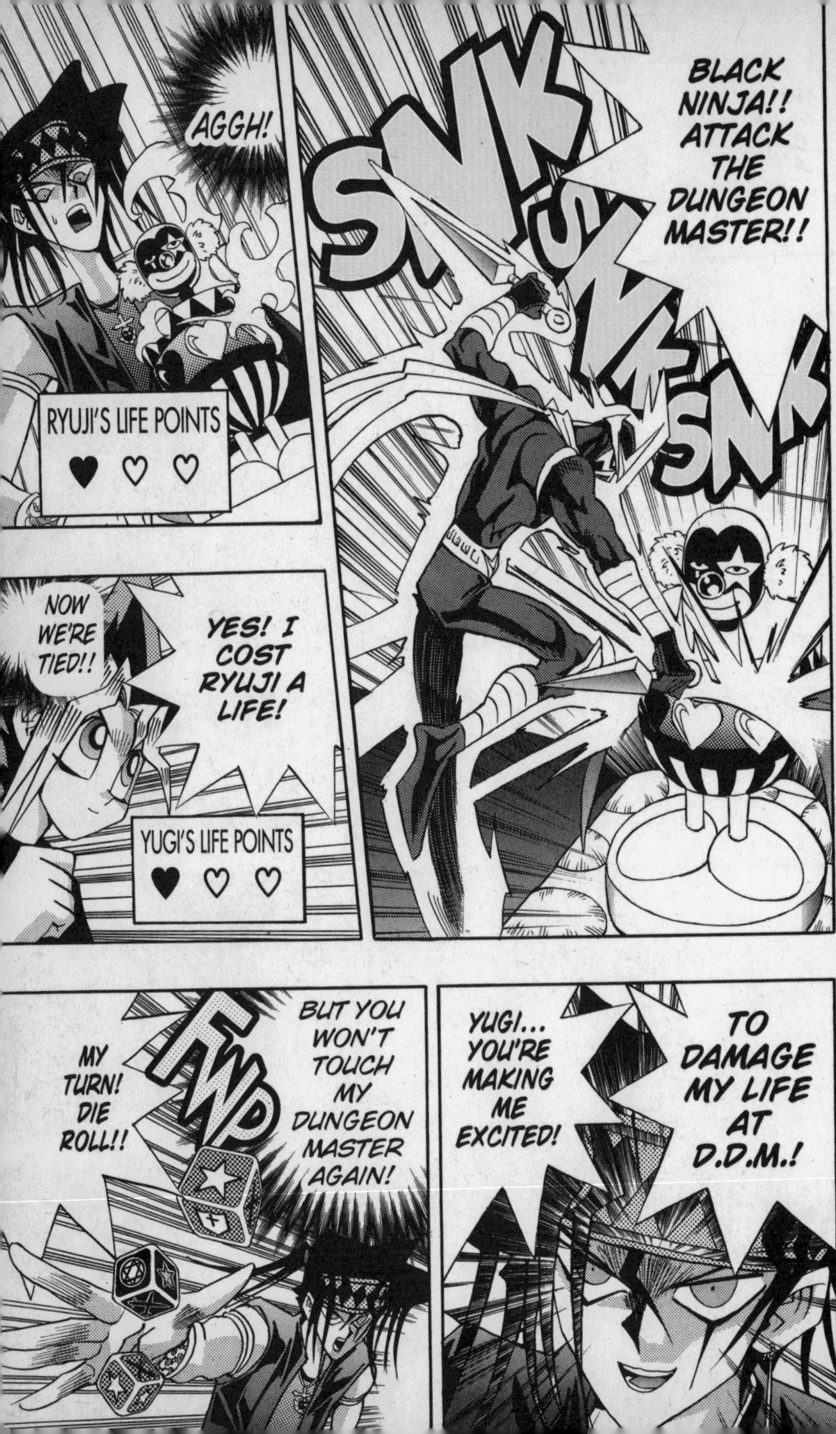
BLACK NINJA!! ATTACK THE DUNGEON MASTER!!
SNK
SNK
SNK
AGGH!
RYUJI'S LIFE POINTS
YES! I COST RYUJI A LIFE!
NOW WE'RE TIED!!
YUGI'S LIFE POINTS
TO DAMAGE MY LIFE AT D.D.M.!
YUGI... YOU'RE MAKING ME EXCITED!
BUT YOU WON'T TOUCH MY DUNGEON MASTER AGAIN!
FWP
MY TURN! DIE ROLL!!

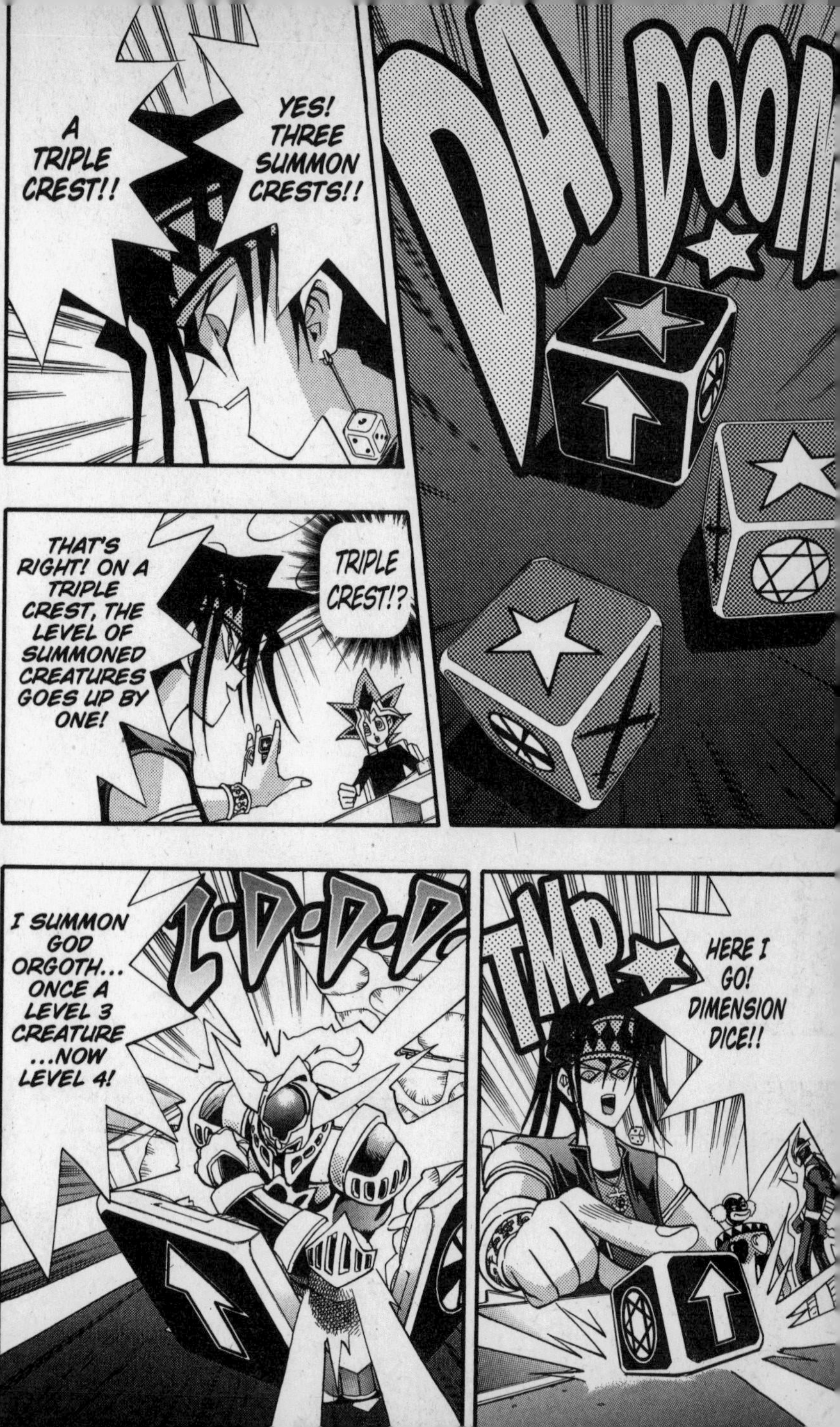
DA DOOM
YES! THREE SUMMON CRESTS!!
A TRIPLE CREST!!
TRIPLE CREST!?
THAT'S RIGHT! ON A TRIPLE CREST, THE LEVEL OF SUMMONED CREATURES GOES UP BY ONE!
TMP
HERE I GO! DIMENSION DICE!!
Z-D-D-D
I SUMMON GOD ORGOTH... ONCE A LEVEL 3 CREATURE ...NOW LEVEL 4!

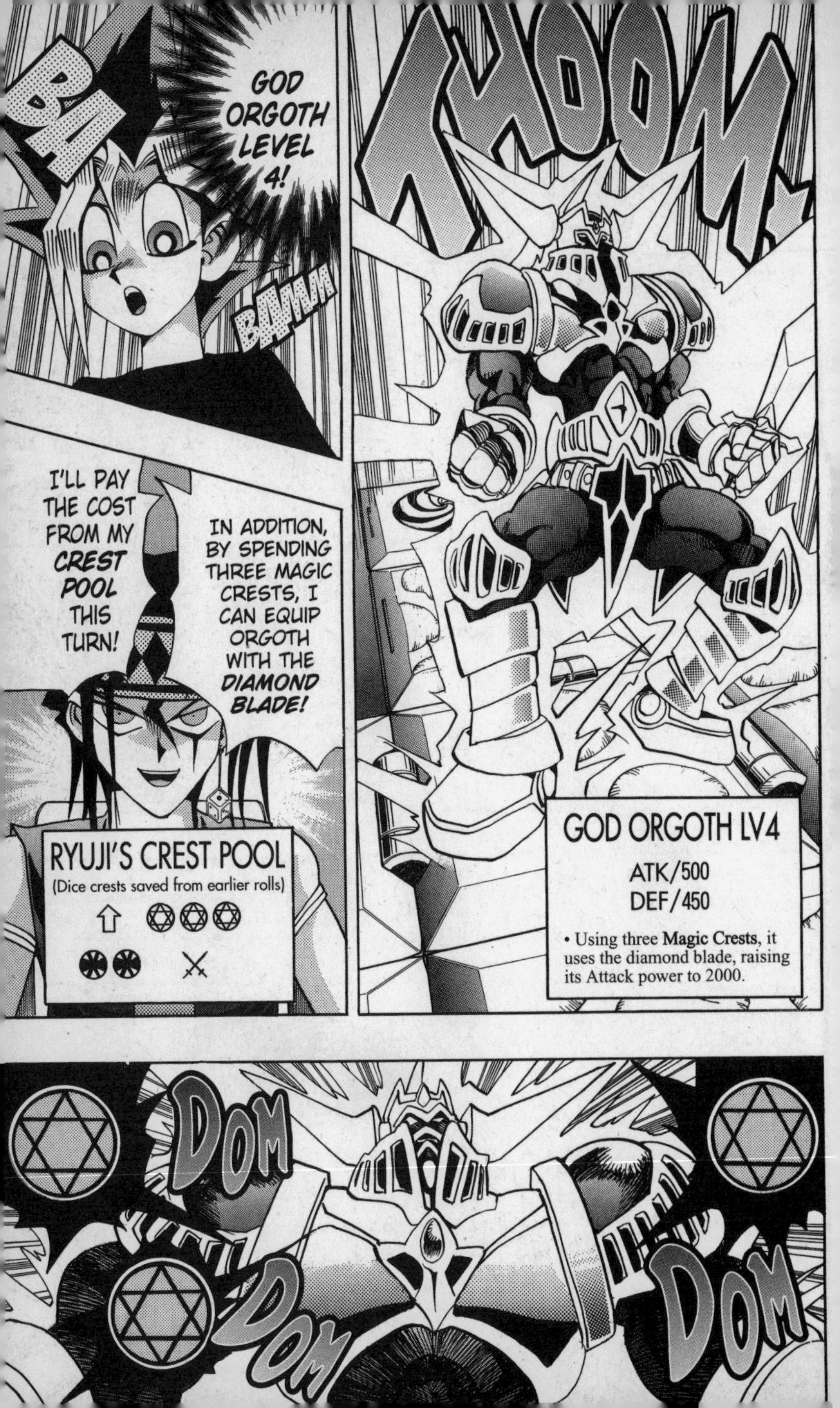
BA
GOD ORGOTH LEVEL 4!
BAMM
I'LL PAY THE COST FROM MY CREST POOL THIS TURN!
IN ADDITION, BY SPENDING THREE MAGIC CRESTS, I CAN EQUIP ORGOTH WITH THE DIAMOND BLADE!
RYUJI'S CREST POOL
(Dice crests saved from earlier rolls)
KHOOM
GOD ORGOTH LV4
ATK/500
DEF/450
• Using three Magic Crests, it uses the diamond blade, raising its Attack power to 2000.
DOM
DOM
DOM

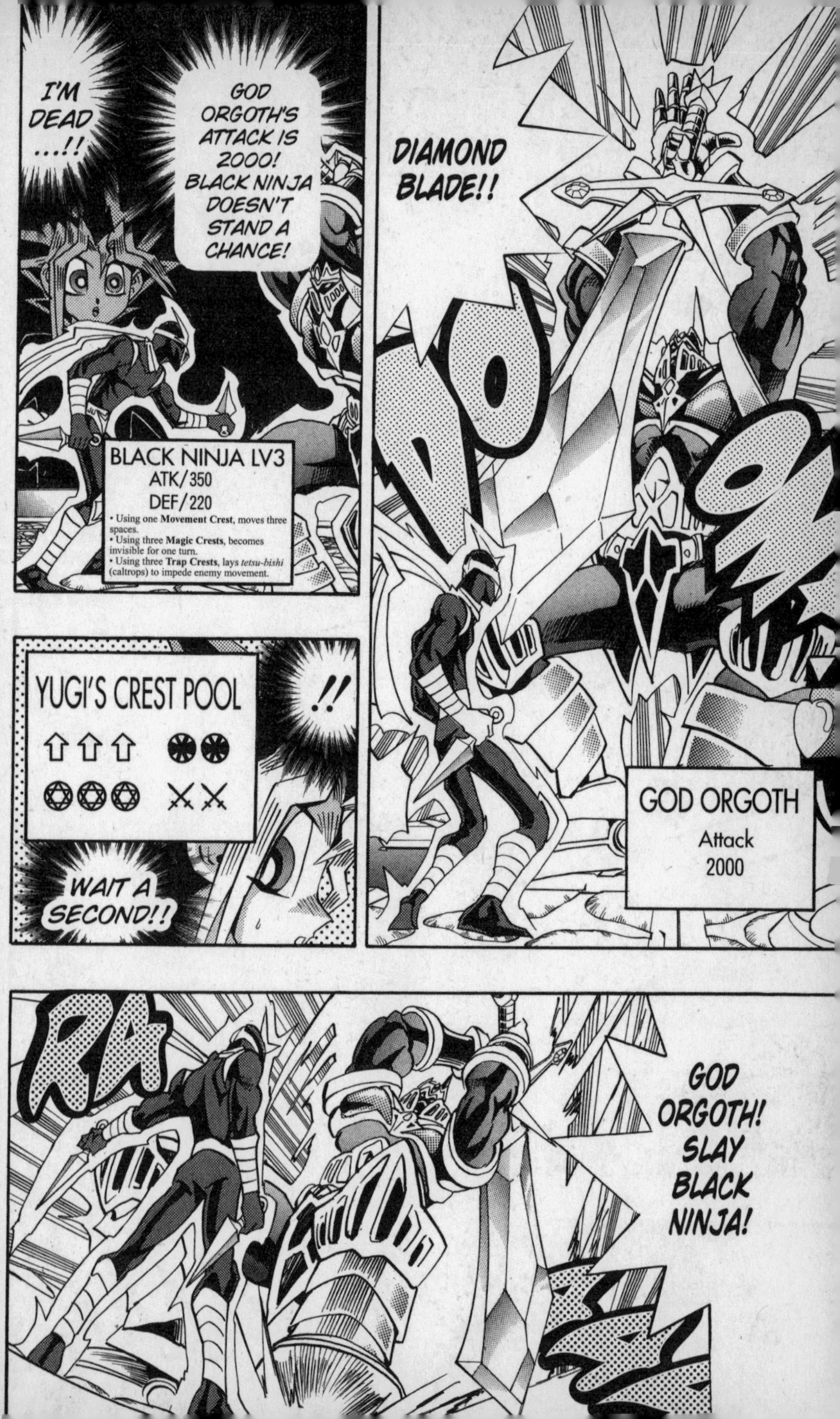
DIAMOND BLADE!!
GOD ORGOTH
Attack
2000
GOD ORGOTH'S ATTACK IS 2000! BLACK NINJA DOESN'T STAND A CHANCE!
I'M DEAD ...!!
BLACK NINJA LV3
ATK/350
DEF/220
• Using one Movement Crest, moves three spaces.
• Using three Magic Crests, becomes invisible for one turn.
• Using three Trap Crests, lays tetsu-bishi (caltrops) to impede enemy movement.
!!
YUGI'S CREST POOL
WAIT A SECOND!!
GOD ORGOTH! SLAY BLACK NINJA!
RA

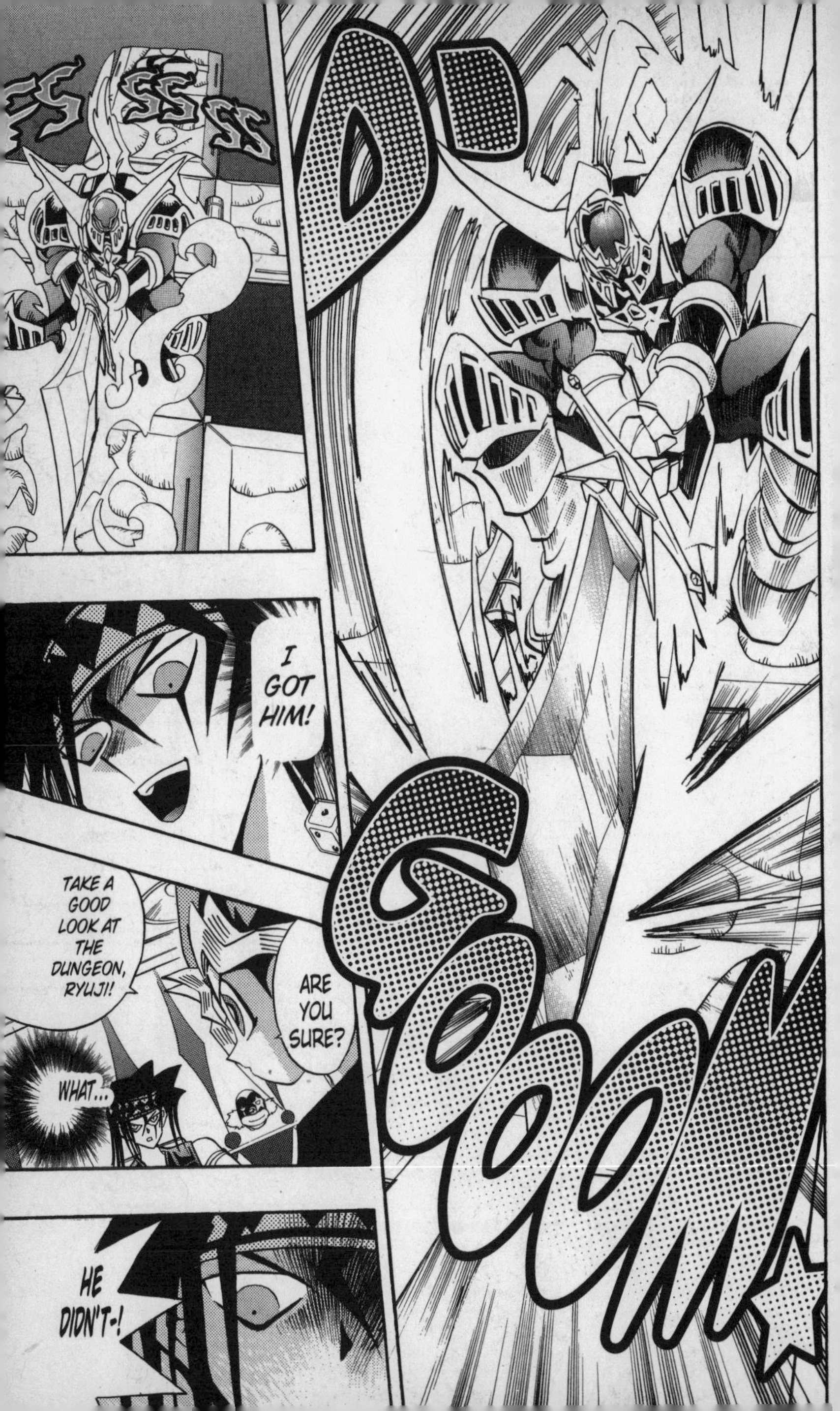
I GOT HIM!
ARE YOU SURE?
TAKE A GOOD LOOK AT THE DUNGEON, RYUJI!
WHAT...
HE DIDN'T-!

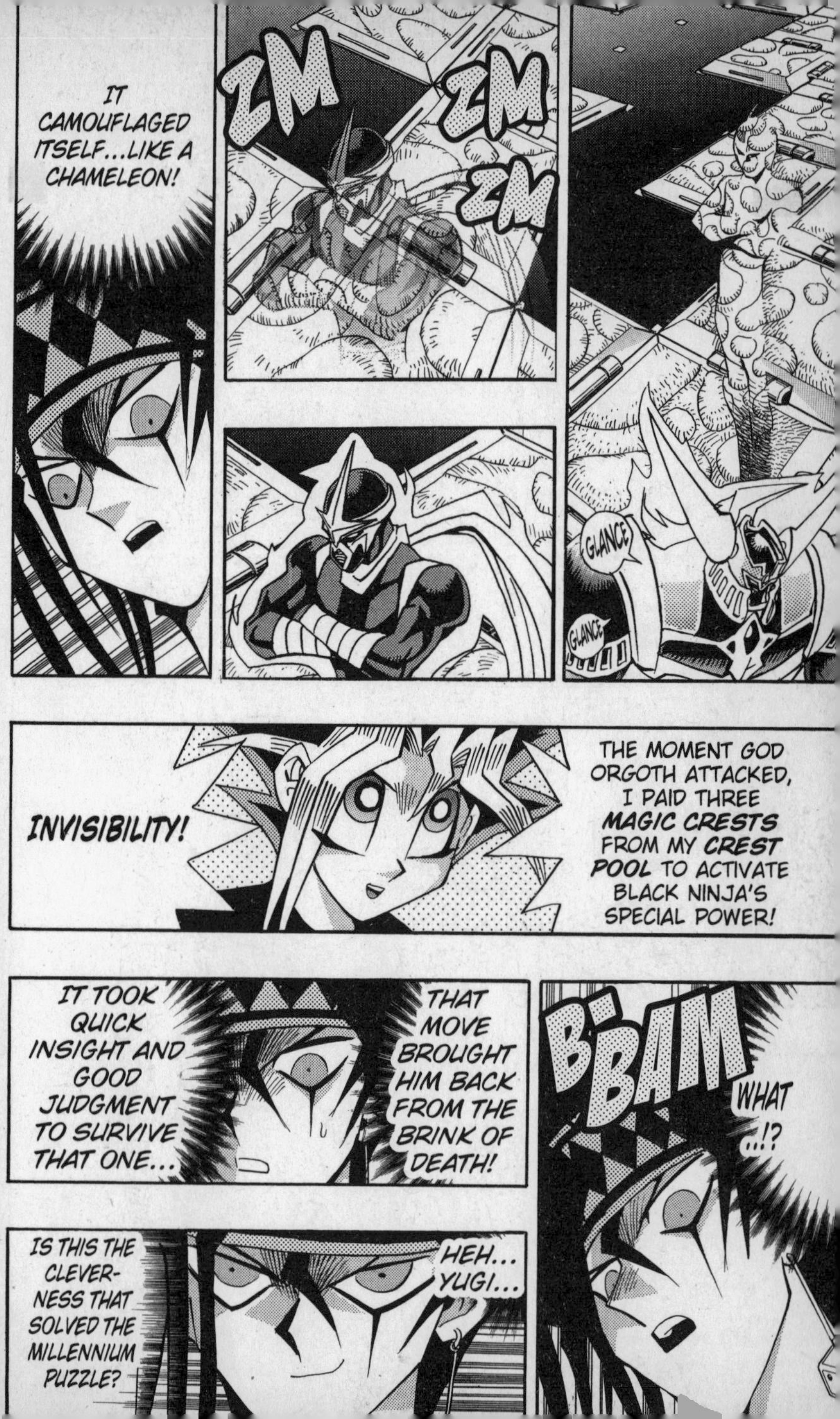
GLANCE
GLANCE
ZM ZM ZM
IT CAMOUFLAGED ITSELF...LIKE A CHAMELEON!
THE MOMENT GOD ORGOTH ATTACKED, I PAID THREE MAGIC CRESTS FROM MY CREST POOL TO ACTIVATE BLACK NINJA'S SPECIAL POWER!
INVISIBILITY!
B-BAM
WHAT ...!?
THAT MOVE BROUGHT HIM BACK FROM THE BRINK OF DEATH!
IT TOOK QUICK INSIGHT AND GOOD JUDGMENT TO SURVIVE THAT ONE...
HEH... YUGI...
IS THIS THE CLEVER-NESS THAT SOLVED THE MILLENNIUM PUZZLE?

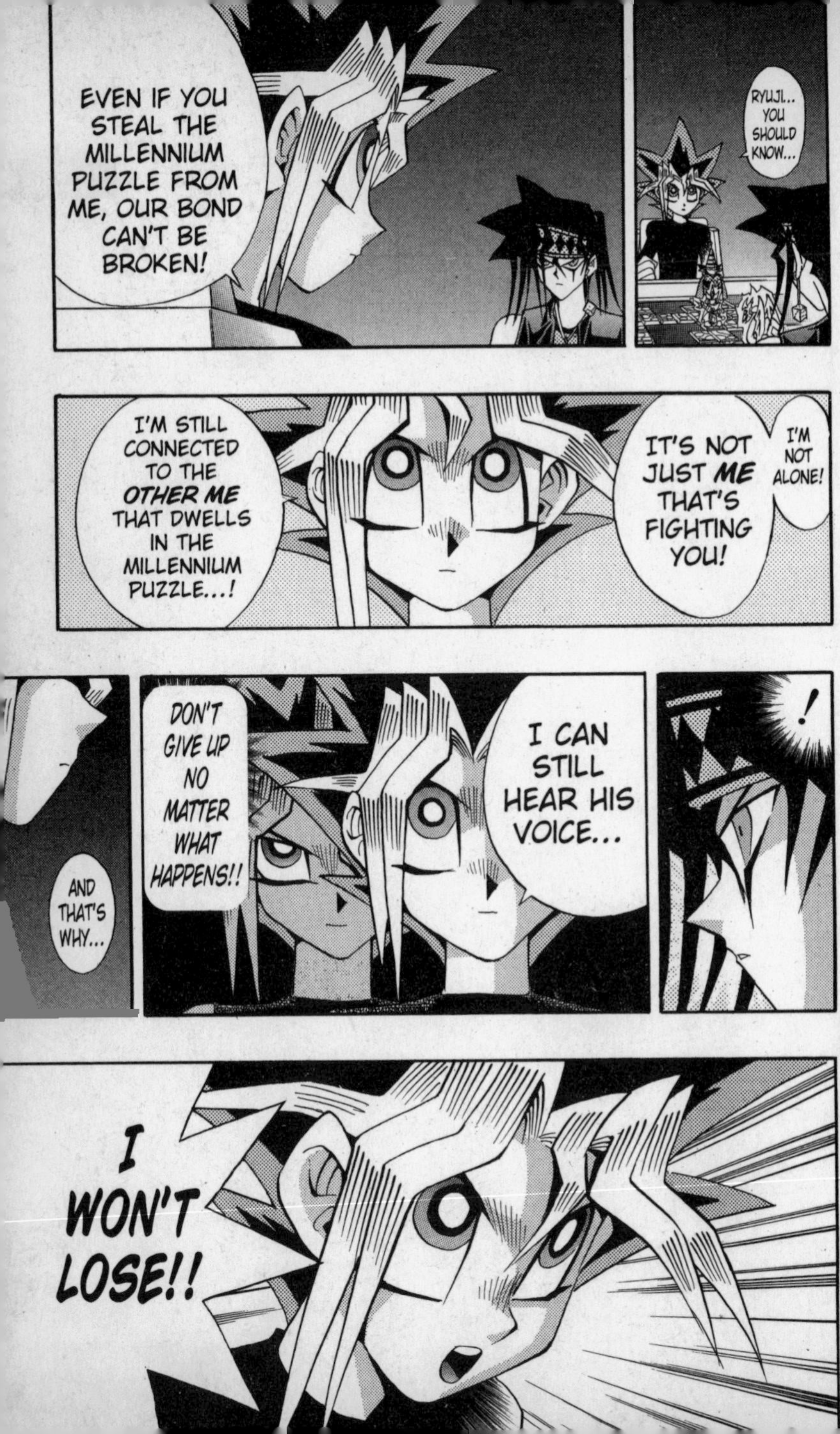
RYUJI... YOU SHOULD KNOW...
EVEN IF YOU STEAL THE MILLENNIUM PUZZLE FROM ME, OUR BOND CAN'T BE BROKEN!
I'M NOT ALONE!
IT'S NOT JUST ME THAT'S FIGHTING YOU!
I'M STILL CONNECTED TO THE OTHER ME THAT DWELLS IN THE MILLENNIUM PUZZLE...!
!
I CAN STILL HEAR HIS VOICE...
DON'T GIVE UP NO MATTER WHAT HAPPENS!!
AND THAT'S WHY...
I WON'T LOSE!!

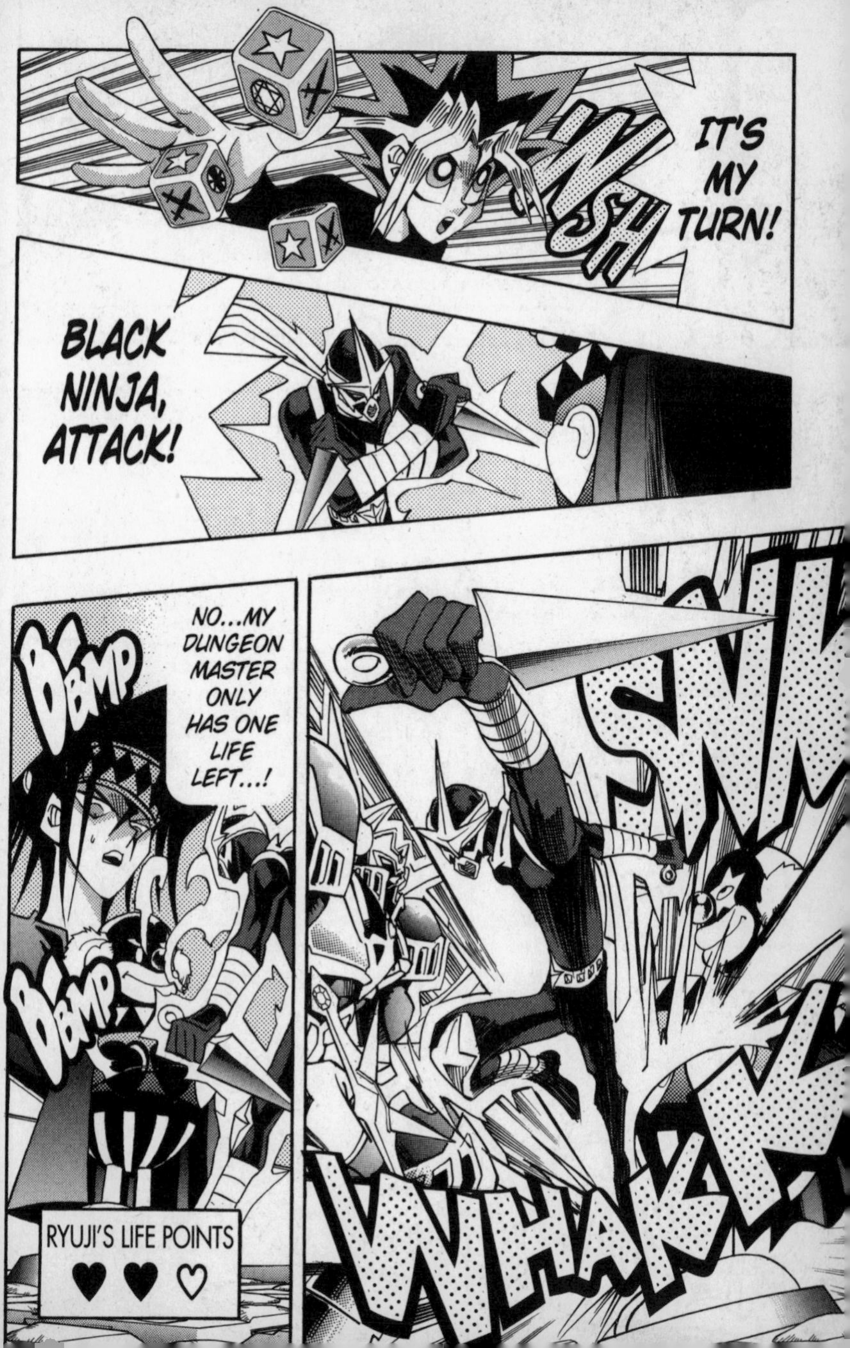
IT'S MY TURN!
WSH
BLACK NINJA, ATTACK!
WHAK
NO...MY DUNGEON MASTER ONLY HAS ONE LIFE LEFT...!
RYUJI'S LIFE POINTS

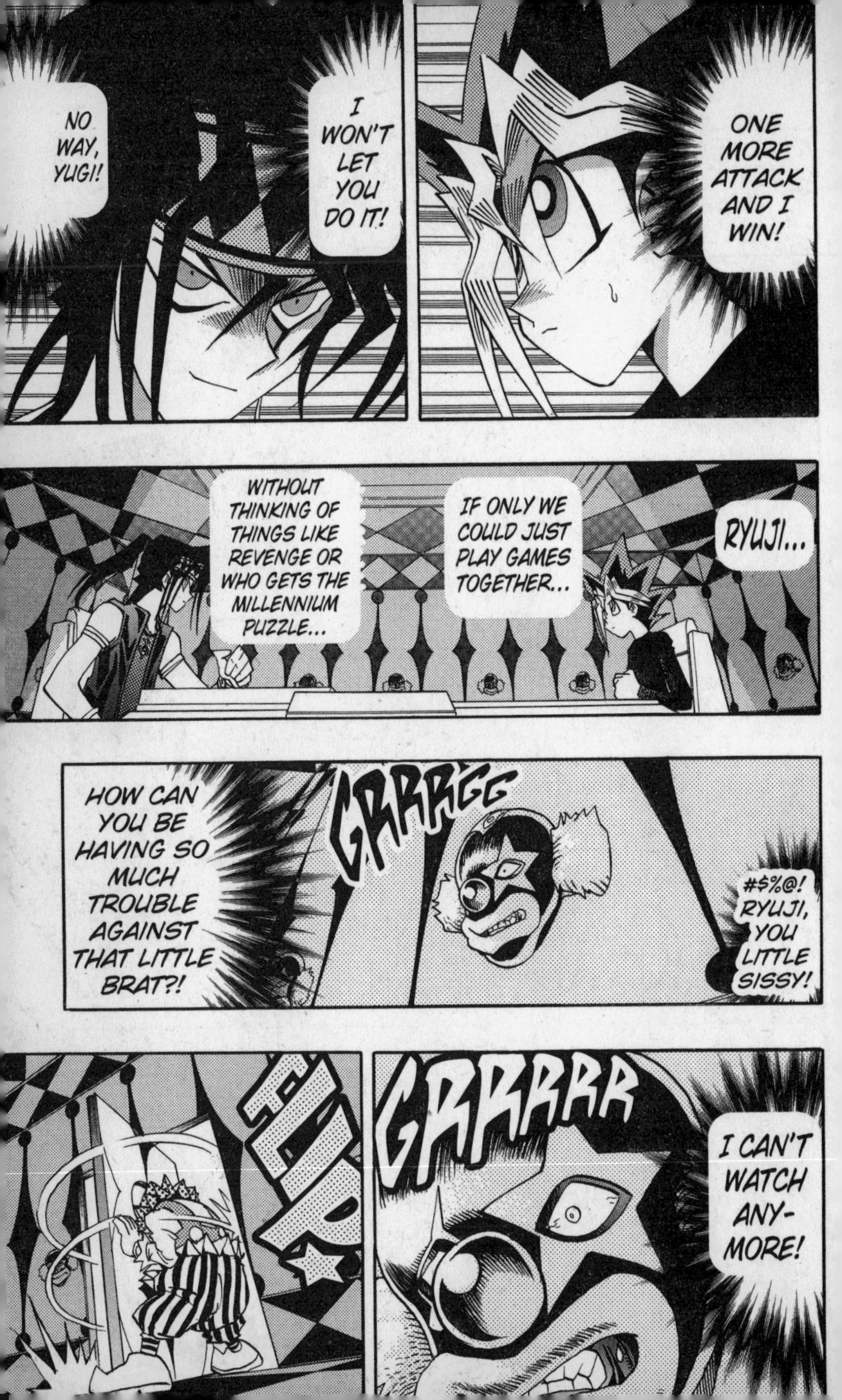
ONE MORE ATTACK AND I WIN!
I WON'T LET YOU DO IT!
NO WAY, YUGI!
RYUJI...
IF ONLY WE COULD JUST PLAY GAMES TOGETHER...
WITHOUT THINKING OF THINGS LIKE REVENGE OR WHO GETS THE MILLENNIUM PUZZLE...
GRRRGG
#$%@! RYUJI, YOU LITTLE SISSY!
HOW CAN YOU BE HAVING SO MUCH TROUBLE AGAINST THAT LITTLE BRAT?!
GRRRRR
I CAN'T WATCH ANY-MORE!

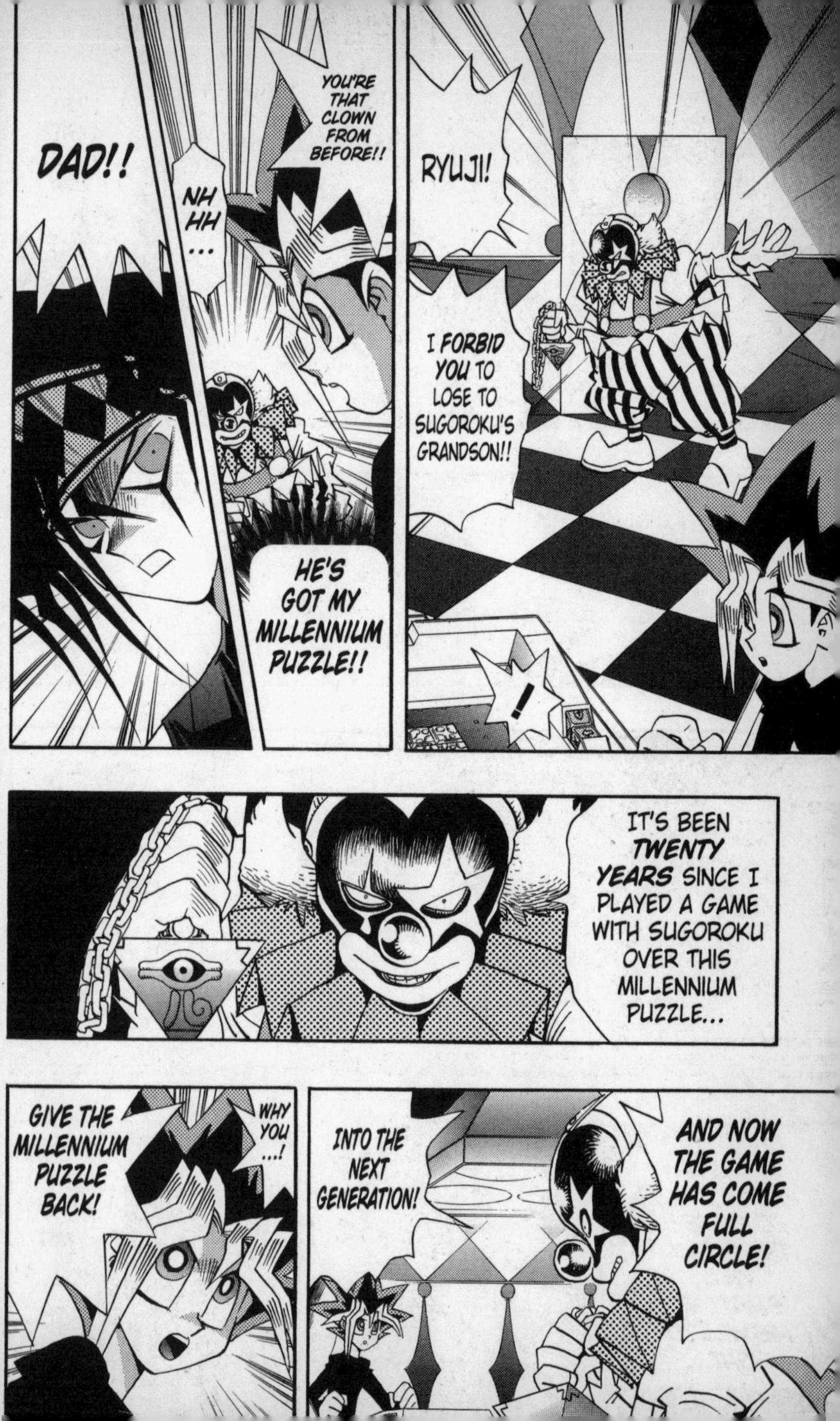
RYUJI!
I FORBID YOU TO LOSE TO SUGOROKU'S GRANDSON!!
!
YOU'RE THAT CLOWN FROM BEFORE!!
NH HH...
HE'S GOT MY MILLENNIUM PUZZLE!!
DAD!!
IT'S BEEN TWENTY YEARS SINCE I PLAYED A GAME WITH SUGOROKU OVER THIS MILLENNIUM PUZZLE...
AND NOW THE GAME HAS COME FULL CIRCLE!
INTO THE NEXT GENERATION!
WHY YOU...!
GIVE THE MILLENNIUM PUZZLE BACK!

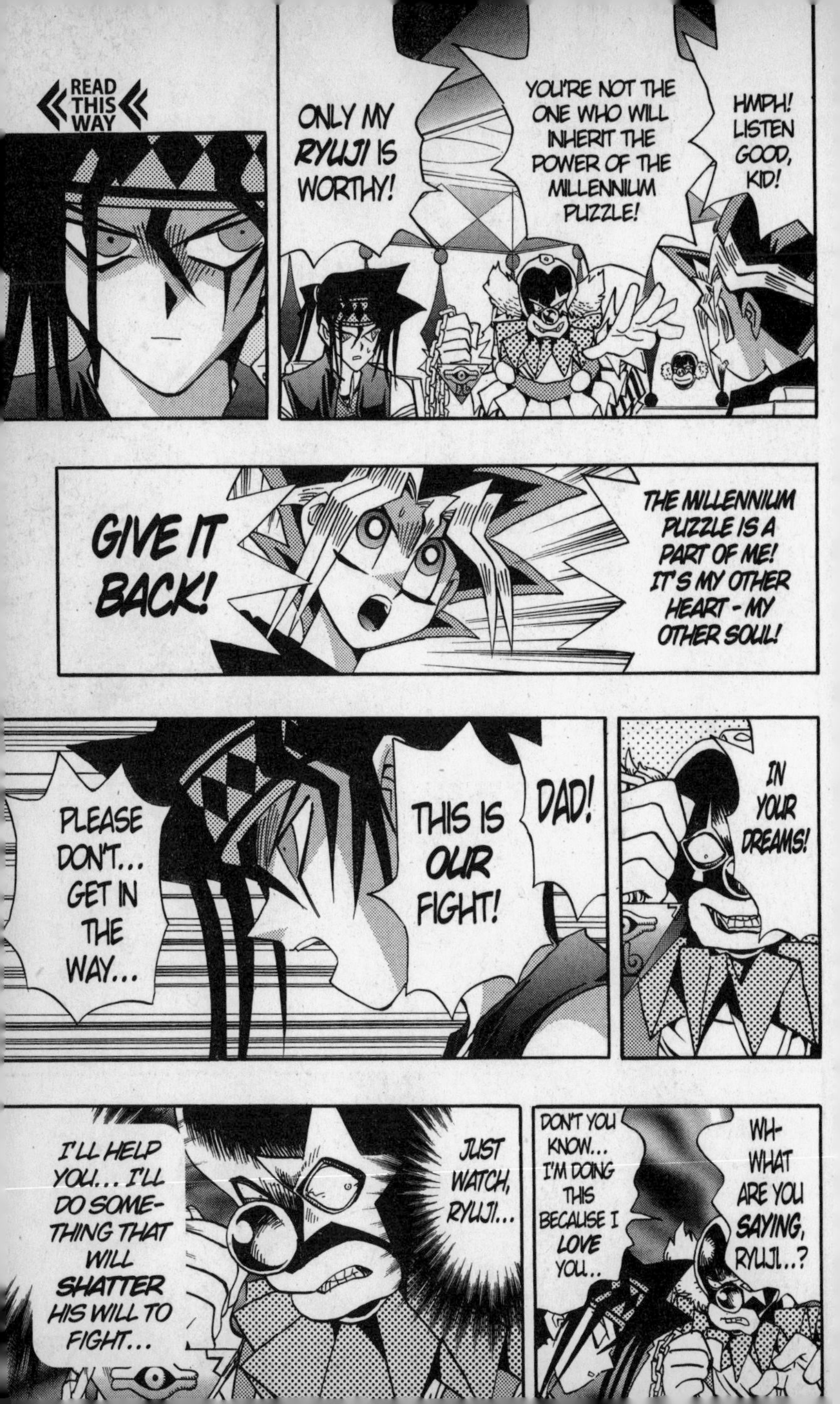
READ THIS WAY
HMPH! LISTEN GOOD, KID!
YOU'RE NOT THE ONE WHO WILL INHERIT THE POWER OF THE MILLENNIUM PUZZLE!
ONLY MY RYUJI IS WORTHY!
THE MILLENNIUM PUZZLE IS A PART OF ME! IT'S MY OTHER HEART - MY OTHER SOUL!
GIVE IT BACK!
IN YOUR DREAMS!
DAD!
THIS IS OUR FIGHT!
PLEASE DON'T... GET IN THE WAY...
WH-WHAT ARE YOU SAYING, RYUJI...?
DON'T YOU KNOW... I'M DOING THIS BECAUSE I LOVE YOU...
JUST WATCH, RYUJI...
I'LL HELP YOU... I'LL DO SOME-THING THAT WILL SHATTER HIS WILL TO FIGHT...

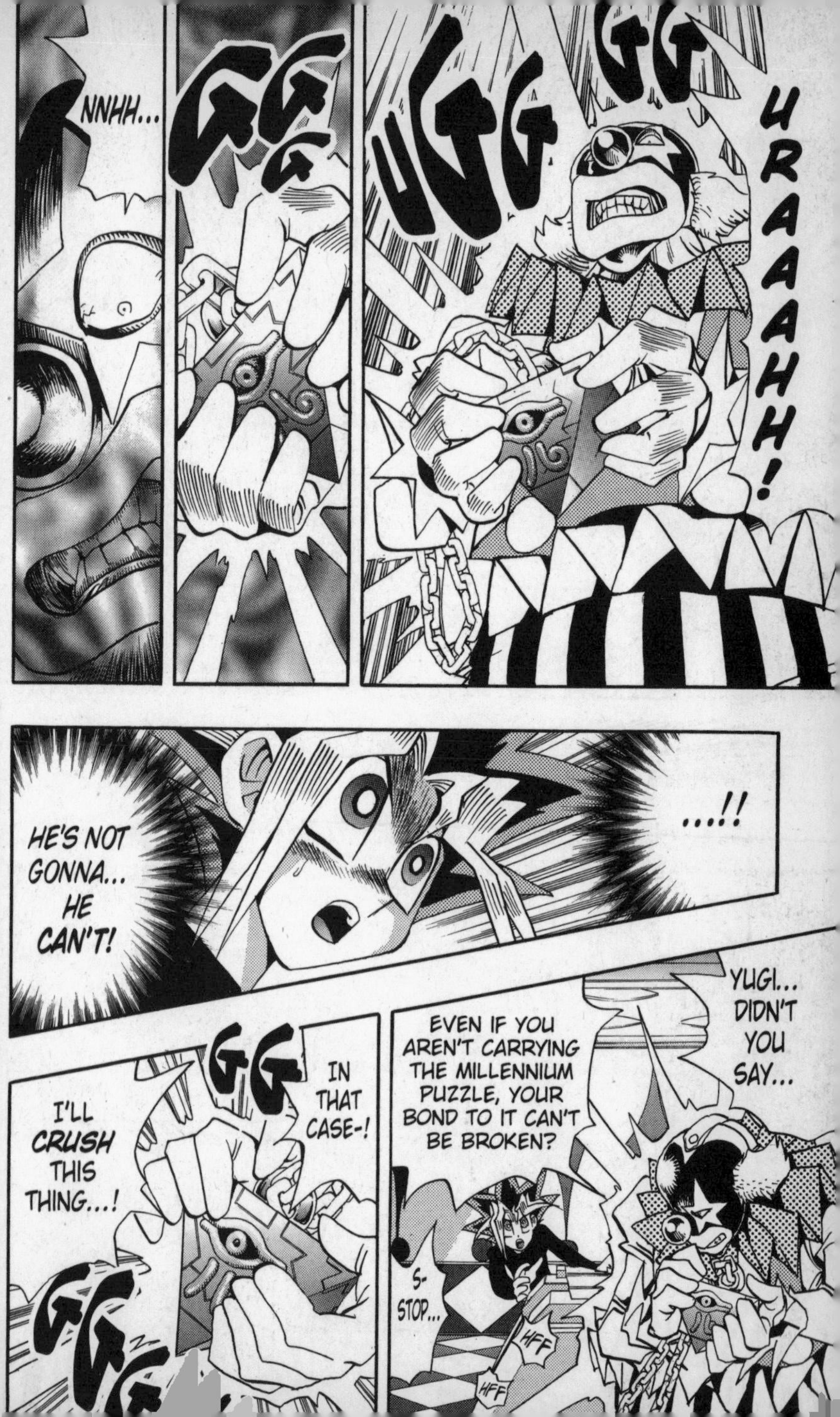
GG
UGG
URAAAAHH!
GGG
NNHH...
...!!
HE'S NOT GONNA... HE CAN'T!
YUGI... DIDN'T YOU SAY...
EVEN IF YOU AREN'T CARRYING THE MILLENNIUM PUZZLE, YOUR BOND TO IT CAN'T BE BROKEN?
S-STOP...
HFF
HFF
GG
IN THAT CASE-!
I'LL CRUSH THIS THING...!
GGG

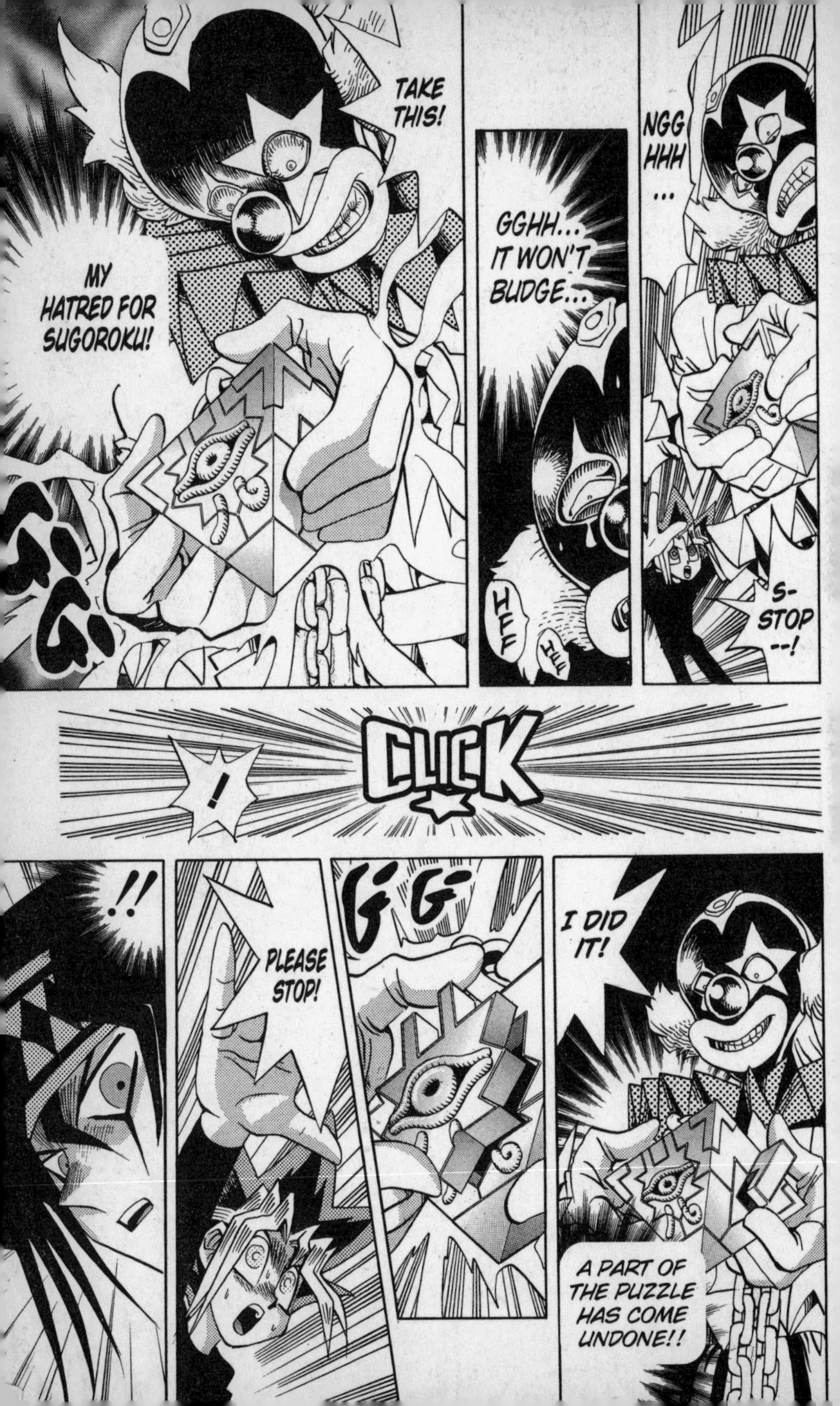
TAKE THIS!
MY HATRED FOR SUGOROKU!
GG
GGHH... IT WON'T BUDGE...
HEF
HEF
NGG HHH ...
S-STOP --!
!
CLICK
!!
PLEASE STOP!
GG
I DID IT!
A PART OF THE PUZZLE HAS COME UNDONE!!

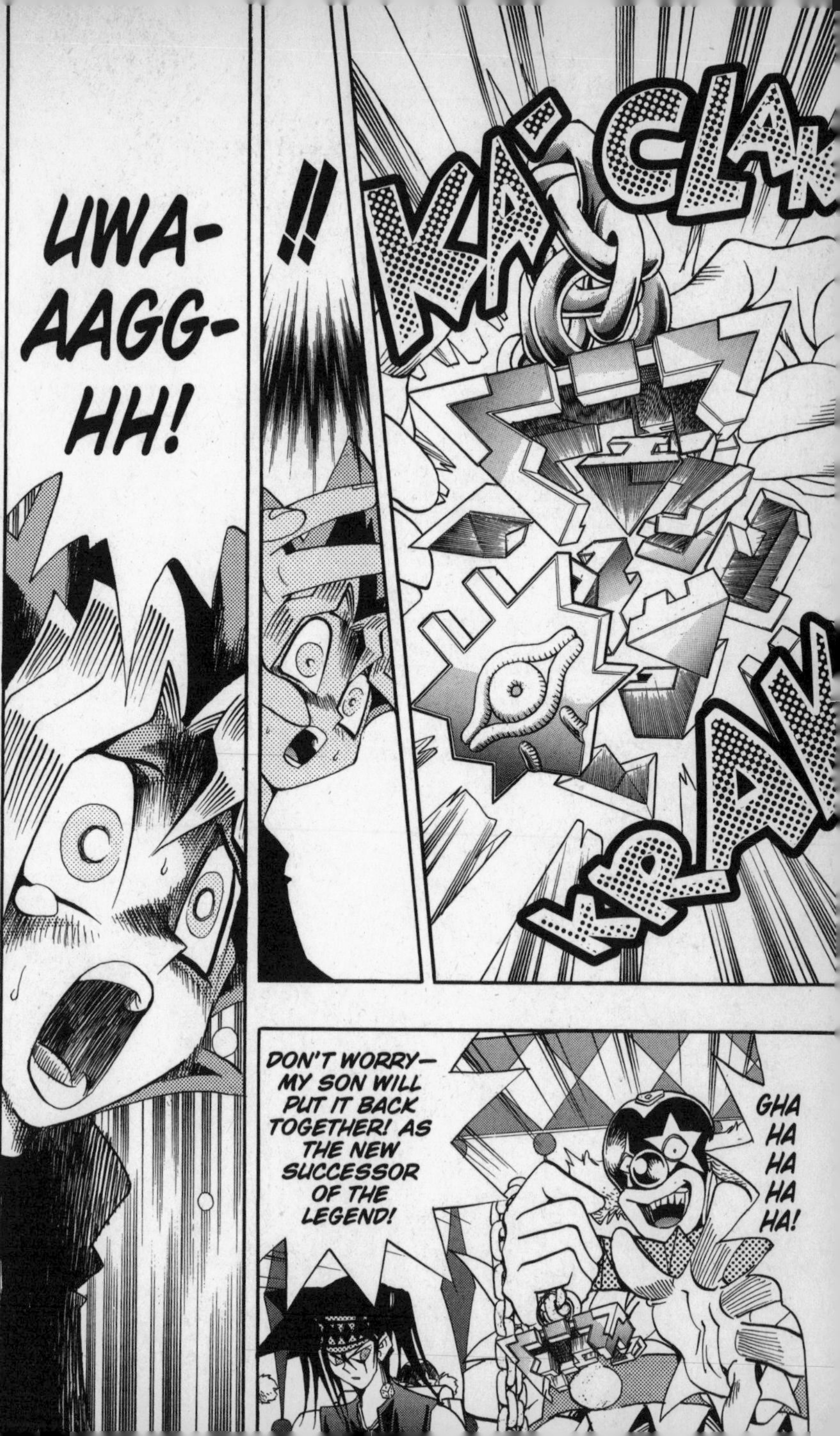
KA-CLAK
KRAK
!!
DON'T WORRY— MY SON WILL PUT IT BACK TOGETHER! AS THE NEW SUCCESSOR OF THE LEGEND!
GHA HA HA HA HA!
UWA-AAGG-HH!

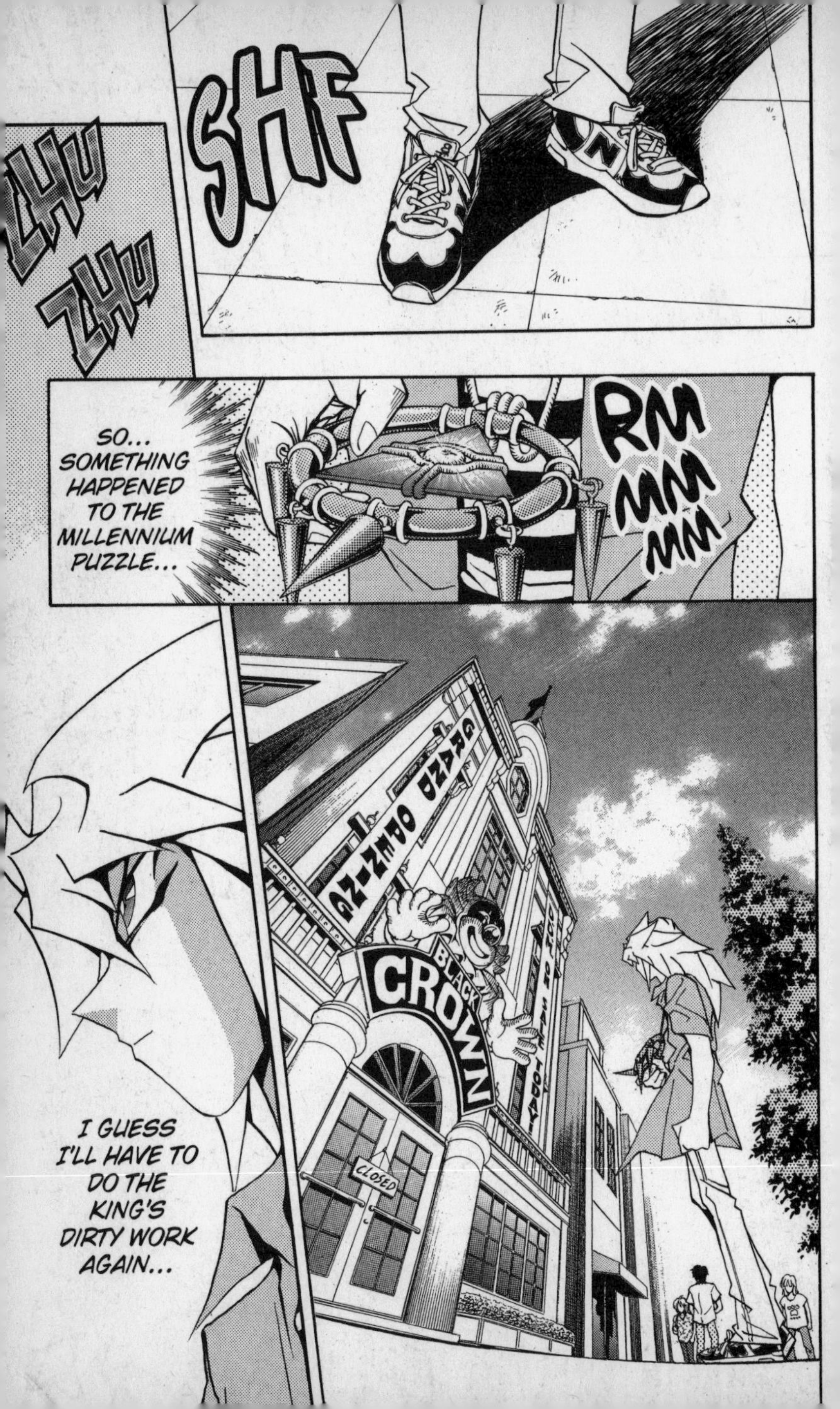
SHF
ZHU ZHU
RM MM MM
SO... SOMETHING HAPPENED TO THE MILLENNIUM PUZZLE...
GRAND OPENING
BLACK CROWN
ON SALE TODAY!
CLOSED
I GUESS I'LL HAVE TO DO THE KING'S DIRTY WORK AGAIN...

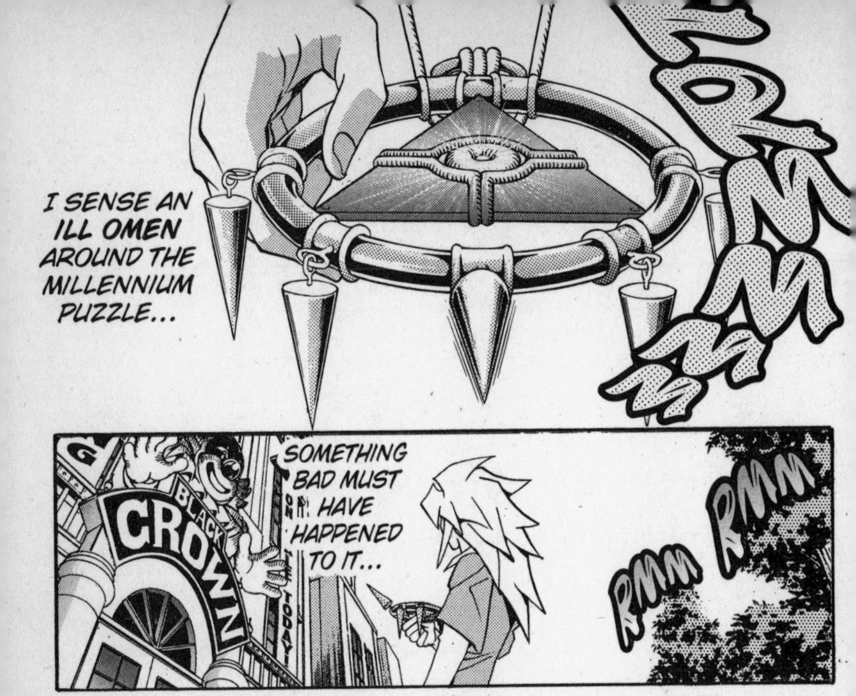
I SENSE AN ILL OMEN AROUND THE MILLENNIUM PUZZLE...
RMM RMM
SOMETHING BAD MUST HAVE HAPPENED TO IT...
BLACK CROWN

Duel 82: The Calling of the Powers

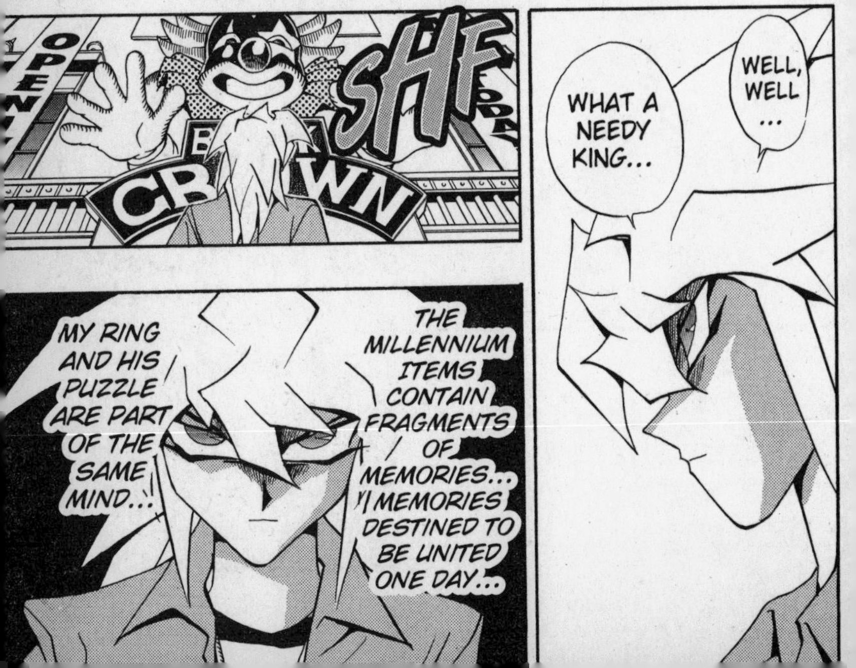
WELL, WELL ...
WHAT A NEEDY KING...
SHF
CROWN
OPEN
THE MILLENNIUM ITEMS CONTAIN FRAGMENTS OF MEMORIES... MEMORIES DESTINED TO BE UNITED ONE DAY...
MY RING AND HIS PUZZLE ARE PART OF THE SAME MIND...

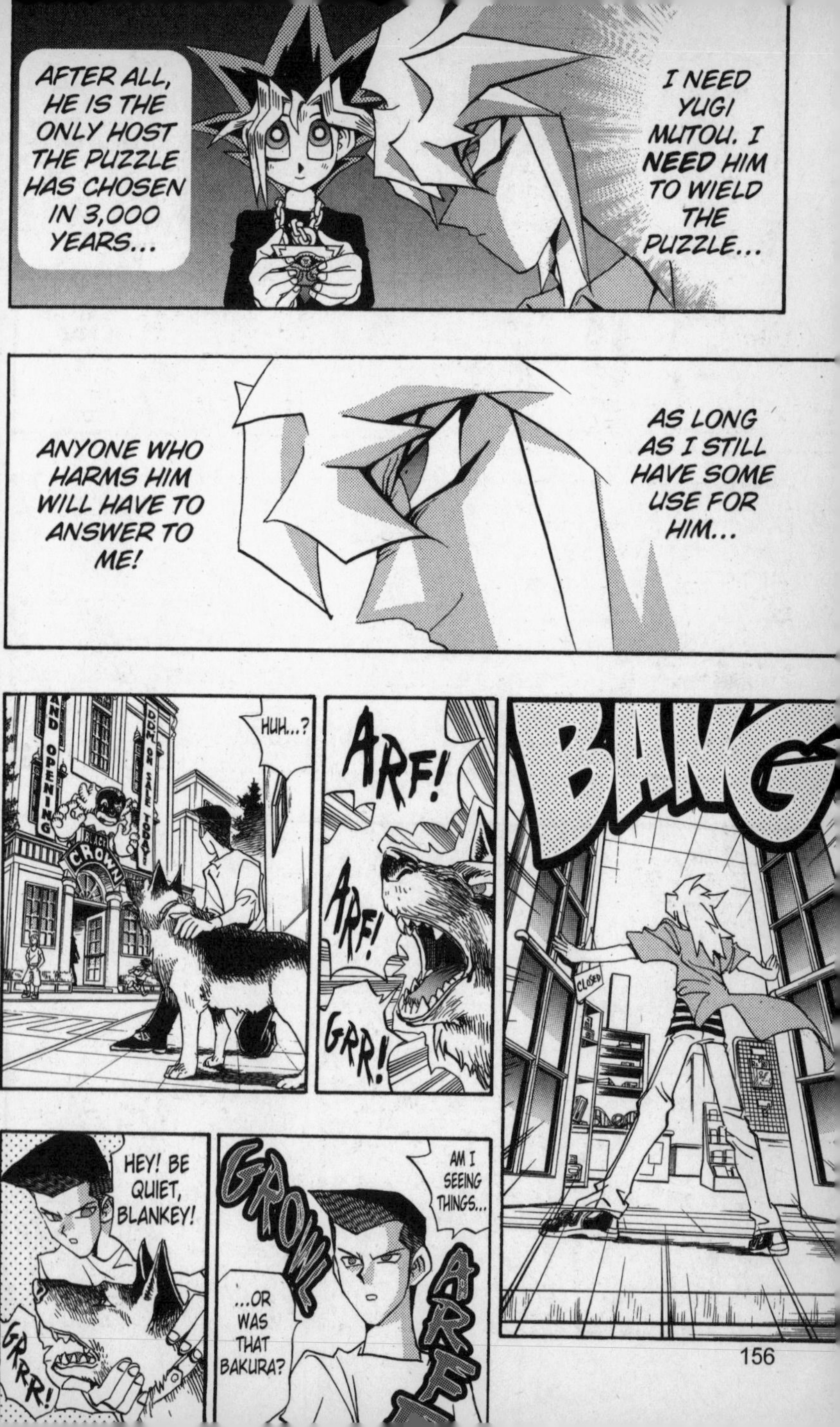
I NEED YUGI MUTOU. I NEED HIM TO WIELD THE PUZZLE...
AFTER ALL, HE IS THE ONLY HOST THE PUZZLE HAS CHOSEN IN 3,000 YEARS...
AS LONG AS I STILL HAVE SOME USE FOR HIM...
ANYONE WHO HARMS HIM WILL HAVE TO ANSWER TO ME!
BANG
CLOSED
ARF!
ARF!
GRR!
HUH...?
AND OPENING
D.D.M. ON SALE TODAY!
BLACK
CROWN
AM I SEEING THINGS...
...OR WAS THAT BAKURA?
GROWL
ARF
HEY! BE QUIET, BLANKEY!
GRRRR!

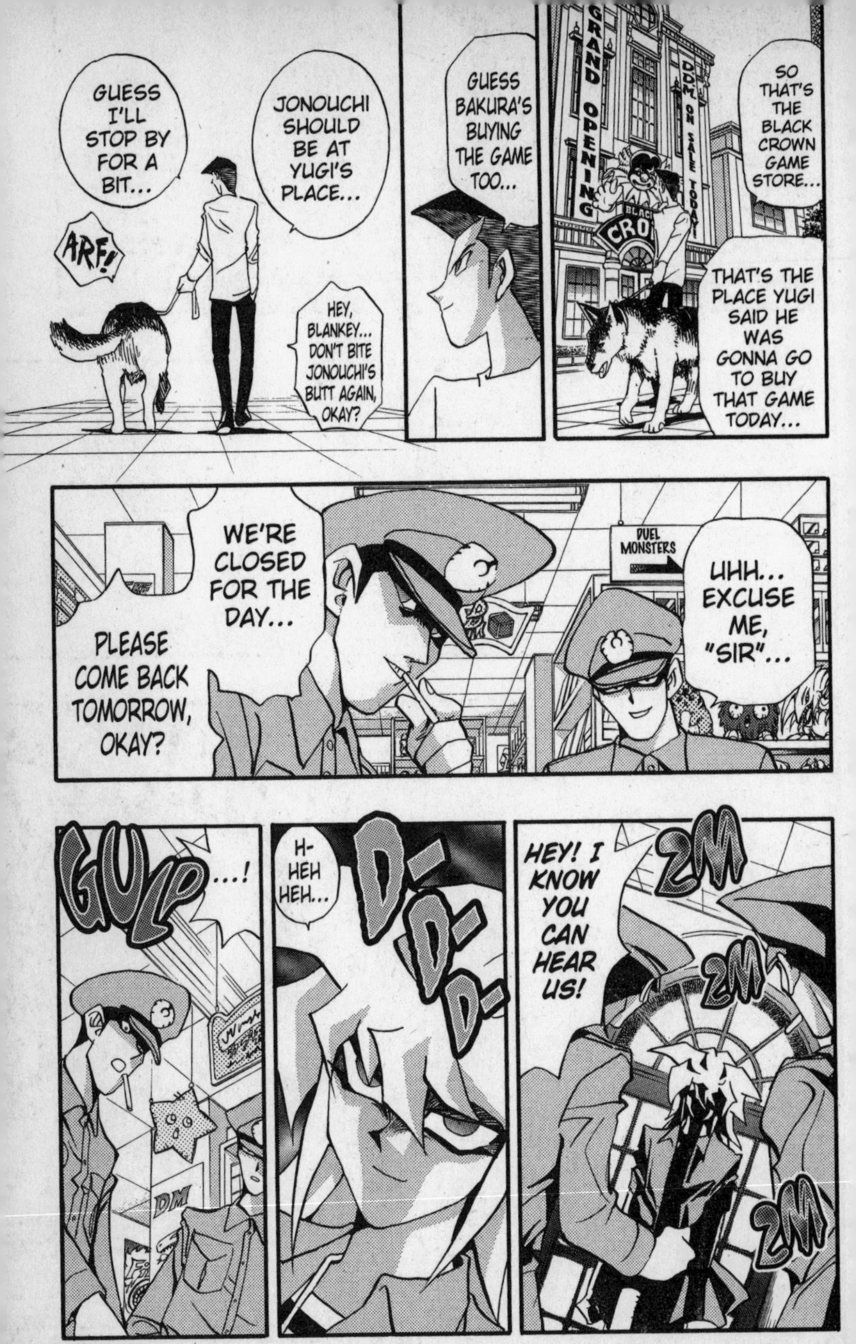
GRAND OPENING
DDM ON SALE TODAY!
SO THAT'S THE BLACK CROWN GAME STORE...
THAT'S THE PLACE YUGI SAID HE WAS GONNA GO TO BUY THAT GAME TODAY...
GUESS BAKURA'S BUYING THE GAME TOO...
JONOUCHI SHOULD BE AT YUGI'S PLACE...
GUESS I'LL STOP BY FOR A BIT...
HEY, BLANKEY... DON'T BITE JONOUCHI'S BUTT AGAIN, OKAY?
ARF!
DUEL MONSTERS
UHH... EXCUSE ME, "SIR"...
WE'RE CLOSED FOR THE DAY...
PLEASE COME BACK TOMORROW, OKAY?
HEY! I KNOW YOU CAN HEAR US!
ZM
ZM
ZM
H-HEH HEH...
D-D-D-
GULP...!
DM

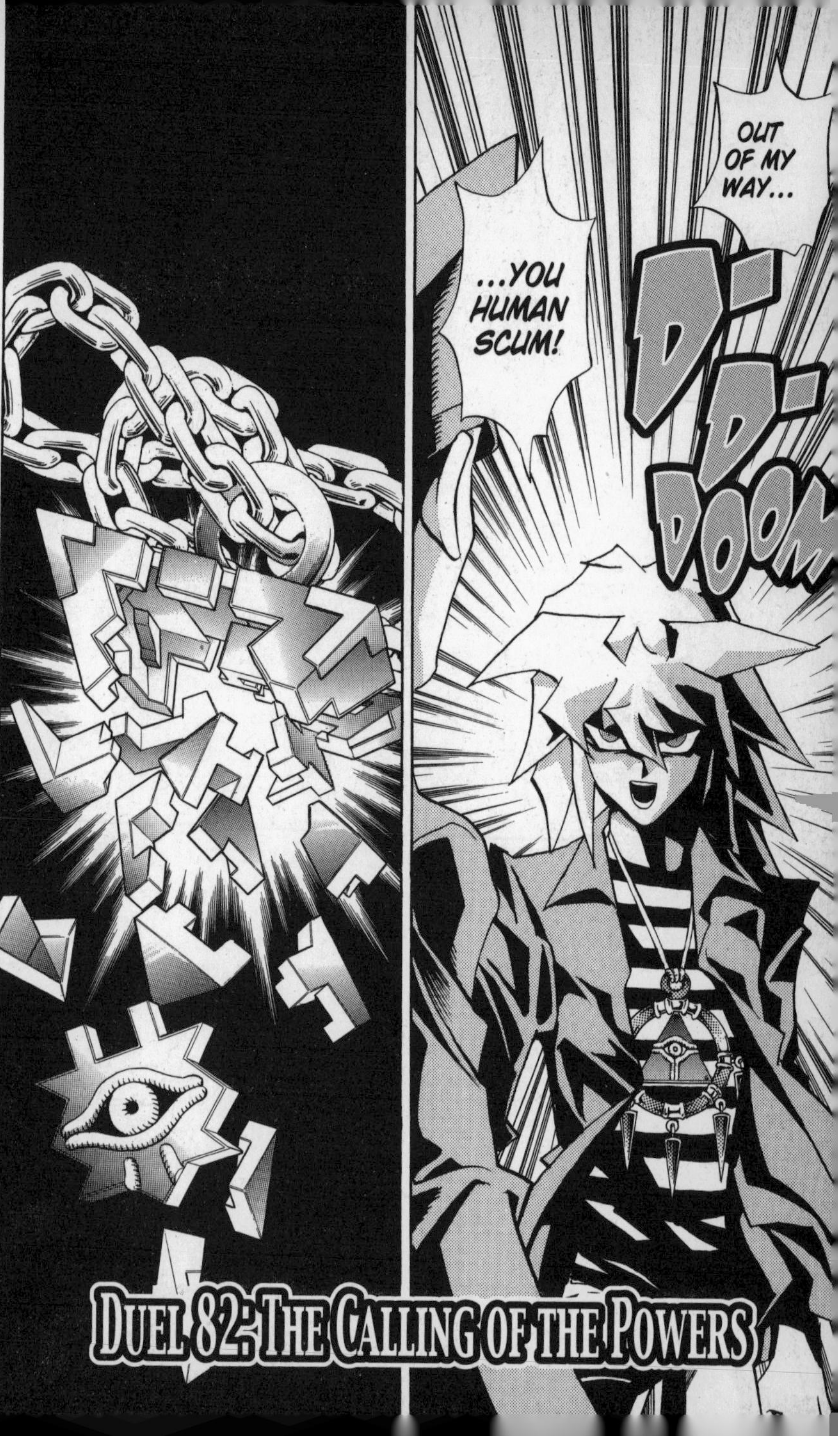
OUT OF MY WAY...
...YOU HUMAN SCUM!
D-D-DOOM

Duel 82: The Calling of the Powers

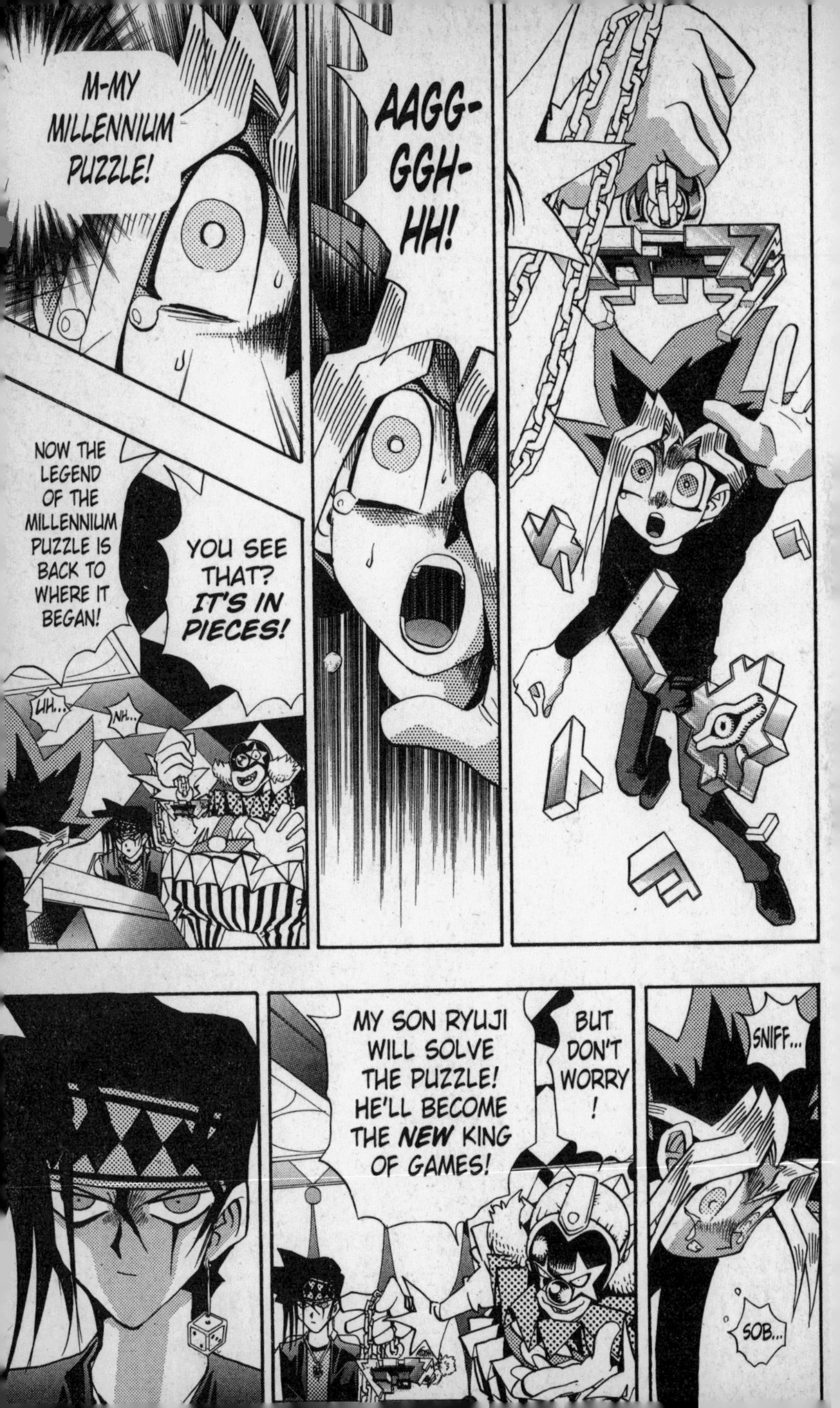
AAGG-GGH-HH!
M-MY MILLENNIUM PUZZLE!
YOU SEE THAT? IT'S IN PIECES!
NOW THE LEGEND OF THE MILLENNIUM PUZZLE IS BACK TO WHERE IT BEGAN!
NH...
UH...
SNIFF...
SOB...
BUT DON'T WORRY!
MY SON RYUJI WILL SOLVE THE PUZZLE! HE'LL BECOME THE NEW KING OF GAMES!

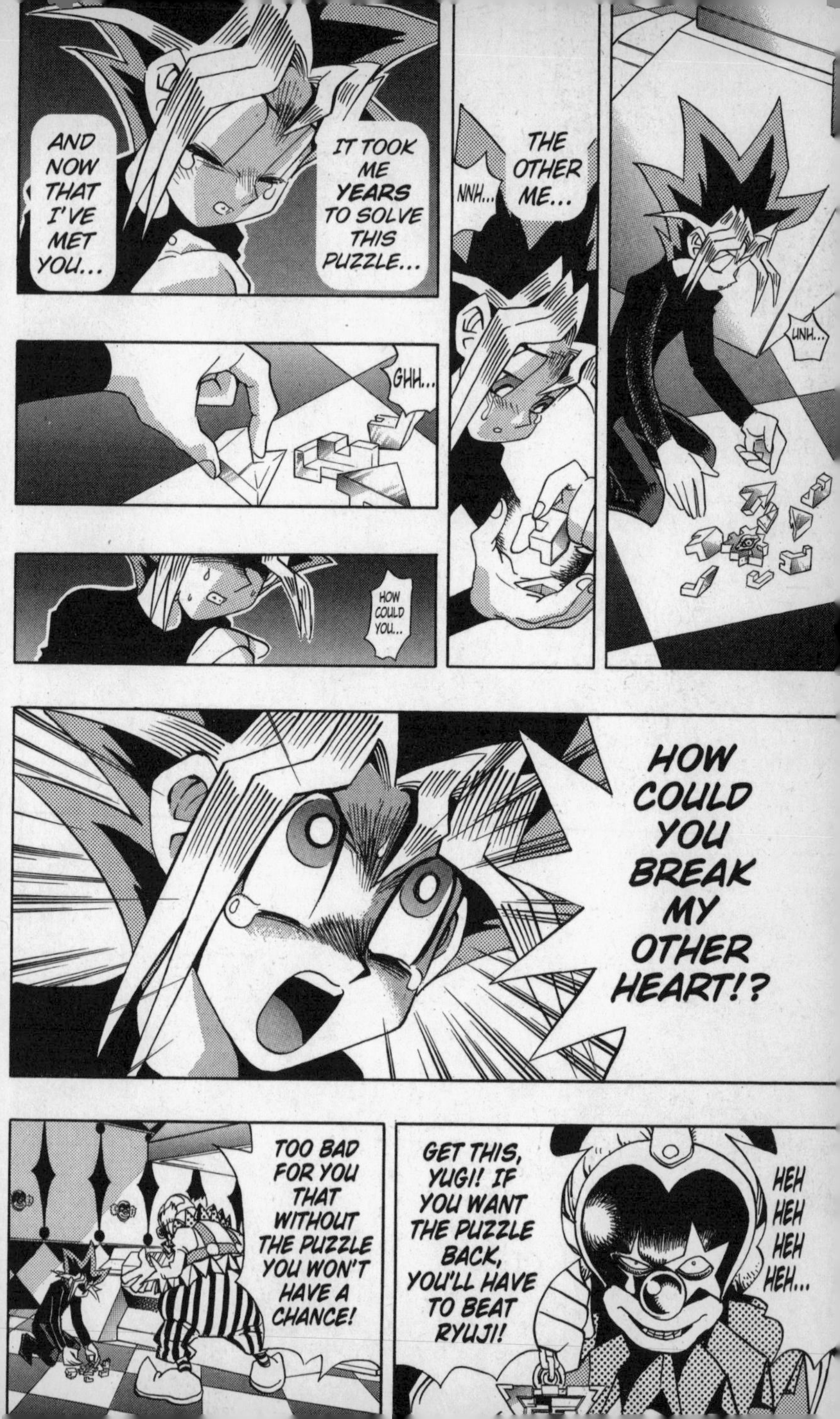
UNH...
THE OTHER ME...
NNH...
IT TOOK ME YEARS TO SOLVE THIS PUZZLE...
AND NOW THAT I'VE MET YOU...
GHH...
HOW COULD YOU...
HOW COULD YOU BREAK MY OTHER HEART!?
HEH HEH HEH HEH...
GET THIS, YUGI! IF YOU WANT THE PUZZLE BACK, YOU'LL HAVE TO BEAT RYUJI!
TOO BAD FOR YOU THAT WITHOUT THE PUZZLE YOU WON'T HAVE A CHANCE!

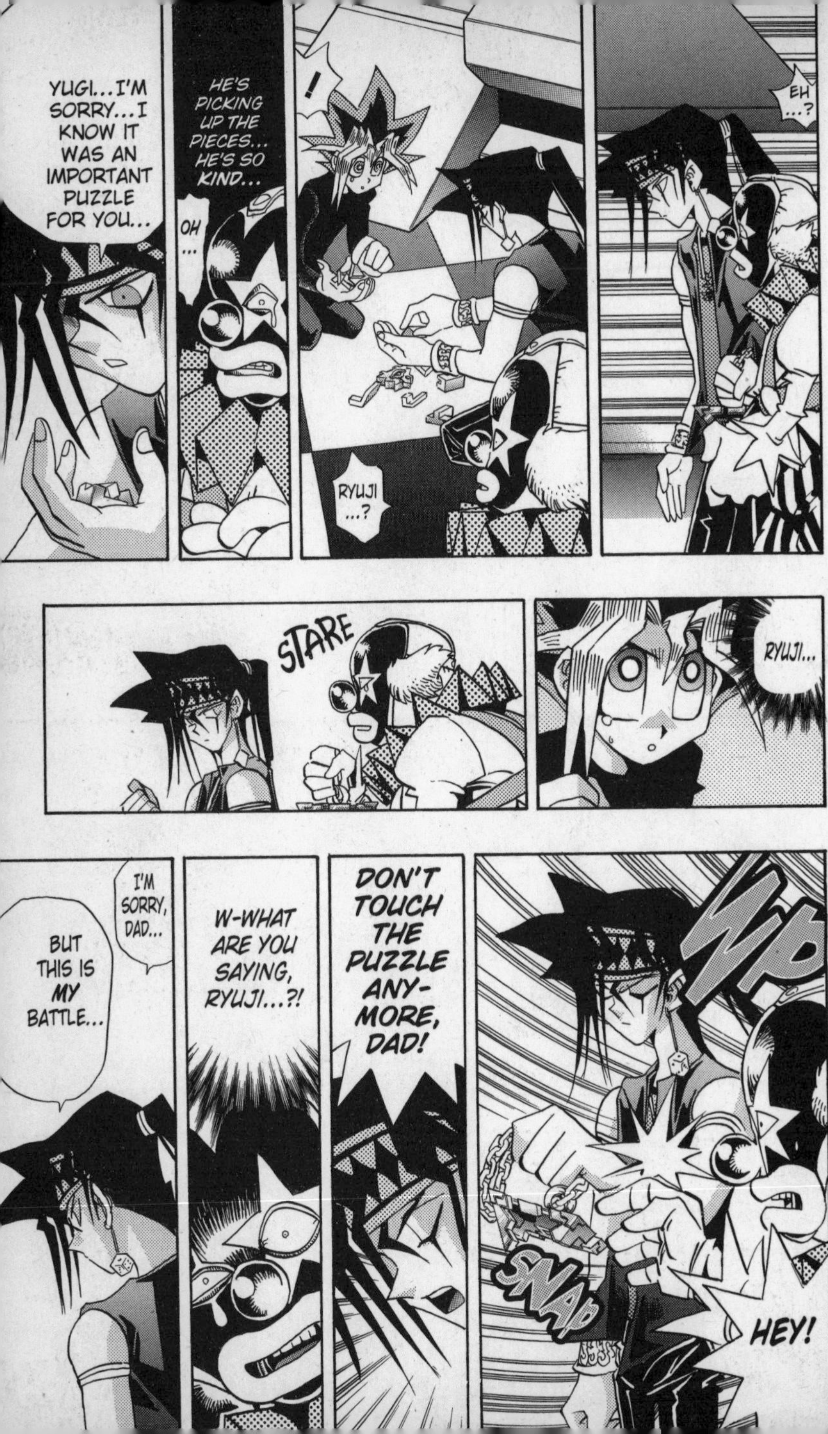
EH ...?
!
RYUJI ...?
HE'S PICKING UP THE PIECES... HE'S SO KIND...
OH ...
YUGI...I'M SORRY...I KNOW IT WAS AN IMPORTANT PUZZLE FOR YOU...
RYUJI...
STARE
SNAP
HEY!
DON'T TOUCH THE PUZZLE ANY-MORE, DAD!
W-WHAT ARE YOU SAYING, RYUJI...?!
I'M SORRY, DAD...
BUT THIS IS MY BATTLE...

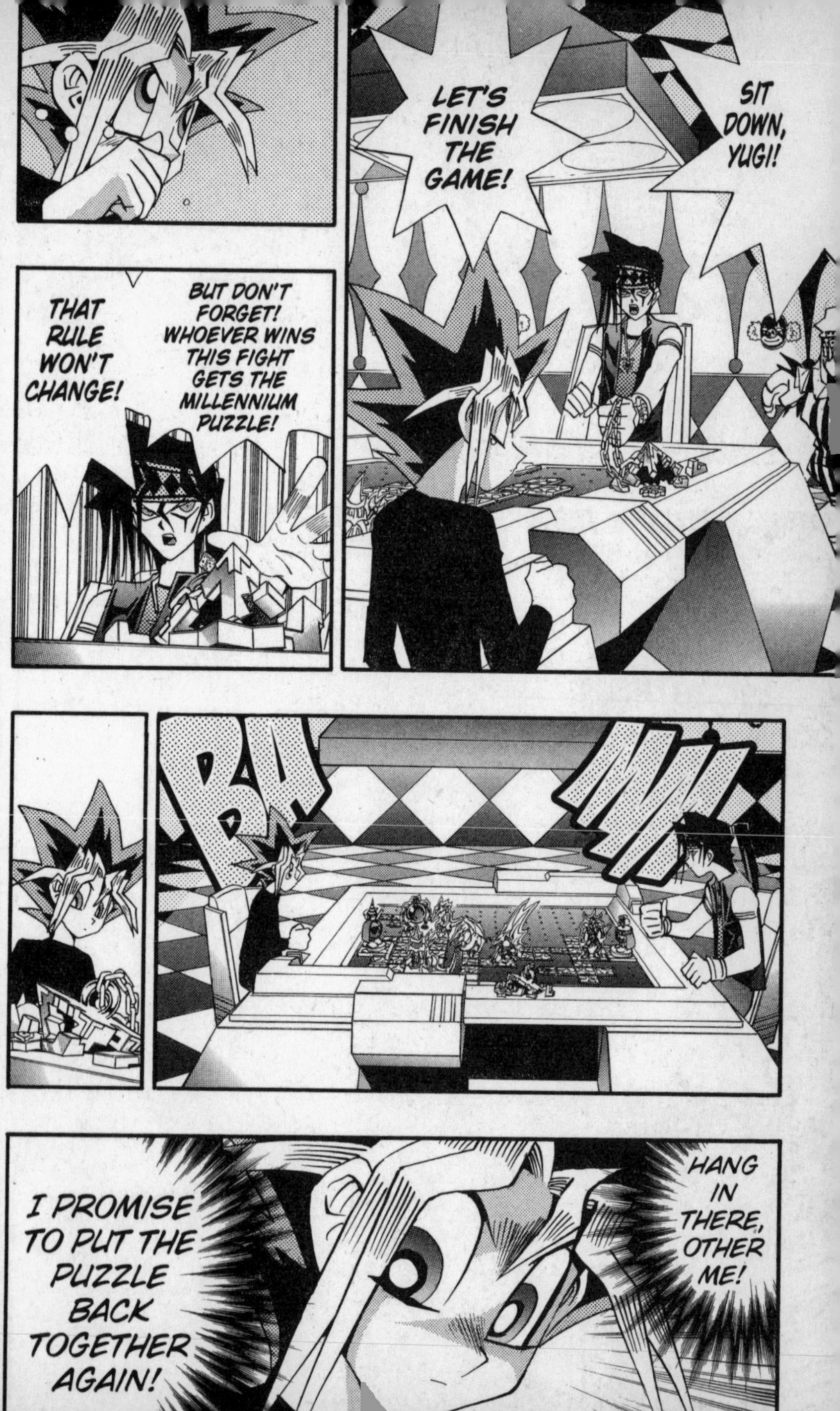
SIT DOWN, YUGI!
LET'S FINISH THE GAME!
BUT DON'T FORGET! WHOEVER WINS THIS FIGHT GETS THE MILLENNIUM PUZZLE!
THAT RULE WON'T CHANGE!
BAMM
HANG IN THERE, OTHER ME!
I PROMISE TO PUT THE PUZZLE BACK TOGETHER AGAIN!

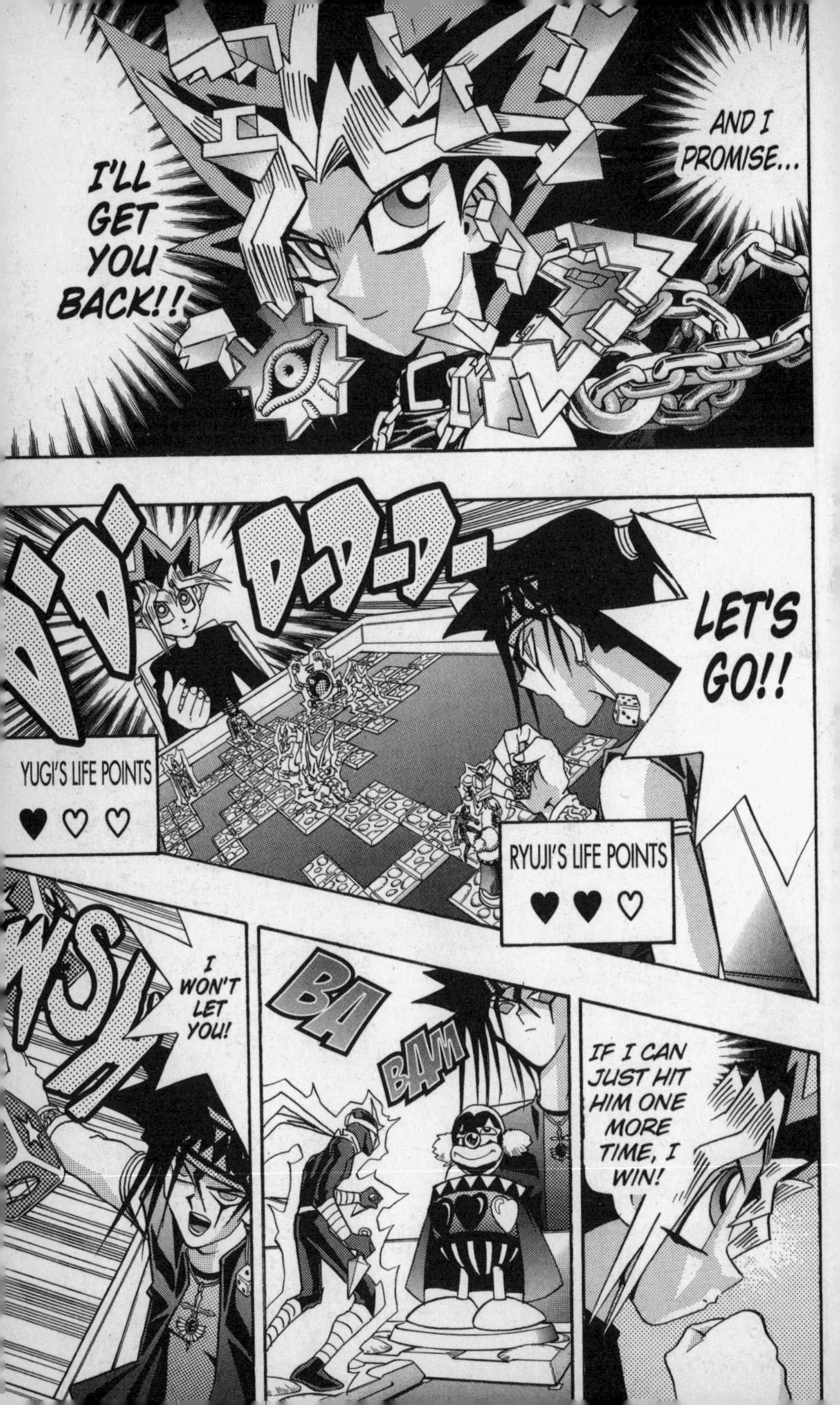
AND I PROMISE...
I'LL GET YOU BACK!!
LET'S GO!!
D..D..D..
RYUJI'S LIFE POINTS
YUGI'S LIFE POINTS
IF I CAN JUST HIT HIM ONE MORE TIME, I WIN!
BA
BAM
I WON'T LET YOU!

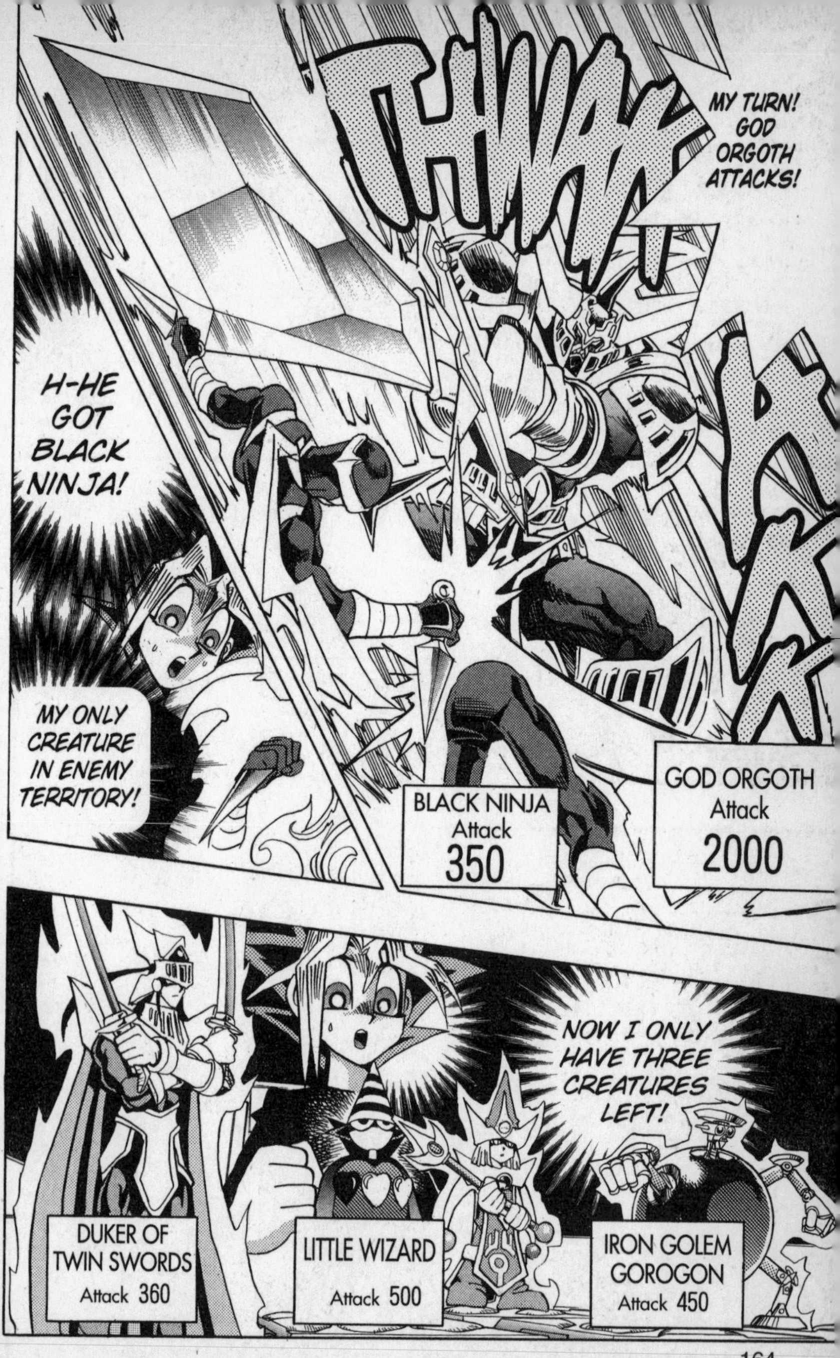
THWAK
MY TURN! GOD ORGOTH ATTACKS!
H-HE GOT BLACK NINJA!
GOD ORGOTH Attack 2000
BLACK NINJA Attack 350
MY ONLY CREATURE IN ENEMY TERRITORY!
NOW I ONLY HAVE THREE CREATURES LEFT!
IRON GOLEM GOROGON Attack 450
LITTLE WIZARD Attack 500
DUKER OF TWIN SWORDS Attack 360

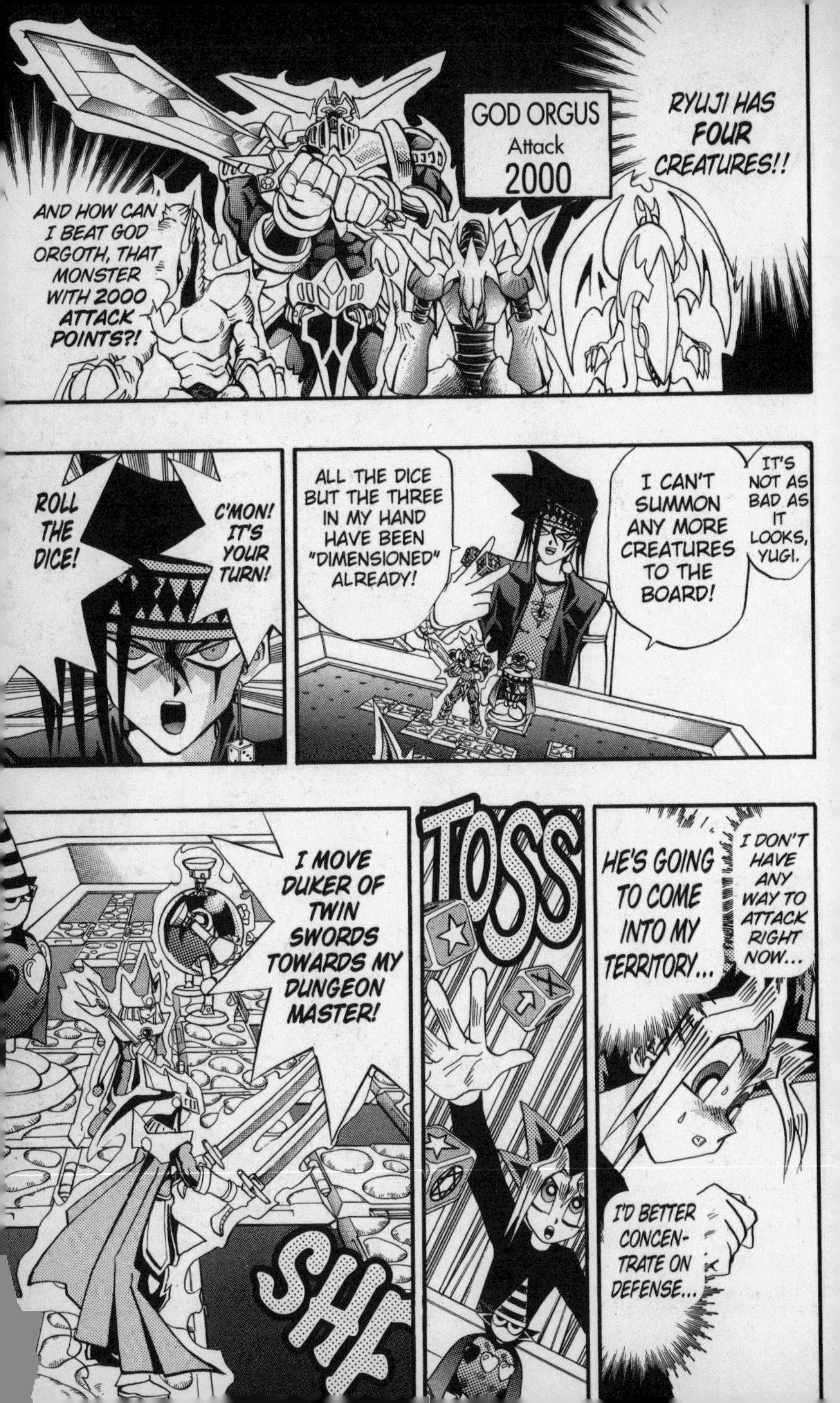
RYUJI HAS FOUR CREATURES!!
GOD ORGUS
Attack
2000
AND HOW CAN I BEAT GOD ORGOTH, THAT MONSTER WITH 2000 ATTACK POINTS?!
IT'S NOT AS BAD AS IT LOOKS, YUGI.
I CAN'T SUMMON ANY MORE CREATURES TO THE BOARD!
ALL THE DICE BUT THE THREE IN MY HAND HAVE BEEN "DIMENSIONED" ALREADY!
C'MON! IT'S YOUR TURN!
ROLL THE DICE!
I DON'T HAVE ANY WAY TO ATTACK RIGHT NOW...
HE'S GOING TO COME INTO MY TERRITORY...
I'D BETTER CONCEN-TRATE ON DEFENSE...
TOSS
I MOVE DUKER OF TWIN SWORDS TOWARDS MY DUNGEON MASTER!
SHF

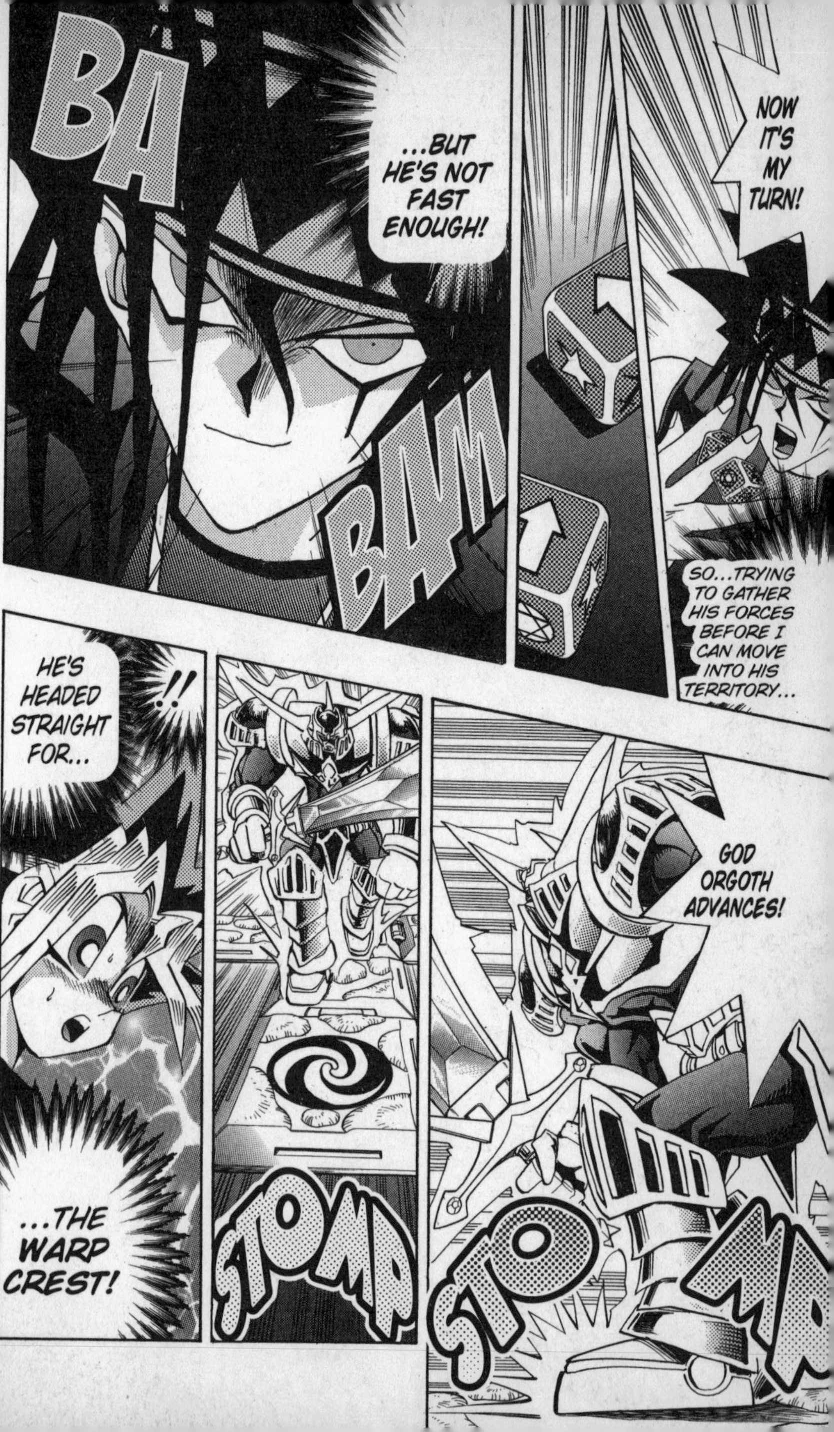
NOW IT'S MY TURN!
SO...TRYING TO GATHER HIS FORCES BEFORE I CAN MOVE INTO HIS TERRITORY...
BA
...BUT HE'S NOT FAST ENOUGH!
BAM
GOD ORGOTH ADVANCES!
STOMP
STOMP
!!
HE'S HEADED STRAIGHT FOR...
...THE WARP CREST!

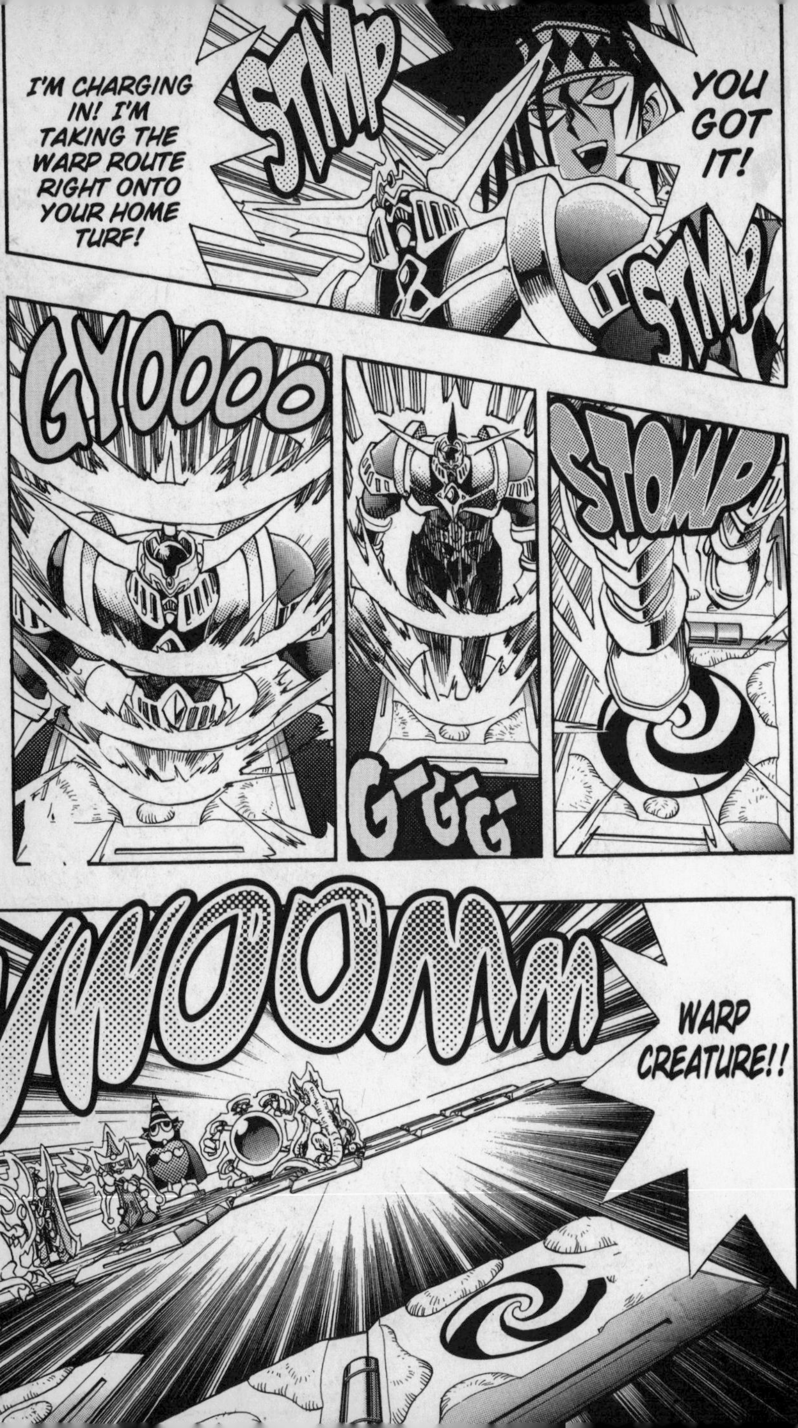
YOU GOT IT!
STMP
I'M CHARGING IN! I'M TAKING THE WARP ROUTE RIGHT ONTO YOUR HOME TURF!
STMP
STOMP
G-G-G
GYOOOO
WARP CREATURE!!
VWOOMM

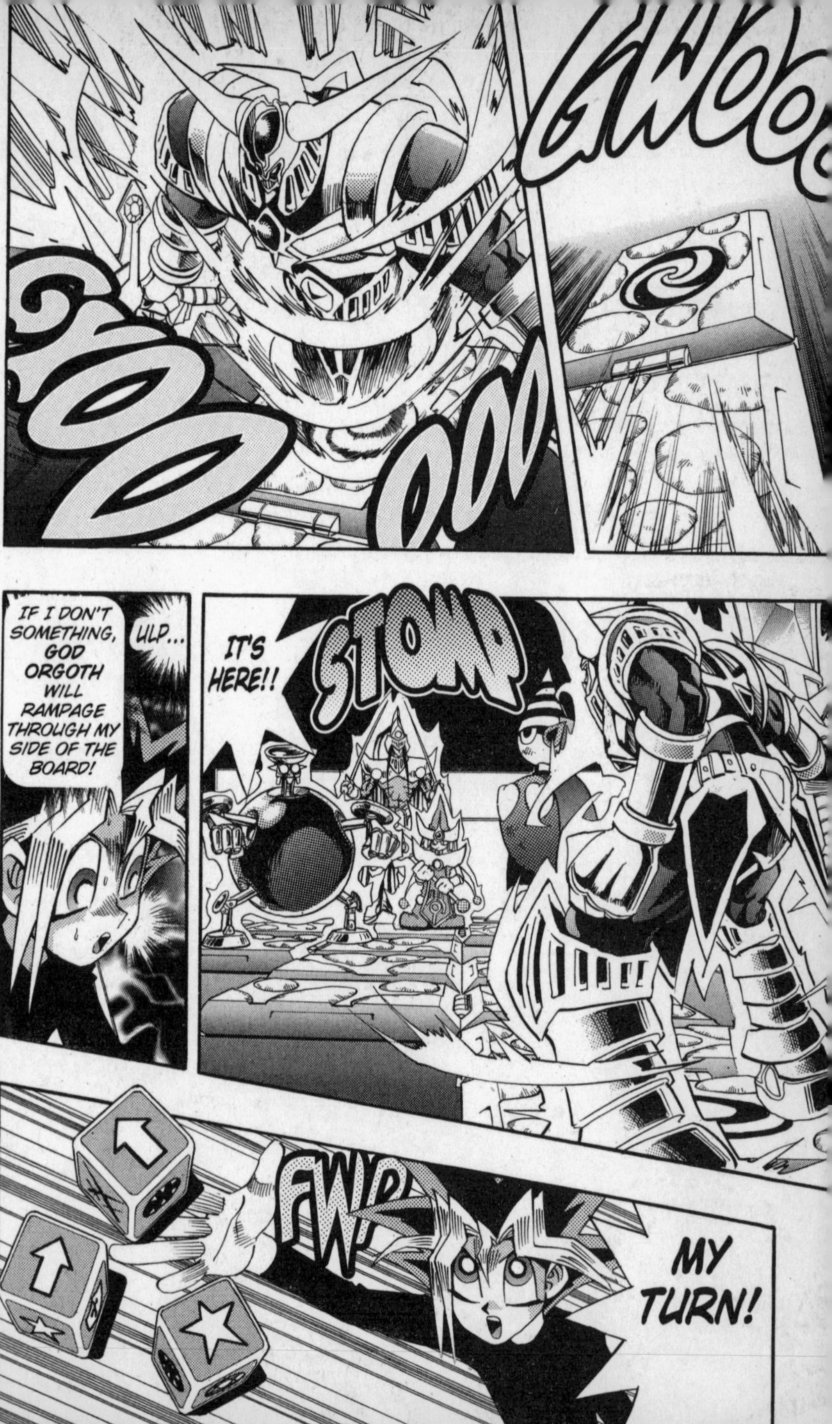
STOMP
IT'S HERE!!
ULP...
IF I DON'T SOMETHING, GOD ORGOTH WILL RAMPAGE THROUGH MY SIDE OF THE BOARD!
FWP
MY TURN!

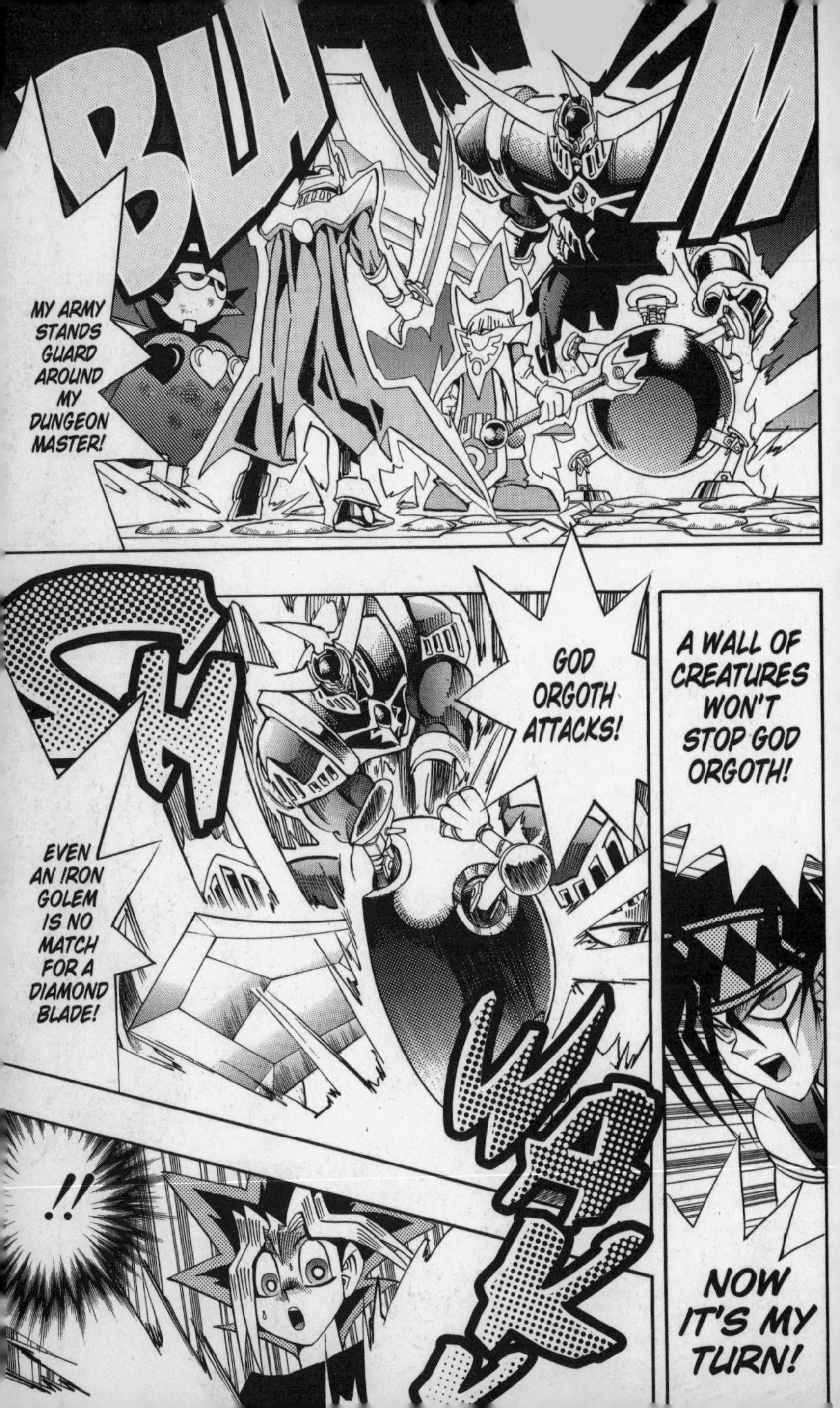
MY ARMY STANDS GUARD AROUND MY DUNGEON MASTER!
A WALL OF CREATURES WON'T STOP GOD ORGOTH!
GOD ORGOTH ATTACKS!
EVEN AN IRON GOLEM IS NO MATCH FOR A DIAMOND BLADE!
NOW IT'S MY TURN!
!!

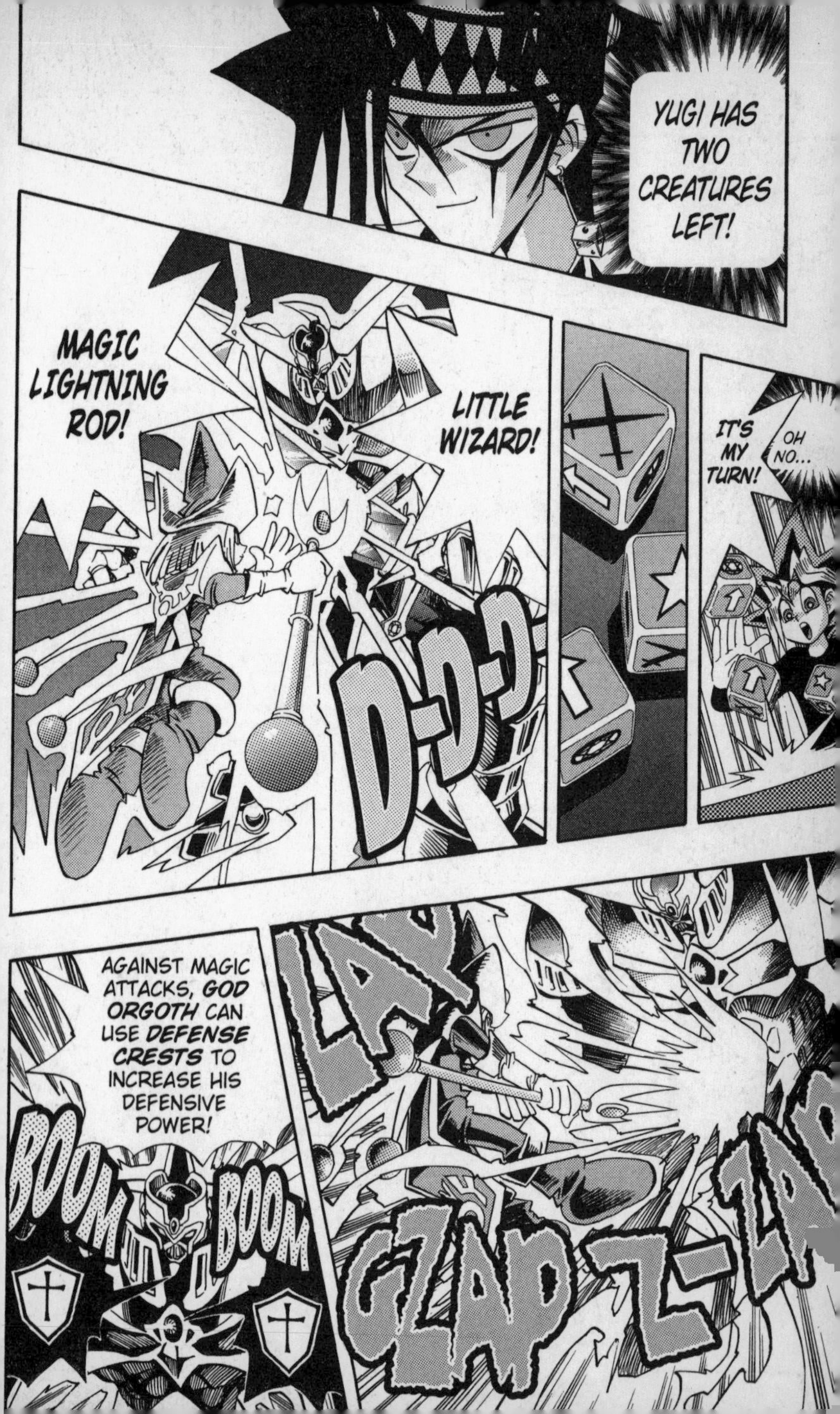
YUGI HAS TWO CREATURES LEFT!
OH NO...
IT'S MY TURN!
LITTLE WIZARD!
MAGIC LIGHTNING ROD!
D-D-D
Z-ZAP
GZAP
AGAINST MAGIC ATTACKS, GOD ORGOTH CAN USE DEFENSE CRESTS TO INCREASE HIS DEFENSIVE POWER!
BOOM
BOOM

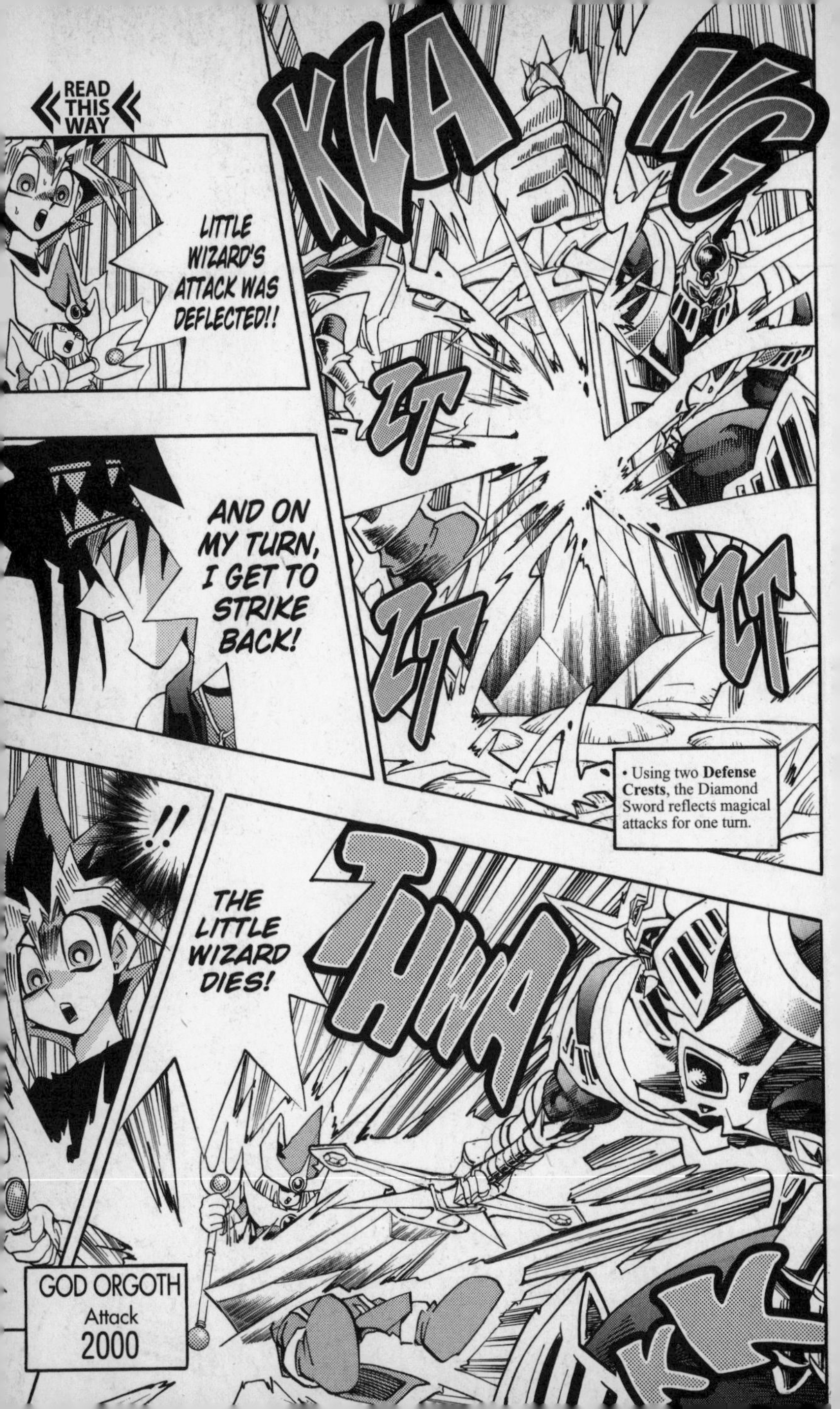
READ THIS WAY
KLANG
ZT
ZT
ZT
• Using two **Defense Crests**, the Diamond Sword reflects magical attacks for one turn.
LITTLE WIZARD'S ATTACK WAS DEFLECTED!!
AND ON MY TURN, I GET TO STRIKE BACK!
THWA
!!
THE LITTLE WIZARD DIES!
GOD ORGOTH
Attack
2000

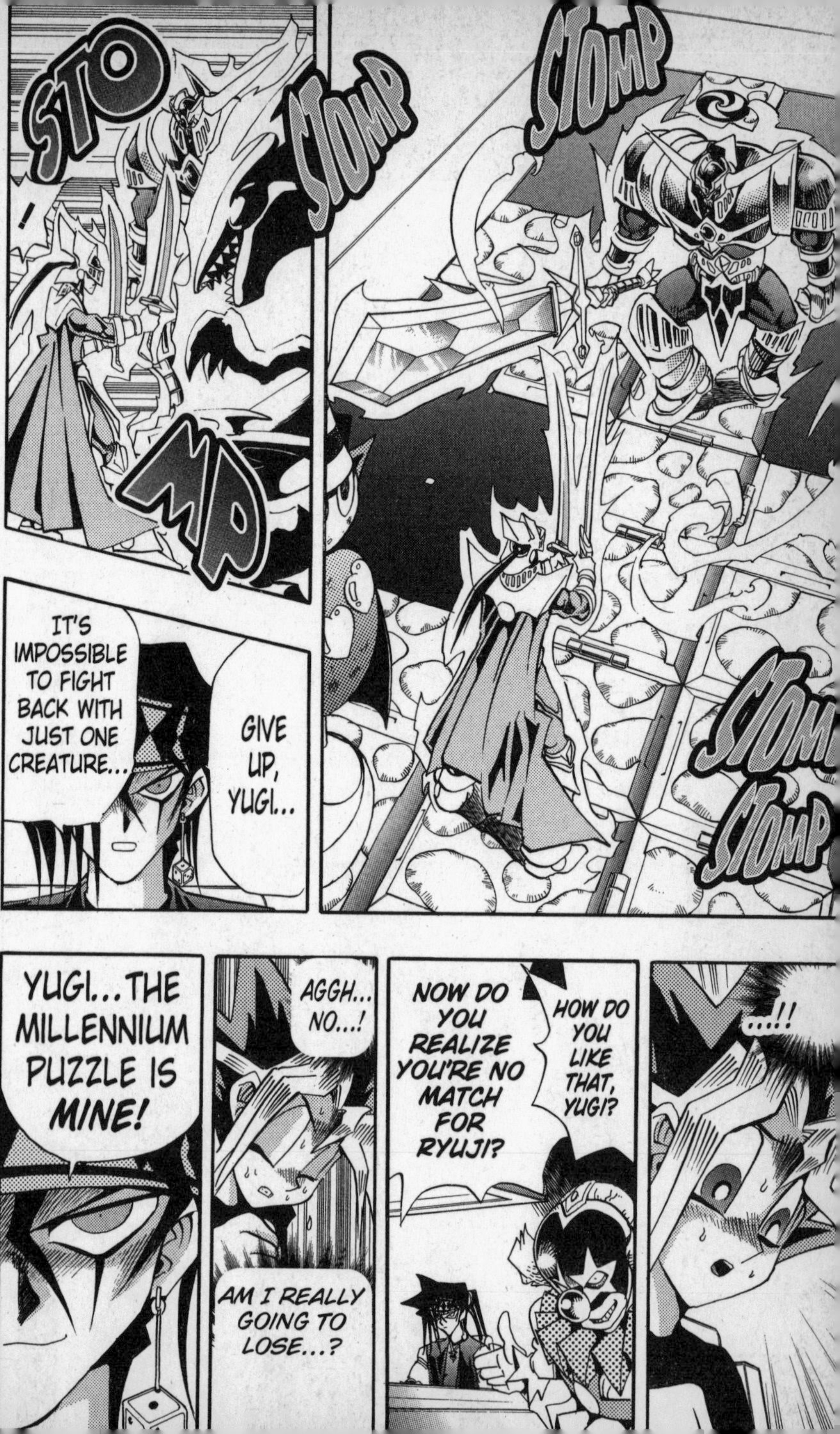
STOMP
STOM
STOMP
STOMP
STO
MP
!
GIVE UP, YUGI...
IT'S IMPOSSIBLE TO FIGHT BACK WITH JUST ONE CREATURE...
...!!
HOW DO YOU LIKE THAT, YUGI?
NOW DO YOU REALIZE YOU'RE NO MATCH FOR RYUJI?
AGGH... NO...!
AM I REALLY GOING TO LOSE...?
YUGI... THE MILLENNIUM PUZZLE IS *MINE!*

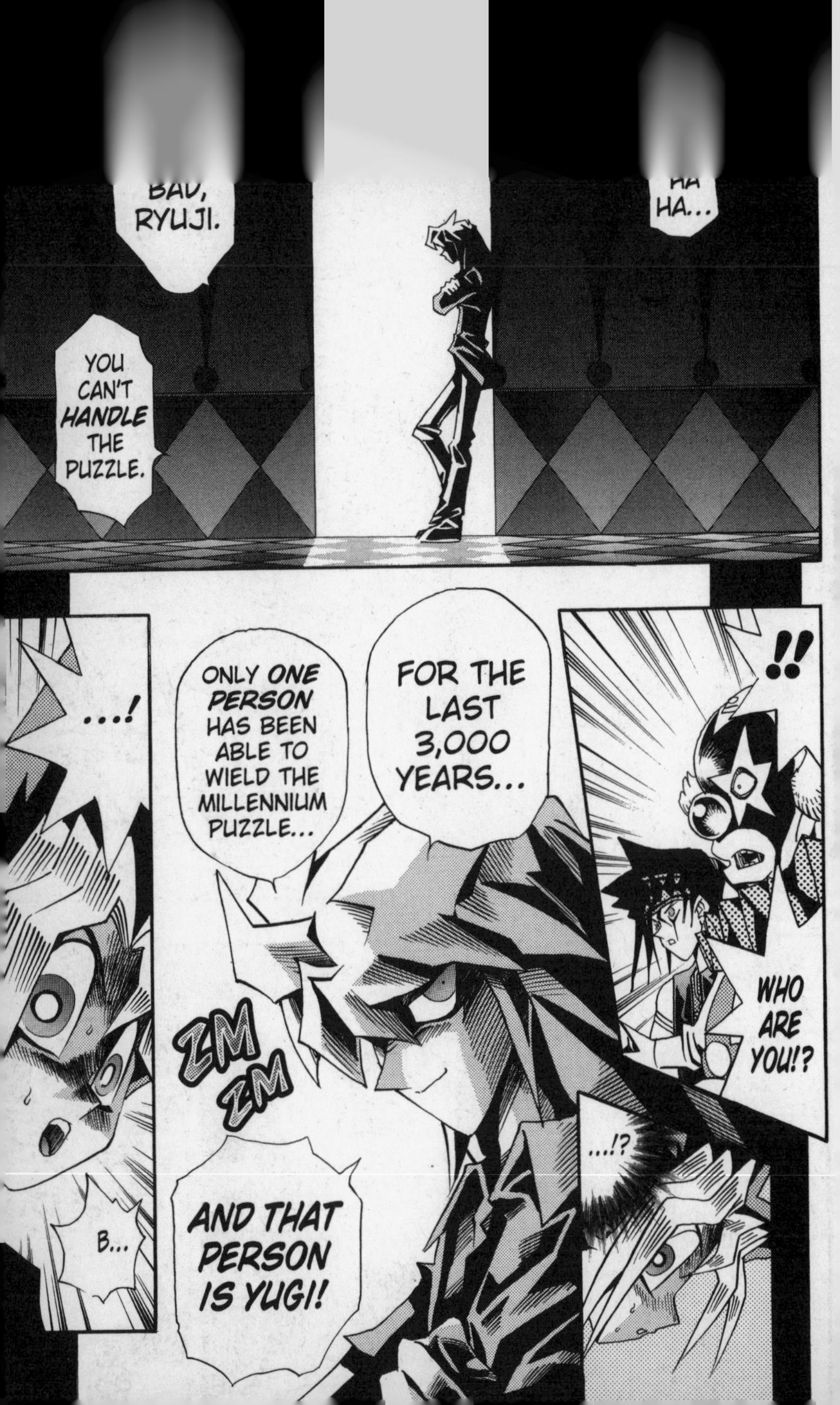
HA HA...
BAD, RYUJI.
YOU CAN'T *HANDLE* THE PUZZLE.
!!
WHO ARE YOU!?
...!?
FOR THE LAST 3,000 YEARS...
ONLY *ONE PERSON* HAS BEEN ABLE TO WIELD THE MILLENNIUM PUZZLE...
ZM ZM
AND THAT PERSON IS YUGI!
...!
B...

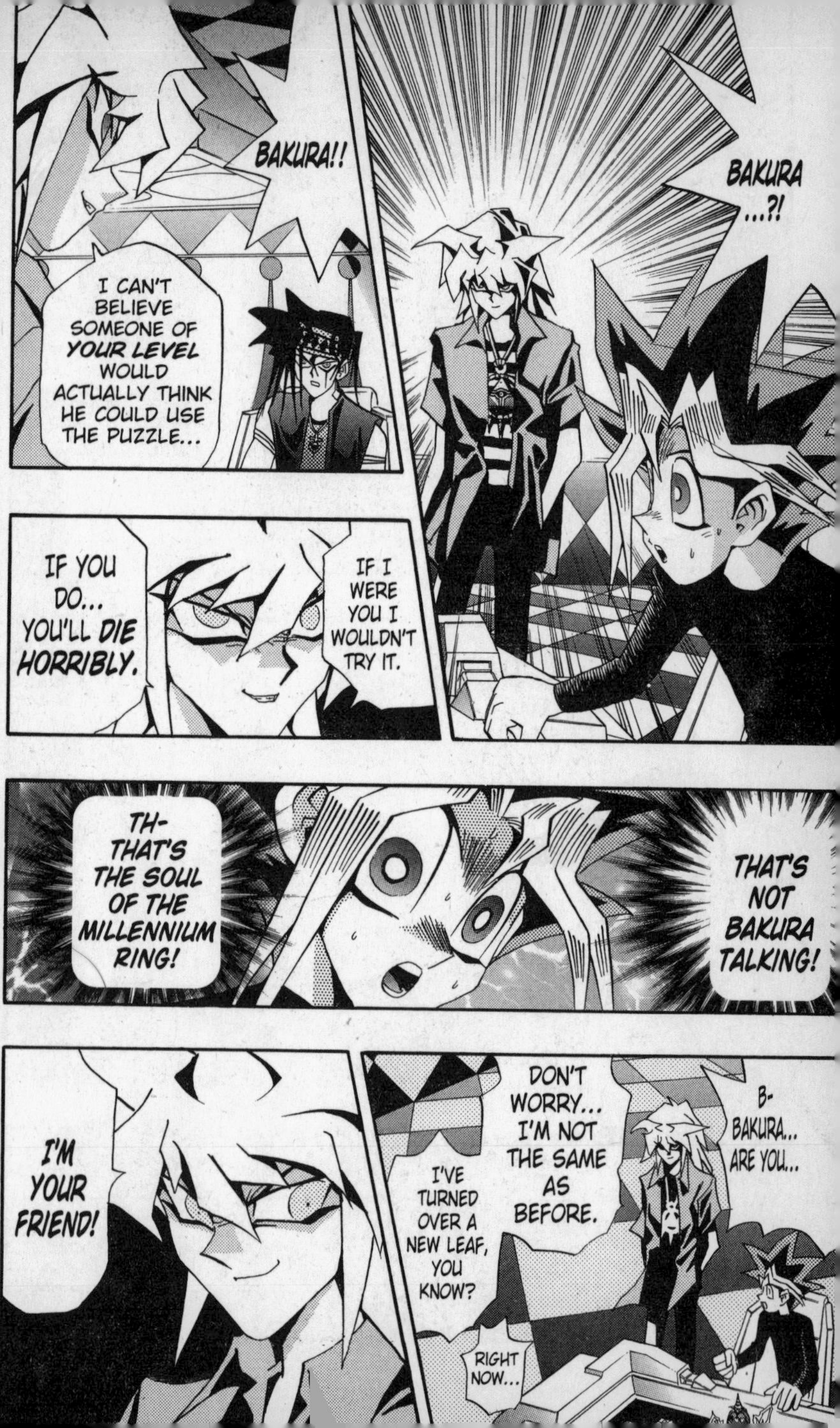
BAKURA ...?!
BAKURA!!
I CAN'T BELIEVE SOMEONE OF YOUR LEVEL WOULD ACTUALLY THINK HE COULD USE THE PUZZLE...
IF I WERE YOU I WOULDN'T TRY IT.
IF YOU DO... YOU'LL DIE HORRIBLY.
THAT'S NOT BAKURA TALKING!
TH-THAT'S THE SOUL OF THE MILLENNIUM RING!
B-BAKURA... ARE YOU...
DON'T WORRY... I'M NOT THE SAME AS BEFORE.
I'VE TURNED OVER A NEW LEAF, YOU KNOW?
RIGHT NOW...
I'M YOUR FRIEND!

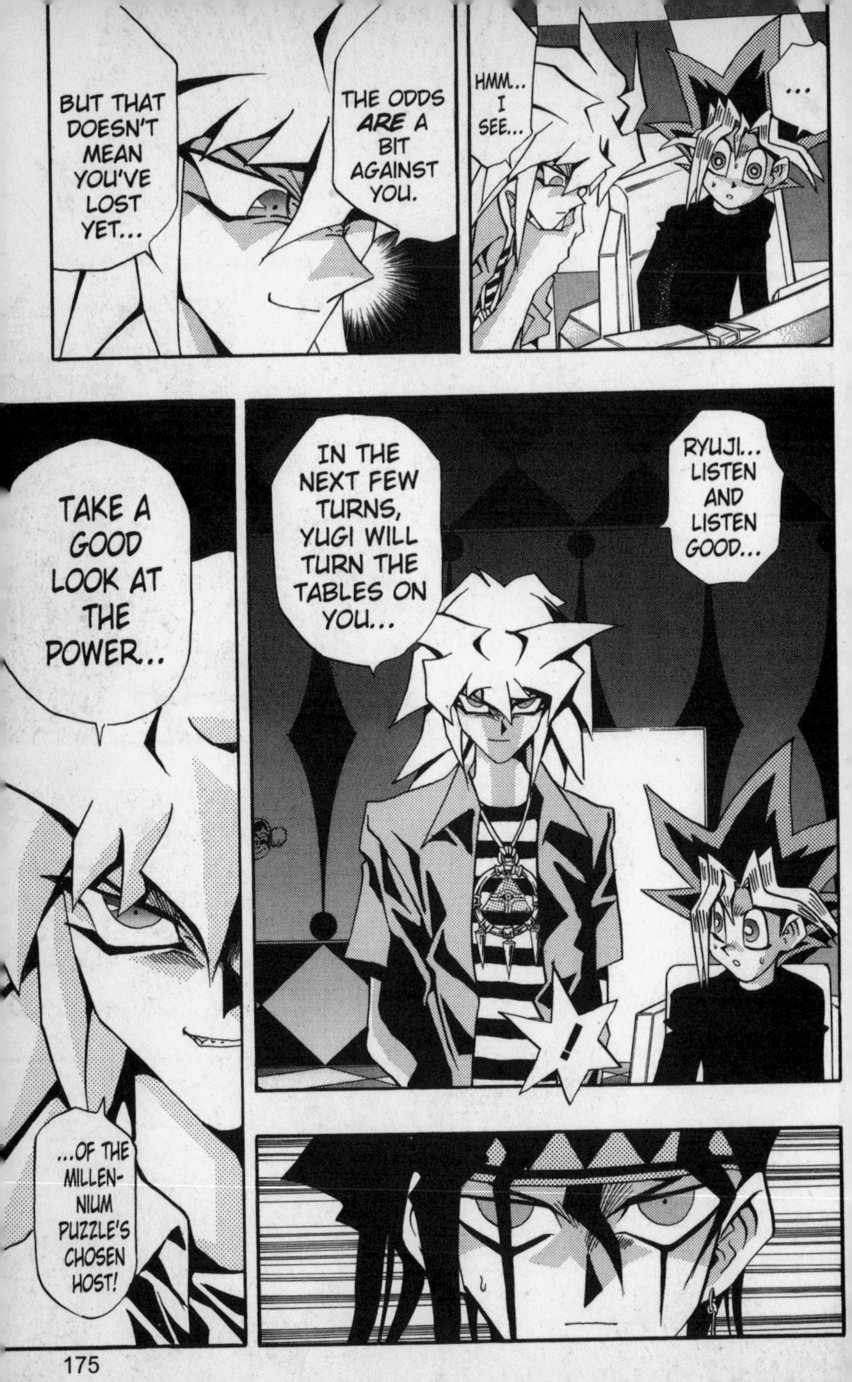
...
HMM... I SEE...
THE ODDS ARE A BIT AGAINST YOU.
BUT THAT DOESN'T MEAN YOU'VE LOST YET...
RYUJI... LISTEN AND LISTEN GOOD...
IN THE NEXT FEW TURNS, YUGI WILL TURN THE TABLES ON YOU...
!
TAKE A GOOD LOOK AT THE POWER...
...OF THE MILLEN-NIUM PUZZLE'S CHOSEN HOST!

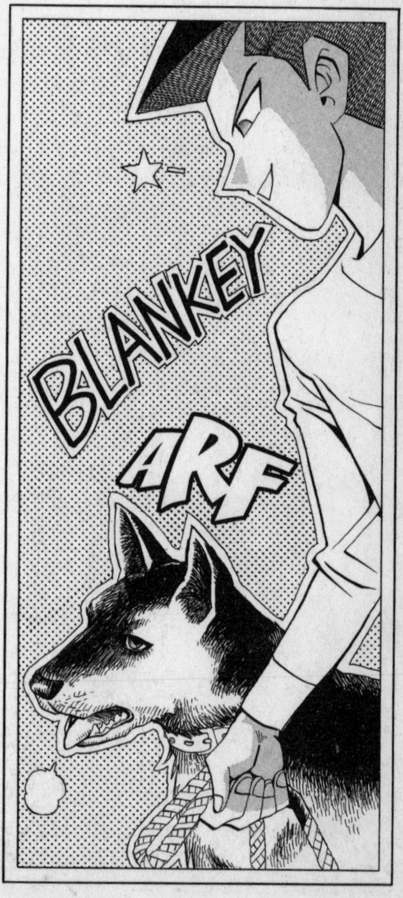
BLANKEY
ARF

Duel 83: Solve the Puzzle!!

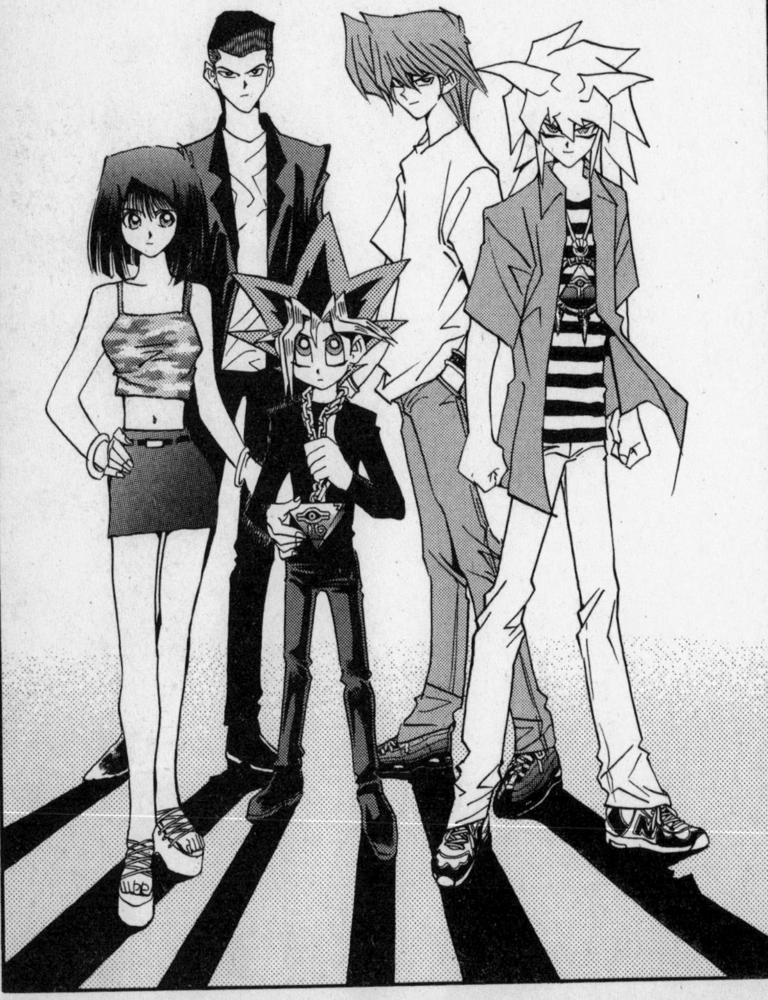

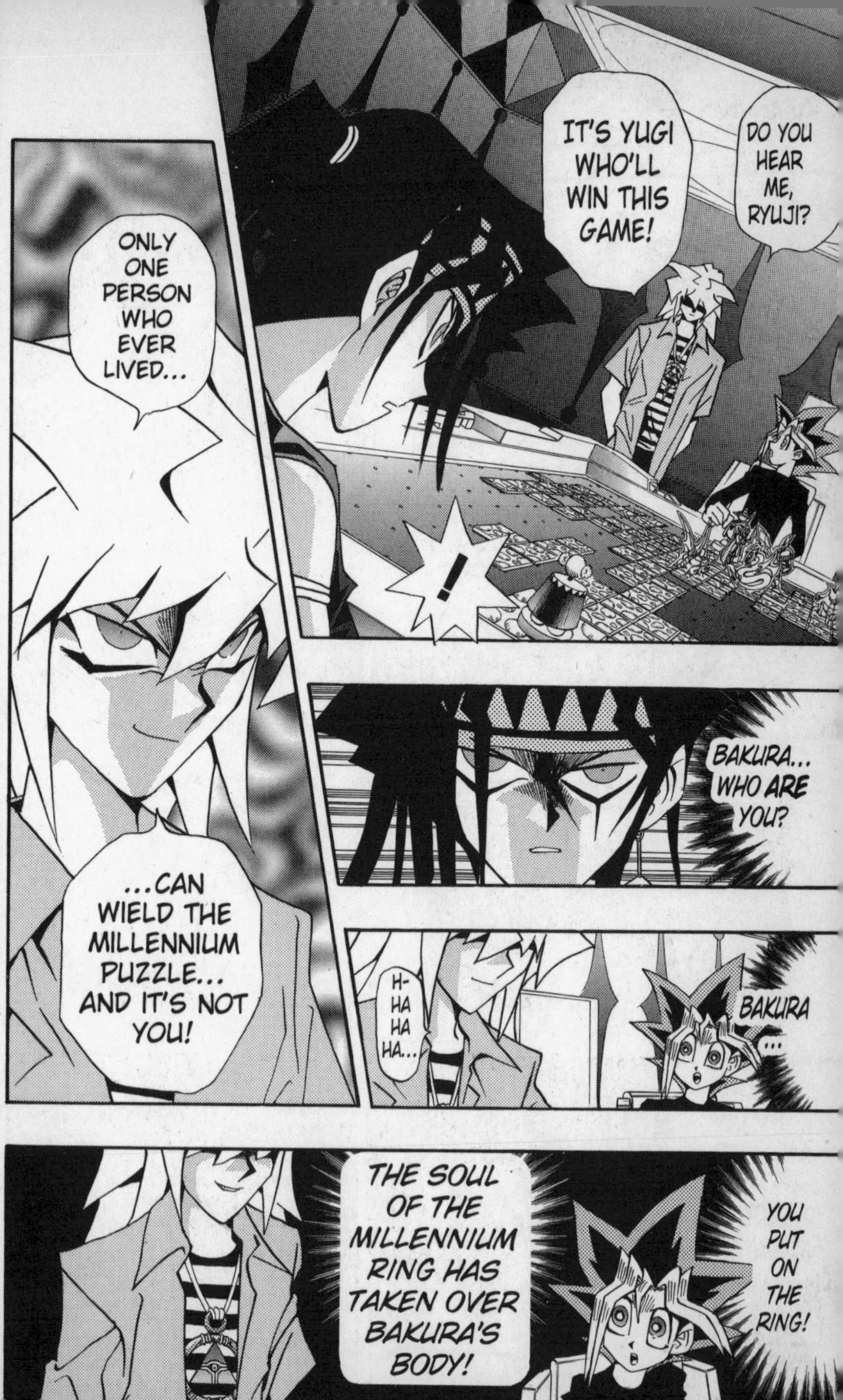
DO YOU HEAR ME, RYUJI?
IT'S YUGI WHO'LL WIN THIS GAME!
!
BAKURA... WHO ARE YOU?
BAKURA ...
H-HA HA HA...
ONLY ONE PERSON WHO EVER LIVED...
...CAN WIELD THE MILLENNIUM PUZZLE... AND IT'S NOT YOU!
YOU PUT ON THE RING!
THE SOUL OF THE MILLENNIUM RING HAS TAKEN OVER BAKURA'S BODY!

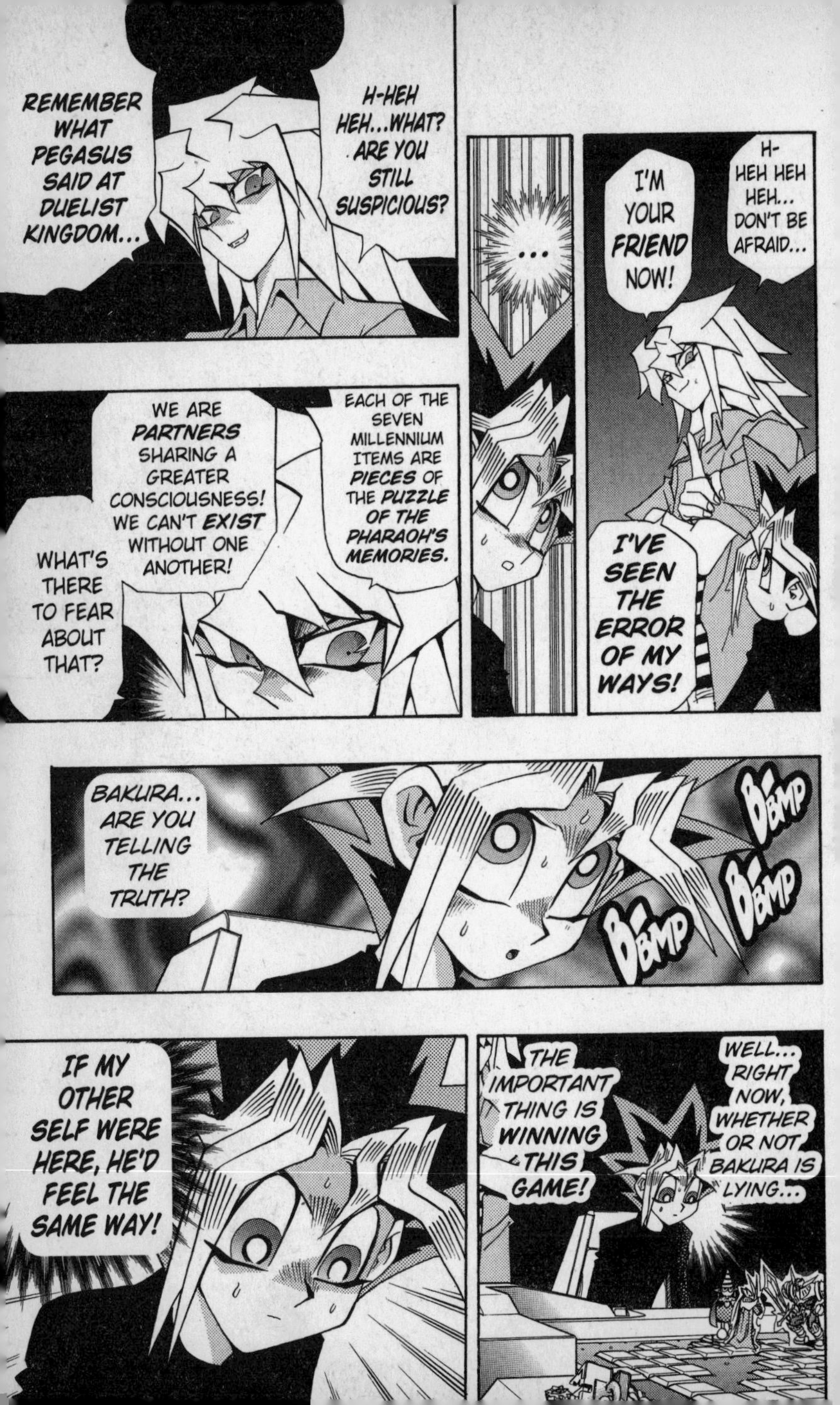
H-HEH HEH HEH... DON'T BE AFRAID...
I'M YOUR FRIEND NOW!
I'VE SEEN THE ERROR OF MY WAYS!
...
H-HEH HEH...WHAT? ARE YOU STILL SUSPICIOUS?
REMEMBER WHAT PEGASUS SAID AT DUELIST KINGDOM...
EACH OF THE SEVEN MILLENNIUM ITEMS ARE PIECES OF THE PUZZLE OF THE PHARAOH'S MEMORIES.
WE ARE PARTNERS SHARING A GREATER CONSCIOUSNESS! WE CAN'T EXIST WITHOUT ONE ANOTHER!
WHAT'S THERE TO FEAR ABOUT THAT?
B-BMP
B-BMP
B-BMP
BAKURA... ARE YOU TELLING THE TRUTH?
WELL... RIGHT NOW, WHETHER OR NOT BAKURA IS LYING...
THE IMPORTANT THING IS WINNING THIS GAME!
IF MY OTHER SELF WERE HERE, HE'D FEEL THE SAME WAY!

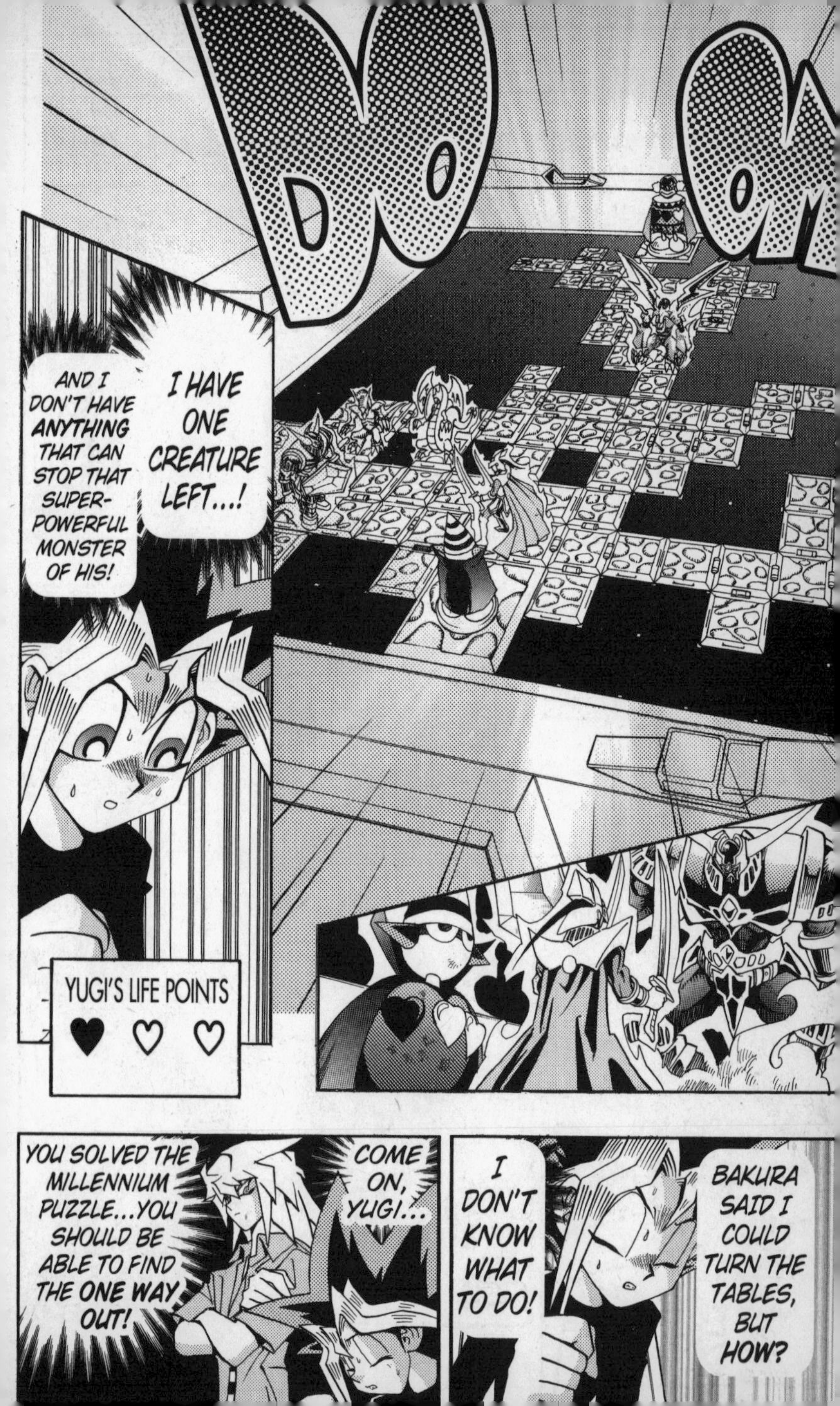
DOOOM
I HAVE ONE CREATURE LEFT...!
AND I DON'T HAVE **ANYTHING** THAT CAN STOP THAT SUPER-POWERFUL MONSTER OF HIS!
YUGI'S LIFE POINTS
♥ ♡ ♡
BAKURA SAID I COULD TURN THE TABLES, BUT HOW?
I DON'T KNOW WHAT TO DO!
COME ON, YUGI...
YOU SOLVED THE MILLENNIUM PUZZLE...YOU SHOULD BE ABLE TO FIND THE **ONE WAY** OUT!

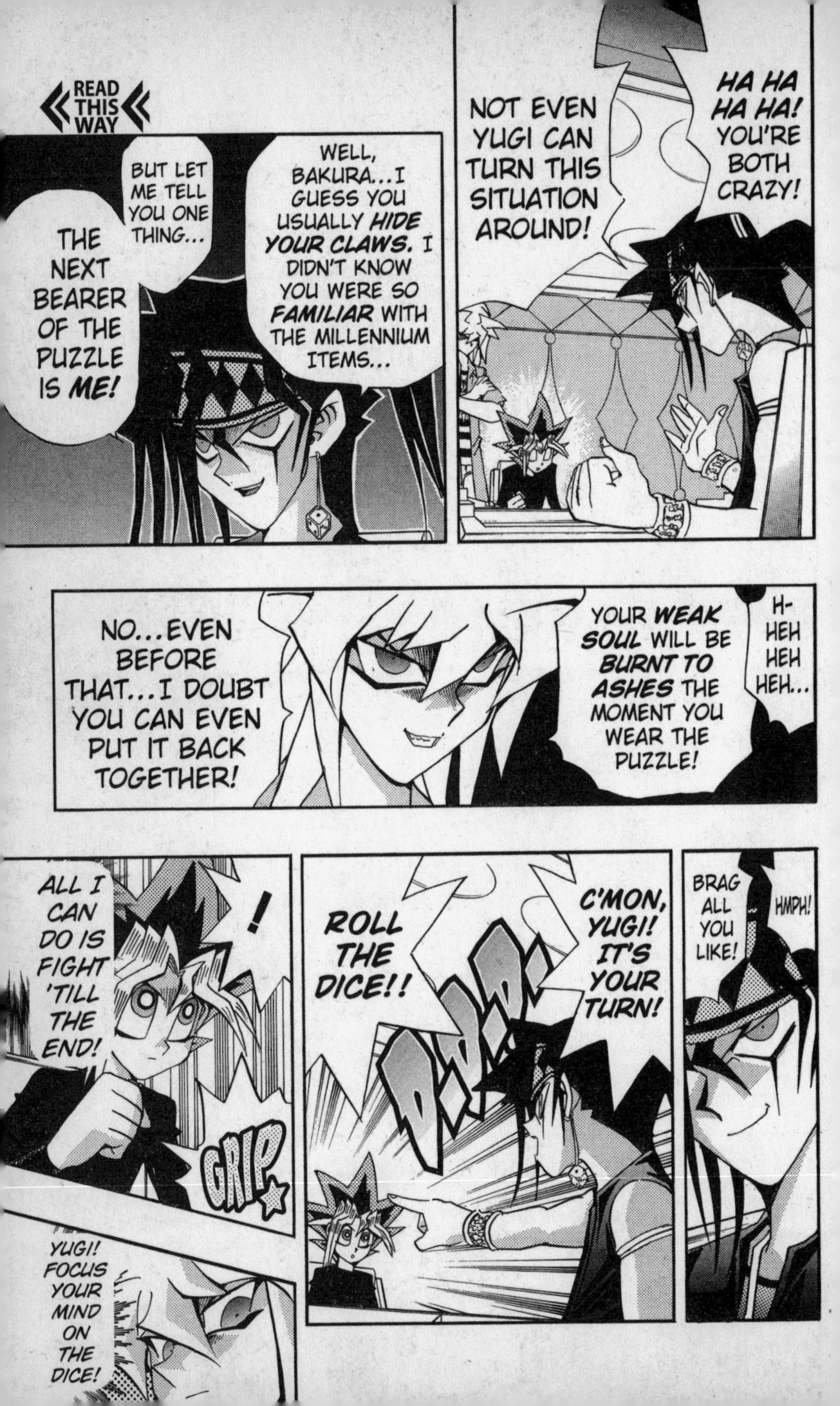
READ THIS WAY
HA HA HA HA! YOU'RE BOTH CRAZY!
NOT EVEN YUGI CAN TURN THIS SITUATION AROUND!
WELL, BAKURA...I GUESS YOU USUALLY HIDE YOUR CLAWS. I DIDN'T KNOW YOU WERE SO FAMILIAR WITH THE MILLENNIUM ITEMS...
BUT LET ME TELL YOU ONE THING...
THE NEXT BEARER OF THE PUZZLE IS ME!
H-HEH HEH HEH...
YOUR WEAK SOUL WILL BE BURNT TO ASHES THE MOMENT YOU WEAR THE PUZZLE!
NO...EVEN BEFORE THAT...I DOUBT YOU CAN EVEN PUT IT BACK TOGETHER!
HMPH!
BRAG ALL YOU LIKE!
C'MON, YUGI! IT'S YOUR TURN!
ROLL THE DICE!!
!
ALL I CAN DO IS FIGHT 'TILL THE END!
GRIP
YUGI! FOCUS YOUR MIND ON THE DICE!

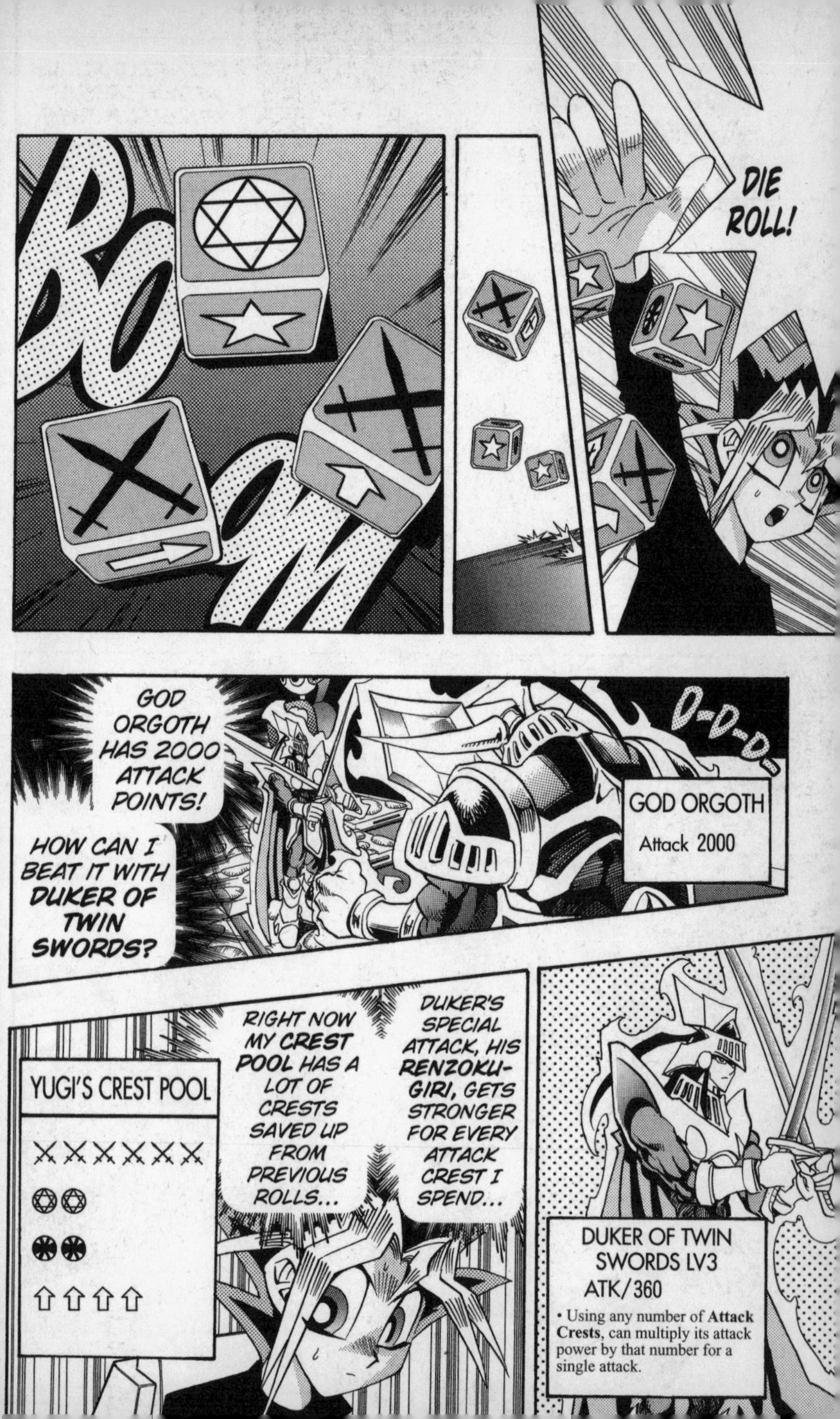
DIE ROLL!
BOOM
GOD ORGOTH HAS 2000 ATTACK POINTS!
HOW CAN I BEAT IT WITH DUKER OF TWIN SWORDS?
D-D-D-
GOD ORGOTH
Attack 2000
DUKER OF TWIN SWORDS LV3
ATK/360
• Using any number of Attack Crests, can multiply its attack power by that number for a single attack.
DUKER'S SPECIAL ATTACK, HIS RENZOKU-GIRI, GETS STRONGER FOR EVERY ATTACK CREST I SPEND...
RIGHT NOW MY CREST POOL HAS A LOT OF CRESTS SAVED UP FROM PREVIOUS ROLLS...
YUGI'S CREST POOL

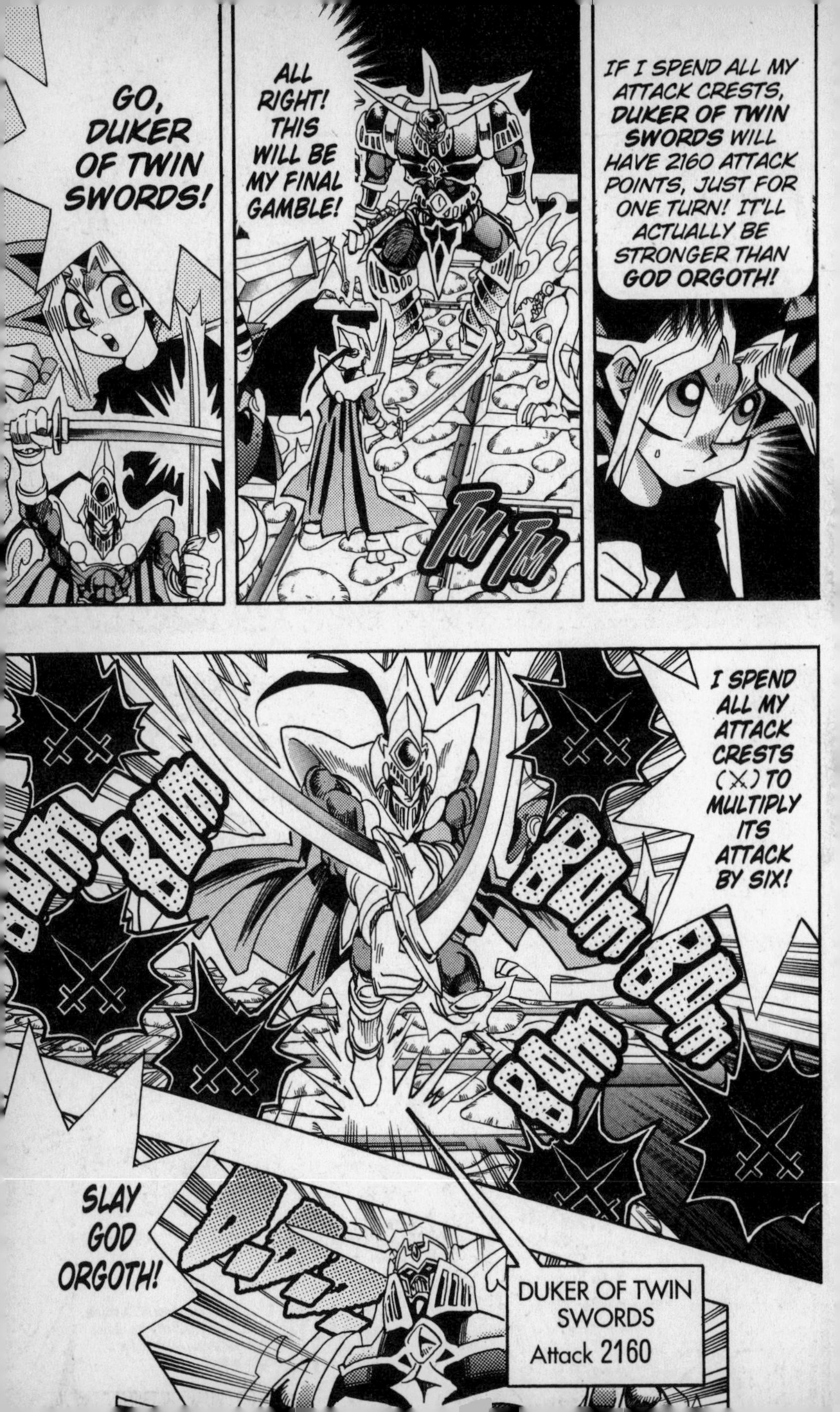
IF I SPEND ALL MY ATTACK CRESTS, DUKER OF TWIN SWORDS WILL HAVE 2160 ATTACK POINTS, JUST FOR ONE TURN! IT'LL ACTUALLY BE STRONGER THAN GOD ORGOTH!
ALL RIGHT! THIS WILL BE MY FINAL GAMBLE!
TM TM
GO, DUKER OF TWIN SWORDS!
I SPEND ALL MY ATTACK CRESTS (⚔) TO MULTIPLY ITS ATTACK BY SIX!
BOM BOM BOM
BOM BOM
SLAY GOD ORGOTH!
DUKER OF TWIN SWORDS
Attack 2160

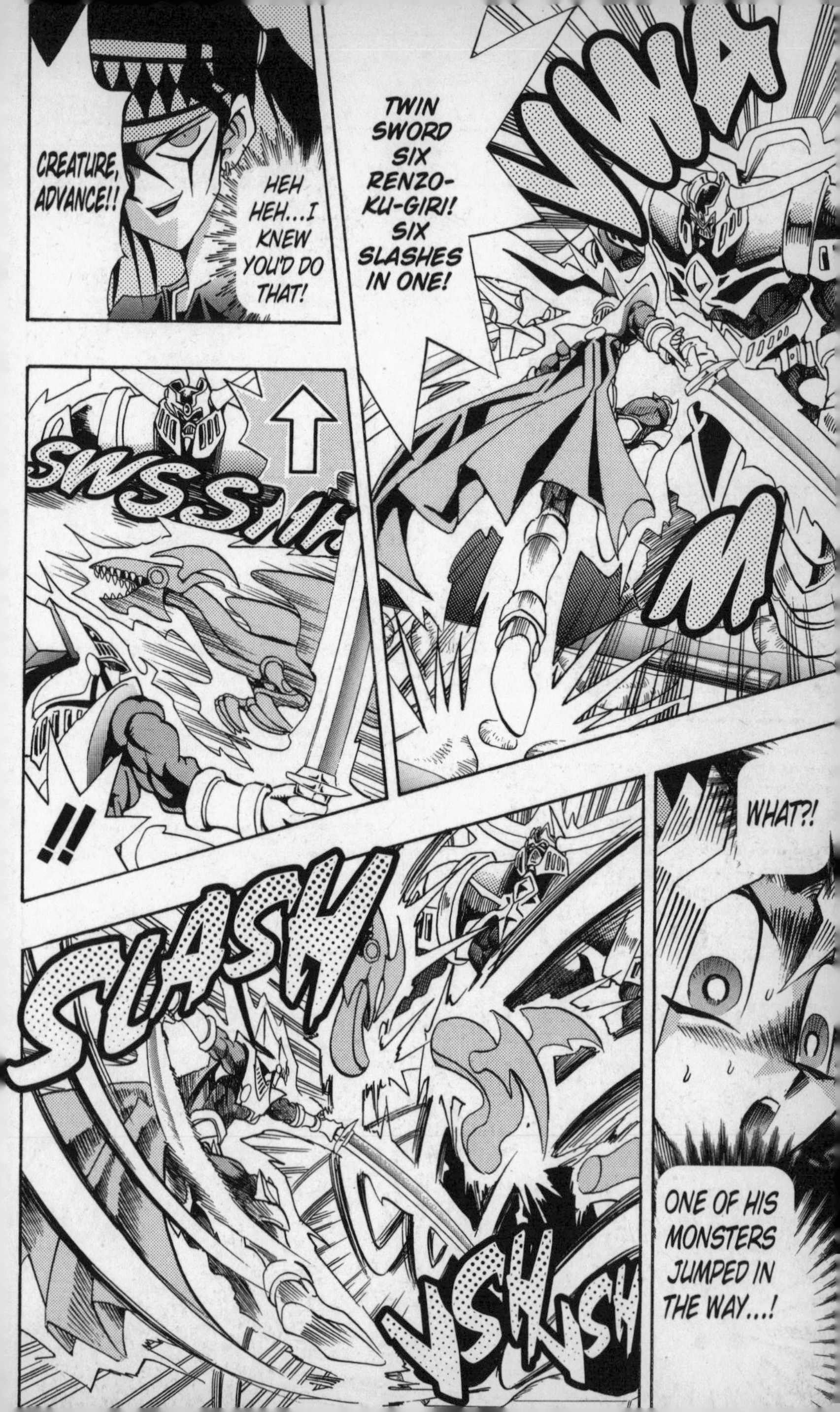
TWIN SWORD SIX RENZO-KU-GIRI! SIX SLASHES IN ONE!
HEH HEH...I KNEW YOU'D DO THAT!
CREATURE, ADVANCE!!
SWSSH!!
!!
WHAT?!
ONE OF HIS MONSTERS JUMPED IN THE WAY...!
SLASH
VSHSH

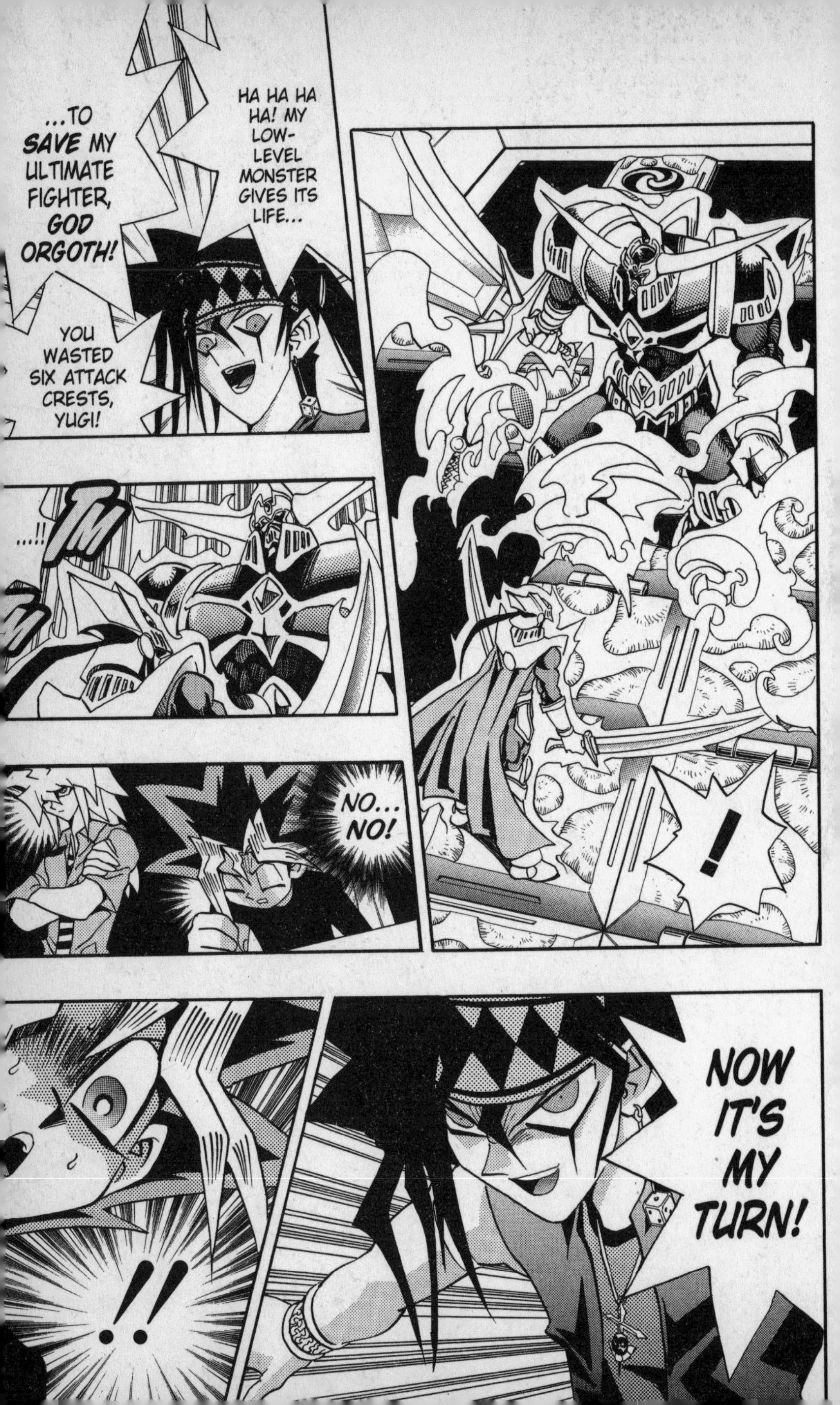
HA HA HA HA! MY LOW-LEVEL MONSTER GIVES ITS LIFE...
...TO SAVE MY ULTIMATE FIGHTER, GOD ORGOTH!
YOU WASTED SIX ATTACK CRESTS, YUGI!
!
...!!
NO... NO!
NOW IT'S MY TURN!
!!

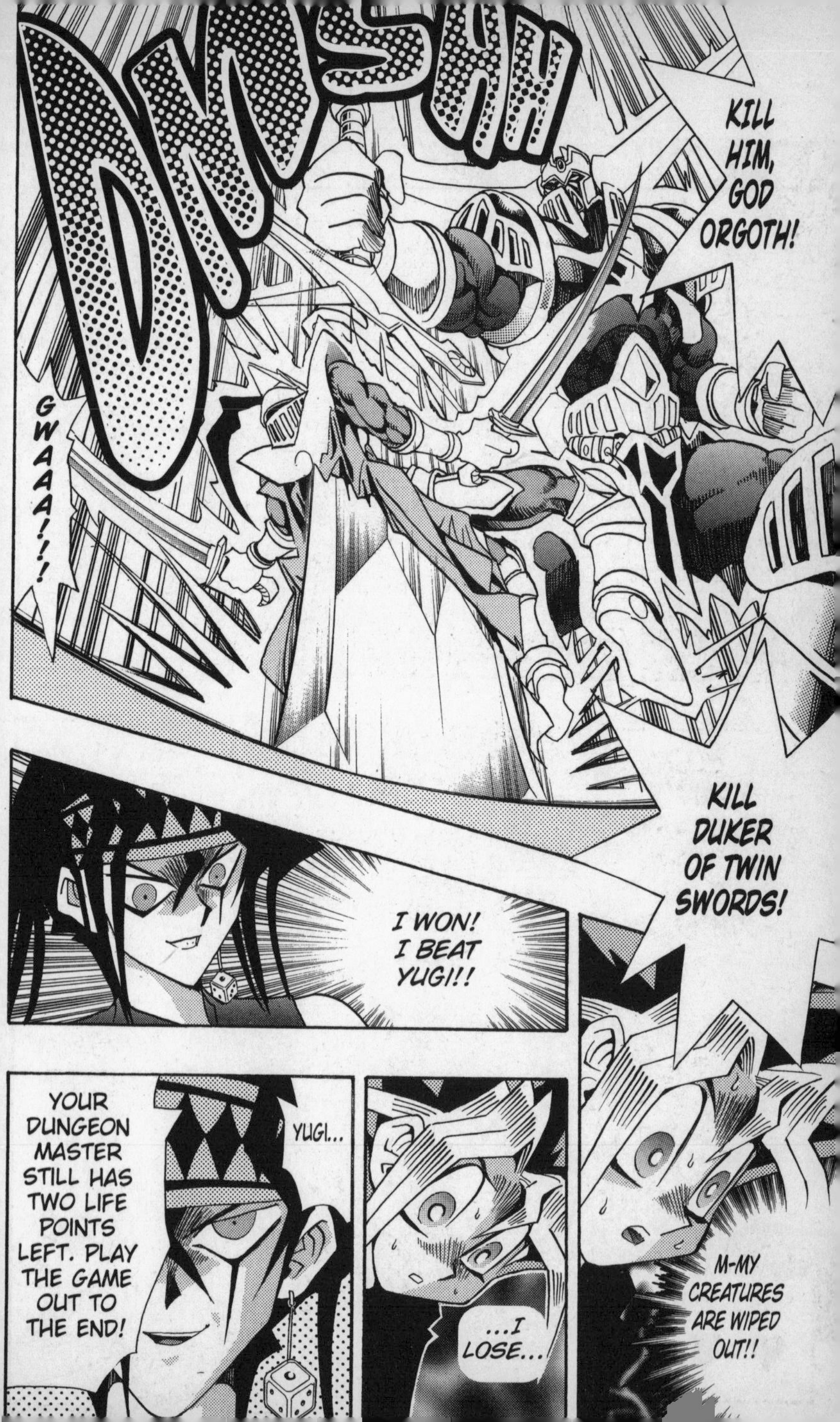
KILL HIM, GOD ORGOTH!
GWAAAA!!!
KILL DUKER OF TWIN SWORDS!
I WON! I BEAT YUGI!!
M-MY CREATURES ARE WIPED OUT!!
...I LOSE...
YUGI...
YOUR DUNGEON MASTER STILL HAS TWO LIFE POINTS LEFT. PLAY THE GAME OUT TO THE END!

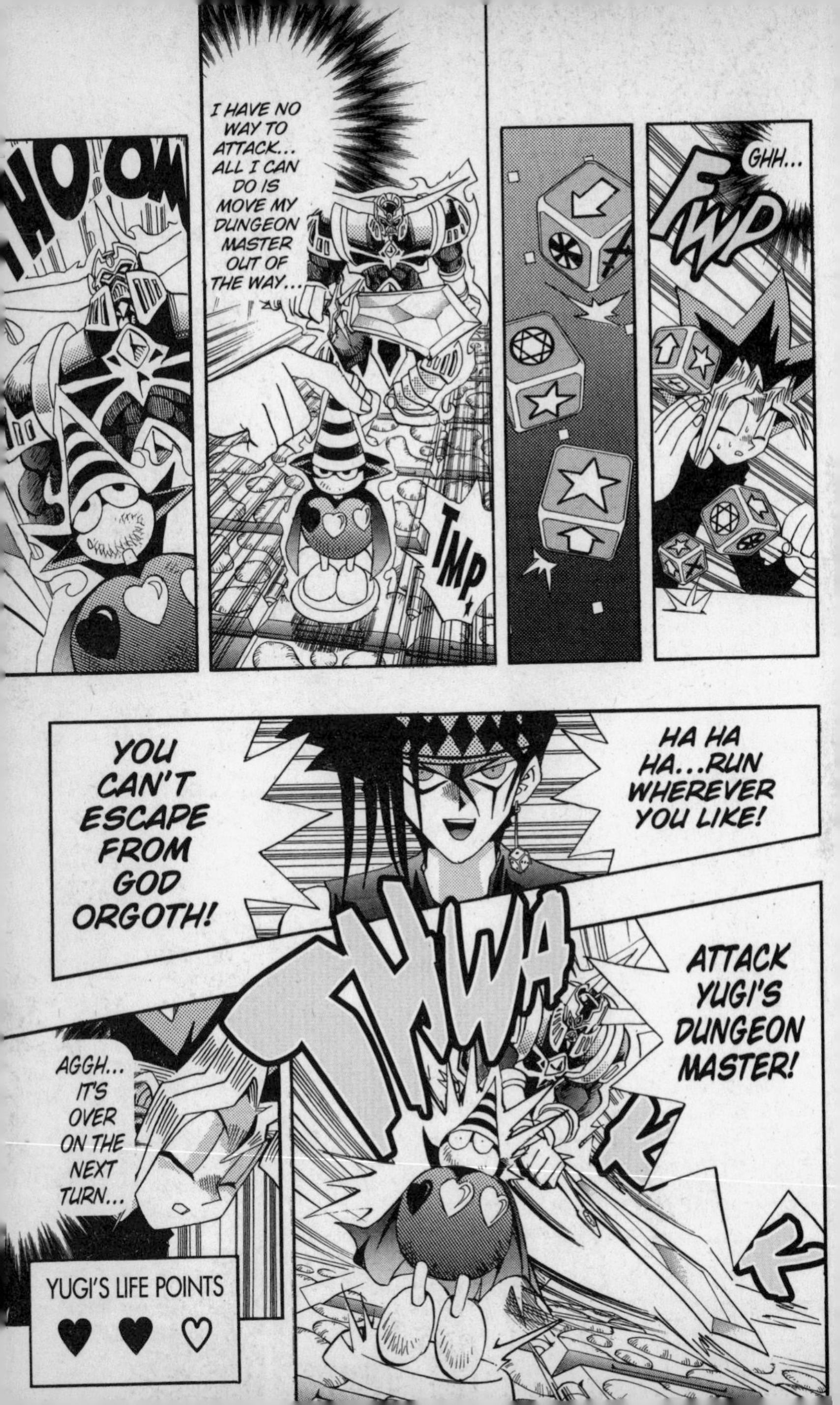
GHH...
FWP
I HAVE NO WAY TO ATTACK... ALL I CAN DO IS MOVE MY DUNGEON MASTER OUT OF THE WAY...
TMP
HA HA HA...RUN WHEREVER YOU LIKE!
YOU CAN'T ESCAPE FROM GOD ORGOTH!
ATTACK YUGI'S DUNGEON MASTER!
THWA
AGGH... IT'S OVER ON THE NEXT TURN...
YUGI'S LIFE POINTS

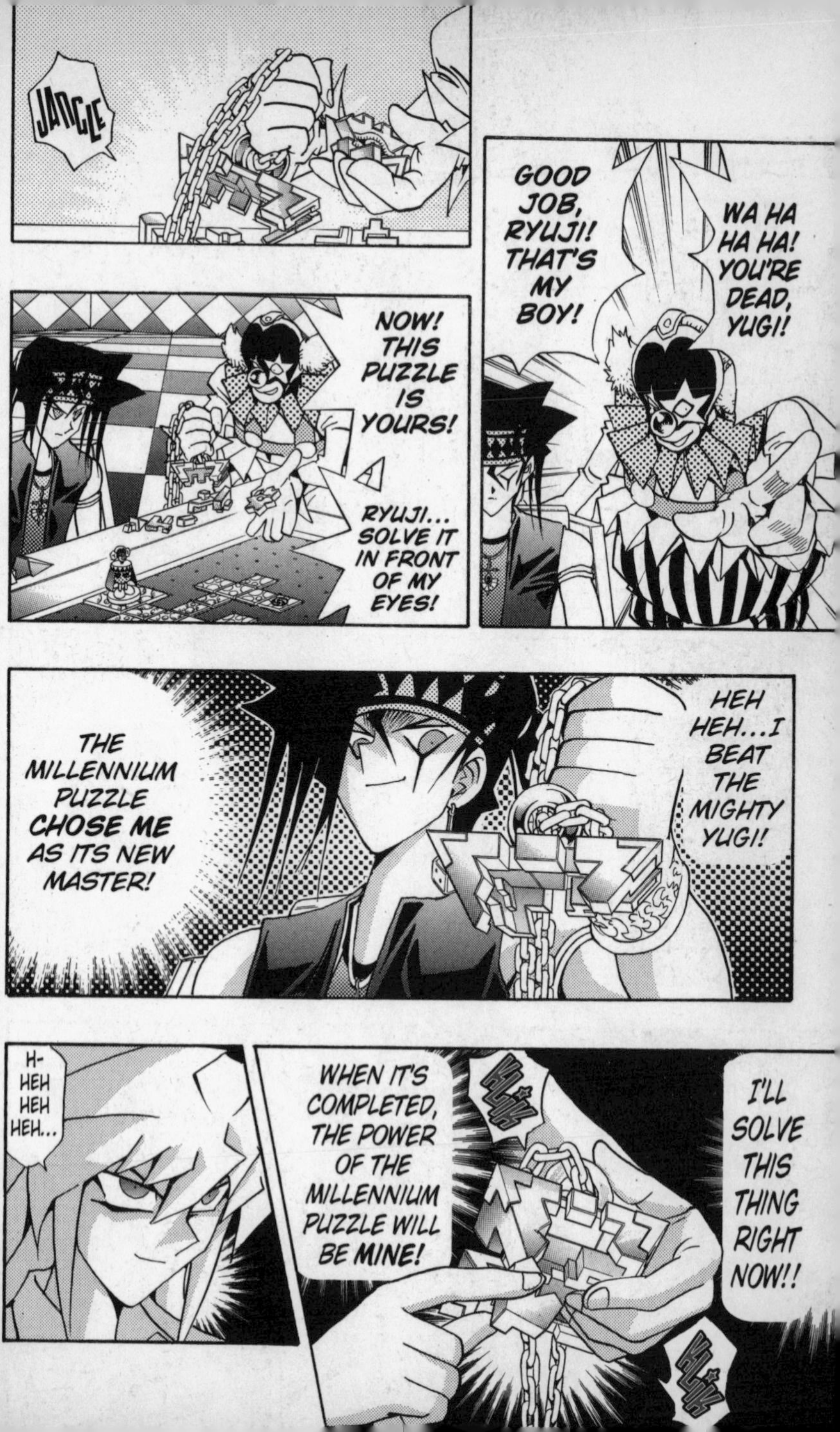
JANGLE
NOW! THIS PUZZLE IS YOURS!
RYUJI... SOLVE IT IN FRONT OF MY EYES!
GOOD JOB, RYUJI! THAT'S MY BOY!
WA HA HA HA! YOU'RE DEAD, YUGI!
HEH HEH...I BEAT THE MIGHTY YUGI!
THE MILLENNIUM PUZZLE CHOSE ME AS ITS NEW MASTER!
I'LL SOLVE THIS THING RIGHT NOW!!
KLIK
WHEN IT'S COMPLETED, THE POWER OF THE MILLENNIUM PUZZLE WILL BE MINE!
KLIK
H-HEH HEH HEH...

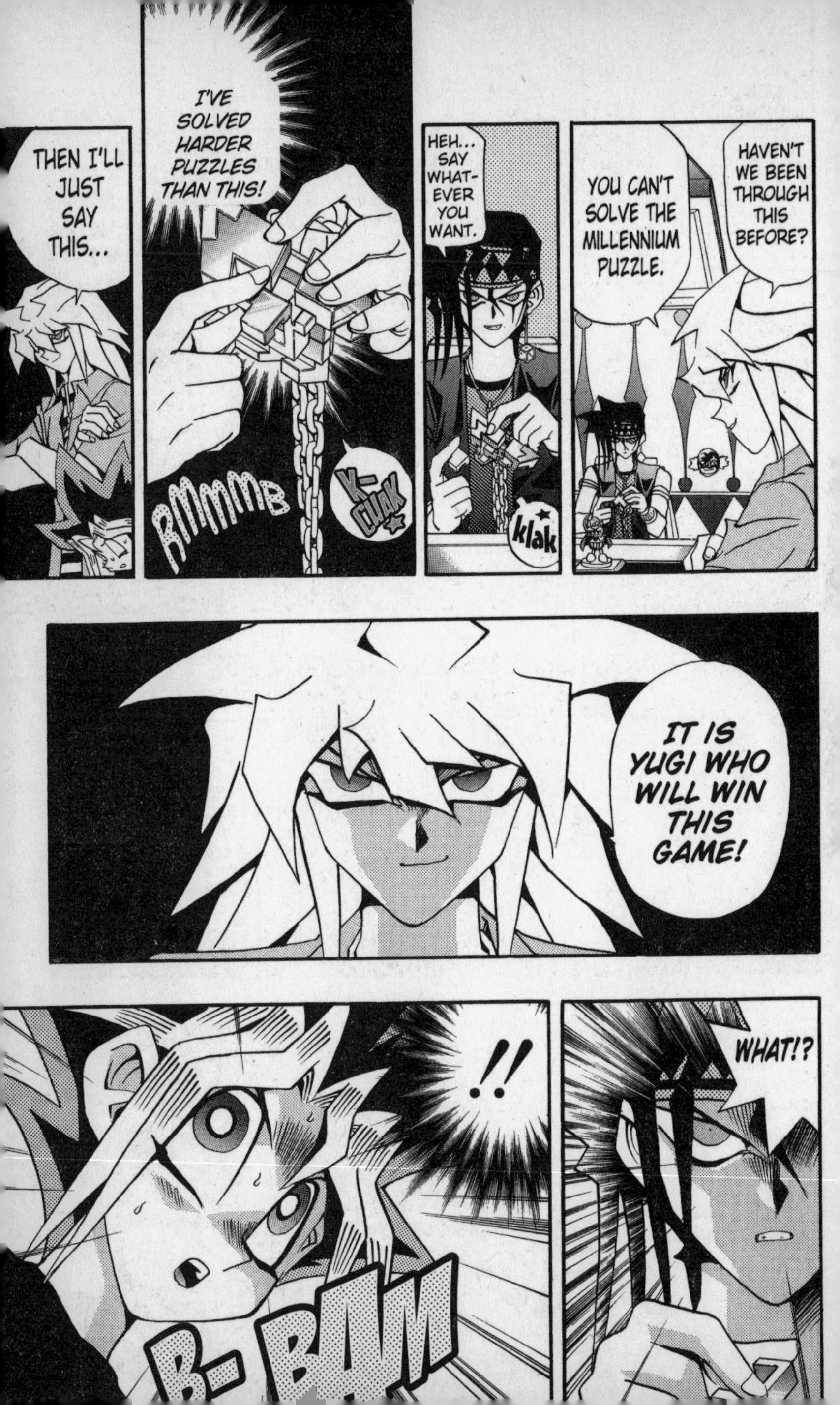
HAVEN'T WE BEEN THROUGH THIS BEFORE?
YOU CAN'T SOLVE THE MILLENNIUM PUZZLE.
HEH... SAY WHAT-EVER YOU WANT.
klak
I'VE SOLVED HARDER PUZZLES THAN THIS!
K-CHAK
RMMMB
THEN I'LL JUST SAY THIS...
IT IS YUGI WHO WILL WIN THIS GAME!
WHAT!?
!!
B-BAM

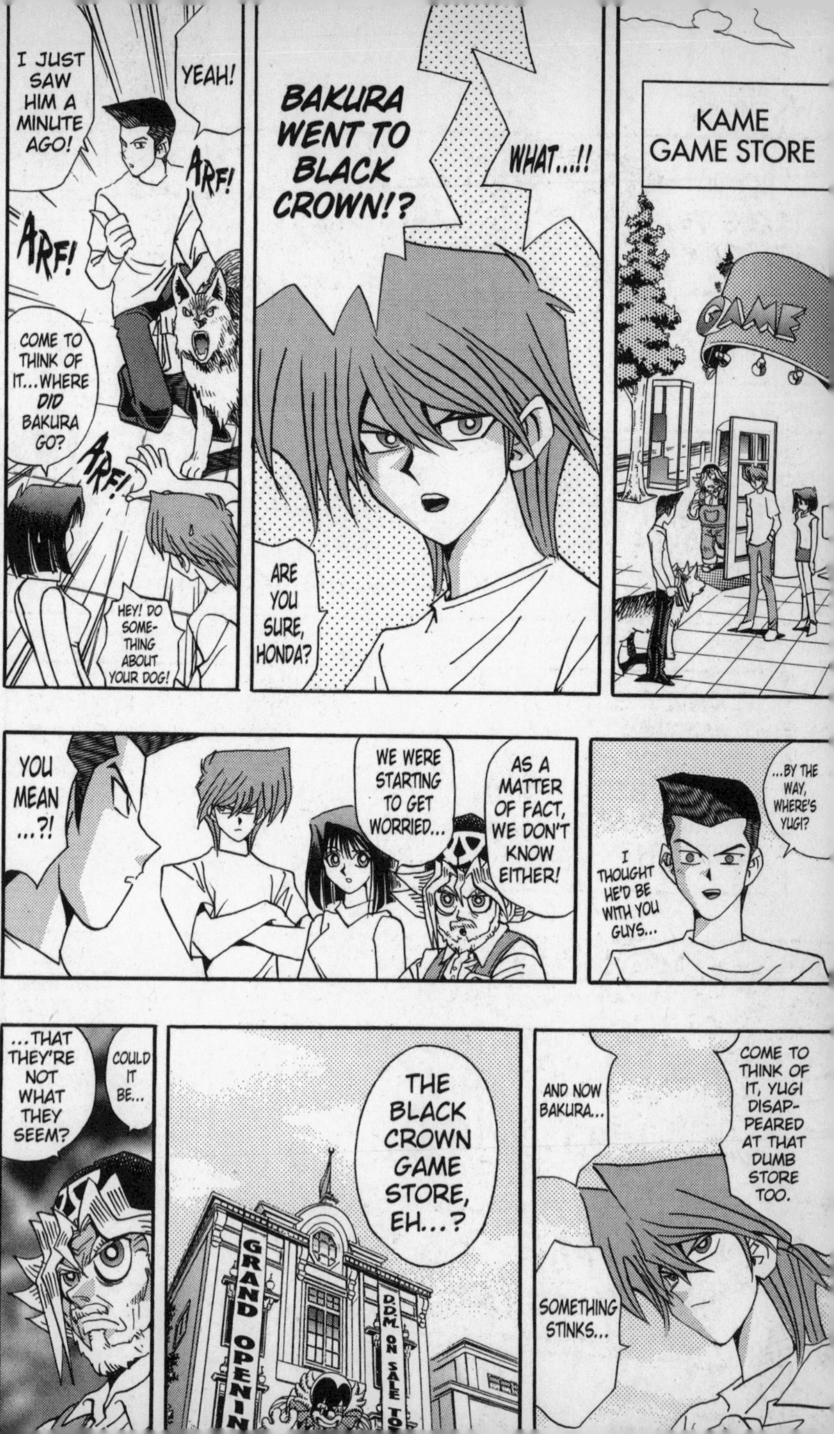
KAME GAME STORE
GAME
WHAT...!!
BAKURA WENT TO BLACK CROWN!?
ARE YOU SURE, HONDA?
YEAH!
I JUST SAW HIM A MINUTE AGO!
ARF!
ARF!
COME TO THINK OF IT... WHERE DID BAKURA GO?
ARF!
HEY! DO SOME-THING ABOUT YOUR DOG!
...BY THE WAY, WHERE'S YUGI?
I THOUGHT HE'D BE WITH YOU GUYS...
AS A MATTER OF FACT, WE DON'T KNOW EITHER!
WE WERE STARTING TO GET WORRIED...
YOU MEAN ...?!
COME TO THINK OF IT, YUGI DISAP-PEARED AT THAT DUMB STORE TOO.
AND NOW BAKURA...
SOMETHING STINKS...
THE BLACK CROWN GAME STORE, EH...?
GRAND OPENIN
D.D.M. ON SALE TO
COULD IT BE...
...THAT THEY'RE NOT WHAT THEY SEEM?

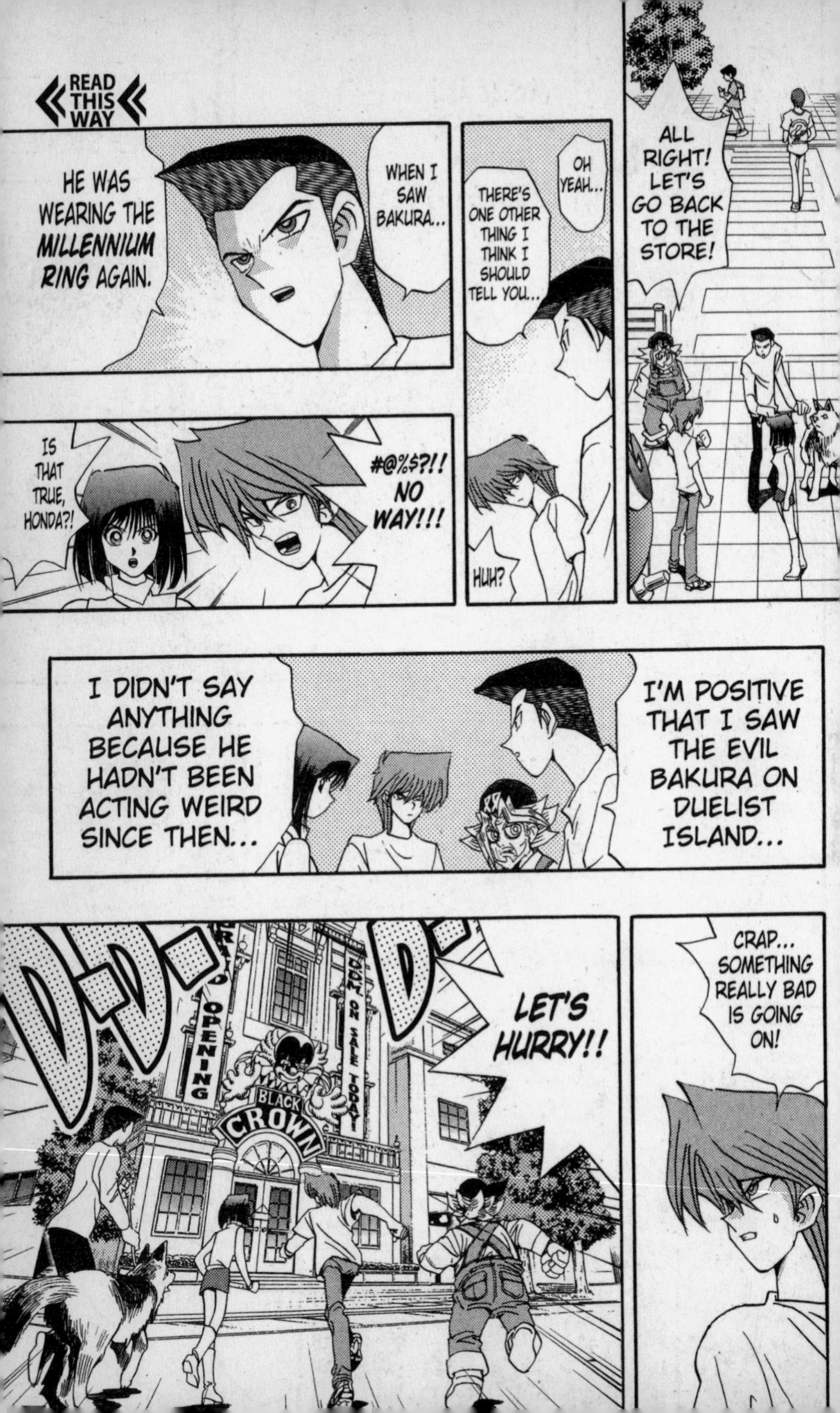
READ THIS WAY
ALL RIGHT! LET'S GO BACK TO THE STORE!
OH YEAH...
THERE'S ONE OTHER THING I THINK I SHOULD TELL YOU...
HUH?
WHEN I SAW BAKURA...
HE WAS WEARING THE MILLENNIUM RING AGAIN.
#@%$?!! NO WAY!!!
IS THAT TRUE, HONDA?!
I'M POSITIVE THAT I SAW THE EVIL BAKURA ON DUELIST ISLAND...
I DIDN'T SAY ANYTHING BECAUSE HE HADN'T BEEN ACTING WEIRD SINCE THEN...
CRAP... SOMETHING REALLY BAD IS GOING ON!
LET'S HURRY!!
OPENING
ON SALE TODAY!
BLACK CROWN

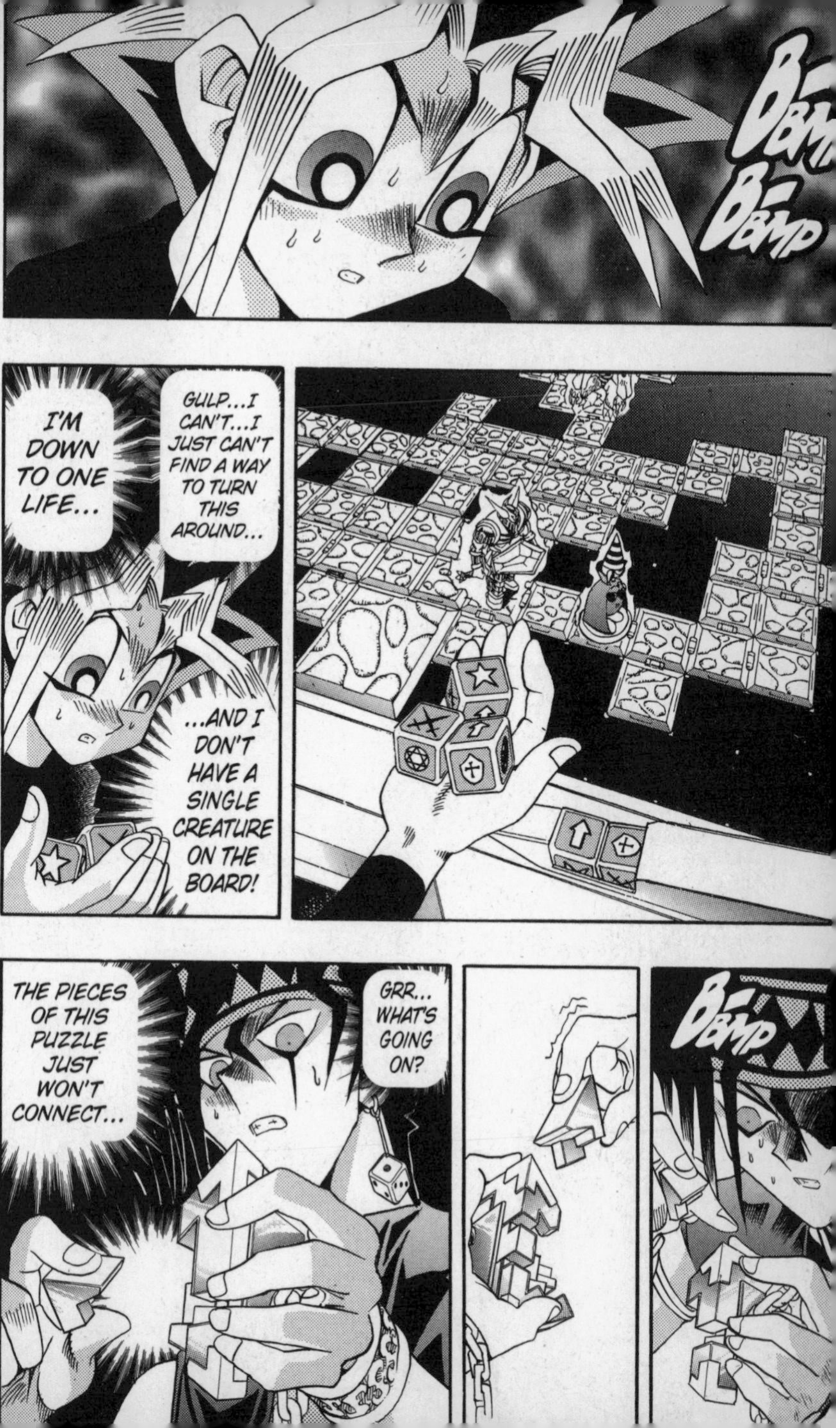
B-BBMP B-BBMP
GULP...I CAN'T...I JUST CAN'T FIND A WAY TO TURN THIS AROUND...
I'M DOWN TO ONE LIFE...
...AND I DON'T HAVE A SINGLE CREATURE ON THE BOARD!
B-BBMP
GRR... WHAT'S GOING ON?
THE PIECES OF THIS PUZZLE JUST WON'T CONNECT...

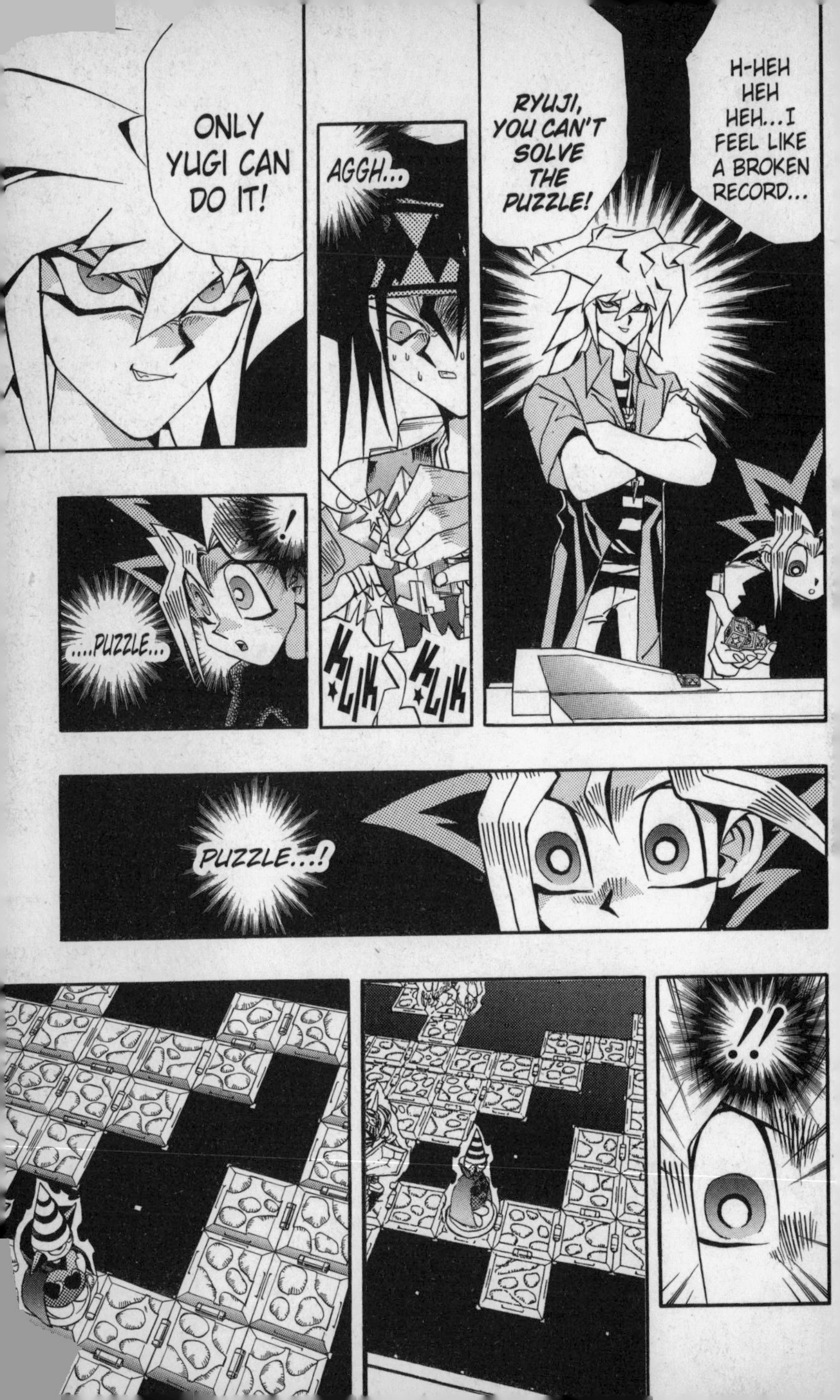
H-HEH HEH HEH...I FEEL LIKE A BROKEN RECORD...
RYUJI, YOU CAN'T SOLVE THE PUZZLE!
AGGH...
KLIK
KLIK
ONLY YUGI CAN DO IT!
!
....PUZZLE....
PUZZLE...!
!!

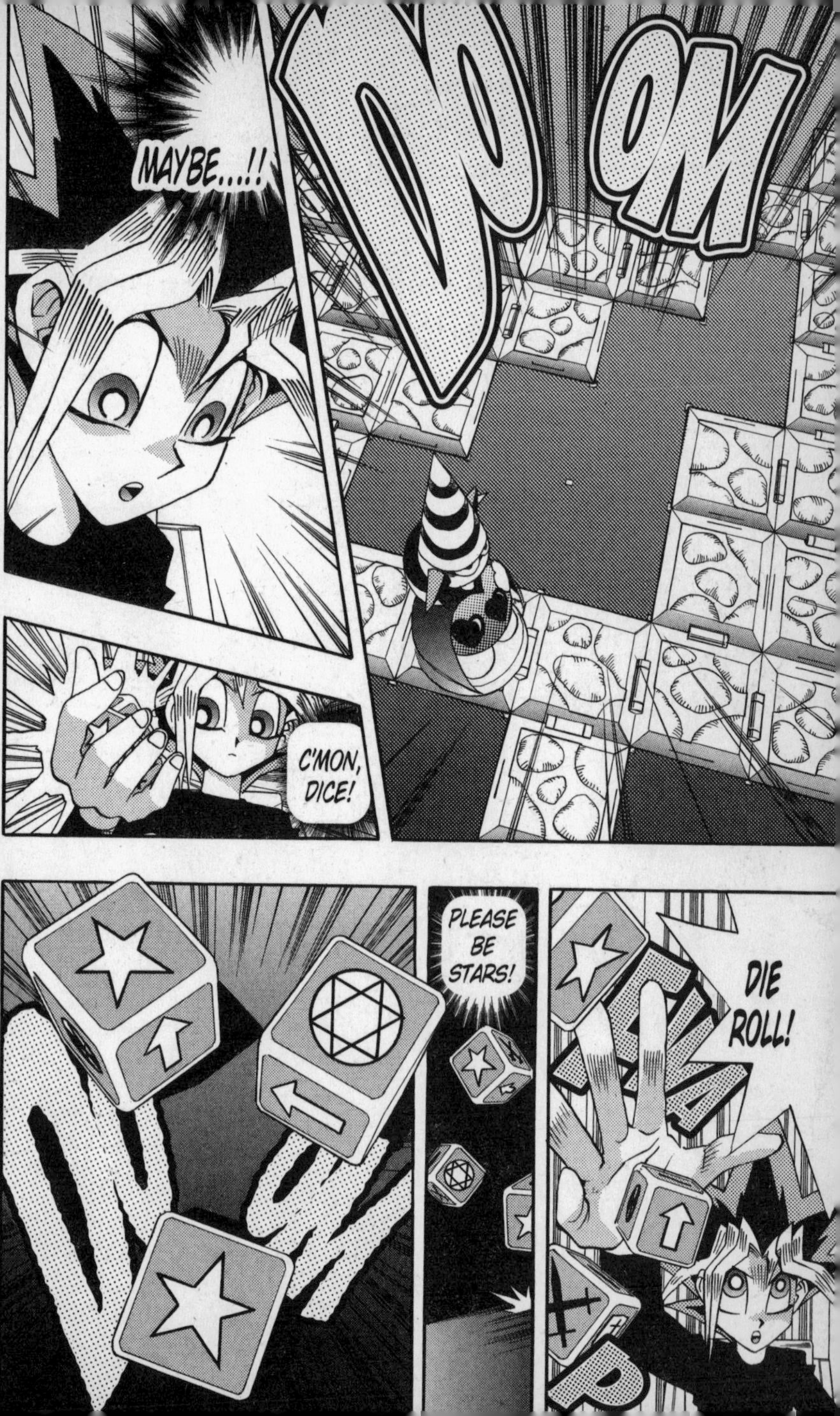
DOOM
MAYBE...!!
C'MON, DICE!
DIE ROLL!
PLEASE BE STARS!

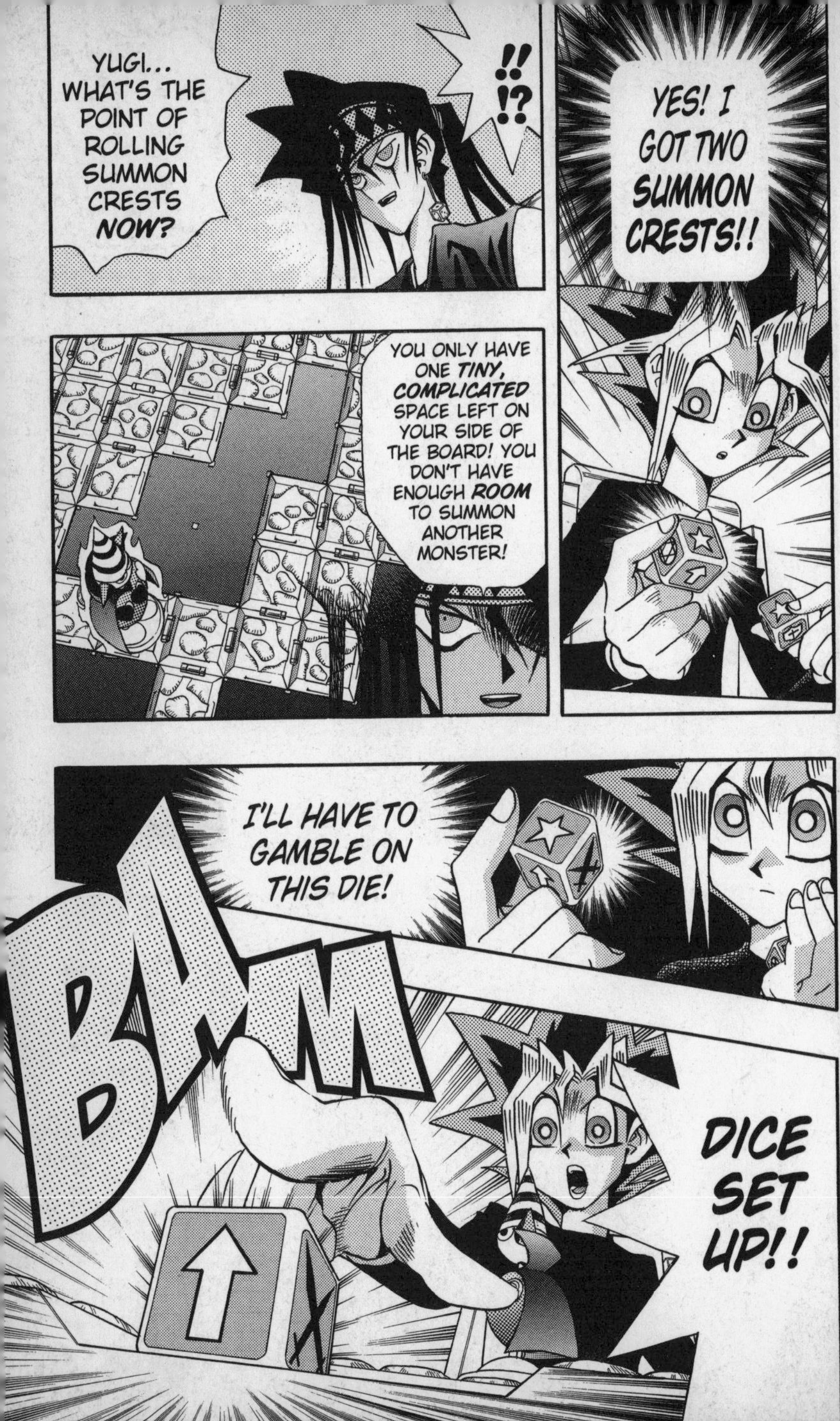
YES! I GOT TWO SUMMON CRESTS!!
YUGI... WHAT'S THE POINT OF ROLLING SUMMON CRESTS NOW?
!!
!?
YOU ONLY HAVE ONE TINY, COMPLICATED SPACE LEFT ON YOUR SIDE OF THE BOARD! YOU DON'T HAVE ENOUGH ROOM TO SUMMON ANOTHER MONSTER!
I'LL HAVE TO GAMBLE ON THIS DIE!
BAM
DICE SET UP!!

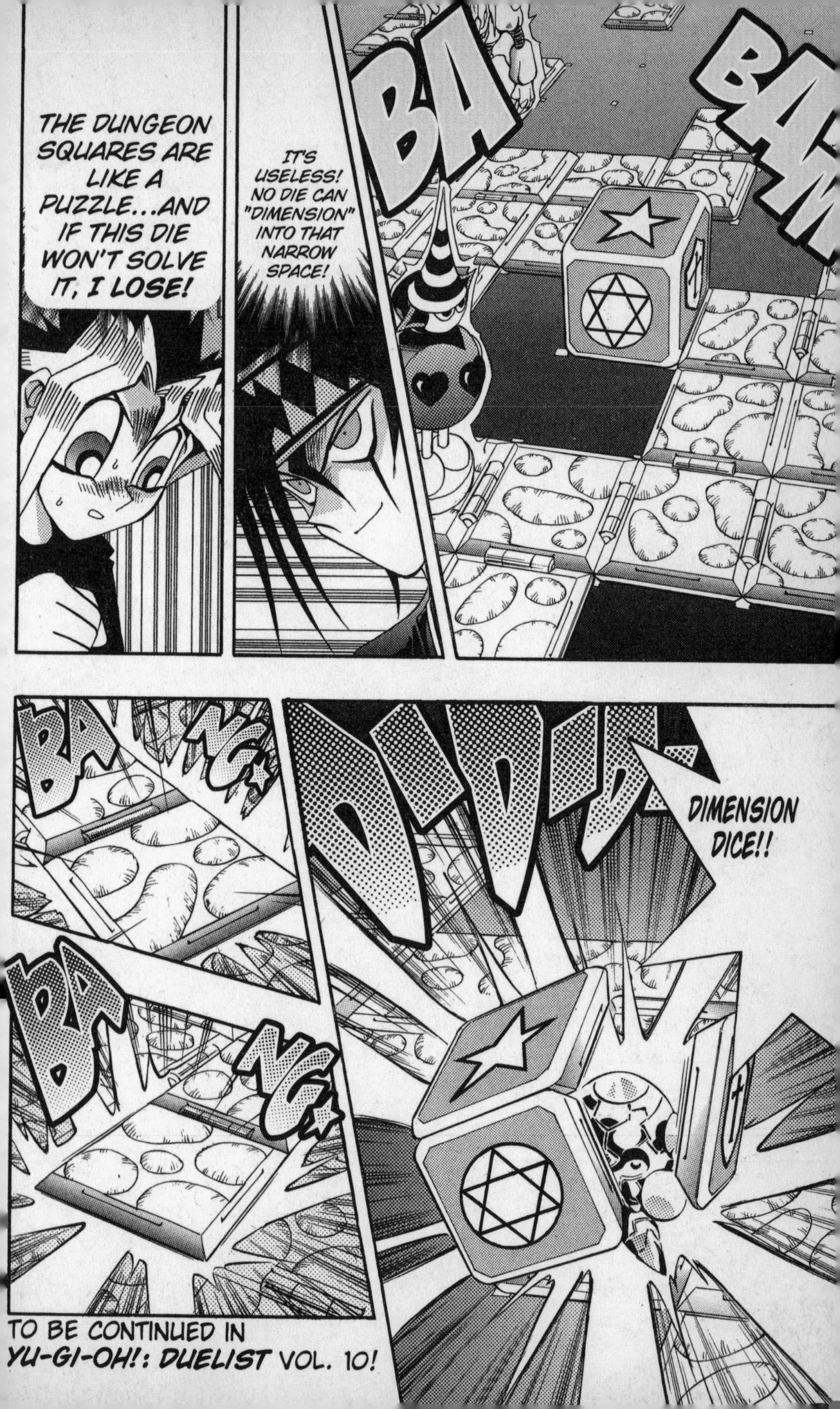
BA
IT'S USELESS! NO DIE CAN "DIMENSION" INTO THAT NARROW SPACE!
THE DUNGEON SQUARES ARE LIKE A PUZZLE...AND IF THIS DIE WON'T SOLVE IT, I LOSE!
DIMENSION DICE!!
BANG☆
BANG☆
TO BE CONTINUED IN
YU-GI-OH!: DUELIST VOL. 10!

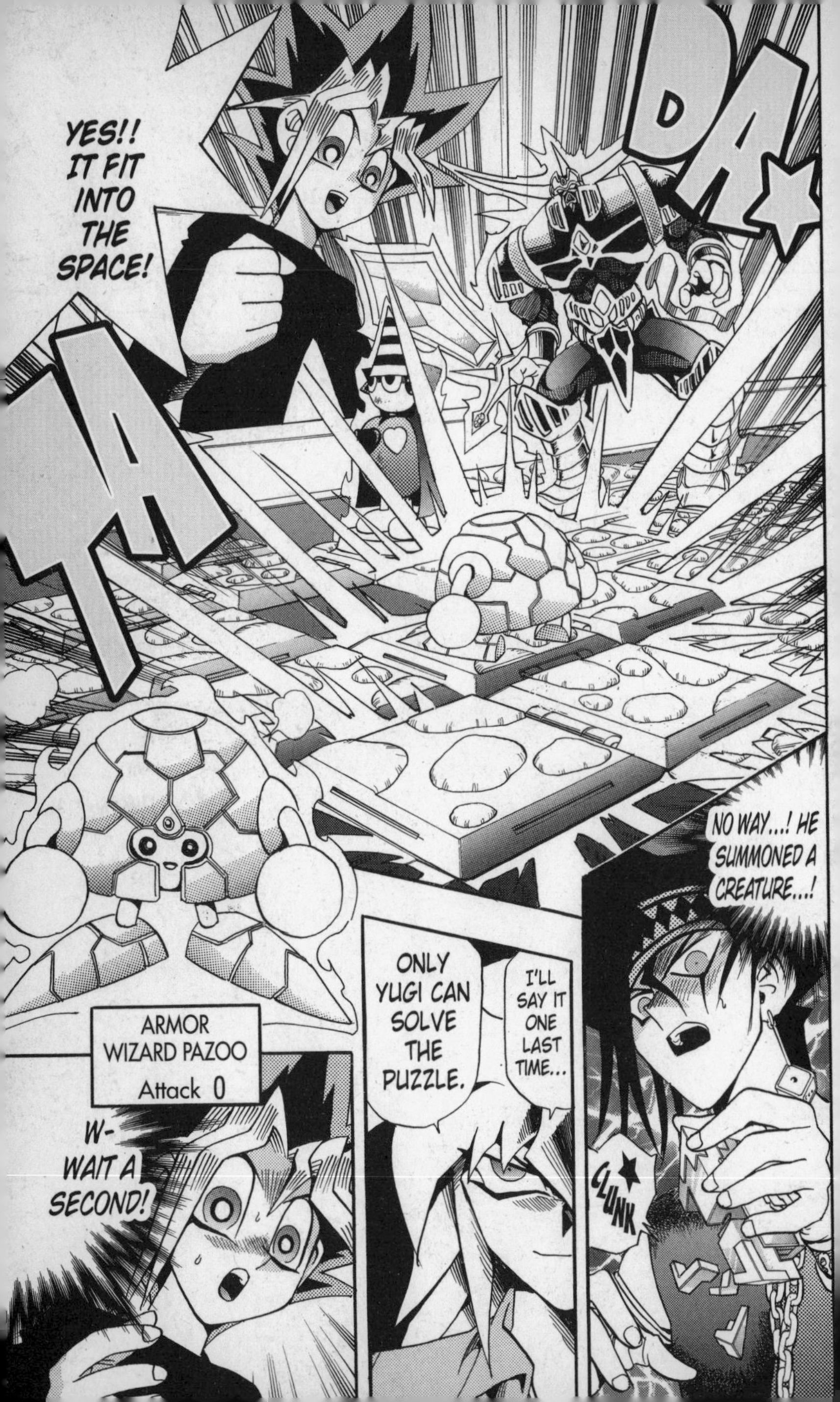
DA☆
YES!! IT FIT INTO THE SPACE!
TA
ARMOR WIZARD PAZOO Attack 0
NO WAY...! HE SUMMONED A CREATURE...!
CLUNK
I'LL SAY IT ONE LAST TIME...
ONLY YUGI CAN SOLVE THE PUZZLE.
W- WAIT A SECOND!

MASTER OF THE CARDS

The "Duel Monsters" card game first appeared in volume two of the original **Yu-Gi-Oh!** graphic novel series, but it's in **Yu-Gi-Oh!: Duelist** (originally printed in Japan as volumes 8-31 of **Yu-Gi-Oh!**) that it gets really important. As many fans know, some of the card names are different between the English and Japanese versions.

No cards appear in this volume, so instead of listing new cards, we'll look back at the decks used by Yugi and Jonouchi's opponents in the "Duelist Kingdom" story arc (**Yu-Gi-Oh!: Duelist** vol. 1-7). Some cards only appear in the **Yu-Gi-Oh!** video games, not in the actual collectible card game. There are other differences too: the Field Cards (Forest, Sogen, Wasteland, Umi and Mountain) aren't actually cards in the manga. (See **Yu-Gi-Oh!: Duelist** vol. 1 p.131 for details.)

DINOSAUR RYUZAKI
He may be the runner-up of the All-Japan Duel Monsters championship, but Dinosaur Ryuzaki's deck is pretty simple. Don't forget that he owned the Red-Eyes Black Dragon before Jonouchi did!

FIRST APPEARANCE IN DUELIST	JAPANESE CARD NAME	ENGLISH CARD NAME
Vol. 1, p.15	*Nitô o Motsu King Rex* (Two-Headed King Rex)	Two-Headed King Rex
Vol. 2, p.188	*Sword Dragon*	Sword Dragon (NOTE: Not a real game card. Called "Sword Arm of Dragon" in the video games.)
Vol. 2, p.192	*Megazaura*	Megasaurus (NOTE: Not a real game card. Called "Megazowler" in the video games.)
Vol. 3, p. 10	*Wild Raptor*	Uraby
Vol. 3, p.12	*Shikabane o musaboru Ryû* (Corpse Devouring Dragon)	Crawling Dragon #2
Vol. 3, p.14	*Red-Eyes Black Dragon*	Red-Eyes Black Dragon

INSECTOR HAGA
Armed with tons and tons of bugs, Haga has an attack deck with insect-themed power-ups. Don't forget to use "Forest" for your field card!

FIRST APPEARANCE IN DUELIST	JAPANESE CARD NAME	ENGLISH CARD NAME
Vol. 1, p.16	*Basic Insect*	Basic Insect
Vol. 1, p.16	*Messiah no Arijigoku* (Ant Lion/Sand Trap of the Messiah)	Infinite Dismissal
Vol. 1, p.17	*Kakitsuki Insect Armor* (Firearms Insect Armor)	Insect Gun Armor (NOTE: Not a real game card. Called "Insect Armor with Fire" in the video games.)
Vol. 1, p.124	*Killer Bee*	Killer Needle
Vol. 1, p.133	*Hercules Beetle*	Hercules Beetle
Vol. 1, p.137	*Laser Cannon Armor*	Laser Cannon Armor
Vol. 1, p.140	*Gokibóru* (Roach Ball)	Pillroach (NOTE: Not a real game card. Called "Gokibore" in the video games.)
Vol. 1, p.140	*Kyuketsunomi* (Blood-drinking Flea)	Giant Flea
Vol. 1, p.140	*Big Ant*	Big Ant (NOTE: Not a real game card. Called "Big Insect" in the video games.)
Vol. 1, p.152	*Larvae Moth*	Larvae Moth
Vol. 1, p.156	*Shinka no Mayu* (Cocoon of Evolution)	Cocoon of Evolution
Vol. 1, p.168	*Great Moth Yondanshinka* (Great Moth Fourth-Stage Evolution)	Great Moth

RYOTA KAJIKI
Any fish, water or sea serpent cards will be at home in the deck of this pelagic duelist. Don't forget to use "Umi" (sea) for your field card!

FIRST APPEARANCE IN DUELIST	JAPANESE CARD NAME	ENGLISH CARD NAME
Vol. 2, p.44	*Devil Kraken*	Devil Kraken (NOTE: Not a real game card. Called "Fiend Kraken" in the video games.)
Vol. 2, p.52	*Kurage Jellyfish* (Sea Moon Jellyfish)	Jellyfish
Vol. 2, p.58	*Leviathan* (NOTE: Japanese text reads: Sea Dragon God)	Leviathan (NOTE: Not a real game card. Called "Kairyu-shin" (Sea Dragon God) in the video games.)
Vol. 2, p.63	*Megalodon*	Megalodon (NOTE: Not a real game card)

PLAYER KILLER OF DARKNESS
Despite his evil theme, the first of the Player Killers is basically a defensive player, so load your deck up with DEF-boosting Spell Cards.

FIRST APPEARANCE IN DUELIST	JAPANESE CARD NAME	ENGLISH CARD NAME
Vol. 3, p.60	Yamikuramashi no Shiro (Castle Which Disappears into the Darkness)	Castle of Dark Illusions
Vol. 3, p.61	Yami (Darkness)	Yami (NOTE: In the manga, "yami" isn't a card, it's a condition of the battlefield.)
Vol. 3, p.77	Card o karu Shinigami (Card-Hunting Death God/Grim Reaper)	Reaper of the Cards
Vol. 3, p.85	Yamimakai no Haō (Supreme Ruler of the Dark Demon World)	King of Yamimakai
Vol. 3, p.97	Barox	Barox (NOTE: Not a real game card)
Vol. 3, p.97	Dark Chimera	Dark Chimera (NOTE: Not a real game card)
Vol. 3, p.98	Chaos Shield	Yellow Luster Shield
Vol. 3, p.106	Metal Guardian	Metal Guardian (NOTE: Not a real game card)

BANDIT KEITH
Like any professional card-player, Keith has several different decks prepared for different situations. When he fights Jonouchi he uses a Machine deck.

FIRST APPEARANCE IN DUELIST	JAPANESE CARD NAME	ENGLISH CARD NAME
Vol. 7, p.107	Furikoyaiba no Gomonkikai (Pendulum Blade Torture Machine)	Pendulum Machine
Vol. 7, p.116	TM-1 Launcher Spider	Launcher Spider
Vol. 7, p.119	Devilzoa	Zoa
Vol. 7, p.122	Metalka Mahōhansha Sōkō (Metal Change: Magic-reflecting Armor)	Metalmorph
Vol. 7, p.125	Shubi Fūji (Defense Seal)	Stop Defense
Vol. 7, p.142	Revolver Dragon	Barrel Dragon
Vol. 7, p.156	Toki no Kikai Time Machine (Time Machine)	Time Machine
Vol. 7, p.160	Slot Machine AM-7	Slot Machine
Vol. 7, p.163	Megatron	Space Megatron
Vol. 7, p.174	7 Card Slot Machine Power Unit	7 Completed
Vol. 7, p.176	Sphere Bomb Kyūtai Jigen Bakudan (Sphere Bomb Spherical Time Bomb)	Blast Sphere
Vol. 7, p.182	Bandit Tōzoku (Bandit Thief)	Pillager

MAI SHIRANUI
Mai's deck is very specialized; it has only a few monsters, but lots of Spell and Trap cards. "Harpie Lady Sisters" isn't a separate card in the manga.

FIRST APPEARANCE IN DUELIST	JAPANESE CARD NAME	ENGLISH CARD NAME
Vol. 1, p.208	Harpie Lady	Harpy Lady
Vol. 2, p.10	Dengeki Muchi (Electric Shock Whip)	Electro-Whip
Vol. 2, p.11	Cyber Bondage	Cyber Bondage (NOTE: Not a real game card. Called "Cyber Shield" in the video games.)
Vol. 2, p.19	Mangekyō: Karei naru Bunshin (Kaleidoscope: Splendid Doppelganger)	Kaleidoscope (NOTE: Called "Elegant Egotist" in the actual card game.)
Vol. 6, p.195	Ginmaku no Mirror Wall (Mirror Wall of the Silver Screen)	Mirror Wall
Vol. 7, p.19	Harpy no Hanebōki (Harpy's Feather Brush)	Harpy's Feather Duster
Vol. 7, p.23	Harpies' Pet Dragon	Harpies' Pet Dragon
Vol. 7, p.32	Yūwaku no Shadow (Shadow of Seduction)	Shadow of Eyes
Vol. 7, p.56	Shisha Sosei (Resurrection of the Dead)	Monster Reborn

GHOST KOZUKA
"Call of the Haunted" is the centerpiece of Kozuka's zombie deck (but technically, he gets the card from Bandit Keith).

FIRST APPEARANCE IN DUELIST	JAPANESE CARD NAME	ENGLISH CARD NAME
Vol. 3, p.38	Medusa no Bōrei (Medusa's Ghost)	Medusa's Ghost (NOTE: Not a real game card. Called "The Snake Hair" in the video games.)
Vol. 3, p.39	Yoroi Musha Zanki (Armored Warrior Zanki)	Zanki (NOTE: Not a real game card)
Vol. 3, p.41	Chi o hau Dragon (Dragon Which Crawls on the Earth)	Crawling Dragon
Vol. 3, p.43	Murder Circus	Crass Clown
Vol. 3, p.46	Undead no Yobigoe (Call of the Undead)	Call of the Haunted
Vol. 3, p.47	Murder Circus Zombie	Clown Zombie
Vol. 3, p.47	Dragon Zombie	Dragon Zombie
Vol. 3, p.47	Yoroi Musha Zombie (Armored Warrior Zombie)	Armored Zombie
Vol. 3, p.63	Ghost Oh Pumpking	Pumpking the King of Ghosts

THE LABYRINTH BROTHERS
Mei and Kyū, the Labyrinth Brothers, fight with the
same dungeon-themed deck.

FIRST APPEARANCE IN DUELIST	JAPANESE CARD NAME	ENGLISH CARD NAME
Vol. 4, p.111	*Meikyū Heki Labyrinth Wall* (Labyrinth Wall)	Labyrinth Wall
Vol. 4, p.122	*Shadow Ghoul*	Shadow Ghoul
Vol. 4, p.122	*Yūgō* (Fusion)	Polymerization
Vol. 4, p.124	*Wall Shadow*	Wall Shadow
Vol. 4, p.126	*Jirai Gumo* (Land Mine Spider)	Jirai Gumo
Vol. 4, p.127	*Meikyū no Masensha* (Demon/Magic Tank of the Labyrinth)	Labyrinth Tank
Vol. 4, p.142	*Meikyū Henge* (Labyrinth Apparition) (NOTE: The kanji for "Henge" can also be read as "Henka," meaning "change.")	Magical Labyrinth
Vol. 4, p.157	*Raimashin Sanga* (Thunder Demon God Sanga)	Sanga of the Thunder
Vol. 4, p.160	*Suimashin Sūga* (Water Demon God Sūga)	Suijin
Vol. 4, p.161	*Dungeon Worm*	Dungeon Worm (NOTE: Not a real game card)
Vol. 4, p.165	*Monster Tamer: Jigoku no Mamonotsukai* (Monster Tamer: Demon User of Hell)	Monster Tamer
Vol. 4, p.171	*Fūmashin Hyūga* (Wind Demon God Hyūga)	Kazejin (NOTE: "Kaze" is Japanese for "wind.")
Vol. 4, p.171	*Gate Guardian* (NOTE: Japanese text reads: Guard/Protection Demon God)	Gate Guardian
Vol. 4, p.189	*Mahō Kaishō* (Magic Liquidation/Dissolution)	De-Spell
Vol. 5, p.12	*Force*	Ryoku (NOTE: "Ryoku" is Japanese for "strength.")

KAIBA
Kaiba's deck contains many powerful monsters, such as the Blue-Eyes White Dragons, but it doesn't neglect Spell and Trap cards either. Is his trust in his dragons a strength or a weakness?

FIRST APPEARANCE IN DUELIST	JAPANESE CARD NAME	ENGLISH CARD NAME
Vol. 2, p.108	*Minotaurus*	Battle Ox
Vol. 2, p.110	*Blue-Eyes White Dragon*	Blue-Eyes White Dragon
Vol. 2, p.120	*Shubi Fūji* (Defense Seal)	Stop Defense
Vol. 2, p.141	*Grappler*	Grappler (NOTE: Not a real game card. Called "Grappler" in the video games.)
Vol. 2, p.148	*Kōgeki no Muryokuka* (Nullification of Attack)	Negate Attack
Vol. 3, p.134	*Gyakuten no Megami* (Goddess of Reversal)	Gyakutenno Megami
Vol. 3, p.170	*Centaurus*	Mystic Horseman
Vol. 3, p.171	*Minocentaurus*	Rabid Horseman
Vol. 5, p.79	*Gargoyle Powered*	Ryu-Kishin Powered (NOTE: "Ryu-Kishin" is Japanese for "Dragon Ogre/Fierce God.")
Vol. 5, p.93	*Fukushū no Swordstalker* (Swordstalker of Vengeance)	Swordstalker
Vol. 5, p.98	*Lamp no Masei La Jinn* (La Jinn, Magical/Demon Spirit/Holy Creature of the Lamp)	La Jinn the Mystical Genie of the Lamp
Vol. 5, p.100	*Magic Lamp*	Ancient Lamp
Vol. 5, p.118	*Yami Dōkeshi no Saggi* (Saggi the Dark Clown)	Saggi the Dark Clown
Vol. 5, p.118	*Shi no Deck Hakai* (Deck Destruction of Death) [NOTE: Symbol on card means "death"]	Crush Card
Vol. 5, p.130	*Holy Elf no Shukufuku* (Blessing of the Holy Elf)	Gift of the Mystical Elf
Vol. 5, p.138	*Yūgō* (Fusion)	Polymerization
Vol.5, p.146	*Blue-Eyes Ultimate Dragon*	Blue-Eyes Ultimate Dragon
Vol. 5, p.184	*Shisha Sosei* (Resurrection of the Dead)	Monster Reborn
Vol. 6, p.60	*Rude Kaiser*	Rude Kaiser
Vol. 6, p.62	*Saiminjutsu* (Hypnotism)	Mesmeric Control
Vol. 6, p.100	*Yami no Jubaku* (Binding Curse/Cursed Chains of Darkness)	Shadow Spell

PEGASUS
Combining deceptively cute cards like "Toon World" with sinister black magic like "Relinquished," Pegasus's deck is more like two decks in one. He also has several anti-dragon cards.

FIRST APPEARANCE IN DUELIST	JAPANESE CARD NAME	ENGLISH CARD NAME
Vol. 1, p.24	*Dragonzoku Fûin no Tsubo* (Dragon Clan Sealing Jar)	Dragon Capture Jar
Vol. 1, p.32	*Tsubo Majin* (Jar Golem/Djinn)	Dragon Piper
Vol. 1, p.35	*Elekids*	Oscillo Hero #2
Vol. 1, p.42	*Holy Doll*	Rogue Doll
Vol. 1, p.52	*Illusionist No Face*	Illusionist Faceless Mage
Vol. 1, p.54	*Genwaku no Manako* (Eye of Enchantment)	Eye of Deception (NOTE: Not a real game card. Called "Eye of Illusion" in the anime.)
Vol. 6, p.59	*Toon Alligator*	Toon Alligator
Vol. 6, p.61	*Parrot Dragon*	Parrot Dragon
Vol. 6, p.64	*Yogen* (Prophecy)	Prophecy
Vol. 6, p.72	*Dark Rabbit*	Dark Rabbit
Vol. 6, p.74	*Yami no Energy* (Dark Energy)	Negative Energy (NOTE: Not a real game card. This card has different art and effects from the game card named "Dark Energy.")
Vol. 6, p.79	*Toon World*	Toon World
Vol. 6, p.83	*Blue-Eyes Toon Dragon*	Blue-Eyes Toon Dragon
Vol. 6, p.96	*Shining Castle*	Shine Palace
Vol. 6, p.108	*Copycat*	Doppelganger (NOTE: Not a real game card)
Vol. 6, p.112	*Devil Box*	Bickuribox (NOTE: "Bickuribox" is Japanese for "Jack-in-the-Box.")
Vol. 8, p.41	*Yumi o hiku Mermaid* (Bow-wielding Mermaid)	Red Archery Girl
Vol. 8, p.43	*Ningyô no Namida* (Mermaid's Tear)	Mermaid's Tear (NOTE: Not a real game card)
Vol. 8, p.52	*Dragon Egger*	Ryu-Ran (NOTE: "Ryu-Ran" is Japanese for "Dragon Egg.")
Vol. 8, p.55	*Wana Utsushi* (Trap Transfer)	Trap Displacement (NOTE: Not a real game card)
Vol. 8, p.63	*Toon Mermaid*	Toon Mermaid
Vol. 8, p.63	*Toon Dragon Egger*	Manga Ryu-Ran (NOTE: "Manga Ryu-Ran" is Japanese for "Comic Dragon Egg.")
Vol. 8, p.73	*Gorgon no Manako* (Gorgon's Eye)	Gorgon's Eye
Vol. 8, p.75	*Toon Demon*	Toon Summoned Skull
Vol. 8, p.101	*Mahô o Uchikesu Kekkai* (Magic-Negating Force Field)	Magic Neutralizing Force (NOTE: Not a real game card)
Vol. 8, p.114	*Dark-Eyes Illusionist*	Dark-Eyes Illusionist
Vol. 8, p.119	*Illusion no Gishiki* (Ritual of Illusion)	Black Illusion Ritual
Vol. 8, p.120	*Sacrifice*	Relinquished
Vol. 8, p.139	*Time Boma*	Jigen Bakudan (NOTE: "Jigen Bakudan" is Japanese for "Time Bomb.")
Vol. 8, p.160	*Sengan no Jakyôshin* (Thousand-Eyes Evil/Heretical God)	Thousand-Eyes Idol
Vol. 8, p.160	*Yûgô* (Fusion)	Polymerization
Vol. 8, p.160	*Thousand-Eyes Sacrifice*	Thousand-Eyes Restrict

IN THE NEXT VOLUME...

Can Yugi beat Ryuji Otogi at "Dungeon Dice Monsters," or will he lose the Millennium Puzzle forever? Then, a mysterious Egyptian woman comes to Japan with a strange prophecy. Could the collectible card game "Duel Monsters" really be of ancient Egyptian origin? But Ishizu Ishtar has come to deliver more than information. "The God of the Obelisk" is one of the three most powerful cards in the world...and she's giving it to Seto Kaiba!

COMING NOVEMBER 2005!

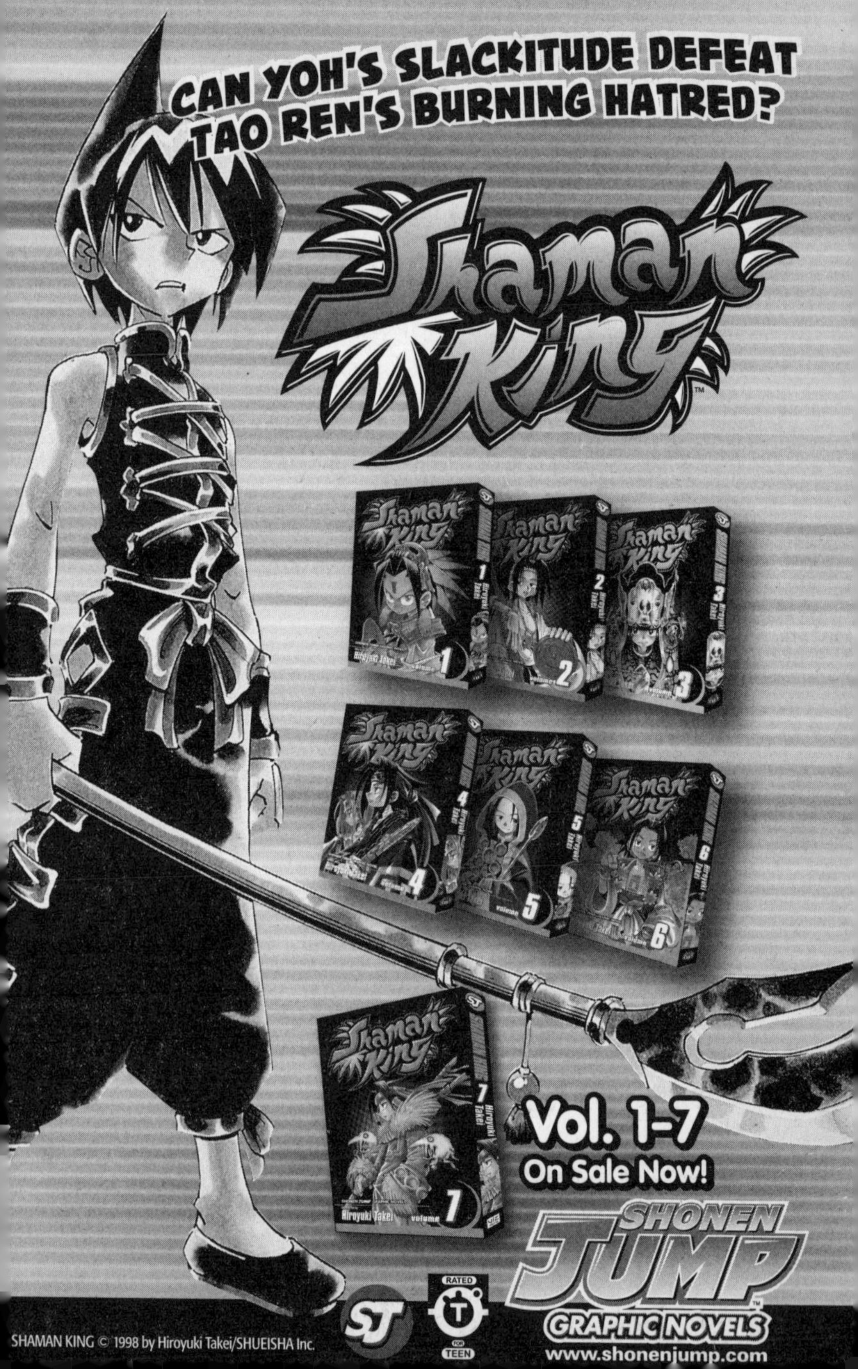
CAN YOH'S SLACKITUDE DEFEAT TAO REN'S BURNING HATRED?
Shaman King™
Vol. 1-7
On Sale Now!
SHONEN JUMP GRAPHIC NOVELS
RATED T FOR TEEN
www.shonenjump.com
SHAMAN KING © 1998 by Hiroyuki Takei/SHUEISHA Inc.

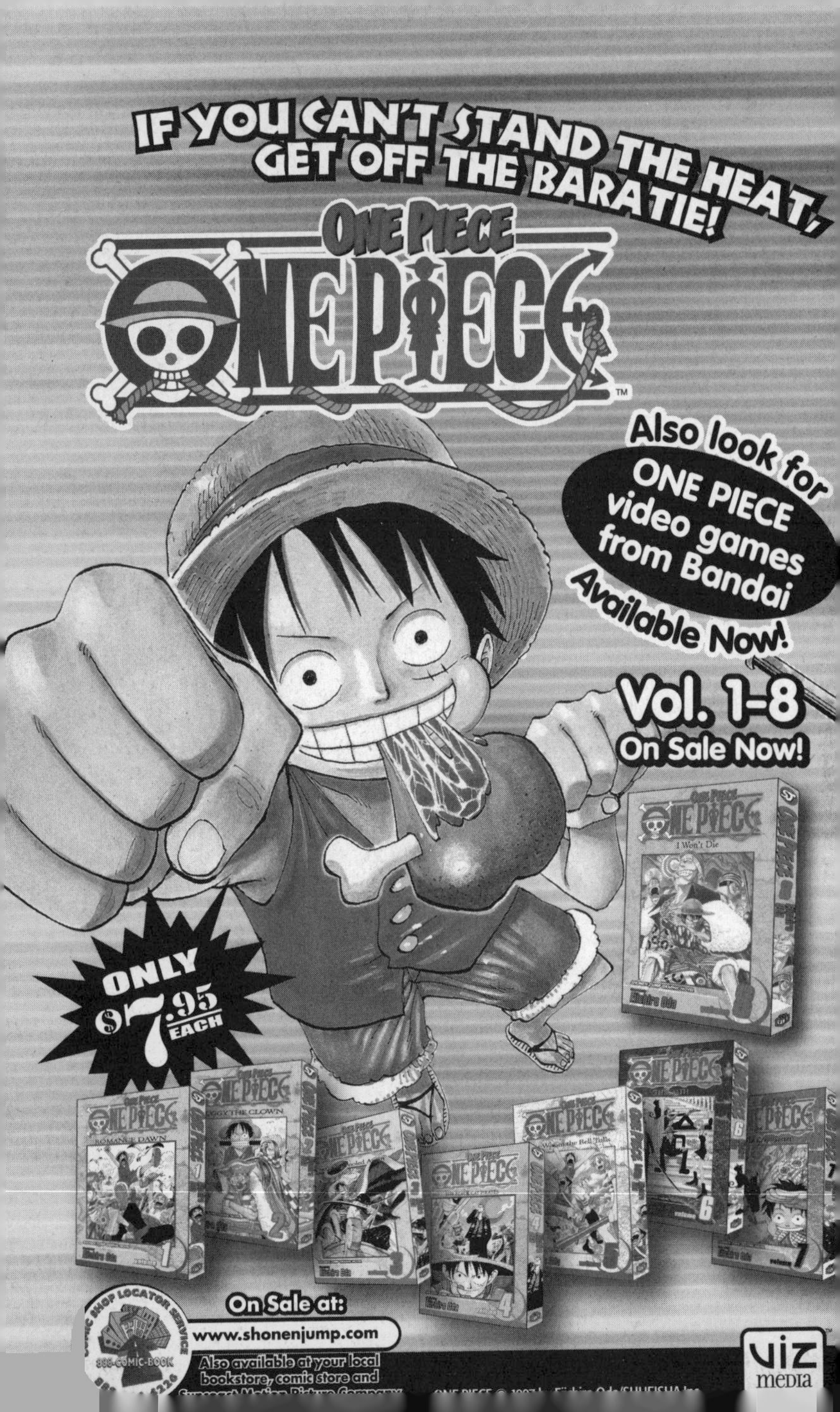

IF YOU CAN'T STAND THE HEAT, GET OFF THE BARATIE!
ONE PIECE
ONE PIECE
Also look for ONE PIECE video games from Bandai Available Now!
Vol. 1-8
On Sale Now!
ONLY $7.95 EACH
On Sale at:
www.shonenjump.com
Also available at your local bookstore, comic store and
COMIC SHOP LOCATOR SERVICE
888-COMIC-BOOK
VIZ media

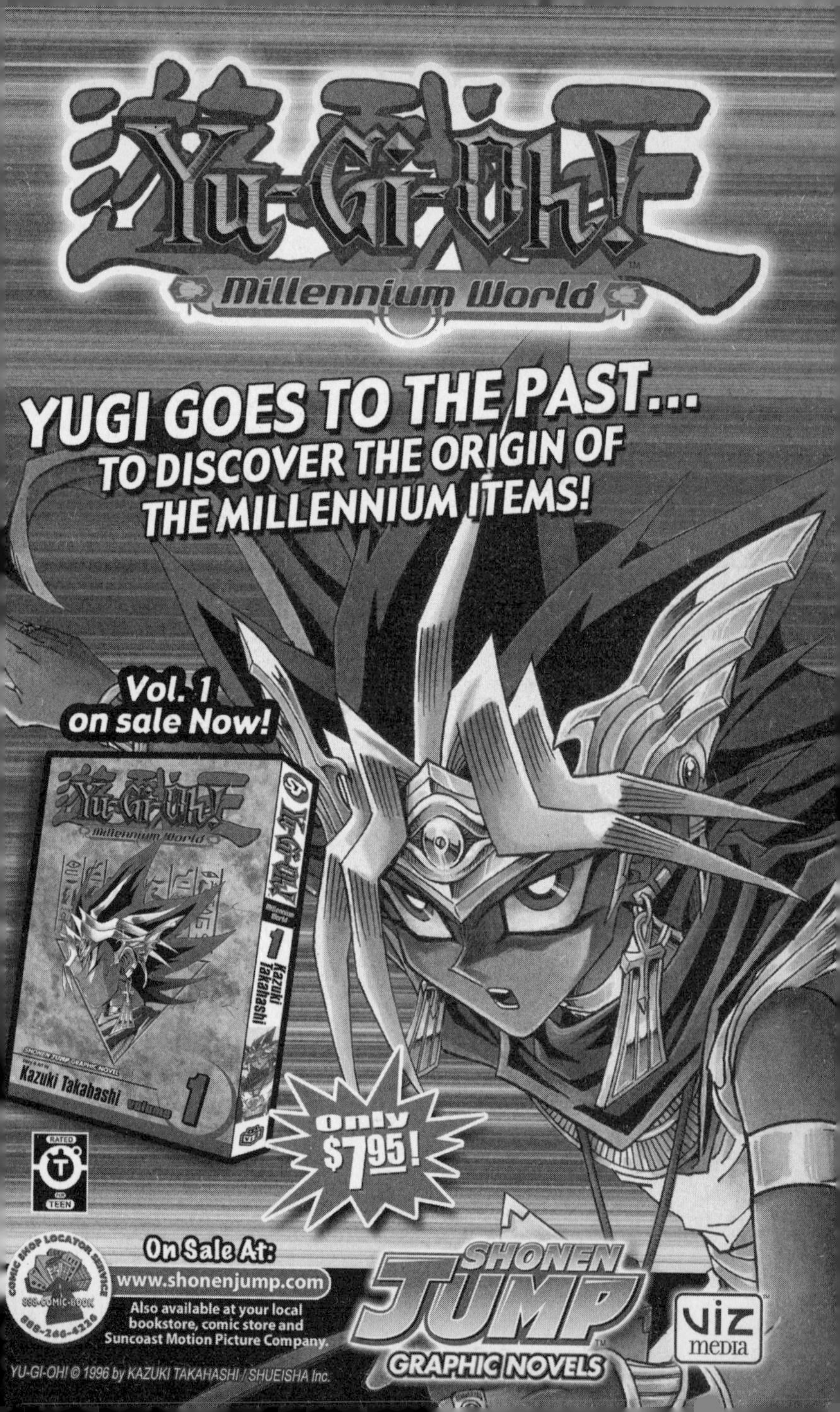

YU-GI-OH!
Millennium World
YUGI GOES TO THE PAST...
TO DISCOVER THE ORIGIN OF THE MILLENNIUM ITEMS!
Vol. 1
on sale Now!
Only $7.95!
RATED T FOR TEEN
On Sale At:
www.shonenjump.com
Also available at your local bookstore, comic store and Suncoast Motion Picture Company.
COMIC SHOP LOCATOR SERVICE
888-COMIC-BOOK
888-266-4226
SHONEN JUMP
GRAPHIC NOVELS
viz media
YU-GI-OH! © 1996 by KAZUKI TAKAHASHI / SHUEISHA Inc.

Check us out
on the web!

www.shonenjump.com

SHONEN JUMP
THE WORLD'S MOST POPULAR MANGA

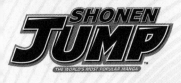

COMPLETE OUR SURVEY AND LET US KNOW WHAT YOU THINK!

☐ Please do NOT send me information about VIZ and SHONEN JUMP products, news and events, special offers, or other information.

☐ Please do NOT send me information from VIZ's trusted business partners.

Name: ______________________________

Address: ______________________________

City: ______________ **State:** ________ **Zip:** ______________

E-mail: ______________________________

☐ **Male** ☐ **Female** **Date of Birth (mm/dd/yyyy):** ___/___/_____ (**Under 13? Parental consent required**)

1 Do you purchase SHONEN JUMP Magazine?

☐ Yes ☐ No **(if no, skip the next two questions)**

If **YES**, do you subscribe?

☐ Yes ☐ No

If **NO**, how often do you purchase SHONEN JUMP Magazine?

☐ 1-3 issues a year

☐ 4-6 issues a year

☐ more than 7 issues a year

2 Which SHONEN JUMP Graphic Novel did you purchase? (please check one)

☐ Beet the Vandel Buster	☐ Bleach	☐ Dragon Ball
☐ Dragon Ball Z	☐ Dr. Slump	☐ Eyeshield 21
☐ Hikaru no Go	☐ Hunter x Hunter	☐ I"s
☐ Knights of the Zodiac	☐ Legendz	☐ Naruto
☐ One Piece	☐ Rurouni Kenshin	☐ Shaman King
☐ The Prince of Tennis	☐ Ultimate Muscle	☐ Whistle!
☐ Yu-Gi-Oh!	☐ Yu-Gi-Oh!: Duelist	☐ YuYu Hakusho
☐ Other ______________		

Will you purchase subsequent volumes?

☐ Yes ☐ No

3 How did you learn about this title? (check all that apply)

☐ Favorite title	☐ Advertisement	☐ Article
☐ Gift	☐ Read excerpt in SHONEN JUMP Magazine	
☐ Recommendation	☐ Special offer	☐ Through TV animation
☐ Website	☐ Other ______________	

4 Of the titles that are serialized in SHONEN JUMP Magazine, have you purchased the Graphic Novels?

☐ Yes ☐ No

If **YES**, which ones have you purchased? (check all that apply)

☐ Dragon Ball Z ☐ Hikaru no Go ☐ Naruto ☐ One Piece
☐ Shaman King ☐ Yu-Gi-Oh! ☐ YuYu Hakusho

If **YES**, what were your reasons for purchasing? (please pick up to 3)

☐ A favorite title ☐ A favorite creator/artist ☐ I want to read it in one go
☐ I want to read it over and over again ☐ There are extras that aren't in the magazine
☐ The quality of printing is better than the magazine ☐ Recommendation
☐ Special offer ☐ Other

If **NO**, why did/would you not purchase it?

☐ I'm happy just reading it in the magazine ☐ It's not worth buying the graphic novel
☐ All the manga pages are in black and white unlike the magazine
☐ There are other graphic novels that I prefer ☐ There are too many to collect for each title
☐ It's too small ☐ Other ______

5 Of the titles NOT serialized in the Magazine, which ones have you purchased?
(check all that apply)

☐ Beet the Vandel Buster ☐ Bleach ☐ Dragon Ball ☐ Dr. Slump
☐ Eyeshield 21 ☐ Hunter x Hunter ☐ I"s ☐ Knights of the Zodiac
☐ Legendz ☐ The Prince of Tennis ☐ Rurouni Kenshin ☐ Whistle!
☐ Yu-Gi-Oh!: Duelist ☐ None ☐ Other ______

If you did purchase any of the above, what were your reasons for purchase?

☐ A favorite title ☐ A favorite creator/artist
☐ Read a preview in SHONEN JUMP Magazine and wanted to read the rest of the story
☐ Recommendation ☐ Other

Will you purchase subsequent volumes?

☐ Yes ☐ No

6 What race/ethnicity do you consider yourself? (please check one)

☐ Asian/Pacific Islander ☐ Black/African American ☐ Hispanic/Latino
☐ Native American/Alaskan Native ☐ White/Caucasian ☐ Other

THANK YOU! Please send the completed form to:

VIZ Survey
42 Catharine St.
Poughkeepsie, NY 12601

All information provided will be used for internal purposes only. We promise not to sell or otherwise divulge your information.